Buddhism in America

ALSO AVAILABLE FROM BLOOMSBURY

Silver Screen Buddha: Buddhism in Asian and Western Film, Sharon A. Suh
Sacred Objects in Secular Spaces: Exhibiting Asian Religions in Museums,
edited by Bruce M. Sullivan
The Daoist Tradition, Louis Komjathy

Buddhism in America

Global religion, local contexts

SCOTT A. MITCHELL

Bloomsbury Academic
An imprint of Bloomsbury Publishing Plc

B L O O M S B U R Y
LONDON · OXFORD · NEW YORK · NEW DELHI · SYDNEY

Bloomsbury Academic

An imprint of Bloomsbury Publishing Plc

50 Bedford Square	1385 Broadway
London	New York
WC1B 3DP	NY 10018
UK	USA

www.bloomsbury.com

BLOOMSBURY and the Diana logo are trademarks of Bloomsbury Publishing Plc

First published 2016

British Library Cataloguing-in-Publication Data
A catalogue record for this book is available from the British Library.

ISBN: HB: 978-1-4725-8192-1
PB: 978-1-4725-8193-8
ePDF: 978-1-4725-8194-5
ePub: 978-1-4725-8195-2

Library of Congress Cataloging-in-Publication Data
A catalog record for this book is available from the Library of Congress.

Cover design by Dani Leigh
Cover images: pamelaoliveras/Raj's Photography/Martin Holtkamp/Getty Images

Typeset by Newgen Knowledge Works (P) Ltd., Chennai, India

For Cleo

Contents

CONTENTS

List of Figures

Acknowledgments

There is one name on the cover of this book, which is, of course, a lie. An idea, a written draft even, may be the work of a solitary author, but it requires the patient assistance of untold others to bring that idea to completion, to print. Legend has it that Jack Kerouac wrote *On the Road* on a single reel of paper in three weeks—if true, we have his editor to thank for turning those free-form thoughts into the coherent finished novel. Likewise, I have my editor, Lalle Pursglove—and her whole team at Bloomsbury—to thank for the book now in your hands.

If it's cliché to say we learn more from our students than they do from us that is only because it's true. I am indebted to my students who have, over the years, taught me so much. I am especially grateful to Dan Bammes, Thomas Calobrisi, Diana Clark, Carole Gallucci, Matthew Hamasaki, Chenxing Han, Ahmed Hassanein, Amparo Marles, Be Scofield, Anne Spencer, Diana Thompson, and Colette Walker.

The thoughtful advice and feedback from Courtney Bruntz, Ann Gleig, Aaron Proffitt, and Natalie Quli have made this a much better book. I am also grateful to my friends and colleagues in the academy and at the Institute of Buddhist Studies who have, over the years, shaped my thinking: Daniel Friedrich, Daijaku Kinst, David Matsumoto, Victoria Montrose, and Eisho Nasu. And, of course, Richard Payne, who I owe so much.

Thanks also to Ben and Phil for helping me build a desk, Jenny and Mikie for baseball updates and cookies, Linda for raising me to be more, Sally for childcare, and Cleo for midday dance parties. And, really, without Dana, none of this would have been possible.

Introduction

Convergence and divergence

The Buddhist flag

In 1885, a group of Buddhist leaders met in Colombo, Sri Lanka, and designed a flag meant to symbolize the Buddhist religion. The flag was composed of five vertical bars of color—blue, yellow, red, white, and orange—each representing a different aspect of the Buddhist teachings or a Buddhist value. A sixth vertical bar was a combination of the five colors, a representation of "pure light," unifying the different aspects or teachings of Buddhism. Among the flag's creators were Migettuwatte Gunananda Thera, a Theravada monk who regularly debated with Christian missionaries; Peter De Abrew, a philanthropist and member of the Theosophical Society; and Don Carolis Hewavitharana, father of Anagarika Dharmapala. The Hewavitharana family was among the wealthiest merchants in the then British-controlled Ceylon, and Dharmapala had been raised with an English education. However, as an adult, he was an outspoken critic of British imperialism and contributed to a growing nationalist movement on the island that overlapped in important ways with an ongoing Buddhist revivalist movement, one that hoped to strengthen Buddhism against Christian missionaries and revive Buddhist institutions across South and Southeast Asia.

Dharmapala's work in reviving Buddhist pilgrimage sites in India was supported by one of the founders of the Theosophical Society, Colonel Henry Steel Olcott, an American who had fought in the US Civil War. The Theosophical Society was a perennialist spiritual organization that hoped to unify the world's religions; Olcott himself had a deep interest in Buddhism, having converted to the religion in 1880. Olcott offered his own input on the Buddhist flag, noting that it should be the same size as a standard national flag for easy adoption. In 1889, along with Dharmapala, he took the flag with him on a trip to Japan and presented it to the emperor and various Japanese Buddhist leaders. From there the flag was disseminated widely across Buddhist Asia and the West. While not universally accepted across all Buddhist traditions, it has become a common symbol for Buddhism in the modern era.

The Buddhist flag can be read as a product of its time, of specific persons in a specific place for particular ends, namely the promotion of a religion that was, in some ways, under siege from outside colonial forces. It can also be read as an overt attempt to reconcile differences. That is, recognizing that the Buddhist tradition had developed into an ever-widening array of schools and lineages over the course of its two-and-a-half millennia history, those who designed and promoted the flag were searching for a way to unify these disparate strands under a common set of values. The flag is a product with local significance, influenced by transnational forces, created within an ongoing discourse between the East and the West, and ultimately distributed across Buddhist cultures via global communication and trade networks.

Buddhism in the United States is much the same—it is the product of specific persons, the result of ongoing discourses between the East and the West. Without pre-existing communication and trade networks, it would never have come into being. It is complex, diverse, and multifaceted. Indeed, it is arguable that there is no such thing as American Buddhism in the singular but rather a complex set of related practices, communities, and discourses, which from a great distance bear a family resemblance, a cluster of *Buddhisms* in America. As Gregory (2001, 239) has commented, it is like an elephant and we, as scholars, teachers, students, and practitioners, are the blind men stumbling along trying to describe it.

Scope and aim of this volume

How, then, do we discuss such an impossibly large topic, one that necessarily includes dozens of Buddhist lineages, each reflecting unique communities of persons and histories? One strategy might be to focus on major traditions, traditions that have had some significant impact in the United States. Of course, this strategy requires some criteria for judging which traditions have been more impactful than others, a system that would necessarily be arbitrary, leaving out groups that might be small in number, say, but have as much of a right to representation as other larger, more visible groups.

An alternate approach would be thematic. Here one could identify one or any number of themes that presumably impact a wide spectrum of Buddhist traditions and explore how different communities have been affected by such issues. By addressing the theme first, one could isolate a few exemplary cases and trust that other traditions not mentioned somehow fit into the interpretive framework. Indeed, this is a common approach to the subject and is arguably one reason why many scholars have focused their attention on the processes of acculturation, assimilation, and Americanization. From this point of view, questions regarding how different Buddhist traditions have become "more American" or adapt their practices to suit the dominant culture's norms become foregrounded. A drawback to the Americanization theme, however, is that it leaves the issue of "Americanness" untheorized. That is, it takes American culture as a fixed entity against which Buddhist practices or attitudes can be judged. American culture, of course, is as diverse and complex as Buddhism itself and is best understood as a network of discursive realms with both contested boundaries and microlevel regional variation. Thus, how "American Buddhism" is enacted will depend very much on which "America" one is referring to.

In sum, the study of US Buddhism is deceptively simple, obscuring a deep complexity. Whereas at most 1 percent of the population self-identifies as Buddhist (Wuthnow and Cadge 2004, 364), and whereas there is at most only 150 years of US Buddhist history (not including preceding colonial contacts in Asia), this small percentage of the population and relatively short history betrays a complex diversity of traditions with connections to virtually all parts of Asia. Any book-length treatment of the subject will necessarily cover only part of the story, and one must strike a balance between breadth and depth of coverage. In what follows, I hope to accomplish this by focusing on the theme of convergence and divergence, and by employing a translocative analysis. The term translocative calls our attention both to how persons and cultures cross temporal and spatial boundaries as well as create homes in or are impacted by local contexts. By tracing how a wide and disparate set of cultural discourses converge and diverge, I hope to gesture toward the breadth of the tradition. By choosing specific examples from this breadth, by attending to specific persons and events in some detail, I hope to provide depth. Ultimately, the aim of this book is not so much to be the definitive word on the subject, but to start conversations and to provide the reader with the methodological tools to contribute her own voice to the ongoing discussion of what the elephant of US Buddhism may be.

A focus on convergence and divergence will highlight the ways in which different cultural discourses (both in Asia and the West), strands of Buddhist thought, persons and practices, have come together over the past several centuries, providing both continuity through time and across borders as well as allowing for new interpretations and articulations of the tradition. Thus, at the intersection of European colonial and Asian nationalist discourses we see the beginnings of Buddhist modernism, a discourse that converged with Victorian-era culture at the end of the nineteenth century at the time of Buddhism's first foray into the United States. At the same time, we can also recognize how strands of the tradition diverge from and create new articulations of Buddhist practice and identity. In the post–World War II years, a convergence of Beat Generation poets and Japanese American Buddhists began a conversation that eventually led to a divergence between two communities whose interests and ideals were no longer in sync. This approach allows us to see multiple sources of influence, relationships between communities and persons, and potential future trajectories of the various strands that make up the diversity of Buddhism in the United States. These themes will be clarified by relying on Tweed's translocal analysis, which in turn is based on his theory of religion articulated in *Crossing and Dwelling*. Here, Tweed defines religions, in part, as confluences of cultural flows that cross boundaries and construct homes (2008a, 54). His translocal analysis (2011, 2015) highlights both the movement of religious practices and persons as well as how religions establish themselves, or make homes, in specific contexts on a varying level of scales, from the local to the global. From this point of view, we can approach US Buddhism as a set of practices and traditions that emerge as a result of local circumstances within global cultural networks, as exemplified by the

Buddhist flag, a product of local invention with translocal significance. These themes will become apparent in this book, which is divided into three parts.

Part One focuses on history, beginning, appropriately, with a short introduction to Buddhism intended to orient the reader to the general contours of the tradition. The remaining three chapters focus on Buddhism's move from East to West, exploring the cultural and historical contexts in which US Buddhism developed over the past two centuries. As such, Buddhism per se is not foregrounded but instead the focus is on broad cultural movements and discourses within and against which Buddhist persons and institutions interacted and developed. The Enlightenment, Romanticism, and Victorian American culture are the focus of Chapter 2, culminating with the nineteenth-century introduction of Buddhism into American culture. This period is defined by European colonial contact with Buddhism and Asian culture more generally, the discursive construction of "the Orient" as a field of study, and the Victorian fascination with "the Other," a set of cultural discourses that defined in important ways how Buddhism was presented to nineteenth-century Americans. In Chapter 3, we will examine the establishment of the first US Buddhist communities by Chinese and, later, Japanese immigrants, tracing their experiences through the post–World War II years. These are decidedly different stories from the grand Romantic narratives of the nineteenth century, though those certainly come to bear in the sudden interest in Buddhism on the part of young seekers, poets, and artists in the 1950s and 1960s, ushering in what has been called the Zen boom. We begin Chapter 4 with the passage of the Hart-Celler Act of 1965, a sweeping reform of early-twentieth-century immigration laws that unintentionally allowed for a large number of Asian Buddhist immigrants from the late 1960s to the present to establish communities in the United States. The 1965 Immigration Act was not passed in a vacuum, of course, but came at a time of rising political and cultural interest in Asia on the part of many Americans, carrying the Zen boom forward to the end of the century. Thus, by the turn of the twenty-first century, we find the wide diversity of Buddhist institutions and traditions in the United States built on centuries of East-West cultural exchange.

The present diversity of US Buddhist traditions is the subject of Part Two. The first three chapters are devoted to the three traditionally defined "vehicles" (yana) of Buddhism: Theravada, Mahayana, and Vajrayana. I have chosen this organizational scheme to highlight the historic trajectory of these traditions and their connections to larger trends in Asia and the West. By bringing into conversation communities usually viewed in isolation, useful comparisons can be made as well as points of divergence noted. Chapter 5 focuses on US Theravada Buddhism, its connections to South and Southeast Asia, and the growing influence of both insight meditation and mindfulness meditation. Chapter 6 traces the history of US Mahayana Buddhism somewhat chronologically from the first communities established in the late nineteenth century through the latter half of the twentieth. Chapter 7 focuses on Vajrayana Buddhist traditions from both Tibet and Japan, with special emphasis on the popularity of Tibetan Buddhism and new religious movements. Far from exhaustive, Part Two is intended to paint in broad strokes the variety of US Buddhist experiences as a foundation for further exploration.

Each chapter in this part begins with an overview of the history, core doctrines, and practices of the respective tradition before highlighting important communities, lineages, practice centers, and topical themes. One recurring theme across these chapters is the tension between maintaining religious tradition and adapting to changing historical circumstances. Nowhere is this tension more pronounced perhaps than at the intersection of religious and secular discourses that reimagine or undermine traditional conceptualizations of religion and often give rise to wholly new forms of spiritual practice. This will be the focus of Chapter 8, a short reflection on non- and pan-sectarian forms of Buddhism, secularism, and new avenues of practice and research.

Part Three presents a series of reflections on theoretical and developmental issues that can be used to frame the study of US Buddhism. These frames can be understood as both methods or disciplinary fields (e.g., media studies) and issues US Buddhists wrestle with as they build homes in their new American contexts (e.g., reactions to media representations of Buddhists). Chapter 9 frames questions of authority and authenticity in Buddhist media and art, exploring both how Buddhist ideas have proliferated into the broader culture and Buddhist responses to the deployment of Buddhism into commercial spaces. The construction of Buddhist identities is the subject of Chapter 10, which explores the intersection of race, gender, sexual orientation, and religion in the construction of social identity with specific attention paid to academic tropes that have been used to study US Buddhism. Social theory is an important component in the articulation of various engaged Buddhist movements, the subject of Chapter 11, wherein we will explore the history of Buddhist political activism and Buddhist responses to ecological crises and restorative justice both inside and outside the *sangha*. That US Buddhism is a product of modernity and globalization should go without saying, and no book on the subject would be complete without a discussion of the various ways in which the tradition has been shaped by various Eastern and Western modernist discourses and made possible by the space-time compression of globalization that allows for the rapid spread of information and persons across the globe, the subject of the concluding chapter.

While the above summary points to a certain logic in this book's presentation, chapters are nevertheless intended to stand on their own and may be read out of order. Each chapter includes an outline and summary, discussion questions, and suggestions for further reading as well as case studies and breakout text. Appendices include a timeline, lineage outline, and a glossary of Buddhist terms.

Counting and categorizing Buddhists and Buddhism

Just how many Buddhists are there in the United States? This is a notoriously difficult question to answer, and it depends entirely on how one defines "Buddhist"—or, for that matter, how one defines religious identity. Most surveys taken in the past few decades have relied on one of two methods: membership numbers as reported by religious organizations or self-identification. A prime example of the former approach is a 2010 report by the Association of Statisticians of American Religious Bodies (ASARB) who contacted religious congregations to get membership numbers. From this report, we can estimate that there are fewer than one million US Buddhists.[1] Membership numbers, however, are misleading: these types of surveys are necessarily better at finding large organizations with listings in local phone books or on the internet; when contacted, minority religious bodies tend to overestimate their numbers to look larger than they are; and, finally, many people who attend religious services or self-identify as religious may not actually belong to any particular organization. For these reasons, self-identification may seem a better choice for determining overall numbers.

The 2008 Pew Forum Religious Landscape Survey is an example of this approach based on a telephone survey that asked "What is your religion, if any?" and reported that 0.7 percent (a little over two million) of Americans self-identified as Buddhist (Lugo 2008). This survey suffers from a host of limitations we will discuss in Chapter 8; for now it is merely important to note that to claim a religious affiliation – to claim "I am *this* religion but *not that* religion"—is hardly universal, especially in Buddhist cultures where one may engage in religious and spiritual practices from any number of traditions simultaneously. From this point of view, one's religious identity is pragmatic and fluid, choosing the appropriate rites, rituals, or codes of conduct appropriate for any given situation.[2]

As something of a corrective, an unrelated Pew Forum report on Asian American religion from 2012 asked a different set of questions. In addition to the standard "what is your present religion?" question, the survey also asked about various practices and beliefs and the general importance of religion in people's lives (Lugo and Cooperman 2012). These questions reveal more about the lived experience of religion rather than the black and white dichotomy of one religion or another. Taken together, such surveys can be used to estimate that the total number of Buddhists in the United States hovers at around 1 percent, with more than half of US Buddhists being of Asian descent.

However, these surveys should also remind us that the sorts of questions we ask will determine the kinds of information we receive. The ASARB survey asks questions about congregational membership. From this, we can learn a great deal about *where* Buddhists are located to the extent that most (but certainly not all) Buddhists are likely to reside in places where they can congregate, that is, where there are other Buddhists and Buddhist communities (Figure 1). However, this information necessarily overlooks those Buddhists who live at a distance from major practice centers and potentially misses smaller communities spread across the country. Therefore, however helpful the location of Buddhist centers might be in telling one story about US Buddhism, this information is nevertheless incomplete. Surveys that ask about religious self-identification reveal a great deal about a particular type of Buddhist (viz., one who claims such an identity), and when compared with other data (both practice patterns and more general demographics), helps tell the story of what many Buddhist lives look like. However, these surveys are also incomplete. They are focused on self-identified Buddhists and overlook those who Tweed has called "Buddhist sympathizers" and "night-stand Buddhists" (1999; 2002). These are persons who may engage in

FIGURE 1 *Locations of US Buddhist centers and communities according to 2010 ASARB survey. (Data sourced from http://www.rcms2010.org.)*

particular kinds of Buddhist-derived practices such as meditation or have been deeply influenced by Buddhist thought through books by teachers such as the Dalai Lama but, for whatever reason, do not identify as Buddhists. Perhaps they identify as "spiritual but not religious," non-religious, or have a dual identity such as belonging to a Christian church or identifying as Jewish as well as Buddhist. Regardless, these varied engagements with Buddhism call into question self-identification as a measure of how Buddhist ideas and practices spread into the broader culture. This tells yet another story about US Buddhism, one that defies easy categorization.

In this book, it is important to know general demographic patterns, preliminary numbers, and the geographic spread of US Buddhism; however, we should not lose sight of other stories and other voices, of the ways in which Buddhism has had an impact on American culture that greatly surpasses its relatively small numbers (Tweed 2008b; Wuthnow and Cadge 2004).

A note on terminology

The subject of this book is Buddhism—Buddhist persons, practices, communities, and discourses—that happens to be located in the United States, a subject I refer to as *US Buddhism*. Scholarship has vacillated between "Buddhism in America" and "American Buddhism," a dichotomy with potentially divisive connotations, discussed below. Moreover, "American" may refer either to US citizenship specifically or to the whole of North (and often South) America, subjects beyond the scope of this book. Therefore, the subject of this book is located within the bounded category of the United States; I will make reference to pan-American crossings where appropriate and trust that the reader will understand that the historical and theoretical perspectives provided may also be of relevance to other cultural contexts, particularly those in the larger Anglophone world (e.g., the United Kingdom, Australia, New Zealand) and especially Canada. Indeed, a growing body of literature dedicated to Canadian Buddhism has emerged over the last decade, attesting to the unique specificity of Buddhist experiences, experiences that at times overlap but are also in need of their own focused attention (Hori et al. 2010; Harding et al. 2014).

The dichotomy between Buddhism in America and American Buddhism has found expression in an ongoing debate about race that has dominated the field for many decades now. This discourse has divided US Buddhists into Asian or Asian American Buddhists *in* America over and against *American* Buddhists (usually white, usually converts), two communities often portrayed as having had little to do with one another. One way that this finds clearest expression is by explicitly labeling the ethnicity of one group (Asian Americans) while not doing the same for another (white Americans/converts); moreover, by equating "whiteness" with "convert," we overlook both those white Americans who were born and raised in the tradition (and therefore cannot be converts) as well as those Asian Americans who adopted a Buddhist identity in adulthood (and therefore are the definition of convert). In short, this dichotomy is not without its problems, and as a result of its prevalence in the literature, it can be difficult to discuss US Buddhism without unintentionally perpetuating certain stereotypes (Prebish 1993; Numrich 2003; Hickey 2010, 2015).

To avoid this problem, I have elected to refer to communities not by the ethnicity or convert status of their largest member base but instead to their respective self-described traditions or lineages. My use of ethnic and racial identifiers is thus specific and used when it is germane to the subject at hand, such as when discussing events during the 1950s and 1960s within Japanese American Buddhist communities when predominately white American converts began seeking the teachings, leading to the establishment of new lineages and communities of practice. Half a century later, these new lineages are best referred to as just that—by their lineage—rather than by the fact that some of their original members happened to be white and converts. That these lineages diverged from a Japanese American community should in no way imply that the Japanese American Buddhist community is in some sense "not American"; nor should we mistakenly assume that these two communities are no longer in contact. Rather, they are merely two different expressions of Buddhism in the United States with a shared history and an ongoing relationship.

This dichotomy also presumes that there are only two racial groups practicing US Buddhism—Asian and white—and thus obscures African American, Hispanic and

Latino/a Americans, and Native Americans who have also been attracted to Buddhism. My use of terms such as "non-Asian Buddhists" is meant to reflect this broader diversity. My use of the term "white" as opposed to "Euro-American" is meant to highlight the way in which whiteness is a constructed racial category, as will become clear in Chapter 10.

In general, I have chosen to use Sanskrit for Buddhist terms used throughout this text with the exception of Chapter 5, which focuses on Pali-based Theravada Buddhism. I have elected to avoid using diacritics; however, they are used in the glossary. Transliteration schemes employed are pinyin for Chinese, Revised Hepburn for Japanese, and McCune-Reischauer for Korean. Tibetan terms are rendered phonetically with Wylie transcriptions included in the glossary.

PART ONE

Histories

FIGURE 2 *Japanese American Historical Plaza, Portland, Oregon. (Photo by author.)*

1

A short introduction to Buddhism

Chapter summary and outline

This chapter provides a basic overview of the historical development and spread of Buddhism from its origins in India and across precolonial Asia. Attention is paid to foundational doctrines and practices, the development of Buddhist textual canons, and the origins and locations of different Buddhist practice traditions and lineages in precolonial Asia.

The life of the Buddha

The first turning of the wheel of the Dharma

Creating a community: The *Sangha*

The development of Mahayana and Vajrayana

Major Buddhist schools in precolonial Asia

Discussion questions

Suggestions for further reading

The life of the Buddha

The world of sixth century BCE India was in the process of profound social, cultural, and political change. Centuries prior, Indo-Aryan peoples had moved into the Ganges river valley, bringing with them religious customs and solidifying a caste-based social hierarchy that was integrated into the broader cultural landscape. At the top of this hierarchy was a priestly caste (*brahmin*) responsible for manipulating the will of the gods through rituals performed according to Vedic texts. Below the *brahmin* were warrior-kings (*kshatriya*), merchants, and artisans, and, finally, the lower social realms of laborers, slaves, and outcastes. Caste was determined by the immutable workings of karma; thus there was little one could do to effect or change one's position in the social hierarchy. On a political level, beyond larger city-states, the subcontinent was divided into small republican territories and various feudal kingdoms ruled over by the wealthy *kshatriyas*. The Ganges valley and northern parts of the subcontinent were becoming increasingly prosperous, allowing for greater social stability, urbanization, and the possibility of new ways of thinking about the social order and modes of religious practice. Thus developed a space for new religious movements, including those characterized by *sramana*, wandering religious practitioners who often undertook ascetic practices and challenged the *brahmins'* exclusive right of access to religious power. *Sramana* generally left the comforts of home-life to wander the forests and collect alms for support. This was the religious and political world into which Gautama Siddhartha, the man who would become the Buddha, was born.[1]

As is true of most historical religious figures, legends and myths surround his life, recorded in various canonical texts (Robinson and Johnson 1997, 11ff). It is said that his mother, Maya, dreamed that a white elephant entered her side, after which she became pregnant. As delivery neared, she retired to a garden in Lumbini near Kapilavastu (present-day Nepal) and gave birth while standing upright and holding onto a tree branch for support. The birth itself was painless, and it was greeted by miraculous events; flowers rained from the sky and the earth shook. The newborn immediately took seven steps, lotus flowers blossoming from his footsteps, pointed to the earth and the sky and declared this to be his final birth.

Seven days later, Siddhartha's mother died. As was custom, his father, a *kshatriya* named Suddhodana who ruled over a small kingdom on the present-day India-Nepal border, married his wife's sister, Mahaprajapati. Asita the sage examined the boy and predicted that he would either grow to be a world-ruling king or an awakened master. Desiring his son to become the former, Suddhodana conspired to shield his son from all suffering and prepare him for political greatness. Thus, Siddhartha was raised in virtual isolation from the world, pampered and given whatever luxuries he desired. For nearly thirty years, Siddhartha was content in this life, eventually marrying and fathering a son of his own. However, he was also restless and desired to know more about the world outside his father's walls.

Journeying in the countryside beyond his palace, Siddhartha came into contact with an elderly man, a diseased man, and a rotting corpse. He at once became unable to reconcile how people could lead lives of pleasure while aware that ultimately all will succumb to old-age, sickness, and death. On a subsequent trip outside his palace, he saw a *sramana* and understood that others were attempting to understand the nature of suffering and life and death. Siddhartha knew that he could no longer find joy or happiness in his life at home, sequestered behind the walls of his father's compound. And so he left his home behind, ventured out into the wilderness, and became a *sramana* himself.

The path he took was one of extreme asceticism. Along with other forest-dwelling renunciants, he engaged in yogic disciplines that involved depriving the mind and body of all sensory pleasures while enduring any number of physical hardships. With a lack of food, Siddhartha became emaciated, near death, meditating in extreme heat without shelter or while submerged under icy waterfalls. For five years, he engaged in these practices with single-minded determination to uncover the answers to his questions about the root causes of suffering but ultimately came to believe that the ascetic path was fruitless.

While canonical sources differ slightly on what brought about this change, what is clear is that Siddhartha realized that the path of extreme pleasure he lived in his father's palace was ultimately empty and temporary; and the path of extreme asceticism was also ultimately fruitless, giving him no answers to his questions. Accordingly, he took a small amount of food to regain his strength—an action that caused his *sramana* colleagues to abandon him, claiming that he had given up the path to live in abundance. Siddhartha then sat beneath a *bodhi* tree and resolved not to be moved until he attained final and complete awakening. Over the course of a single night, he attained release, an event that is as imbued with legend as his birth. It is said that the great demon king Mara, seeing that someone was about to conquer death, set his armies of desire after Siddhartha, attempting to seduce him away from the path. Siddhartha was ultimately victorious, however, remaining immobile against Mara's armies. By sunrise, he had attained awakening, becoming the Buddha (Gethin 1998, 22–24).

The round of rebirth

Buddhist cosmology takes for granted that beings are endlessly reborn into one of six realms of existence, *samsara*, depending on their karma. These realms are: (1) various hell realms including eight hot and eight cold; (2) the realm of hungry ghosts, *preta*, beings doomed to suffer unquenchable hunger and thirst; (3) the realm of animals; (4) the realm of humans; (5) the realm of *asuras*, variously defined as angry or wrathful demigods; and (6) the heavenly realms of the gods. None of these realms is permanent, and all of them have their advantages and drawbacks. Thus, while the drawbacks of the hell realms may be obvious (unimaginable suffering), they are nevertheless impermanent; one will eventually be reborn elsewhere. Conversely, whereas the heavenly realms may appear to be an ideal place to be born—and indeed there are numerous examples of beings born in these realms and being able to practice the dharma free from distraction—generally speaking the gods are too self-absorbed to be bothered with any religious commitments. Thus, the human realm is the ideal realm to be born into, a location with enough imperfection to motivate one to practice without too much suffering to get in the way.

The content of this experience under the *bodhi* tree is quite detailed in the Buddhist canon (Robinson and Johnson 1997, 17–19). First, Siddhartha progressed through a series of evermore refined states of mental clarity and equanimity. These would allow him to eventually have an insight into the workings of karma and his past lives. Karma was understood broadly to be the mechanism by which peoples' destinies were assured, binding them to the round of rebirth, or *samsara*. Siddhartha saw that karma was also a moral force, that actions had positive, negative, and neutral qualities, and how this web of causes and conditions bound all sentient beings to the round of rebirth and was thus a cause of suffering. Not only was he able to see his own past lives and karmic conditions but the karmic causes and conditions of all sentient beings throughout the cosmos. The inherently interconnected nature of these conditions and the subsequent suffering they produce forms the heart of the Buddha's awakening and informs subsequent Buddhist philosophy.

It should be noted here that the basic outline of the Buddha's life above (and the remaining forty-five years of his teaching career) are not unique to the historical Buddha. The canonical texts go out of their way to note that the truths the Buddha would eventually teach were not his, nor were they revealed to him; rather, they are absolute truths that exist regardless of whether anyone teaches them. The Buddha himself is merely the latest in a long line of Buddhas, stretching back an infinite number of eons, who also realized these truths. The texts name a number of previous Buddhas, and their biographies are remarkably consistent across time: each of them are born into lives of luxury, they all marry and have a son, they all reject the home life and endure austerities before attaining Buddhahood, they all die in roughly the same way. The historical Buddha, named Sakyamuni (the sage of the Sakya clan), will impart these teachings to our world, and after a certain number of millennia, these teachings

FIGURE 3 *Buddha Sakyamuni, Central Tibet, circa eleventh century. (Los Angeles County Museum of Art.)*

will be forgotten, will disappear from this world; and at that time, a new Buddha will be born. Thus, while Sakyamuni Buddha is generally revered as a very special Buddha, he has never been understood by the tradition to be the "founder" of the religion. Despite this, however, it is undeniable that following his awakening, the Buddha would go on to create a new community that would have a profound impact on the social and religious world of the Indian subcontinent before being exported to nearly all parts of Asia.

The first turning of the wheel of the dharma

For a time, the Buddha remained under the *bodhi* tree; he believed that humanity was simply not ready to understand the dharma (teachings) he had discovered. People were too attached to their behaviors and desires. According to tradition, the god Brahma intervened, noting that while certainly some would not understand, others were ready to hear the dharma. The Buddha then agreed to teach, representing a crucial point in his biography where an explicit choice is made, born out of compassion, to lead others to awakening. Rising from his seat, he went out in search of the *sramanas* with whom he had previously practiced. Seeing him from a distance, they first conspired to reject him, believing that he had strayed from the ascetic path. As he drew closer, however, they realized that a change had come over him, that he had become something more than the *sramana* they knew. And after hearing what he had to say, they became his first monastic disciples. This is considered the first turning of the wheel of the dharma and the content of this sermon contains the fundamental teachings of Buddhism.

The Buddha first taught the Four Noble Truths: (1) the truth of *duhkha* or suffering; (2) the cause of *duhkha*, desire (*trisna*) or attachment; (3) the solution to the problem of *duhkha*, nirvana; and (4) the way (*marga*) toward nirvana, the Eightfold Path.

The first noble truth of *duhkha*, or suffering, is often the most challenging. *Duhkha* is etymologically related to the condition of a chariot wheel being out of alignment. This has led modern interpreters to suggest that *duhkha* might be better translated as "out of alignment," or a generalized feeling of dissatisfaction. This is true, to be sure, but the precise quality, causes, and types of *duhkha* were something the Buddha spent a considerable amount of time discussing; *duhkha* refers to something more than merely a generalized feeling of unhappiness. It is the feeling of longing or desire to be with those one loves; it is also the opposite desire to distance oneself from those one dislikes. It is both the easy-to-grasp feeling of loss when something pleasurable comes to an end as well as the existential angst caused by the awareness of one's mortality. There is suffering in desiring pleasurable things. There are both physical and psychological types of suffering. To exist at all in the realm of *samsara* is to experience *duhkha*. And as a result of one's karmic conditions, upon death one is assured rebirth in *samsara*, trapped as it were in a never-ending round of rebirth, suffering, death, and rebirth.

The cause of suffering, the second noble truth, is grasping, clinging, and attachments—most specifically our attachment to the idea of self. This is not to say that the Buddha advocated a type of nihilism or a destruction of the self. Rather, the

Buddha's teachings implore us to investigate the nature of what we think of as the self, and, above all, recognize its impermanence. Pre-Buddhist Indian thought generally took for granted the notion of some permanent self, ego, soul, or essence that was bound to *samsara*. According to the Buddha, however, the opposite is true, there is no self: the doctrine of *anatman*. The Buddha deconstructed the self into the five *skandhas* of form, sensation or feeling, perception, mental formations, and consciousness, revealing that none of these can exist without the others, none of them are permanent, and it is our delusional clinging to ideas about the permanence of the self and the body that lead to suffering. Once we are able to release our attachment to these notions of permanence, we will be freed from our connection to *samsara*.

The constructed nature of the self and its relationship to the world is arguably the core insight the Buddha had on the night of his awakening, expressed in the teaching of *pratityasamutpada*, or conditioned origination. In one formulation, this teaching is summarized as:

When this is, that is.
From the arising of this comes the arising of that.
When this isn't, that isn't.
From the cessation of this comes the cessation of that.[2]

Pratityasamutpada is further elaborated as a twelve-fold chain of causation, with each link giving rise to the next as such: from (1) ignorance comes (2) volitional actions that lead to (3) consciousness and (4) name and form to (5) the six internal sense-bases to (6) sensory contact to (7) sensation or feeling that leads to (8) thirst or attachment to (9) grasping or clinging, which leads to (10) the process of becoming, which leads to (11) birth or rebirth, which leads to (12) old age and death, thus, *duhkha*. This formula for explaining the constructed nature of the self in relationship to the external world, as well as transcending one life while spanning multiple rebirths, is the basis for an understanding of the self that is inherently interdependent. Our experience of the world is reducible to the five *skhandas*, leading to the awareness of our selves being impermanent and, simultaneously, existing only because of the existence of others. Thus, we can understand how the self is both impermanent and deeply interconnected.

It is our attachment to this idea of a permanent self that is the root cause of suffering. Without this, suffering ceases. Thus, there is a solution to the problem of suffering, the third noble truth, nirvana, most commonly translated as awakening or enlightenment. From the Sanskrit "to blow out" as in "a flame blown out by the wind," nirvana is more properly translated as "extinction," specifically the extinction of the desires that allow one to be freed from the round of rebirth. These translations, like *duhkha* as suffering, rarely do justice to the complexity of the concept. Is nirvana an experience? A state of being? A realm into which one enters, implied by its juxtaposition with *samsara*? Yes. And definitely no. It is a state, in classical Buddhist texts, defined as an escape from *samsara* in the sense that one is no longer bound to the realm of *samsara*, and therefore one is not reborn post-mortem.

Whereas nirvana as extinction of desires may appear at first glance quite mundane, Buddhas and advanced practitioners are described as possessing a range of supernatural powers such as the ability to see others' past lives and projecting images of themselves across great distances. Despite these depictions, awakening is also clearly something to be attained by ordinary sentient beings; the path of practice may be arduous, but it is nevertheless attainable.

The path to nirvana—however it is defined—was clearly laid out in the fourth noble truth as the Eightfold Path:

1. Right views

2. Right intention

3. Right speech

4. Right conduct

5. Right livelihood

6. Right effort

7. Right mindfulness

8. Right concentration

While modern interpreters are fond of describing Buddhism as a path of practice rather than mere belief (orthopraxy as opposed to orthodoxy), it is clear from the Eightfold Path that both are necessary. One must cultivate proper understandings about the world and our place within it, including right views on the nature of the self (or lack of it). Moreover, one's practice must be supplemented with proper ethical behavior. Without right conduct, without cultivating appropriate speech acts or even having an acceptable job, progress along the path is impossible. One of the most important contributions to religious discourse the Buddha made was his explicitly moral interpretation of karma. That is, karma was not mechanistically predeterminative; rather, one necessarily suffers the results of bad behavior while at the same time being free to behave better and create positive future conditions. The Eightfold Path is often likened to a three-legged stool representing grounding in wisdom, ethics, and mental training; without one leg, the whole thing collapses.

Orthodoxy, from the Greek for "right belief," is adherence to the central beliefs, tenets, or creeds of a particular religious faith. Orthopraxy, then, refers to right practice, that is, adhering to proper (usually ritual) behavior.

While these basic concepts and moral outlooks might betray simplicity, they have also been the basis for an ongoing Buddhist discourse for over two thousand years. As one might imagine, this discourse has created a dizzying array of responses to these teachings and an even wider array of approaches to putting them into practice.

Creating a community: The *sangha*

Following the first turning of the wheel of the dharma, the Buddha began a lengthy teaching career, traveling across the Indian subcontinent for over forty years. As a result, the general outline of teachings and approaches to understanding the fundamental nature of reality would become further clarified and nuanced. And, importantly, a community of followers would grow around the Buddha—what would become known as the *sangha*.

His former *sramana* coreligionists were his first followers, and he ordained them as monks or *bhiksu*. As with any religious community, the *sangha* needed rules to function and maintain harmony. As the community grew, these rules became more complex and specific and would eventually be codified into what are called the *vinaya* (Gethin 1998, 91–94). *Vinaya* regulations, in their various manifestations, remain to this day the standard that Buddhist monastics follow, governing not only ethical and social behavior but also basic, everyday rules for how to live together in community. These rules were not a part of the Buddha's awakening, nor did he deliver them to the *sangha* all at once; rather, they developed over time as pragmatic responses to problems that arose in the community. As the *sangha* grew, the *vinaya* allowed for stability, which in turn led to the growth of large monastic complexes and Buddhist universities.

Originally, the *sangha* was exclusively male—men who had left behind family and caste to enter into a celibate monastic community. As this community grew and attracted wider attention, women too—including the Buddha's stepmother, Mahaprajapati, and his wife, Yasodhara—sought membership. At first, the Buddha resisted the idea, perhaps reflecting normative gender roles and biases of the day. The women were undaunted, however, and eventually the Buddha allowed for the establishment of a female monastic order. The order of nuns, *bhiksuni*, while in many ways subordinate to the male order (Chapter 10) was nevertheless unorthodox for a time in India when religious pursuits were generally the sole purview of men and provides some of the earliest examples of women's religious experiences in world history. As we will see later, as Buddhism developed and spread out of India, multiple *vinaya* traditions developed, and the *bhiksuni* order was spread to all parts of Buddhist Asia. Sometime between the eleventh and thirteenth centuries, the nun's lineage disappeared in South and Southeast Asia; efforts to reestablish the order have become an important issue in modern Buddhism.

As the community grew, it attracted the attention of powerful political forces as well. Early in the development of the *sangha*, patronage became an important factor in allowing the community some stability, and in addition to hundreds (perhaps thousands) of monastic followers, the Buddha also attracted lay followers. Thus, the term *sangha* is sometimes clarified to mean the four-fold *sangha* of monks, nuns, laymen, and laywomen. Whereas rules for monastics are complex and detailed, regulations for laypersons are less so; nevertheless, the Buddha did provide teachings for laypersons, basic codes of ethical conduct, and gave advice to kings on how to rule their countries in accordance with the dharma.

For the next forty-five years, the Buddha and his community traveled across the country spreading the dharma. While in the area of Vaisali, the Buddha hinted to one of his senior disciples, Ananda, that he could live another eon if requested to do so; Ananda did not understand what the Buddha was implying and so did not make the request. As a result, three months later, the Buddha ate some tainted food and passed away in Kusinagari. Having attained full awakening, the Buddha is said to have passed into *parinirvana*, leaving behind all conditioned states. His body was cremated, and his relics were divided among the eight kingdoms who were instructed to build reliquaries (*stupa*) for veneration of his remains (Figure 4).

Following the Buddha's death, the *sangha* held the First Buddhist Council, led by the disciple, Mahakasyapa. Another disciple, Upali, was relied upon to recite the full *vinaya* monastic codes; Ananda recited the sutras. Sutras are, strictly speaking, the words of the Buddha, and accordingly each one begins with the words "Thus have I heard" followed by the time, location, and those present for a teaching delivered by the Buddha. Once the monks at the First Council agreed on the content of the *vinaya* and sutras, these bodies of teachings became the basis for the Buddhist canon, known as the

FIGURE 4 *Great Stupa, Sanchi, Madhya Pradesh, India, third to first century BC. (Getty Images.)*

tripitaka or "three baskets." The *tripitaka* was committed to memory by the *sangha*, recited orally and passed on to future generations for some centuries before the canon was formally written down.

It is fair to say that the dharma was not systematized; rather, the Buddha imparted teachings in a proscriptive way, focusing on the essential facts of how to progress along the path (*marga*) to awakening in a largely narrative format. Following the Buddha's *parinirvana*, perhaps in response to challenges from outside the community, the *sangha* began to systematize the Buddha's teachings into an ever-expanding group of texts known as the *Abhidharma*, a body of literature that forms the third basket of the *tripitaka*. Unlike the sutras, the *Abhidharma* presents us with a more thoroughgoing and organized philosophy based on the sutras and often in the form of lists. The unnamed authors of these texts sought to reconcile differences between what the *sangha* understood to be the conventional versus the ultimate understandings of the dharma; that is, the Buddha's use of figurative language and metaphors for persons at the beginning of the path versus literal language used for the more advanced. As these textual commentaries grew, so did divergent opinions about what constituted the conventional or the ultimate; as a consequence, different philosophical schools of thought developed. It should be stressed here that these different schools were not distinct denominations as we would understand the term in a Protestant Christian context; rather, they represented different schools of thought, positions held by monastics often residing in the same monastery, and so long as the *sangha* was united by a common monastic code, monks could live and practice together despite differences of opinion (Robinson and Johnson 1997, 56). These differences of opinion would lay the philosophical groundwork for the development of what are known as the mainstream schools of Indic Buddhism.

In the third century BCE, King Asoka united a large part of India. In a series of stone pillars and edicts, Asoka is described as renouncing the bloodshed caused by his various military campaigns and turning instead to the dharma. According to the Buddhist tradition, he was a great supporter of Buddhism, specifically charging Buddhist monks with the task of spreading the religion. For example, the fourth century CE Pali text *Dipavamsa* notes that Asoka was responsible for bringing Buddhism to Sri Lanka (and, conveniently, supported the Pali canonical tradition, which was then becoming dominant on the island). While the archaeological evidence and traditional accounts do not always match on this point, it is no doubt true that having a large, stable kingdom fostered trade, which in turn allowed for the spread of Buddhism well beyond its birthplace. By the beginning of the Common Era, Buddhism had already spread across most of the Indian subcontinent and was well on its way to the rest of Asia.

The development of Mahayana and Vajrayana

By the beginning of the Common Era, a profound change came over the Buddhist tradition. The causes of this change are both complex and still a matter of some scholarly debate (Silk 2002; Williams 2009, 21–44). An earlier generation of scholars believed that a large movement of lay followers challenged the authority of monastics advocating for different approaches to the path of practice, a theory that has fallen out of favor. There is some evidence that lay followers were engaged with monastic institutions that relied on the former for financial support, but there is little evidence that this support was organized into a movement to challenge doctrinal understanding in Buddhist institutions. Moreover, as discussed earlier, divergent opinions on interpreting the Buddhist canon were already evident in the immediate century after the Buddha's death. These philosophical differences would eventually include different interpretations of the *vinaya* expressed at the Second Buddhist Council that would lead to further divisions at the Third Buddhist Council held during the reign of Asoka. Within this context, a new body of texts, which would profoundly impact the development of Buddhism, was being composed and attributed to the Buddha.

> The Sanskrit *dharma* (Pali *dhamma*), from the root "to hold" or "maintain," literally means factor or element. In this sense, dharma can refer to a constituent element of matter—both physical and mental phenomenon. "To maintain" may also reference maintaining specific doctrines, beliefs, or practices, and it is in this sense that dharma-as-teaching is more widely known.

These texts are generally referred to as *prajñaparamita*, or the perfection of wisdom. In part, they were a response to an earlier generation of *Abhidharma* texts that sought to reduce all of phenomenal existence to a series of atomistic parts (dharma). The problem, according to the *prajñaparamita*, was that these atomistic parts retained a semblance of "self-ness" that was fundamentally at odds with the Buddha's teaching of no-self. *Prajñaparamita* literature, and various schools of thought that supported it, argued that all of existence is without any inherent, independent existence—all is marked by *sunyata*, or emptiness. A later text, known as the *Heart Sutra*, in English, would sum up these teachings by stating simply, "form is emptiness, emptiness is form," a terse phrase that has been the subject of endless commentary (Gethin 1998, 234–237).

A concomitant development at this time was the clarification of the bodhisattva path. Bodhisattva literately means "awakening being" and was an epitaph given to the Buddha before he became the Buddha; in other words, in past incarnations and in his life as Gautama Siddhartha, he was the "bodhisattva," a buddha-to-be, whose karma was inexorably leading him toward full and final nirvana. In broader Buddhist literature, all future Buddhas are also considered bodhisattvas, and because there is only ever one Buddha at a time, the term bodhisattva is necessarily limited to whoever is to be the next Buddha. In this schema, those who followed the Buddha (both his disciples as well as subsequent generations of monks) were not on the path to becoming Buddhas themselves but rather an *arhat*, a state of awakening, which is, for all intents and purposes, nearly identical to that of the Buddha without actually being a Buddha or embodying all the superhuman qualities usually attributed to a supremely enlightened being. As the *sangha* grew and developed, however, the term bodhisattva came to be applied to anyone who was on the path toward full and complete Buddhahood (Gethin 1998, 226–231). The path itself became further clarified doctrinally and textually, referring to persons, both physical and cosmic, who had forsaken final nirvana in order to remain in the realm of *samsara* to be of service to other suffering sentient beings. It was assumed that a bodhisattva was one who would willingly give up complete release until all suffering had ended. This path of practice, as well as associated quasi-mythical figures, was detailed in texts such as the *Avatamsaka Sutra* and the *Lotus Sutra* as well as commentarial literature such as the eighth-century treatise *Bodhicaryavatara* by the Indian Buddhist monk Santideva.

The final chapter of the *Avatamsaka Sutra*, which at one point was likely a stand-alone sutra, the *Gandavyuha*, symbolically details the bodhisattva path in the story of Sudhana. Seeking a spiritual teacher (*kalyanamitra*), Sudhana visits fifty-two different beings—including twenty women, a prostitute, a slave, the Buddha's mother, and several celestial bodhisattvas—representing the fifty-two stages of the bodhisattva path. Each being displays specific spiritual abilities or is reflective of a particular spiritual state of being and in some ways reflects the growing sense that the fruits of Buddhist practice are to be found not only in monastic life but in ordinary lay life as well. A cornerstone of these practices is *upaya* or skillful means. *Upaya* is the central concern of the *Lotus Sutra* wherein the Buddha explains differences arising in approaches to practice as different teachings aimed at different persons because, while sentient beings suffer, the causes of their sufferings differ requiring different remedies. A bodhisattva therefore skillfully meets a person where they are, guiding them toward awakening in a way specific to their circumstances. Within the *Lotus Sutra* a chapter is dedicated to the bodhisattva of compassion Avalokitesvara who is seen manifesting himself in all manner of physical forms, responding to the cries of suffering beings throughout the cosmos. Avalokitesvara would later become an extremely popular figure in East Asian Buddhism as Guanyin, where she is more often depicted in female form (Yü 2000).

These texts, along with the broader genre of *prajñaparamita* literature, differed from earlier Buddhist texts in that they were composed in Sanskrit, the same sacred language of the preexisting Vedas. This literature would form the foundation for what is now known as the Mahayana (lit. "great vehicle"). By the beginning of the Common Era, the Mahayana schools were distinguishing themselves rhetorically from rival schools with the pejorative term "hinayana"—the "lesser vehicle"—a term that those schools never adopted for themselves seeing as it was obviously insulting and they generally ignored the new movement regardless (Robinson and Johnson 1997, 83). It should be stressed here that modern scholarship has begun to embrace the term "mainstream schools" rather than the derogatory hinayana to refer to the non-Mahayana schools of Indian Buddhism.

Esoteric refers to secret teachings or knowledge held by a select group or inner circle; in the Buddhist context, it may also refer to the correct understanding of a text's or ritual's meaning that is passed from a teacher to a disciple.

Sometime around the seventh to eighth centuries another body of literature, and undoubtedly representing a much older practice tradition, began to develop within Indian Mahayana Buddhism (Wayman 2013). Based in part on preexisting ritual practices, including the recitation of the names of Buddhas and complex visualization and meditation practices, as well as Indian yogic practices, these texts would later be labeled tantra. Tantra as a class of texts are defined in the Buddhist tradition by their use of esoteric practices including the recitation of *mantra* and *dharani*, the performance of rituals such as the *homa* fire ritual, and the construction of elaborate *mandala* used during visualization meditations (Figure 5). Each of these practices is meant to clarify or purify the body, speech, and mind of defilements and are not unrelated to the broader philosophical and cosmological worldview of Mahayana texts and practices, which took for granted the existence of multiple world systems inhabited by an endless array of cosmic Buddhas and bodhisattvas who could be appealed to for spiritual support or teachings. Undoubtedly influenced by the broader tantric movement in India, many of these texts, such as the *Guhyasamajatantra* and the *Cakrasamvaratantra*, directly challenged social and religious taboos regarding dietary restrictions and sexual mores (Robinson and Johnson 1997, 127–128). Buddhism's transmission to Tibet coincided with a time when the tantras were well regarded and flourishing in India, and many Indian Buddhists were compiling commentaries on the tantras. Whereas this tradition, in the modern era, is sometimes referred to as a separate tradition of Buddhism—Vajrayana—it is clear that tantric practices have played a major role in the development of Mahayana Buddhism across East Asia (Wedemeyer 2013).

FIGURE 5 *Buddhist monk making sand mandala. (Getty Images.)*

As early as the third century BCE, Buddhism began to spread from its birthplace in northeastern India across the subcontinent and throughout Asia in no small part due to the royal patronage of King Asoka (Figure 6). Over the centuries, as monastics followed trade routes and pilgrims made their way back to India, new Buddhist schools of thought and practice developed both in India and across Buddhist Asia. Initially, mainstream Buddhist schools dominated India and Sri Lanka from where they found their way into what is now Burma, Laos, Thailand, and parts of Indonesia. The distinction between the mainstream schools and the rising Mahayana was not as clear-cut as it may be today, thus it is important to note that there is evidence of Mahayana (and even Vajrayana) thought, iconography, and practice throughout Southeast Asia.

Initially, however, early Mahayana was primarily practiced in the northwest from where it spread into central Asia along the Silk Road. Buddhism arrived in China by the second century of the Common Era, and monks began establishing monasteries and translating texts almost immediately. Over the centuries, there was continued contact between Buddhist India and China as pilgrims traveled to Indian monasteries and Buddhist universities and brought new texts and teachings with them back to China, texts that were then translated and commented upon. In great monastic

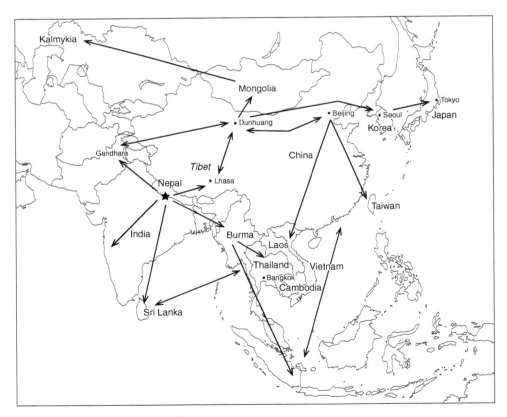

FIGURE 6 *Buddhism's spread across Asia.*

complexes along the Silk Road, new texts were composed that have no corollary in Sanskrit, thus leading to the development of wholly new Chinese Buddhist traditions. Simultaneously, tantric texts found their way over the Himalayas onto the Tibetan plateau where they would come to have an enormous impact on the whole of Chinese Buddhism. By the fourth century of the Common Era, Buddhism had found its way into Korea and into Japan by the sixth. Chinese Buddhist schools and culture continued to influence East Asian Buddhism for centuries to come, with monastics traveling back to China to receive new teachings and most of the major Chinese schools having Korean and Japanese equivalents. By the fourteenth century, Buddhism's influence had waned considerably in its homeland. Once-thriving centers of Buddhist learning were in decline by the time of the Muslim conquest of India such that Buddhism had all but vanished from India by the colonial period while thriving throughout the rest of Asia.

Major Buddhist schools in precolonial Asia

The history of Buddhism in the United States begins in colonial Asia. By the nineteenth century, most of Buddhist Asia was either directly under European control or was indirectly influenced and affected by colonial politics and economics. Whereas there had been minimal contact between Buddhist Asia and European cultures as far back as the third century BCE, there was no sustained, substantive, or systematic exchange of ideas or cultures until the colonial era, when European powers (and accompanying ways of organizing and categorizing the world) came to dominate Asia. This relationship brought both an exchange of ideas and the ability for persons to more easily move between the East and the West. What, then, were the major strains of Buddhism in Asia that would come to define the colonial-era East-West exchange?

As we have seen, while mainstream Buddhist schools commingled with rising Mahayana and tantric texts and practices, it was the mainstream schools that eventually came to dominate South and Southeast Asia. Following the death of the Buddha, several competing mainstream schools and canons of Pali texts existed across the region. By the fifth century CE, owing in large part to royal actions to purge non-mainstream and competing teachings and Buddhaghosa's exegetical work (see Chapter 5), a Pali canon began to form (Collins 1990). Over the ensuing centuries, Sri Lanka, Burma, Cambodia, and Thailand would all become major hubs of Pali-based Buddhism, and by the eleventh century what would eventually come to be known as Theravada began to dominate the region. Due to its close proximity to both Southeast Asia and China, Vietnam had a more eclectic set of Buddhist influences, with Mahayana forms dominating. Unlike the rest of the region, Thailand was never directly colonized by a European power, though it is hard to ignore how colonialism effected the construction of the modern, democratic country. Thai Buddhism has had a large influence on Buddhism in the United States as a result of Thai immigrants to the United States and US-born teachers traveling to Thailand to receive teachings or ordination.

Mahayana Buddhism began entering Tibet in the seventh century, and tantric texts and practices had a major impact. By the twelfth century, Buddhism dominated the religious and political landscape. The greater Tibetan plateau is an enormous stretch of land that has had a large cultural impact on China, Mongolia, Bhutan, Nepal, and parts of central Asia and eastern Russia. And it is the Tibetan form of tantric or Vajrayana Buddhism that is most familiar to the United States, largely as a result of the Chinese invasion of Tibet in 1959 and subsequent popularity of the 14th Dalai Lama. In part because of his popularity, Tibetan Buddhism is often referred to in the singular, which betrays the complexity and diversity of the tradition. There are in fact several branches of Tibetan Buddhism, with the Nyingma, Kagyu, Sakya, and Gelug traditions being the largest. Of these, the Dalai Lama is the spiritual head of only the Gelug tradition while historically being the political leader of the nation as a whole. Like Thailand, Tibet was never a European colony; unlike Thailand, Tibet is far more remote and less strategically important on the world's political stage. Thus, the country remained relatively isolated during the colonial period, at times acting as a romantic stand-in for Western idealizations of a mythic spiritual realm immune to the corrupting influences of the modern world (popularly known as the Shangri-la myth, see Lopez 1998).

Due to Buddhism's longevity in China, as well as its relationships to other parts of Buddhist Asia, Chinese Buddhism is complex and diverse. The Indian Mahayana schools of Madhyamaka and Yogacara would be extremely influential in the development of Chinese Buddhism; over the centuries several distinct schools of thought developed in China. Many of these schools began as explicit attempts to systematize the large body of texts and teachings imported into China, thus leading to the creation of hierarchies of teachings and associated textual traditions. Among the most influential Chinese Buddhist schools were the Vinaya, Huayan, Tendai, Chan (Zen), and Pure Land schools. However, it must be remembered that Chinese religious life is highly syncretic; thus, in general, Chinese culture has been defined simultaneously by Confucian, Daoist, and Buddhist thought, and it would not be uncommon for a person to identify with or participate in practices derived from all three. And as syncretistic as religious life may have been in general, the same is true for different Buddhist schools. While there may have been times and places where specific teachers or even monasteries loudly claimed affiliation with one particular Buddhist lineage, this did not prohibit participation in other forms of practice. It is common, for example, for a monastery to have both a Chan meditation hall alongside a Pure Land recitation hall.

All the major schools of Chinese Buddhism have played a part in the development of Korean Buddhism. However, by the time the Korean peninsula was annexed by Japan in 1910, the Sŏn and Vinaya schools were the dominant forms, and they would unite as the Chögye Order in 1935. Korea's status as a Japanese colony and the subsequent rise of Protestant Christianity have seemingly eclipsed studies of Korean Buddhism; it has only been in the last few decades that scholars have taken an active interest in the study of Korean Buddhism, and there are few Korean Buddhist traditions in the United States. To the extent that the vast majority of Korean Americans are practicing

Christians, Korean American Buddhists are a minority within a minority population (Suh 2004).

Buddhism came to Japan from China via Korea in the sixth century. Initially, the esoteric Chinese schools of Tendai and Shingon dominated Buddhist thought and practice with Tendai having especially close ties to the ruling powers. By the thirteenth century, political tides would turn in Japan leading to the development of wholly new schools of Buddhism, some imported by pilgrims to China, including Zen. During the intervening centuries, Pure Land, Zen, and Nichiren forms of Buddhism would grow in influence and importance and, unlike their mainland antecedents, would grow increasingly sectarian in character. Japanese Buddhism played an especially important role in the development of Buddhism in the United States, beginning as early as the 1880s.

DISCUSSION QUESTIONS

1. How did changing political and cultural contexts in pre-Buddhist India allow for the development of new religious movements?

2. Does the Buddhist tradition consider Sakyamuni Buddha to be the religion's founder? Why or why not?

3. What forms of Buddhism are predominant in South Asia? East Asia? Central Asia?

SUGGESTIONS FOR FURTHER READING

Gethin, Rupert. 1998. *The Foundations of Buddhism*. Oxford University Press.

Kapstein, Matthew T. 2013. *Tibetan Buddhism: A Very Short Introduction*. New York: Oxford University Press.

Keown, Damien. 2013. *Buddhism: A Very Short Introduction*. New York: Oxford University Press.

Lopez, Donald S., ed. 2005. *Critical Terms for the Study of Buddhism*. Chicago: The University of Chicago Press.

Robinson, Richard H., and Willard L. Johnson. 1997. *The Buddhist Religion: A Historical Introduction*. 3rd ed. Belmont, CA: Wadsworth.

Williams, Paul. 2009. *Mahāyāna Buddhism: The Doctrinal Foundations*. London; New York: Routledge.

2

Nineteenth-century foundations

Chapter summary and outline

Colonialism in Asia brought the West into direct contact with Buddhism while defining the relationship between East and West. The convergence of nineteenth-century Western discourses (the Enlightenment and Romantic eras, Orientalism) with Asian Buddhist reform movements gave birth to Buddhist modernism, which came to the United States by the century's end and was on full display at the World's Parliament of Religions in 1893. These discourses set the stage and terms of debate for Western engagements with the Buddhist tradition for the century ahead.

Introduction: The White City

From May through October 1893, the White City gleamed along the banks of Lake Michigan, encompassing the area around Jackson Park in Chicago, Illinois. Buildings constructed for the express purpose of the World's Columbian Exposition were covered in white stucco or made of marble, and the widespread use of electric lights seemed to make the buildings glow, even at night (hence the name, the White City). Intended to showcase exhibits from the world over, the Beaux-Arts neoclassical architecture symbolically represented what the organizers believed to be the height of human civilization. Along the Midway Plaisance leading up to Jackson Park was an anthropological exposition, "an illustrated encyclopedia of civilization" (Ketelaar 1990, 141). At its end, closest to the White City, were villages representing Northern European cultures. Moving further west, one came to Middle Eastern, East Asian, African, and, finally, Native American cultures. This blatant structuring of human civilizations, culminating in the White City, was certainly not unusual for the time, and was in no small part based on a simplistic misreading of Charles Darwin's theory of evolution applied to humanity. Indeed, this was the subtext of the World's Columbian Exposition, a showcase for the supposed superiority of Western culture generally and American exceptionalism specifically.

A few miles north of the main Exposition, in what is now the Art Institute of Chicago, the first World's Parliament of Religions was convened in September 1893. Organized in part by John Henry Barrows, a Presbyterian minister and professor at the University of Chicago, delegates from the "ten major world religions" (variously defined) were invited to attend in a spirit of "universal brotherhood." Delegates included a cadre of Japanese Buddhist leaders, the Sinhala Buddhist revivalist Anagarika Dharmapala, Hindu teacher Swami Vivekenanda, and representatives from other religious traditions including Islam and various Christian denominations. Despite the stated objectives of the organizers for "brotherhood," it was also clearly evident that Barrows' intention was to showcase Christianity's superiority, that by bringing the world's religions into conversation, their refracted light would be unified in the light of heaven (Ketelaar 1990, 140–141). Delegates from Asian countries living under colonial rule had other designs and hoped to use the event to showcase their own traditions' superiority or actively critique the Parliament's intentions. Pun Kwang Yu, a Chinese delegate representing Confucianism, openly criticized the very category of religion as "spreading falsehoods and errors" (149).

The World's Parliament of Religions looms large in the study of US Buddhism, often referred to as a pivotal event in the history of the tradition, one that "radically changed the entire landscape" of US Buddhism (Prebish 1998, 4). At the same time, the event was quickly forgotten following the Exposition. As the country slipped into World War I and the Great Depression, hopes for universal brotherhood and peace seemed out of reach. The World's Parliament of Religions can, nevertheless, be read as a symbolic referent to the cultural moment when Buddhism entered US public life. The events of 1893 were the result of ongoing modernist discourses in the Victorian world that themselves were the result of European colonial projects in Asia; these discourses came into direct contact with emerging nationalist discourses in the Pacific world in which religion and religious identity were playing an increasingly greater role.

The Victorian turn to the East

To begin, it is important to note that "Buddhism" as we know it is a relatively recent invention. Placing its construction in the colonial period will help illuminate how

Buddhism was transformed into a modern world religion, and how this transformation is an integral aspect of its history and practice in the United States.

Colonial origins

Rudyard Kipling opens his 1889 poem "The Ballad of East and West" with the following refrain:

Oh, East is East and West is West, and never the twain shall meet,
Till Earth and Sky stand presently at God's great Judgment Seat;
But there is neither East nor West, Border, nor Breed, nor Birth,
When two strong men stand face to face, though they come from the ends of the
    earth! (Kipling 1994, 245)

The sense that "East" and "West" have specific borders representing two mutually opposing cultural spheres is a direct result of the colonial era in which Kipling was raised. For centuries prior to the colonial period, the borders between European and Asian cultures were permeable and shifting. Within decades of the passing of the historical Buddha, monks and pilgrims began leaving his birthplace and spreading the dharma through the Gandharan region into Central Asia from where it spread throughout East Asia; simultaneously, Buddhism had found its way to Sri Lanka before the beginning of the Common Era and easily spread through most of Southeast Asia. There are references to Buddhism and Buddhist monks in the accounts of Alexander the Great as he pushed the Hellenistic world into the Indian subcontinent. Narrative elements from the Buddha's life story spread throughout the ancient world, eventually transforming themselves into the story of Barlaam and Josaphat, a widely known medieval European Christian allegory, translated into Latin, Arabic, and even Middle English by the eleventh century (MacQueen 1998). Thus, for hundreds of years, Buddhist pilgrims and monks, merchants and tradespersons, came into contact with the full range of European and Near Eastern peoples and cultures.

This fluidity between East and West, and the inherent power relations between them, changed dramatically during the colonial period. Beginning as early as the fifteenth century with Portuguese exploration and trade across Africa, the Near East, and, later the New World, various European powers and commercial ventures began increasing trade networks around the globe. Most were public-private ventures, such as Christopher Columbus' voyages that led him to the Americas, funded by Italian business interests with the support of the Spanish royal family. As time progressed, private corporations became increasingly important such as the East India Company and Hudson Bay Company that controlled trade in India and North America respectively. Very often, Christian missionaries quickly followed, including Jesuits who landed in Japan in the sixteenth century having been dispatched there after Portuguese traders had already made contact. Commercial networks were inherently competitive, at times resulting in open conflict. Such conflicts necessitated the intercession of military forces, which soon came to dominate colonial outposts across Asia. It was during this time that the rhetorical distinctiveness between "the Occident" and "the Orient" was born.

Since at least the 1970s, much scholarly attention has been paid to the discursive processes of colonialism and Orientalism and their effects on the peoples and cultures of the Near and Far East (Clarke 1997; King 1999; Said 1978). As European powers expanded outside Europe, discourses developed to justify such expansion, among them being the explicit defining of both European (Occidental) and Asian (Oriental) cultures. These definitions were distinct from earlier eras of cultural exchange in several important ways. First, they relied on geopolitical borders that were created by the West. That is, the Occident was defined as the political and cultural world west of the Ural Mountains in Russia. North Africa and the Ottoman Empire became the Near East, and everything east of that became the Far East, collectively labeled the Orient. Second, a concomitant development during the colonial period was the emergence of the nation-state as the de facto norm of political organization which displaced premodern feudal kingdoms and empires. This model of social organization would quickly spread to the Near and Far East, and it goes without saying that many modern national borders are the direct result of the dissolution of colonial empires, such as the border between India and Pakistan. Third, and most important for our present purposes, "East" and "West" became defined as mutually opposed cultural realms with the East in a subservient position to the West. The Occident was almost always gendered masculine, a culture of rationalism and progressive forward thinking. The Orient was cast in the feminine, a culture of inward-looking mysticism and a degenerate shadow of past cultural glory. This inherent power imbalance was then used to justify the civilizing influence of European colonial control.

Postcolonial theory

Following from the work of Edward Said, Gayatri Spivak, and others, postcolonial studies has emerged as an important critical framework and lens with which to study the cultural impact of colonialism, the human consequences of imperial rule, and the legacy of domination between colonizer and colonized. In the specific case of religion, scholars have focused on how European frameworks and methods have defined the subjects of study in such a way as to minimize the perspective of native informants and perpetuate unequal power dynamics between religious cultures.

The ability to name "the Other" is a hallmark of the Orientalist project. For Said, Orientalism refers to both the corporate institutions that managed colonial territories as well as rhetorical discourses used to justify colonialism. Managing colonies required naming and labeling colonial lands, persons, and cultures—the "systemic accumulation of human beings and territories" (Said 1978, 123)—in relationship to and employing European terms and categories. In its discursive form, Orientalism is concerned with constructing an image of the Orient that can be thoroughly analyzed, *known* in some sense, by the colonizer. The opening scene of Kipling's 1901 novel *Kim*, for example, takes place in and around a British museum in what is now Pakistan, where a young Tibetan lama is taken on a tour of religious and cultural artifacts by the museum's curator. Abe relates this fictional account of a "native" being so bereft of his own tradition that he needs an "outsider" to explain the significance of his own culture to him as emblematic of the larger colonial project that collected and housed Asian art and artifacts for display to a largely European audience (Abe 1995). The collection and labeling of such artifacts allows for the colonizer to understand at a distance "the other," now safely rendered in his own language, thus "creating a textualized, homogeneous and limited group of world religions largely constructed in its own (modern, Western) image" (King 1999, 82). When confronted with a dizzying array of cultural practices that bear some resemblance to one another, the colonizer deploys the category of "religion"—and its many subcategories—to contain them. In this way, various ritual and ethical practices across Asia that bear a family resemblance came to be called "Buddhism"; once constructed as a religion, Buddhism was then juxtaposed against Christianity. Whereas the former is defined by idol worship and a pantheon of gods akin to the paganism of pre-Christian Europe, and thus backward facing and regressive, the latter is defined as a civilizing, moral force, progressive and forward facing. It was in this context that Buddhism as a distinct religious tradition—that is, an object of study—emerged.

Thus, by the Victorian Era (1837–1901), European and American interests dominated global trade and cultural production. It was said that the sun never set on the British Empire; and even where the United Kingdom did not have direct control, it exerted huge influence, such as in mainland China, leading to the Opium Wars of the mid-nineteenth century. The United States, meanwhile, had a different experience with colonialism, owing in part to the fact that it was itself a former colony. Nevertheless, Thomas Jefferson's desire to create an "empire for liberty" out of the North American continent, a desire aided greatly by the Louisiana Purchase (1803) and near genocide of indigenous peoples, can be read as a type of colonialism. Moreover, by the latter half of the nineteenth century, the United States was beginning to look beyond its continental boarders, leading to conflicts with Spain and the opening of Japan.

Enlightenment and Romanticism

The underlying philosophical discourse of the day was crafted in the Enlightenment, beginning in the late seventeenth century. With foundations in philosophy and science set by Descartes and Newton, Enlightenment Era thinkers were free to question the foundations of premodern European society including political systems and revealed religions. Such thinking paved the way for rational empiricism, modern science, the rise of the nation-state, and secular republican forms of government.

Post-Reformation Europe saw the development of modern philosophy and science, and René Descartes (1596–1650) is widely considered to be the father of modern philosophy. In an era of increasing criticism of church doctrine, Descartes pursued philosophical and mathematical truths guided by skeptical empiricism and the "natural light" of reason. His most well-known contribution, *cogito ergo sum* or "I think, therefore I am," set the stage for latter philosophical thinking in Europe that took for granted what has been subsequently called a Cartesian dualism between mind and body. For our present purposes, the consequences of Descartes' *cogito* to subsequent philosophy are not as important as his methods; guided not by adherence to church authority or doctrine but rather by a method of skepticism and doubt, Descartes' method allowed subsequent thinkers to openly question preexisting assumptions about the natural world and search for empirical truth in the physical world. While at university, Isaac Newton (1642–1727) supplemented his formal studies based on Aristotelian philosophy with the work of Descartes and other contemporary philosophers and scientists, including Johannes Kepler (1571–1630). Kepler's observations of planetary orbits and Descartes' methods would lead Newton to develop the law of universal gravitation, the foundation of modern science. Newton's work in this regard would become the standard model of the universe until developments in quantum physics some three centuries later.

Later philosophers criticized Descartes while employing his basic methods; Newton's physical laws and empirical method allowed for the rise and diversification of modern science. Whereas Newton's and Kepler's initial observations were of orbiting planets, their methods allowed for scientists to explore the physical world writ large, including the natural and biological sciences as exemplified by the nineteenth-century work of Darwin, whose theory of evolution provides the basis for modern biology. Other philosophers in the early seventeenth century would apply these methods not only to the physical world but to social, political, and economic systems as well. French philosophers such as Voltaire and Jean-Jacques Rousseau and British and Scottish philosophers such as Thomas Hobbes, John Locke, and Adam Smith laid the groundwork for modern economic systems, ideals of equality and personal freedom, natural law, and republican forms of government. Locke's *Two Treatises of Government* is echoed in Jefferson's *Declaration of Independence*. Thus, one direct result of the rise of rational empiricism and modern philosophy was the intellectual justification for the American Revolution which sought independence for the American colonies from the United Kingdom. In many ways, the American Revolution was a gamble (a small collection of ill-funded colonies versus the largest empire on the planet), but its unlikely success was seen as something of an inspiration for the French Revolution, however short lived, in 1789. Both revolutions employed rhetorics and discourses forged in the Enlightenment.

The Enlightenment was in many ways profoundly destabilizing for premodern Christianity. First, rational empiricism and modern science undermined Christian cosmologies, histories, and soteriology and relegated them to the category of *faith* as opposed to *reason*. Secondly, and perhaps more importantly, secular governments that separated church and state undermined the political and economic support of religious institutions altogether. And, finally, this process of secularization created a distinct category of social life explicitly labeled as *religious*. What was once a broad set of social customs, attitudes, and practices embedded throughout the culture became, in the modern age, a distinct and separate sphere of activity, something internal, personal, and private. As a result of this destabilization, many Christian institutions responded either by reinterpreting their tradition (giving rise to a literalist interpretation of Biblical texts and the quest for the historical Jesus) or by increased missionary activity at home and in the colonies. By the nineteenth century in England and the United States, the Victorian period brought with it a return to or refocusing on Christian morality, arguably a return to a more modest and conservative mood in response to the perceived amorality of the previous century.

Colonialism in many ways contributed to what has been called the space-time compression of modernity (Chapter 12) (Tweed 2012). As we move further in time from the beginning of the nineteenth century to the present, the ability for persons to travel to distant lands or communicate with others around the globe becomes easier and faster. A consequence of this ease of access to the Orient as well as the displacement of traditional Christian perspectives and institutions was an increased interest in non-Christian religious and spiritual practices. Whereas the Enlightenment was dominated by the pursuit of pure reason, the subsequent Romantic period, which the Victorian era inherited, rejected rationalism in favor of intuitive and emotive direct experiences with both the natural world and the transcendent. In Victorian England and America, this manifested itself, in part, in new spiritualist movements, including a fascination with mysticism, esotericism, and the occult, variously defined.

This fascination would have an impact on Buddhism as Europeans and Americans sent to live or work in Asian colonies came in contact with non-Christian traditions first hand. As part of the larger Orientalist project, this interest expressed itself in the collection and translation of texts, work that would allow for the first translations of Buddhist texts into European languages and give rise to a new academic field of Buddhist studies or Buddhology. Eugène Burnouf, for example, compiled the monumental *Introduction à l'histoire du Bouddhisme indien* in 1844, a 600-page work that sought to catalog the whole of the Buddhist tradition, and included 147 Sanskrit Buddhist texts. While an admirable attempt at understanding the Buddhist tradition, Burnouf's work suffers from being purely textual; that is, it is the result of Orientalist scholarship that sought to locate the true or authentic core of Buddhist teachings in its texts and ancient languages while actively ignoring the voices of living Buddhists (King 1999, 146). Such translations found their way to the Americas as well; Ralph Waldo Emerson published a translation of the *Lotus Sutra* from Burnouf's French by Elizabeth Palmer Peabody in the Transcendentalist newsletter, *The Dial* (Blum 2009, 226). Not all colonial-era translations were conducted in Europe, of course. In the late 1800s, a British civil servant serving in Sri Lanka, T. W. Rhys Davids founded the Pali Text Society and dedicated himself to translating Theravada Buddhist texts. He was assisted in this work by his wife, Caroline Rhys Davids, who took over as president of the society following his death. Their careers helped lay the groundwork for modern Buddhist scholarship in addition to providing some of the first translations of Buddhist texts into European languages.

The Buddha's cause in Sri Lanka

Colonel Henry Steel Olcott (1833–1907), after having been discharged from the US Army following the Civil War, moved to New York where he set up a law practice and began investigating spiritualist events and organizations around New England. It was during this time that he met Helena Blavatsky (1831–1891). Blavatsky had been in the United States for a very short time but had already created a name for herself as a powerful medium and was well on her way to creating a new spiritualist movement. Together with Olcott and others, in 1875 they founded the Theosophical Society.

According to the Society, theosophy was an ancient spiritual practice, most recently revealed to Blavatsky by Himalayan masters ("mahatmas") during her seven-year journey into Tibet. The Society devoted itself to the study of comparative religion, philosophy, and science; the promotion of universal brotherhood; and the investigation of unexplained natural and psychic phenomenon, especially the latent powers of the human mind. Placing itself within a cosmic evolutionary model of spiritual development, Blavatsky argued that humanity was heading toward the perfection of consciousness, and that the Theosophical Society was the latest iteration of other, often-hidden and unseen, groups over the millennia who had helped guide human civilizations toward this end. The Theosophical Society argued a kind of perennialism that was part of larger religious discourses of the time, a strategy aimed at reconciling apparent differences between religious traditions by proposing universalistic alternatives. Much of this rhetoric looked to the ancient past as sources of spiritual inspiration; Blavatsky's mahatmas, advanced spiritual beings believed to be located deep in the Himalayas, filled this role for the Theosophical Society (Washington 1995).

Perennialism is a philosophy of religion that argues that all religions are based on the same fundamental, universal truth and that the apparent diversity of religions is the result of human interpretations of that universal truth. Whereas this perspective may be comforting in the face of discord that stems from religious difference, perennialism makes false equivalences between what are in fact very different approaches to spiritually, ethics, and behavior.

A recurrent theme in Orientalist literature is the notion that contemporary Asian cultures are degenerate shadows of once-great civilizations, and the degenerative effects of modernity have obscured ancient high culture and lost spiritual wisdom. The causes of degeneration vary (though they are often explicitly linked with racial hierarchies and blamed on Semitic or non-European cultural influence, see Clarke 1997, 78); but this degeneration is often juxtaposed against anxieties about the modern age. For those dismayed by rapid technological advances, the increasing importance of rationalism or science, the apparent decline in virtuous morality, or a first-hand experience of modern warfare (such as the US Civil War), the allure of some ancient civilization and its forgotten wisdom was potent. This desire manifested itself in idealized accounts of various Near and Far Eastern cultures and is expressed clearly in the myth of Shangri-la, a hidden Himalayan kingdom or Tibetan Buddhist utopia. Such idealizations were grafted onto Tibet itself, a nation largely isolated from the forces of colonialism or modernity until relatively late. Due to this isolation, "there remained, occasionally peeking above the surface, this mythic image of Tibet—a physically esoteric land concealing an even more esoteric body of mystical knowledge" (Hackett 2013, xiv). This mythic image was a powerful draw for late-nineteenth- and early-twentieth-century spiritual seekers who made numerous attempts to travel to the Himalayas, as Blavatsky claimed to have done herself.

This somewhat indirect connection to Tibet provides us with one way in which the activities of Blavatsky and Olcott, as well as the Theosophical Society more generally, overlap with the history of Buddhism. A more direct connection came as a result of Blavatsky's and Olcott's decision to move the Theosophical Society's headquarters to India. For several years in the late 1870s, Olcott had been corresponding with Hindu and Buddhist reformers in the British colonies, and he became convinced that the Society's future lay in Asia, not the United States. He and Blavatsky arrived in India in 1879. Tensions were rising across the subcontinent and Sri Lanka (then Ceylon) as both Hindu and Buddhist leaders increasingly advocated for religious freedom and other rights, as well as against Christian missionary work considered to be a threat to precolonial religious and cultural customs. In Sri Lanka, these tensions were on full display in publications and public debates between Buddhists and Christians (Prothero 1996, 85–86). Such rhetorical conflicts were feeding a growing Sinhala Buddhist revivalist movement that overlapped with a growing nationalist movement. Olcott was impressed by the Buddhist revivalists, in particular the skills of Migettuwatte Gunananda Thera who had won a debate against a Wesleyan minister in 1873 (Lopez 2002, xiii). Olcott and Blavatsky set sail for Sri Lanka in 1880. Almost immediately after their arrival, they took the three refuges and five lay precepts, publicly declaring themselves to be Buddhist.

Over the next twenty years, Olcott would have a complicated relationship with both the Theosophical Society and various Buddhist institutions and movements in India and Sri Lanka. At first, he advocated quite strongly on behalf of Buddhism. In 1881, in an effort to clarify the Buddhist teachings, he wrote a *Buddhist Catechism*. Based on Christian catechisms laid out in a series of questions and answers, Olcott's was intended to both clarify Buddhist doctrine and to be used in Buddhist educational settings. As a result, the *Buddhist Catechism*, regardless of its authorship and idiosyncrasies, became extremely popular among Buddhist leaders and remains a standard text in many Sri Lankan Buddhist schools to this day. Following a religious riot in 1884, Buddhist leaders requested that Olcott defend their interests to the colonial authorities. In a visit to London, he successfully argued for more religious rights in Sri Lanka, and while not as thoroughly widespread as he would like, the colonial government both recognized Buddhist religious freedom as well as established *vesak* (Buddha's birthday) as an official holiday. These explicit activities on Buddhism's behalf endeared Olcott to many and no doubt helped people overlook his apparent dual-identity as both a Buddhist and theosophist (Prothero 1996, 101–115).

It was on his first trip to Sri Lanka in 1880 that Olcott met Anagarika Dharmapala (1864–1933), who was then fourteen years old. Dharmapala was born Don David Hewavitharana into a family of wealthy merchants. His family's relative prosperity privileged him with a colonial education and caused him to be somewhat ignorant of widespread class, ethnic, and religious disparities in his homeland. As he toured Sri Lanka with Olcott during his first visit, the young Hewavitharana saw the deep poverty of many Sinhalese and was inspired to work toward reestablishing Buddhism. He changed his name to Anagarika Dharmapala (lit., "homeless one," "protector of the dharma") and, later in his life, ordained as a monastic. In his youth, he was inspired by Olcott's bureaucratic and organizational skills, which would prove invaluable following his visit to Bodhgaya—an important pilgrimage site, where the Buddha had attained awakening and had been neglected and fallen into a state of disrepair by the end of the nineteenth century. Dharmapala resolved, in 1891, to restore the site as a major pilgrimage center, and this in turn led to the foundation of the Maha Bodhi Society. In the following year, he established a new journal, the *Maha Bodhi Journal*, and it was his writings therein that caught the attention of the organizers of the World's Parliament of Religions (Kemper 2005).

It is worth noting here that Dharmapala was of course not the only Buddhist reformer responding to colonial occupation in South or Southeast Asia. The Kingdom of Siam, later Thailand, was being pressured by the British to the west and the French to the east to modernize its government and open the country to trade. In response to these pressures, King Mongkut (1804–1868) initiated a number of reforms across Thai society including many to the Buddhist *sangha* (Chapter 5). In Burma, controlled by the British empire, Buddhist reformers initiated programs aimed at the laity with an eye toward empowering lay persons to become experts in the dharma to fend off the decline of Buddhism; these programs included teaching the laity meditation practices including *vipasyana* (P: *vipassana*) (Braun 2013). Across the region, authority shifted from oral traditions and local customs to textual study and knowledge of the Pali canon, reflecting the influence of text-centric Western scholarship. In short, the colonial period had a profound effect on the development of modern Theravada Buddhism which would find its way to the United States a century later.

Whereas Olcott had been embroiled in Theosophical Society's institutional crises through the 1880s, by the decade's end he was simultaneously recommitting himself to the cause of restoring Buddhism. This work expressed itself in a number of ways, including visits to Japan and Burma, the convening of a pan-sectarian Buddhist conference in 1890, and the composition of a fourteen-point "Buddhist platform" that he had hopes of spreading throughout the Buddhist world in an effort to reconcile Buddhist sectarian differences. Following Blavatsky's death in 1891 and subsequent power struggles in the Theosophical Society, Olcott spent an increasing amount of time in India, working at times with Hindu outcastes. Olcott's ambivalence between different religious and spiritual traditions and rhetoric of unifying the world's religions would eventually cause many of his former allies to denounce him. Dharmapala publicly did so in 1899, declaring that Olcott had abandoned Buddhism's cause in Sri Lanka (Prothero 1996, 165).

Despite the failure of his Buddhist platform to be universally accepted, his idiosyncratic *Buddhist Catechism*, and mixed successes later in life, Olcott remains an important and influential figure in late-nineteenth-century Buddhist history. Scholars have identified this period of time with the birth of Buddhist modernism (Chapter 12), and Olcott plays an important role here. The *Catechism* defines Buddhism in several specific ways, including its rejection of superstition, embrace of scientific and rational empiricism, and commitment to gender equality. Here, we can see the beginnings of a specific modernist rhetoric that follows Buddhism down to the present. Whereas it is clear that Olcott was not always successful in his attempts at unifying Buddhism, it is equally clear that his celebrity status helped elevate other Buddhist leaders, including Dharmapala. Dharmapala's work with the Maha Bodhi Society, his speech at the World's Parliament of Religions, and subsequent speaking tours in the United States left a lasting impact on American's understanding of Buddhism. And over the course of the twentieth century, subsequent Buddhist reformers would follow in his wake, employing modernist discourses in an effort to revitalize Buddhism in Sri Lanka, Burma, Thailand, and across Southeast Asia.

It was precisely this spirit of revivalism that attracted Japanese Buddhist leaders who invited Olcott to Japan in 1889.

The Meiji turn to the West

The Tokugawa or Edo Period (1603–1867) in Japan followed a long period of internal warfare and political struggle. The Tokugawa *shogunate* (military government) brought stability and relative prosperity to the nation, but it was at the cost of strict government oversight meant to manage virtually all aspects of social and cultural life, including religion. The desire to control religious institutions was motivated, in part, by two factors. First, during the medieval period, Buddhist institutions had grown increasingly large and influential, at times strong enough to challenge both local warlords and the *shogunate* itself through force of arms. By reigning in and managing these institutions, the Tokugawa *shogunate* was able to maintain peace among various Buddhist denominations. A consequence of this was that Buddhist schools became more sectarian and increasingly had little to do with one another, a marked departure from the syncretistic norm of East Asian Buddhism more generally. Second, as mentioned earlier, in the 1500s, European traders and Jesuit missionaries had begun to arrive on Japanese shores. Early missionary activities were surprisingly successful—successful enough to worry the Tokugawa regime who outlawed Christianity by the 1630s. Japan's awareness of European incursions on the Asian mainland led to a strict isolationist policy that would remain in place throughout the Edo Period.

All of this changed with the arrival of US Commodore Matthew Perry in 1853 who sailed into Tokyo harbor, guns not quite blazing but certainly trained on the imperial palace. The United States at this time was beginning to look beyond its continental borders to secure trade relationships or expand territory, and Perry was on an errand to sign a trade agreement with the nation of Japan. The Japanese, of course, knew that various European countries controlled much of Asia; China and the United Kingdom were in the middle of the Opium Wars, causing concern that Japan could be next. Fearful of being taken over by foreign powers, the government entered into a trade agreement with the United States, one that promptly ruined the Japanese economy, an event that coincided with several natural disasters and pandemics that caused widespread dissent among the populace. When the Tokugawa government reached out to their trade partners for help, they found that the United States had entered its own Civil War. Growing discontent across Japan then led to the overthrow of the *shogunate* and the reinstatement of the emperor, known as the Meiji Restoration, in 1868.

In the short term, the Meiji Restoration was disastrous for Buddhism (Ketelaar 1990). The new government sought to solidify national identity and loyalty around the emperor, in part, by promoting the mythological origins of the nation rooted in Shinto beliefs. By highlighting the divine origins of the imperial family, this nativist movement began actively promoting what was known as State Shinto while trying to rid the nation of foreign influences, including Buddhism. A series of laws passed in the years immediately following the Meiji Restoration weakened government support of Buddhist institutions; Buddhist bells were confiscated by the government and melted down for armaments; Buddhist monks were disrobed and monastic vows regarding marriage and the eating of meat nullified (Jaffe 2001). These persecutions were short-lived, however; a new generation of Buddhist intellectuals began promoting what was termed *shin bukkyo* or "new Buddhism," which would become an essential part of Japanese national identity (Sharf 1995b).

This was the context in which Dharmapala and Olcott sailed in 1889 at the behest of Japanese Buddhist revivalists. While Dharmapala spent most of the trip ill and at the hospital, he was nevertheless able to meet with Japanese Buddhist leaders who established a local chapter of the Maha Bodhi Society. Olcott, meanwhile, was swept up on a grueling three-month tour of the nation, invited to give daily lectures, tours of major institutions, factories, and universities, and an audience with high-ranking religious and political figures. According to his own accounts, his speeches drew crowds of thousands, eager to hear about the virtues of the Buddhist religion and the West's deepening interest in what the East had to offer. As Snodgrass (2003) has noted, large audiences are more a reflection of his hosts' organizational skills than his celebrity, and it is quite likely that most of those in attendance would not have understood his English well enough to grasp what he was saying. Olcott's tour of Japan was more a performance piece intended to showcase to a Japanese audience how its native Buddhism was being embraced by the West.

In this regard, Japanese intellectuals were involved in the same project of construct-ing a modern religion as their South Asian counterparts. Whereas Sinhala Buddhist modernizers were living under direct colonial control, Japanese intellectuals were only threatened by the possibility and thus held the West at a distance. Despite the Meiji government's desire to rid Japan of foreign influence, it is undeniably true that they imported into Japan Western political and cultural institutions and structures. For dec-ades, Japanese students and leaders traveled to European and later American univer-sities to learn about Western philosophy, politics, and culture, knowledge that was then brought home to remake Japan as a modern nation with its own colonial aspirations.

The question of religion was a deeply important part of this overall project of nation-building. Whereas during the early Meiji, State Shinto was promoted as an integral aspect of Japanese identity, it was not framed as a religion per se. Moreover, part of the learning imported to Japan from the West was the aforementioned discourse on rationalism and science. The question of where Buddhism fit into these discourses was then taken up by native Buddhist thinkers and philosophers who rather deliber-ately defined "religion" in modern Japan. One example is Inoue Enryo (1858–1919). Born into a Jodo Shinshu family, educated at Tokyo Imperial University, and founder of a number of important philosophical societies and publications, Inoue was attracted to both Chinese and Western philosophy. His work helped define Buddhism and reli-gion in Meiji-era Japan, in part, by delineating between religion and superstition. In detailed studies of religious mythology, what would later become known as "monster studies," Inoue argued that belief in supernatural beings was irrational; Buddhism, on the other hand, was devoted to an empirical experience of the absolute, expressed in acultural and universalistic terms. Inoue placed the historical Buddha in a pantheon of sages, which included Confucius, Socrates, and Kant as all providing pragmatic orien-tations toward the absolute (Josephson 2006). Importantly, Inoue also advocated for the development of a nationalistic spirit that would enable Japan to strongly counter Western influence; this spirit could be derived from Buddhism, he argued, explicitly joining a Japanese nationalist identity with Buddhist philosophy (Snodgrass 2003, 147). Later thinkers and public intellectuals, many of whom studied with Inoue or at organizations he founded, would elaborate on these themes. Manshi Kiyozawa (1863–1903), for example, not only set the stage for modern Jodo Shinshu thought but was also instrumental in transforming sectarian Buddhist schools into modern universities (Blum 2011). But it was the work of later thinkers such as Nishida Kitaro and Shaku Soen that would have the most direct influence on US Buddhism primarily through Soen's student, D. T. Suzuki (Sharf 1995b).

By the turn of the twentieth century, Japanese Buddhism had undergone profound institutional and doctrinal changes, transforming itself into a modern religion. This transformation was in line with larger cultural and political movements that sought to reshape the Japanese nation into a modern world power, secure against imperial threats from the West. It was within this context that Buddhism was deployed rhet-orically as the "soul of Japan," as the quintessential Japanese religion while remaining universal in appeal, thus superior to Christianity. This desire to define Buddhism as something quintessentially Japanese and simultaneously universal would be on clear display at the World's Parliament of Religions.

The World's Parliament of Religions

As mentioned at the outset, the World's Parliament of Religions was organized by, among others, John Henry Barrows. Promotional literature emphasized the importance of bringing together the world's religions in a spirit of brotherhood; but as Ketelaar has noted, "brotherhood" reflected a universalism that required acceptance of a particular conception of religious truth. For Barrows, the various religions of the world emanated from the "light of heaven" and were refracted by the "prism of man" (Ketelaar 1990, 140–141). In organizing the Parliament, Barrows requested that each delegate speak in English on matters of interest to the American public, including such topics as God, the relationship of man to God, the role of women, ethics, and morality. These terms reflect neither universal human understandings of the transcendent nor humanity's relationship to it; rather, they reflect particular concerns of late Victorian American Christian culture. The very nature of these questions refigures other religious traditions so that they must respond to the Christian host rather than speaking on their own terms. Barrows and the other organizers assumed that the natural superiority of Christianity would rise to the fore, that "it was the 'light and religion of Christ' that had 'led to the chief and noblest development of modern civilization'" (Girardot 2002, 485).

These assumptions were openly challenged. Pun Kwang Yu, as we saw before, called into question the very category of religion. Hirai Kinzo, the only Japanese delegate who had command of English, delivered two talks, the first of which was a strong rebuke of Christianity. In it, he argued that the Japanese associated Christianity with imperial aggression and that this was the reason missionaries had had little success in Japan (Snodgrass 2003, 181). That his arguments appealed to notions of political power, justice, and economics should not be surprising; Japan was at the time hoping to renegotiate unequal trade agreements with the United States. Hirai's comments were directed as much toward international politics as they were toward the fundamental questions of religion.

Despite attempts to challenge the underlying assumptions of the Parliament or to showcase their religions' own superiority, in general the Asian delegates were hampered in their efforts. Most of the delegates were not fluent enough in English to present their papers without translation, and much was lost in the process. Whereas his refutation of the categories of religion and God were, on paper, eloquent and forceful, Pun Kwang Yu's delivered remarks were more or less summaries of the original questions about God and man that Barrows had asked the delegates to prepare. Shaku Soen, a Rinzai Zen Buddhist delegate, prepared an elaborate discussion of the Buddhist doctrine of conditioned origination (*pratityasamutpada*); the translation of his talk, however, borrowed heavily from Theosophical language (Ketelaar 1990, 151). Dharmapala's second paper, "Buddhism and Christianity," argued for a Buddhist origin for all that was good in Christianity; in Barrow's official history and transcripts of the event, this statement was excised (Snodgrass 2003, 190).

The Parliament would have lasting effects on the development of US Buddhism, despite whatever drawbacks or rhetorical failures the delegates may have had in 1893. When we examine how the Parliament was publicized in Asia after the event, for example, it is clear that the Asian delegates used their experience to bolster ongoing reform, revivalist, and nationalist movements. Speaking to a Buddhist group in Yokohama, a Japanese delegate declared that the Parliament "showed the great superiority of Buddhism over Christianity" and that "Western peoples had lost their faith in Christianity and were ready to accept the teachings of our superior religion" (Snodgrass 2003, 247). Having had this opportunity to speak to American audiences, the Parliament was used as a precursor to further public lecture tours by Asian religious thinkers spurred on by pre-existing Victorian interest in non-Christian and occult practices; this led to continued exchanges between East and West and the establishment of new communities in the United States. Dharmapala toured the United States on several occasions in the decades following, allowing him to establish chapters of the Maha Bodhi Society. Soen's student, D. T. Suzuki, attended the Parliament but only to translate his teacher's talks. Nevertheless, his attendance caused him to meet Paul Carus (1852–1919).

A German American philosopher and publisher, Carus was extremely impressed with Soen's talks at the Parliament. The following year, Carus published *The Gospel of Buddha*, a loose collection of translations of Buddhist texts summarizing the Buddhist religion for English-speaking audiences. *The Gospel* was not well received by his contemporaries in the academic study of Buddhism; it reflected a deliberate picking and choosing of original sources that were intended to reveal Buddhism's universality as a "religion of science" superior to other, less-evolved spiritual traditions. Nevertheless, almost immediately upon its US publication, Soen had Suzuki translate it into Japanese, not necessarily because it was a particularly accurate representation of Buddhism but because it reinforced Soen's belief that Americans were willing accept Buddhism over Christianity (Snodgrass 1998). Following the *Gospel's* translation and publication, Suzuki was sent to LaSalle, Illinois, to work with Carus on other publication and translation projects. As a result of this relationship, Suzuki went on to enjoy a long career as a Zen Buddhist teacher. He traveled widely in the United States and Europe, wrote extensively, and participated in the "Zen boom" of the 1950s, laying the foundation for Zen Buddhism's rise in popularity in the latter half of the twentieth century (Iwamura 2010, 25).

Monism is a philosophical postulate that argues for a unity, oneness of origins, or singular essence of all things; that is, monists argue that underlying all apparent differences in matter is a single, unified essence. Buddhism is not monistic; some traditions outright reject monism while others suggest that whereas all phenomena may have the similar characteristic of emptiness (*sunyata*), there are nevertheless discrete elements of phenomena.

Suzuki's Zen Buddhism, however, is a product of its time, reflecting a convergence of Soen's Japanese nationalism and Carus' universalistic *monism*. Following the Parliament, as Japan's imperialist agenda grew and eventually led to the Russo-Japanese War (1904–1905), Soen's writing reflected an ever-growing nationalist spirit including Buddhist justifications for Japanese military aggression. Carus' publishing ventures included two journals, *Open Court Press* and *The Monist*, both of which were devoted, in part, to reconciling religion and science. For Carus, Buddhism was the religion most in line with modern science in that it presented a rational approach to the apprehension of empirical (albeit transcendent) truth, a truth that was singular and universal. We see these trends in Suzuki's representation of Zen Buddhism as well. For Suzuki, Zen is universal in that it apprehends transcendent truths that are gleaned through an experiential path of practice that is necessarily ahistorical and acultural. On the other hand, it is also uniquely and quintessentially Japanese. According to Suzuki, whereas Zen was imported into Japan from China, it was only in Japan that it reached its full flowering; in the transmission of Zen to Japan, Zen becomes clarified and authentic while simultaneously igniting the true spiritual essence of the Japanese. Thus, Zen is the authentic spirit of Japan, effecting and influencing all levels of art, culture, and identity. This perspective is somewhat confusing and misleading. First, it is hard to follow Suzuki's logic that the religion is both universal and particular, dependent on experiences beyond verifiability ("To study Zen means to have Zen experience, for without the experience there is no Zen one can study," [Suzuki 1967, 123]); second,

FIGURE 7 *D. T. Suzuki, 1870–1966. (Alamy Stock Photo.)*

despite his arguments that Zen is the authentic spirituality of Japan, the inspiration for everything from systems of government to the Japanese tea ceremony, Zen Buddhism is a minority tradition in Japan, far outnumbered by other Buddhist traditions who have historically had much wider cultural impact. Its modern influence is in many ways the result of Meiji-era Buddhist revivalist movements (Sharf 1995b).

Thus, the World's Parliament of Religions was a watershed moment not only in its immediate impact but also in its lasting legacy. It was convened at the intersection of several cultural and rhetorical trajectories, including colonial, modernist, nationalist, and Victorian. As European colonial enterprises sought to control the Near and Far East, rising Asian nationalist movements rearticulated religious perspectives and institutions in an attempt to challenge Western powers in the Pacific World. In the late Victorian era, Europeans and Americans had inherited rationalist and scientific discourses that called into question preexisting Christian articulations of truth; this questioning led to both a reaffirmation of Christian faith and a Romantic idealization of non-European sources of spiritual wisdom. The Parliament reflected all of these concerns in numerous ways and provided a launchpad for further discourse and exchange. Moving forward from the Parliament, figures such as Suzuki would have an outsized influence on US Buddhist discourses, influencing such thinkers as Alan Watts, Beat Generation writers, and later American-born Zen Buddhist teachers. However, by the turn of the twentieth century, in addition to these largely rhetorical and intellectual debates about the meaning of Buddhism, Asian immigrants would begin arriving on US shores, bringing with them a living tradition and forever changing the US Buddhist landscape.

DISCUSSION QUESTIONS

1. In what specific ways did rational empiricism undermine premodern religious authority?
2. Perennialism reduces differences between religious traditions by claiming that all religions are reflections of a unifying underlying truth. What are the limitations of this perspective?
3. How did Japanese Buddhists use their experiences at the World's Parliament of Religions for their own revivalist ends?

SUGGESTIONS FOR FURTHER READING

Clarke, J. J. 1997. *Oriental Enlightenment: The Encounter between Asian and Western Thought*. New York: Routledge.

King, Richard. 1999. *Orientalism and Religion Post-Colonial Theory, India and 'the Mystic East'*. New York: Routledge.

Learman, Linda, ed. 2005. *Buddhist Missionaries in the Era of Globalization*. Topics in Contemporary Buddhism. Honolulu: University of Hawai'i Press.

Lopez, Donald S., ed. 1995. *Curators of the Buddha: The Study of Buddhism under Colonialism*. Chicago: University of Chicago Press.

Said, Edward. 1978. *Orientalism*. 1st ed. New York: Pantheon Books.

Snodgrass, Judith. 2003. *Presenting Japanese Buddhism to the West: Orientalism, Occidentalism, and the Columbian Exposition*. Chapel Hill: University of North Carolina Press.

3

From acculturation to the counterculture

Chapter summary and outline

Late-nineteenth- and early-twentieth-century immigration allowed for the establishment of the first US Buddhist communities that faced strong anti-Asian prejudices and immigration exclusion acts culminating in World War II Japanese American internment. The postwar years saw an increase in interest in Buddhism exemplified by Beat Generation poets and artists. Twin cultural trajectories converged in Cold War America, reflecting diverging interests that reshaped the US Buddhist landscape.

Introduction: The Berkeley Study Center

In August 1952, a three-day seminar was hosted by the Berkeley Buddhist Temple, a Jodo Shinshu Buddhist temple affiliated with the Buddhist Churches of America

(BCA). The seminar was organized by young Japanese Americans who were part of a study group at the temple run by the resident minister Kanmo Imamura and his wife Jane. Following World War II internment, the Japanese American community was in a process of rebuilding and readjustment. For the BCA at large, this included the desire to provide Buddhist education in English in the United States. The Berkeley Temple's study group was an outgrowth of this movement. However, the 1952 seminar was broader in scope than the BCA community. Invited speakers included Buddhist priests from both the United States and Canada; Thubten Jigme Norbu, brother of the Dalai Lama; cofounder of the American Academy of Asian Studies, Haridas Chaudhuri; and popular philosopher Alan Watts.

The Berkeley Temple's study group was, before 1952, somewhat limited to the immediate community of Buddhists and Japanese American students who lived at the temple's dormitory while studying at the University of California, a few blocks away. Following this seminar, the temple became publicly visible. Jane Imamura would later write that the 1950s were a time when scholars, linguists, authors, poets, and artists would "hang around" the temple—groups of young men and women, "erudite seekers [who] often engaged in friendly bantering but mostly in serious discussion" (Imamura 1998, 38–39). These scholars, artists, and seekers included Buddhist scholars Dennis Hirota, Alex Wayman, and Robert Jackson, and young and as yet unknown poets Gary Snyder and Jack Kerouac. Their "friendly bantering" would lead to a large volume of essays, dharma talks, poetry, and art, which became the content of an annual journal, the *Berkeley Bussei*. Whereas before the war the *Bussei* was essentially a temple newsletter with community notes and event listings, in the 1950s it was transformed into something of a literary and philosophical journal. Watts contributed essays on Buddhism, religion, and psychology. Snyder, Kerouac, and others contributed poetry. A stage play written by Hiroshi Kashiwagi based on the Buddhist story of Kisa Gotami was published and later performed at the temple, with a young George Takei playing the lead role.

By the beginning of the 1960s, however, the core of the study group had largely moved on to other projects or graduated from university and left the area. Eventually the study group evolved into a graduate school, the Institute of Buddhist Studies. But for a time in the 1950s, the Berkeley Temple was at the intersection of twin trajectories of US Buddhist development. Japanese immigrants had arrived in the United States in the late nineteenth century, bringing Buddhism with them. Communities they established in the early part of the twentieth century continued to serve the Japanese American community through the war years while acclimating to the dominant American religious landscape. As we saw in the previous chapter, there was a growing interest in Asian religions generally and Buddhism specifically throughout the nineteenth century; this interest saw a resurgence following World War II, a time when many young Americans began to look for alternative sources of religious and artistic inspiration. These parallel histories converged in Berkeley in the 1950s.

Gold Rush and picture brides

Early Chinese migration

Shortly after the discovery of gold in 1848 near Sacramento, California, hundreds of thousands of people from the world over migrated to California. Among those hoping to strike it rich were several thousand Chinese immigrants. By the 1870 US Census, there were over 60,000 Chinese living in the United States, mostly along the West Coast. After having been pushed off the gold mining fields by white Americans, many moved east to help in the construction of the transcontinental railroad. By the 1870s, most had returned to large urban areas, such as San Francisco or Los Angeles, where they were by and large forced to settle in ghettoized communities—the first Chinatowns.

While it is undoubtedly true that this first generation of Chinese immigrants brought their religious traditions with them, very little is known about what this religious life would have looked like before the turn of the century. There are reports of "joss houses" in the media of the day—*joss* being a derivative of the Portuguese *deus* and referencing gods or idols that would have been the central object of devotion within a small temple or shrine. Chinese religion being highly syncretic, US joss houses would have undoubtedly contained religious practices derived from local folk customs, Daoism, and Buddhism. In San Francisco, Buddhist temples such as Tin Hou and Kong Chow were established by the 1850s (Chandler 1998, 16), though few of these temples survived into the next century.

Chinese gold miners being forced off the mining fields due to anti-Chinese sentiment was a portent of things to come. During the economically depressed post-Civil War years, politicians and labor leaders blamed Chinese immigrants for keeping wages low, building on a general anti-Asian sentiment at the time. Laws were passed across the country that barred nonwhites from participating fully in public life or becoming US citizens and many were directed at Chinese and other Asian peoples, leading to the passage of the Chinese Exclusion Act of 1882. This law barred immigration from China to the United States until the 1940s, thus stifling the Chinese American population. Whatever religious or social communities they had established in the mid-nineteenth century would eventually be abandoned, and thus there are virtually no Chinese Buddhist communities of this era that survive to the present. In the next chapter, we will explore how the Chinese American Buddhist community has been affected by immigration changes in the latter half of the twentieth century.

Japanese Buddhists would have a similar but quite different experience. As mentioned in the previous chapter, the Meiji Restoration was a turbulent time in Japanese history that saw the reorganization of society at all levels. One important consequence of this period was Japan's relationship to the United States, including immigration laws on both sides of the Pacific, laws that would allow for Buddhism to firmly root itself in the United States.

Japanese Buddhist missions

Since its discovery by colonial powers in the eighteenth century, the Hawai'ian islands were contested by various European and later American interests into the nineteenth century when the islands were unified as the Kingdom of Hawai'i in 1810. By mid-century, Protestant missionaries and plantation owners had settled enough of the islands to displace native populations and hold outsized influence in politics and local economies. Closely aligned with the United States (who annexed the islands as a territory in 1898), agricultural concerns drove the economy and necessitated large labor pools. Early on, many Chinese immigrants had come to work the plantations, and in the 1880s, plantation owners were able to convince the Meiji government to allow its citizens to emigrate from Japan. Such arrangements were quickly replicated on the US mainland, especially in central Californian farming lands that were also experiencing rapid growth. The first Japanese arrived in Hawai'i in 1885 and the West Coast of the mainland a few years later. Labor agreements made between US businesses and the Japanese government targeted specific Japanese prefectures for immigrant workers. It so happened that these prefectures were locations where the dominant form of Buddhism was Jodo Shinshu (Shin Buddhism). Thus, the vast majority of Japanese immigrants at this time came from families with a Shin Buddhist heritage (Nishimura 2008, 91).

The establishment of Japanese Buddhist organizations in the United States happened first in Hawai'i. A Shin Buddhist priest, Soryu Kugai, arrived there in 1889 and began organizing Buddhist groups among the plantation workers. This culminated in the first official temple, dedicated in 1897. That same year, Nasaburo Hirano, a young immigrant to the US mainland, traveled to Kyoto where he persuaded Shin Buddhist leaders to send missionaries to America. Hirano had learned English in Christian-run schools where he and other Japanese immigrants felt pressured to convert. Concerned that they would lose their Buddhist heritage, Hirano hoped to establish a Buddhist presence in North America. Two priests, Eryu Honda and Ejun Miyamoto, were dispatched in 1898. They toured the West Coast, from San Francisco to Vancouver, Canada, and decided to establish a Young Men's Buddhist Association, modeled after Young Men's Christian Associations. A year later, their organization was officially recognized by the Japanese leadership as an overseas mission, reorganized as both the Buddhist Church of San Francisco and the North American Buddhist Mission (NABM). Renamed the Buddhist Churches of America (BCA) during World War II, this community is the longest continually operating Buddhist organization in North America.

The NABM and its Hawai'ian counterpart have remained separate and independent organizations since their founding as a result of Hawai'i's independence from the US mainland. Both organizations, however, are affiliates of the Nishi Honganji branch of Shin Buddhism in Japan, and their US-affiliated temples have similar histories. Many of them were established by small groups of individuals who hosted meetings or services in members' homes. Later, as they grew large enough, they would request the services of an ordained priest or minister, purchase or rent property, and establish a fully functioning temple, often referred to as "churches" reflecting the dominant culture's normative religious language (Kashima 1977, 11–12). By the 1920s, dozens of temples had been established, mainly along the West Coast, including several in Canada (which at the time were affiliated with the NABM [Wilson 2011, 539]). Not all Japanese immigrants were Shin Buddhist, of course, and other Japanese Buddhist organizations were established during this period, following a similar pattern. Over the course of the first few decades of the twentieth century, several Japanese Buddhist temples, missions, and organizations were founded in Hawai'i and on the mainland. Soto Zen Buddhist priest, Kaiseki Kodama, arrived on the big island of Hawai'i in 1914 and began working with local farmers and laborers. A temporary temple was constructed the following year; by 1921, a new temple was finished with a Buddha image installed and official ties made with the Soto Zen hierarchy in Japan. The North American headquarters for Soto Zen Buddhism, which was established in 1922, are located at Zenshuji Soto Mission in Los Angeles. Smaller denominations of Japanese Buddhism, including Shingon, also established temples and missions in the United States, including the Shingon Shu Hawai'i Temple built in 1918 in Honolulu (Figure 8).

As had been the case with their Chinese predecessors, Japanese immigrants soon found themselves on the receiving end of American xenophobia. Anti-Japanese

FIGURE 8 *Kukai statue outside Shingon Shu temple, Honolulu, Hawai'i. (Photo courtesy James C. Clar.)*

sentiment expressed itself in a variety of ways. In Hawai'i, many Buddhist communities, in addition to hosting religious services, served as community centers dedicated to passing Japanese culture on to their children, including Japanese-language schools. By the 1920s, ongoing debates both within the Japanese community and the wider culture regarding the assimilation of immigrants led to direct attacks against Buddhist Japanese schools. Editorials in local newspapers regarded these schools as thoroughly un-American, anti-Christian, and promoting worship not only of the Buddha but the emperor of Japan (Asato 2010, 57). On the mainland, since the end of the Civil War, states across the nation had been passing discriminatory Jim Crow laws, laws usually targeting African Americans. These laws discriminated against other ethnic minorities as well; for the Japanese, this included prohibitions against becoming naturalized citizens or owning property, so-called Alien Land Laws passed in the 1910s and 1920s. Anti-Japanese sentiment was stoked by politicians, including California governors and senators, as well as newspaper publishers and labor leaders. Senator James Phelan, for example, warned a US House of Representatives committee in 1920 that there were dozens of Japanese temples in California, and that "they are regularly attended by 'Emperor worshippers' who believe that their Emperor is the over-lord of all" (Kashima 1977, 32).

Such anti-Japanese sentiment had a number of effects on the nascent Japanese American Buddhist community. Most notably, in the face of racial prejudice and social stigma, the Buddhist church became a refuge, a safe space for Japanese immigrants and their children to meet, speak Japanese, and engage in Japanese cultural customs without fear of reprisal. Prejudice also had the effect of pressuring the community to acculturate or bend its customs toward American norms, effecting changes in both language and religious customs.

The first Japanese immigrants were almost exclusively male—a migrant worker population of men, many of whom did not intend to stay on in America. However, over time, sentiments changed, and many desired to remain in their adopted home and build lives for themselves. This necessarily meant marrying and beginning families. However, the generalized anti-Asian sentiment of the time which led to the passage of the Chinese Exclusion Act of 1882 resulted in passage of several other immigration laws, including the Gentlemen's Agreement of 1907 and the Immigration Act of 1924. The Gentlemen's Agreement was an unofficial agreement between the US government and the Empire of Japan; Japan agreed to not issue passports to the United States, and the United States agreed to allow wives and children of immigrants already in the country to join them. This began what is known as the "picture bride era," a time when a largely bachelor population of Japanese immigrants were joined by their "wives"—often arranged marriages with women whom they had never met but had a photograph of, hence the phrase picture bride. The immigration of women and children obviously had an immediate impact on the broader community, namely the establishment of a first generation of native-born Japanese Americans who were US citizens by birth. The Immigration Act of 1924, together with other early-twentieth-century immigration laws, created an "Asiatic Barred Zone" that prohibited immigration from Asia and enforced strict per-country immigration quotas. Thus, by the 1920s, immigration from Asia virtually ended until changes were enacted in the 1960s.

Despite widespread anti-Japanese sentiment in the early twentieth century, it would be a mistake to view this period as one of exclusion or disengagement from the broader American culture. The mere act of establishing a religious community would have necessitated contact with non-Japanese Americans. More crucially, as covered in the previous chapter, this was a period of increased interest in Asian cultures and religions, and nascent Japanese Buddhist communities attracted the curious and the sympathetic. Finally, whereas the initial inspiration for establishing Buddhist communities in the United States may have been out of concern for Japanese immigrants and their descendants, many Japanese priests and ministers dispatched to North America saw this as an opportunity to spread Buddhism to Americans more generally. These missionaries reached out to non-Japanese converts and experimented with new ways of teaching the dharma.

Yemyo Imamura (1856–1932), who served as the head of the Hawai'ian Shin mission from 1900 to 1932, made a number of attempts at reaching out to the broader culture, including inviting Henry Steel Olcott to give a lecture in 1901 and inviting important local business and political leaders to Shin Buddhist ceremonies (Ama 2011, 39). Imamura was interested in propagating a pan-sectarian version of Shin Buddhism throughout Hawai'i, one that was rooted in their particular denomination but that was of appeal beyond the narrow confines of one sect. He was aided in this regard by Ernest and Dorothy Hunt who had moved to Hawai'i in 1915. The Hunts worked closely with Imamura, and were ordained as priests in 1924. Hunt was especially well known in Hawai'i, both inside and outside the Buddhist community, for converting Anglo-Americans (Ama 2011, 70–72; Tanabe 1998). Together, the Hunts popularized a Shin Buddhist worship service and song culture that has had a lasting impact in both Hawai'i and the mainland. Rinzai Zen teacher Soen Shaku, in addition to sending D/T. Suzuki to the United States, also invited his disciple Nyogen Senzaki (1876–1958) with him on a speaking tour early in the twentieth century. Soen left Senzaki in San Francisco, alone and penniless, famously forcing the young Zen student to make it on his own. In 1919, Senzaki published a collection known as *101 Zen Stories* that would, decades later, be republished as part of *Zen Flesh, Zen Bones*. Scraping by financially, Senzaki established what he later referred to as a "floating *zendo*," setting up practice centers in rented spaces in and around Los Angeles in the years before the war, teaching Zen Buddhism to Japanese and non-Japanese Americans alike (Seager 1999, 38; Busto 2002, 15–21).

White American engagement with, or involvement in, Japanese American Buddhist communities thus took many forms, from assisting in various English-language publication projects, serving as lay leaders, to ordination as ministers or priests. In the case of the NABM, through the first few decades of the twentieth century, a number of white American ministers were ordained, though their levels of long-term commitment to the community or acceptance by the Japanese Buddhist hierarchy remain unclear. Many were ordained by local ministers in the United States, ordinations that may not have been reported to head temples in Japan (Ama 2011, 76). Others like Julius Goldwater were deeply committed to Buddhism. Introduced to the community by the Hunts and Imamura in Hawai'i, he was ordained and recognized by the Honganji in 1926. He supported the Los Angeles temple for a number of years, importantly acting as a steward of members' belongings held at the temple during World War II internment (Prothero 1997).

In 1936, a woman named Gladys Pratt (1898–1986) was ordained in Tacoma, Washington, by Kenju Masuyama who was then the *socho* (bishop) of the NABM and was active in recruiting non-Japanese members to the community. This ordination was reported in the Los Angeles *Times* where she was described as the "first White priestess in Buddhist religion" (Ama 2015). Whether or not Pratt was the "first White priestess" is debatable; it is also a moot point compared to the larger significance of her ordination itself, her decades of service to the Tacoma Buddhist community, and what such ordinations reveal about US Buddhist practice in the early twentieth century. Whereas virtually all ministers who have served in North American Shin Buddhist communities over the last century and half have been ordained in Kyoto, Pratt and others from this time were exceptions. Very often, they were ordained in the United States by local ministers, reflecting the possibility that local communities ordained ministers out of necessity or as a way of rewarding ongoing service. Apart from these ordinations being held in the United States, the ceremonies themselves departed in form and structure from their Japanese antecedents. In Japan, ordinands wear robes appropriate to their denominations and often shave their heads. Pratt did neither; in photographs she appears to be wearing robes more reminiscent of a Theravada tradition. Moreover, her choice in Buddhist name—Sunya—was not the usual Japanese but a Sanskrit term.

Indeed, this is an important characteristic of US Buddhism at the time. As new immigrant communities began to establish themselves and either commingle with Buddhist immigrants from other traditions or attract converts from the wider population, a more generalized or pan-sectarian form of Buddhism began to emerge, what Ama has termed a "universal Buddhism" (Ama 2015). In the case of the NABM, this meant downplaying the unique specificity of the Jodo Shinshu sect as it existed in Japan while refocusing doctrinal and devotional practices to a more generalized Buddhism, including explicit references to Theravada and Pali terms, practices, and a focus on the historical Buddha. The efforts of the Hunts and Imamura in Hawai'i can be seen in this light; attempts by second-generation (*nisei*) Japanese American Buddhists to create nonsectarian Buddhist organizations are another example, one that would prove pivotal in the reestablishment of Buddhism in the postwar years. In many ways, this universal or pan-sectarian view of Buddhism was endemic of the time. Tweed (2012), for example, has documented early-twentieth-century Buddhist hymns and service books that contain references to both Japanese Mahayana as well as South Asian Theravada sources, with contributions coming from Japanese missionaries, Americans, and Europeans alike. While it is hard to judge to what extent such archival ephemera reflects on-the-ground practice, such artifacts reflect a convergence of Pacific and Victorian discourses, another example of universalized forms of Buddhism championed by Olcott and others half-a-world away.

From internment to relocation

The changes in Japan brought on by the Meiji Restoration led directly to the establishment of Japan as a major world power with dreams of empire. Beginning in the 1890s, Japan expanded its influence and power by engaging in military operations in China, Russia, and Korea, and came to dominate large parts of East Asia. Such aggression would stoke anti-Japanese sentiments in the United States, which was concerned about a rising Japanese power in the Pacific. In December 1941, the Empire of Japan attacked a US naval base in Hawai'i, Pearl Harbor.

The effect of this attack on the Japanese American population was immediate and devastating. As we have seen, for four decades prior to the attack, Japanese were considered a suspicious threat, unable to acculturate to American norms. In the years leading up to World War II, the US Federal Bureau of Investigations (FBI) had been monitoring Japanese activity, including Japanese language schools and Buddhist communities. Within hours of the Pearl Harbor attack, community leaders were questioned or arrested by the FBI. Some priests in Hawai'i were sent to the mainland for incarceration; others were deported to Japan. Concerned about their future and knowing their loyalty would be questioned, community and Buddhist leaders burned letters from Japan or destroyed religious objects that might be misunderstood by the authorities as supporting the Empire of Japan. The long-standing general anti-Japanese mood along the West Coast was crystallized by the attack on Pearl Harbor, and in February 1942, President Franklin Roosevelt issued Executive Order 9066 requiring all persons of Japanese descent to be removed from coastal areas along the West Coast as a matter of national security (Williams 2002, 2003).

Regardless of the pretense of the Order or its justifiability either at the time or in hindsight, the forced incarceration of American citizens is a violation of several parts of the US Constitution, especially the Fourth Amendment. Beginning in 1942, all persons of Japanese ancestry were told to vacate their homes and report to service centers. Each person could carry only one bag. As a result, families were forced to give away possessions or store them at local Buddhist churches. They were first sent to Assembly Centers, usually repurposed racetracks where they were housed in horse stables. Later, they were sent to War Relocation Authority detention camps spread out across the United States, including Tule Lake, California; Heart Mountain, Wyoming; and Rohwer, Arkansas. Priests and other community leaders were often separated from their families and held in custody with prisoners of war, though eventually some were allowed to be reunited with their families. All told, some 120,000 men, women, and children were forced from their homes and housed in internment camps for the duration of the war.

Buddhist ministers and priests, Japanese language instructors, and other community leaders were suspected of being part of a potential "fifth column" of Japanese in America who might support an invasion force. Identified as such, this meant long periods of isolation from their families at camps run by the Department of Justice. In 1943, the US government distributed a "Loyalty Questionnaire" to internees, a form that included two questions asking respondents to foreswear loyalty or citizenship to Japan and to serve in the US Armed Forces. Those who refused to sign the form were labeled "no-no boys," an action that created a rift within the community, reflecting the complex feelings of Japanese Americans during the war. On the one hand, many wanted to embrace their new homeland or were citizens by birth and were frustrated by having their Americanness openly questioned and rights rescinded; on the other hand, even if they desired to assimilate to American culture, it was difficult to let go all affinities for their ancestral culture (Kashima 1977, 58; Williams 2003).

Such a protracted state of internment could have been devastating for US Buddhist communities; nevertheless, Buddhism managed to both survive within the camps as well as reestablish itself in the postwar years. In the camps, Buddhists found creative ways to continue their traditions and practices. For example, when Buddhists wanted to celebrate the birth of the Buddha with a *hanamatsuri* service, a service that necessitated a wide assortment of ritual objects, a Buddha image, and flowers, internees improvised; a priest carved a Buddha image out of a carrot, and others made imitation flowers out of paper. A Zen Buddhist priest used discarded and dried peach pits to construct prayer beads (*ojuzu*). And despite being incarcerated, many were able to communicate with family and friends in other camps via letters, allowing for the dissemination of Buddhist teachings across the country (Williams 2003).

Buddhist altars

Altars play an important part in Buddhist practice. Typically, altars contain an image of the Buddha, though in some Japanese traditions this may be replaced by a scroll with a Buddha's name or the title of a sacred text written in calligraphy. Across the Buddhist world, altars are typically decorated with flowers, incense, and offerings of fruit and rice. Prayer beads, called *ojuzu* in Japanese and *mala* in Sanskrit, are often worn or held by practitioners while performing services in front of an altar. In some traditions, beads are counted while chanting.

Arguably, the work of younger Japanese Americans had some of the most long-lasting effects on US Buddhism. Prior to the war, many second-generation Japanese Americans had begun organizing Young Buddhist Associations (YBA) that served the needs of the English-speaking children of the first immigrants. Such groups reestablished themselves in the camps, and many argued for less sectarian or pan-sectarian forms of Buddhism that would have less direct association with Japan and Japanese Buddhist institutions.

Such sentiments reflected the growing desire among the younger generation to acculturate itself to American norms. In 1944, leaders of the NABM convened a series of meetings at the Topaz, Utah, camp to decide the future of their Buddhist organization. It was during these meetings that a decision was made to formally change the group's name to the Buddhist Churches of America and to restructure the governance of the community. New rules were accepted in large part by the support of YBA groups who argued for the renamed organization to be pan-sectarian and to sever ties with Japan (Kashima 1977, 59–61). In some ways, the trend toward pan-sectarianism that began before internment can be read within the larger discourse of universalizing Buddhism as mentioned earlier. In the camps, faced with an uncertain future and having their Americanness directly challenged by incarceration and loyalty oaths, pan-sectarian sentiments can also be read as an explicit attempt among native-born Japanese Americans to reshape their Buddhist communities in line with American norms.

Beginning in January 1945, nine months before the end of the war, the internees began leaving the camps. This most often meant being given $25 and a bus ticket back to their home town. As can be imagined, the resettlement of Japanese Americans was as disruptive as their internment. In most cases, internees returned to the cities they left. Others followed relatives who had either left the West Coast before the war or those who had been released years prior, such as those who had answered the loyalty oath satisfactorily. As a result, new Japanese American communities were established in such cities as Cleveland, Ohio and Seabrook, New Jersey. Following the war, midwestern labor shortages attracted recently released Japanese American internees; and wherever they settled, new Buddhist communities followed (Kashima 1977, 59).

Those who returned to their prewar homes all too often found nothing to return to. In many cases, land had been illegally sold or taken over. Homes were sometimes destroyed. Before the war, many Japanese Americans stored their personal belongings in Buddhist temples, which were in turn watched over by white American friends, such as Goldwater. Following internment, these same temples now became makeshift hostels for evacuees with nowhere else to turn. Thus, the Buddhist institutions that had served the larger Japanese community were called into service once more as a stabilizing force in the uncertain times immediately following the war.

The war years represent a crucial turning point in the history of US Buddhism in part because of the psychological toll taken by the Japanese American community. Having suffered the effects of overt discrimination and racism, having had their status as Americans challenged and called into question, many Japanese Americans in the postwar years retreated into their communities and had limited engagement with the broader culture. There is an oft-cited Japanese expression that loosely translates to "the nail that sticks out get pounded in" which reflects a tendency toward conformity within the Japanese American community at this time. It must be remembered, however, that such proverbs are always contested and are not reflective of universal acceptance on the ground. By the 1950s, many in the community were actively engaging broader cultural and religious trends; and simultaneously, the broader culture was once more turning its attention to the religious traditions of Asia.

Beats, squares, and the counterculture

As discussed, around the turn of the twentieth century, the NABM made explicit attempts to connect with non-Japanese-American sympathizers. These attempts included, in part, the production of English-language publications, such as the NABM-sponsored *The Light of Dharma*. Before the end of its publication in 1907, this periodical included writings by Japanese ministers and missionaries, as well as D. T. Suzuki, Olcott, and Rhys Davids (Tweed 1992, 32). Publications of this sort were revived in the postwar years under new names, including the *Tri-Ratna: Buddha*, the *Buddhist*, and *American Buddhist*. Just as they had before the war, many of these publications included a diverse array of voices, both Eastern and Western. Such publications and explicit attempts to share the dharma outside the Japanese American community would eventually coincide with a growing interest in Buddhism among non-Asian Americans.

In the late 1940s and early 1950s, a new literary and artistic movement was attracting mainstream American attention—the Beat Generation. Jack Kerouac (1922–1969) coined the phrase "Beat generation" in 1948 during late-night discussions over poetry and jazz in New York with Allen Ginsberg (1926–1997) and William S. Burroughs (1914–1997), all of whom were attending Columbia University at the time. Over the following years, individually and at times together, these young men would crisscross North America, hitchhiking or riding box cars, providing Kerouac the raw material for his 1957 novel, *On the Road*. Meanwhile, in San Francisco, a literary movement known as the San Francisco Renaissance had emerged. In 1955, Ginsberg read his epic poem "Howl" at the Six Gallery in San Francisco, an event attended by Kerouac, Gary Snyder (b. 1930) and Philip Whalen (1923–2002), among others. "Howl" captured the cultural dissatisfaction of these literary and arts movements; this reading was both immortalized in Kerouac's 1958 novel *The Dharma Bums* and set off an obscenity trial that thrust the Beats into the national spotlight.

The Beat Generation has had an important impact on the development of US Buddhism. The artistic and spiritual inspiration for much Beat writing overlaps with both an explicit critique of normative postwar American values and an embrace of an exoticized other, often grafted directly onto Asian religions and cultures. Kerouac's *On the Road*, for example, can be read as an extended metaphor of nostalgia for premodern America, an escapist fantasy that rejects Eisenhower-era middle-class suburbia. This was a vision that openly embraced, or appropriated, the subaltern worlds of jazz and recreational drug use while, ironically, glossing over the concurrent and ongoing civil rights movement of the day (Panish 1994). From this point of view, much early Beat writing can be seen as a rejection of or even escape from postwar American culture and an attempt at embracing alternative sources of creative and spiritual inspiration. In some ways, this is a continuation of late-Victorian-era thinking, especially as exemplified by the Transcendentalists who rejected the normative religious thinking of their day. Of course, this rejection prompted criticism, garnering the Beats a "reputation as anti-religious enemies of god and country, or, at best, as dilettantes, fashionable dabblers in the exotic East" (Prothero 1995, 6).

Indeed, the moniker "Beat generation" implies an importance that betrays the in fact small nature of this artistic movement. The Beat movement was never universally accepted, very few artists self-identified as "Beat," and within a few short years, mainstream media was already parodying the Beats as pedantic misfits, stereotyped as the "beatnik." The term beatnik itself was coined by San Francisco *Chronicle* columnist Herb Caen to poke fun at the Beats as irrelevant and anti-American (the *-nik* a direct reference to the Soviet satellite Sputnik launched in 1957). Even erstwhile supporters were critical of the Beats' excesses, as was Alan Watts (1915–1973) in his 1959 essay, "Beat Zen, Square Zen, and Zen." While acknowledging the potential for sharp social criticism in some writers, Watts describes Kerouac as "uneven" and "always a shade too self-conscious, too subjective, and too strident to have the flavor of Zen ... there is a hostility in [his] words which clangs with self-defense. But just because Zen truly surpasses convention and its values, it has no need to say 'To hell with it,' nor underline with violence the fact that anything goes" (Watts 1967, 92). Such critique lays bare the motivating impulse behind much Beat activity at the time, an ongoing critique of normative American culture exemplified in an embrace of alternative religious traditions and the casual acceptance of recreational drug use—what would become hallmarks of the American counterculture through the 1960s and 1970s. Thus, while small in number and short-lived, the Beat Generation would leave a profound mark on American cultural life.

On the one hand, Watts' writings from the 1930s and 1940s, however idiosyncratic, were a major intellectual reference point for Beat writers. On the other hand, local Japanese American communities served as intermediaries between Beat intellectual fascination with Buddhism and living Buddhist communities of practice. And communities such as the Berkeley Buddhist Temple played a key role. Like many BCA temples, the Berkeley Temple housed members' belongings during the war and served as a hostel following internment. In 1946, Kanmo Imamura, son of Yenmo Imamura of the Hawai'ian Shin Mission, was assigned as the temple's resident minister, and together with his wife Jane, sought to reinvigorate the Buddhist community. Jane, a trained musician, worked closely with the community's children and their dharma school and began composing Buddhist songs and developing a music culture at the temple. The temple building that had been used as a post-internment hostel was later used as a dormitory for Japanese Americans studying at the University of California. This connection to the university dovetailed with the Imamuras' interest in education, and by the late 1940s, they were hosting study groups at the temple. These study groups began to expand and attract wider interest and attention not just among the temple's younger generation but the wider community, including Gary Snyder. Soon, the group was supported directly by the BCA national leadership who recognized the importance of educating a new generation of English-speaking Shin Buddhist leaders. The Imamuras' outreach to the broader community included inviting guest speakers to the study group, seminars, and conferences.

Jane Imamura (1920–2011)

Daughter of Issei Matsuura, a Shin Buddhist priest, Jane Imamura was born and raised in the central California city of Guadalupe. She studied music at the University of California, Berkeley, and married Kanmo Imamura shortly before the evacuation of Japanese Americans to internment centers. In 1946, the couple returned to Berkeley where they both worked to reinvigorate the local Buddhist community. Imamura's love of music led to the creation of a lively music culture at the Berkeley Temple as well as the composition of numerous Buddhist songs for the children's program. These songs have become a cornerstone of US Shin Buddhist services for more than half a century and are sung across North America. Together, both Jane and her husband helped to organize what would later become the Institute of Buddhist Studies, one of the first Buddhist graduate schools in North America. Her memoirs, *Kaikyo: Opening the Dharma: Memoirs of a Buddhist Priest's Wife in America*, presents a fascinating glimpse into the establishment of US Buddhism.

Gary Snyder had been studying at Reed College in Portland, Oregon, where he was roommates with Philip Whalen. Both were drawn to classical Chinese painting and Asian religions, an interest that led Snyder to enroll in a graduate program in East Asian languages at the University of California. His time in Berkeley was dramatized as the character of Japhy Ryder in Kerouac's *The Dharma Bums*. What this caricature glosses over, however, was Snyder's relationship with the Imamuras at the Berkeley Temple (Snyder 1996, 153–154). The couple and the young poet were close friends, and Snyder was a regular fixture at their study groups where he joined other Berkeley Temple members as well as a growing number of converts and sympathizers interested in learning more about Buddhism. Enthralled by these meetings, Snyder invited his friends Kerouac, Ginsberg, and Whalen to the study groups as well, and all of them contributed poetry and other writings to the temple newsletter, the *Berkeley Bussei*, years before they were nationally known literary celebrities.

The growing popularity of the *Bussei* prompted the BCA to start its own English-language publication, *American Buddhist*. Like *The Light of Dharma* fifty years earlier, this postwar journal included a wide variety of contributors with an editorial staff that included Taitetsu Unno and Robert Jackson (Masatsugu 2004). Unno was a second-generation Japanese American minister who had been educated in Japan; his writings on Shin and Zen Buddhism have become extremely popular within the American Shin Buddhist community. Robert Jackson studied in Los Angeles with Zen teacher Nyogen Senzaki. The "serious discussions" mentioned by Jane Imamura in the beginning of this chapter quickly became the basis of ongoing debates in the *American Buddhist* regarding what it meant to be a Buddhist in America.

Some white American contributors championed the Buddhism of the Beats while openly critiquing the practices of Japanese American Buddhists. Writing in the *American Buddhist*, Jackson claimed that the Beats had fully embraced the Noble Truth of suffering and that though they did not care to be called Buddhists, they fully under-stood emptiness, wisdom, and compassion while integrating meditation into their lives. Unno responded, arguing that however well intentioned the Beats were, they were seeking wisdom in the wrong place, escaping to mountain hermitages or taking refuge in tranquilizers and drugs (Masatsugu 2008, 424). In one of his contributions, Watts drew a distinction between what he called "temple Buddhism" and "ashram Buddhism"; the former represented by the Protestant church-like model of the BCA and the later by less-organized groups of disciples and philosophers as exemplified by the followers of the historic Buddha. According to Watts, temple Buddhism is accept-able, "so long as it does not supplant or overshadow ashram-Buddhism. But this is just what is happening in ... the American groups of Japanese origin, and it is to be feared that if this course continues, these groups will die out, and fail to make their important contribution to Western life" (Masatsugu 2008, 447). BCA ministers such as David Iwamoto and John Doami responded by championing the BCA model as a space in which to share the teachings, a space that reflected the everyday sense of Buddhist life rather than an Orientalist vision of an exoticized Buddhism apart from the world.

These debates reflect the underlying tensions and cultural discourses of the early Cold War years, a time marked by the rise of the United States as a global and nuclear superpower juxtaposed against the perceived threat of globalized communism. It was in this context that the Eisenhower-era vision of a prosperous middle class and con-formity to American values was brought into focus, a vision sharply criticized by Beats and other public intellectuals. Such critiques often embraced non-European cultures (such as the Beats' embrace of Asian religions) as they did leftist or Marxist ideologies, and were thus denounced as anti-American. Anticommunist campaigns by politicians such as Joseph McCarthy demanded acquiescence to normative American cultural values. Having just endured the internment experience where their loyalty and right to be in the United States was called into question, it is understandable that Japanese Americans would be hesitant to embrace a cultural movement that brazenly called into question those values. But the Beats were doing just that, rejecting conformity in pursuit of experiences derived from subaltern and non-Western sources. In publica-tions such as *American Buddhist* and communities like the Berkeley Buddhist Temple, we see two cultural trends converging and, ultimately, diverging, following different trajectories into the even more turbulent years of the 1960s.

Beginner's Mind

While not a direct consequence of the Beat movement, the late 1950s and early 1960s saw what some writers have called a Zen boom, a period of intense interest in and acceptance of Buddhism in general, Zen in particular. The convergence of this "boom" with the ongoing development of Japanese American Buddhism in such public confer-ences and publications as detailed earlier, points toward two strains of US Buddhist his-tory that, in the decades to come, would diverge in significant ways. Such divergences are perhaps best exemplified by two Japanese Zen Buddhist teachers, Taizan Maezumi (1931–1995) and Shunryu Suzuki (1904–1971). Maezumi immigrated to the United States in 1956 having been assigned to the American Soto Zen headquarters, Zenshuji Soto Mission, in Los Angeles. Suzuki (no relation to D. T. Suzuki) arrived in San Francisco in 1959 where he was assigned to Sokoji Temple, a small Japanese American Soto Zen community. US Soto Zen Buddhist history is very similar to that of the Buddhist Churches of America, as discussed earlier, and both men would have been responsible for attending to a community of primarily Japanese American Buddhists who would have expected them to attend to services and ceremonies, funerals and memorial services.

However, the broader cultural climate was shifting. Whereas the Beat movement itself may have been small and short-lived, it represented a larger cultural current that was both actively questioning American values and searching outside traditional American religions for inspiration. Within a few years of their arrival, both Maezumi and Suzuki attracted the attention of young white American sympathizers and future converts (Prebish 1999, 13–16). Many came to Buddhism looking not for the perceived ritualism and oppressive structures of normative American Protestantism but instead for religious or spiritual experiences, especially as described by Watts, D. T. Suzuki, and Senzaki in by then well-known publications. Maezumi and Suzuki both had been trained in Japanese Soto Zen monasteries, and they began teaching Zen meditation and lecturing in English to a new generation of converts. In addition to his training in Soto Zen Buddhism, Maezumi had been ordained in two other Zen Buddhist lineages; thus, his teaching style diverged from what one might expect to find in a Japanese Zen monastery. In both cases, the very act of teaching traditional Zen meditation practices (*zazen* and *shikantaza*) to non-monastic lay followers was a marked departure from Japanese modes of religiosity (Asai and Williams 1999, 20–21). A consequence of this move was the eventual split of the community.

Varieties of practice

In the popular imagination, Buddhist practice is often reduced to a single practice—meditation—which itself is reduced to a single kind of meditation—seated meditation such as *zazen* and *shikantaza* in the Soto Zen tradition. This overlooks both the wide array of meditation practices—of which seated meditation is just one—and the even wider array of practices across the Buddhist tradition. Of equal importance in most Buddhist traditions is chanting; in the case of Japanese Buddhism, the Shin and other Pure Land schools often engage in *nenbutsu* practice, the recitation of the name of the Buddha Amida. Whereas meditation and chanting became hallmarks of specific sectarian identities in Japan, it is far more common to see them operating together in Buddhist traditions across Asia.

In the case of Suzuki, in 1962, together with new converts, he established the San Francisco Zen Center which catered to the interests and needs of primarily non-Japanese-Americans and has had, historically, little connection to the Japanese American Sokoji Temple to which Suzuki was originally assigned. Over time, the community would establish two training centers, Green Gulch Farm and Tassajara Zen Mountain Center, both in California. The Green Gulch location, in addition to hosting meditation retreats, also grows organic vegetables for a high-end vegetarian restaurant in San Francisco. In 1970, Suzuki's students compiled some of his talks into the widely influential book *Zen Mind, Beginner's Mind*. Maezumi went on to found the Los Angeles Zen Center and the White Plum Asangha, a diverse network of teachers and training centers across the country. Among his many disciples are Bernie Glassman (b. 1939) who is as well known for his socially engaged activities (Chapter 11) as he is for his Hollywood celebrity students, including actor Jeff Bridges. Glassman's student, Joan Halifax (b. 1942), established the Santa Fe-based Upaya Zen Center in 1990. Another student of Maezumi, John Daido Loori (1931–2009), established the Mountains and Rivers Order of Zen Buddhism whose headquarters are located at the Zen Mountain Monastery in upstate New York (Chapter 6). This general current of US Zen Buddhist thought and development was augmented by the work of a third Japanese Zen teacher, Hakuun Yasutani (1885–1973). Disenchanted with Japanese Zen institutions of his day, Yasutani created a new Zen Buddhist school known as Sanbokyodan in 1954 which explicitly drew from both Soto and Rinzai lineages. This lineage would be imparted to Robert Aitken (1917–2010) and Philip Kapleau (1912–2004) whose writings and own practice centers have in turn influenced generations of US Buddhists.

It is important to contextualize this early activity within the larger discourses of the postwar years and the dawning countercultural and civil rights movements of the 1960s. For early immigrants and their children, their US Buddhist experiences were defined by attempts to perpetuate or accommodate traditions in an openly hostile and racially charged environment. Simultaneously, nineteenth-century intellectual engagement with and curiosity in Buddhism laid the groundwork for non-Asian American interest that saw a resurgence, first, in the Beat generation. The civil rights movement provided a political voice to those who had been disenfranchised by American politics and the counterculture openly criticized normative American values. While these various discourses often converged in US Buddhist communities, they also diverged in the establishment of lineages that branched off from the Japanese American communities established nearly fifty years prior, creating a wide diversity of lineages and traditions.

DISCUSSION QUESTIONS

1. How did immigration patterns and laws on both sides of the Pacific affect the establishment of specific Buddhist communities in the United States?

2. Discuss the differences between Japanese Americans' and white Americans' abilities to critique normative Eisenhower-era cultural values. Why might Japanese Americans have wanted to blend in? What were the Beats rebelling against?

3. How did Japanese Americans adapt Buddhist practices while being interned during World War II?

SUGGESTIONS FOR FURTHER READING

Ama, Michihiro. 2011. *Immigrants to the Pure Land: The Modernization, Acculturation, and Globalization of Shin Buddhism.* Honolulu: University of Hawai'i Press.

Busto, Rudiger V. 2002. "Disorienting Subjects: Reclaiming Pacific Islander/Asian American Religions." In *Revealing the Sacred in Asian and Pacific America,* ed. Jane Iwamura and Paul Spickard, 9–28. New York: Routledge.

Chandler, Stuart. 1998. "Chinese Buddhism in America: Identity and Practice." In *The Faces of Buddhism in America,* ed. Charles S. Prebish and Kenneth Tanaka, 14–30. Berkeley: University of California Press.

Imamura, Jane Michiko. 1998. *Kaikyo: Opening the Dharma: Memoirs of a Buddhist Priest's Wife in America.* Honolulu: Buddhist Study Center Press.

Masatsugu, Michael K. 2008. "Beyond this World of Transiency and Impermanence: Japanese Americans, Dharma Bums, and the Making of American Buddhism during the Early Cold War Years." *Pacific Historical Review* 77 (3): 423–451.

Tweed, Thomas A. 1992. *The American Encounter with Buddhism, 1844–1912: Victorian Culture and the Limits of Dissent.* Bloomington: Indiana University Press.

Williams, Duncan Ryûken. 2003. "Complex Loyalties: Issei Buddhist Ministers During the Wartime Incarceration." *Pacific World: Journal of the Institute of Buddhist Studies* 3 (5): 255–274.

Williams, Duncan Ryûken, and Tomoe Moriya, eds. 2010. *Issei Buddhism in the Americas.* Urbana: University of Illinois Press.

4

Diversity and pluralism at century's end

Chapter summary and outline

Substantial social changes both foreign and domestic coincided with revisions to US immigration laws that allowed for a dramatic rise in Asian immigration and mainstream acceptance of Buddhism from the 1960s to the end of the century. These cultural shifts allowed for the proliferation and diversification of the US Buddhist landscape through the introduction of new Asian Buddhist communities and the conversion of non-Asian Americans.

Introduction: The Hart-Celler Act
The US Buddhist landscape of the early 1960s
Convergence and divergence
    New immigrants: China and Tibet
    New immigrants: South and Southeast Asia
    New pilgrims
    Paralellism
The maturation of US Buddhism
A Vesak/Hanamatsuri celebration
Discussion questions
Suggestions for further reading

Introduction: The Hart-Celler Act

In June 1963, speaking to the American Committee on Italian Migration, President John F. Kennedy discussed his plans to send legislation to Congress to alter US immigration

laws, laws that had been in effect for forty years and were based on a quota system
that privileged immigration from Northern and Western Europe. Kennedy hoped that
Congress would accept his recommendations and recognize "that all people can make
equally good citizens, and that what this country needs and wants are those who wish
to come here to build their families here and contribute to the life of our country"
(Kennedy 1963). Following his assassination later that year, President Lyndon Johnson
and Congress pushed this legislation forward resulting in passage of the Immigration
and Nationality Act of 1965, known as the Hart-Celler Act. Signing the bill into law at
the foot of the Statue of Liberty, Johnson spoke of America's openness, of its history
as a people from many cultures coming together to build a new nation. Hart-Celler, he
claimed, would right an injustice, that previous immigration quotas "violated the basic
principle of American democracy—the principle that values and rewards each man on
the basis of his merit as a man." In signing Hart-Celler, he said, "We can now believe
that [immigration quotas] will never again shadow the gate to the American Nation
with the twin barriers of prejudice and privilege" (Johnson 1965).

These idealizations of American values were couched in the ongoing ideological
war with the Soviet Union, and both Kennedy and Johnson believed that by highlighting American openness and equal opportunity, immigrants from Southern and

FIGURE 9 *President Lyndon Johnson at the Statue of Liberty to sign the Hart-Celler Act
into law, 1965. (Getty Images.)*

Eastern Europe would be drawn to the United States thus bolstering the view that Western democracy was preferable to communism. Thus, the Hart-Celler Act was aimed squarely at eastern Europe, and Johnson explicitly claimed that it was "not a revolutionary bill ... It will not reshape the structure of our daily lives, or really add importantly to either our wealth or our power" (Johnson 1965). This prediction was wholly inaccurate.

The Hart-Celler Act was passed during a time of significant political and cultural change in the United States. Following World War II, the United States had emerged as a global super power, both a strong military force and an ideological influence around the world. The anticommunist containment policy led the United States into several clandestine operations and proxy wars in Asia, including Korea and Vietnam. These very visible conflicts point toward the complicated ideological engagements and foreign policies of the Cold War. On the domestic front, a stable economy allowed for a growing middle class that exposed deep racial and economic inequalities that fueled the civil rights movements of the 1960s and served as the cultural bedrock of the 1970s. Into this shifting cultural terrain arrived new immigrants as a result of the 1965 law that would further redefine American demographics and reshape the US Buddhist landscape.

The US Buddhist landscape of the early 1960s

As we saw in the previous chapter, the early twentieth century was a time of restrictive immigration laws and quotas. The Chinese Exclusion Act of 1882, the Asiatic Barred Zone Act of 1917, and the Immigration Act of 1924 had essentially ended immigration from most of Asia while imposing a strict quota system on the rest of the world. This quota system was standardized in 1920s legislation that was directed toward limiting immigration from Eastern and Southern Europe while privileging immigration from Northern and Western Europe, thus preserving late-nineteenth-century ethnic composition of naturalized American citizens. US Supreme Court cases of this era had ruled that Asian immigrants were not eligible for citizenship precisely because they were not white (Chapter 10). Whereas such court decisions and quota systems would be overturned or ratified over the next several decades, very little changed for Asian immigration through World War II. Only highly skilled workers or, in some cases, spouses and children of US citizens were allowed to settle in the United States. As a result, the Asian American population was limited in size and largely restricted to major metropolitan areas along the coasts. Thus, the US Buddhist landscape at the time was necessarily restricted to those parts of the country with a sizable population of Asian immigrants and Asian Americans (Figure 10).

At the same time, the intellectual interest in Asia and Buddhism that began in the colonial era continued through the war and postwar years. In the late nineteenth century, Harvard and other universities began devoting studies to Sanskrit, Pali, and other historic Buddhist languages. American interest in Buddhist cultures dovetailed with an

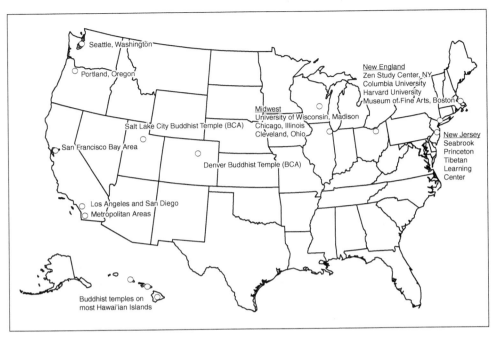

FIGURE 10 *Locations of US Buddhist centers and communities before mid-century "Zen boom."*

interest in Asia generally that was spurred by the Pacific front of World War II, the post-war occupation of Japan, and the anticommunist containment policies of the Cold War. This general awareness of Asia contributed to the establishment of Asian studies, area studies, and even Buddhist studies departments in major research universities. Notably, Richard Robinson at the University of Wisconsin, Alex Wayman at Columbia University, and Masatoshi Nagatomi at Harvard University all helped to establish Buddhist studies in their respective institutions (Prebish 1999, 176–178). Moreover, smaller study centers and new schools were established at this time. D. T. Suzuki, following his work with Paul Carus in Illinois, lectured at universities across the country, including Columbia, and assisted in the establishment of New York City's Zen Study Center. He was also somewhat involved with Alan Watts in the foundation of the California Academy of Asian Studies (now California Institute of Integral Studies) in San Francisco.

Consequently, prior to 1960, the US Buddhist landscape was in some ways defined by its restriction to large metropolitan areas and a distinctly Japanese perspective. Partly as a result of the aforementioned immigration laws, there were very few established Buddhist communities or practice centers aside from Japanese American temples or churches. Thus, in practice, unless one had the means to travel to Asia, one's primary point of contact with a Buddhist community of practice would almost certainly have been Japanese. If one lived in proximity to a college or university, one might be exposed to Buddhism this way. However, arguably scholarship of this era was focused almost entirely on Asia and historical studies (i.e., one would not necessarily be exposed to living traditions in the United States), and was influenced by contemporary Japanese scholarship. For those living in pre-1960s America, exposure to Buddhism would most likely have been through a Japanese lens or an academic one, which in turn was in conversation with Japanese scholarship. Thus, the Japanese point of view regarding Buddhism had an outsized influence on early US Buddhism in both theory and practice.

Furthermore, travel to Asia prior to World War II would have been extremely difficult for the average American. There were no jet airliners to cross the Pacific in a matter of hours; and one would necessarily need the linguistic or social savvy to negotiate international bureaucracies to travel to, say, Burma or Nepal—to say nothing of the actual costs of travel. As World War II ended and the American occupation of Japan began, US servicemen and women had direct access to Japan (and other Asian nations) thus exposing them to Buddhist cultures. Sometimes this contact resulted in marriages that in turn led to spouses entering the United States, which would have an effect on new US Buddhist movements. It also reflected growing US political concerns and ties to Asia, concerns that would allow for greater American travel abroad. Gary Snyder, who we last saw in Berkeley in Chapter 3, was one such traveler who in 1956 left his studies at the University of California to travel to Japan where he studied at the Rinzai Zen Buddhist temple Shokokuji, among other locations (Snyder 1996, 155). By the 1960s, such international interest would include volunteer organizations such as the Peace Corps and nongovernmental agencies providing aid to foreign countries thus allowing for a new generation of Americans to come into contact with Buddhism in Asia.

An underlying factor motivating US interest in Asia in the postwar years, of course, was communism. Following the war, Soviet Russia expanded its influence over Eastern Europe and was looking toward central Asia. The People's Republic of China had a large influence on both the Korean peninsula and in Southeast Asia. The United States, concerned about political and military threats including the development of nuclear weapons, adopted a policy of containment; rather than engaging communist powers in large-scale battle, the United States hoped to contain communism through diplomacy, foreign aid, limited military assistance, and covert operations by the Central Intelligence Agency (CIA). Fundamentally, the Cold War was an ideological one between Western capitalism and Eastern European communism, and immigration policies became a pawn in this larger ideological battle. By highlighting American exceptionalism, idealizations of universal human rights and equality, the Hart-Celler immigration reform act of 1965 was directed squarely at Eastern Europe and those nations who were under the threat or direct rule of the Soviet Union.

In practice, of course, the law had more direct relevance for Asian immigration. Whereas immigration had been effectively prohibited from Asia for over fifty years prior to passage of the law, between the early 1970s and the beginning of the twenty-first century, more than seven million Asians emigrated to the United States (Le 2001). It should be noted that not all Asian immigrants are practicing Buddhists, of course, but it is nevertheless true that this large influx of immigrants in the later twentieth century diversified US demographics more generally and allowed for the establishment of heretofore unrepresented Asian Buddhist traditions.

In Part Two, we will explore in some detail this wide diversity of Buddhist traditions in the United States. For now, we will focus on some founding figures and communities in the decades following Hart-Celler through the end of the twentieth century as well as larger cultural currents that were as responsible for Buddhism's acceptance as any one piece of Congressional legislation.

Convergence and divergence

As discussed in the previous chapter, the 1950s and 1960s represented a time of increased interest in Buddhism on the part of non-Asian Americans. This interest coincides with an increase in Asian immigration. Here we will discuss the foreign and domestic events that motivated both this interest in Buddhism and immigration of Buddhists to the United States.

New immigrants: China and Tibet

Political relations with China and Chinese immigrants have been complicated since the end of the nineteenth century. In the decades leading up to US involvement in World War II, the United States and China became allies against their common enemy Japan, the Chinese Exclusion Act was repealed, and Chinese and other Asian immigrants became eligible for citizenship. However, immediately following the war, Mao Zedong's (1893–1976) communist revolution succeeded in overthrowing the Republic of China; the old nation's government retreated to the island of Taiwan, and the mainland became the People's Republic of China in 1949. Through the 1950s and 1960s, Chinese culture went through radical changes into a socialist republic, and religious institutions, especially Buddhism, suffered greatly during the Cultural Revolution in the late 1960s and early 1970s. During this time, the United States officially recognized only the Republic of China, now displaced to the island of Taiwan. Diplomatic relations changed dramatically following President Richard Nixon's visit to China in 1972, a visit that shifted the tone of the Cold War and allowed for greater trade between the United States, China, and other Asian nations. Increased diplomatic relationships are, of course, a precursor to increased immigration, and since the 1970s, Chinese immigrants have hailed not only from Taiwan and the mainland but from the greater Chinese diaspora, including Hong Kong, Burma, Malaysia, and elsewhere, thus creating a large and internally diverse Chinese American population composed of those with cultural roots in various parts of Asia (Zhou 2003). Social and cultural institutions often form within smaller, mutually exclusive subgroups within this larger community.

More will be said of these communities and traditions in Chapter 6. For now, it is worthwhile to note three organizations that have had an important impact on the history of US Buddhism. Founded in San Francisco in 1968 by Chinese Chan Master Hsuan Hua, the Dharma Realm Buddhist Association (DRBA) has grown from a single monastery serving Chinese Americans to a large international organization. The DRBA includes publishing and translation projects, a sizable monastery in Northern California, a degree-granting university, and relationships with dozens of pan-Buddhist organizations serving a wide diversity of US Buddhists. The work of lay Buddhist C. T. Shen and Chinese Chan monk Sheng Yen in the 1970s led to the establishment of several important Chan Buddhist centers in the United States as well as in Taiwan. Eventually organized under the auspices of Dharma Drum Mountain in Taiwan, the organization has centers and affiliates in more than a dozen states and Canada. Finally, Hsi Lai Temple in Southern California was established in 1988 by Fo Guang Shan (Figure 11). Also based in Taiwan, Fo Guang Shan promotes a self-described version of "humanistic Buddhism" and funds a large charitable network following the vision of its founder, Hsing Yun. Hsi Lai Temple boasts being the largest Chinese temple in the western hemisphere. All three of these organizations, while established initially to meet the needs of Chinese American populations, have grown in size, serve ethnically diverse populations, engage in explicit charitable or engaged practices, and have established links to the broader culture through publication and educational projects (Chandler 1998; Lin 1999; Prebish 1999).

Apart from internal cultural upheaval and complicated political relations with the United States, the Chinese communist revolution also resulted in the eventual invasion and occupation of Tibet. The history of Chinese attitudes toward Tibet, and vice versa, is far too complex to be summarized here (see Sperling 2004). Suffice to say, China has long held that Tibet has always been, or at least should be, part of the nation as a whole; moreover, following normative Marxist ideology, the People's Republic

FIGURE 11 *Hsi Lai Temple, Hacienda Heights, California. (Getty Images.)*

of China considered the leadership of Tibet to be little more than theocratic feudal landlords exploiting the populace. As a result, the People's Liberation Army entered Tibet in 1950; a year later, the region became effectively under control of the central government. Dissatisfaction persisted for several years, eventually resulting in guerrilla combat against the occupying force and open conflict following the uprising of 1959. This was also the year that the 14th Dalai Lama fled Tibet, setting up a government in exile in Dharamsala, India. Since that time, the Dalai Lama has not been allowed to return to his homeland with many Tibetan people living in a global diaspora. Prior to his exile, the Dalai Lama had repeatedly reached out to Western governments for support, but these requests went generally unanswered. However, there is evidence that the CIA was funding and/or training the aforementioned Tibetan guerrillas as part of the anticommunist containment policy during the 1950s (Urubshurow 2013). In addition to this less-than-public program, some refugees from Tibet were allowed into the United States prior to the passage of the Hart-Celler Act. Following further immigration reforms, some several thousand Tibetans have settled in the United States. Tibetan Buddhist communities in the United States remain small to this day; however, the immense popularity of the Dalai Lama and the ongoing crisis in Tibet—including the distressing rise of self-immolations in protest of Chinese occupation (Gyatso 2014)— have shed a large light on the community that betrays its relative small size (Chapter 7).

Certainly adding to the high visibility of Tibetan Buddhism in North America is the Tibetan-derived Shambhala International. Established in the early 1970s as Vajradhatu by a former Tibetan Buddhist monk, Chögyam Trungpa (1939–1987), the community almost certainly benefited from the rising interest in Buddhism at the time with many early converts and supporters coming from the Beat Generation and countercultural movements of the 1960s and 1970s, including poet Allen Ginsberg. While the group went through considerable growing pains following the death of its founder (see below), it remains an important voice in North American Buddhist discourses through its numerous publication ventures and public Buddhists, not the least of which is Pema Chödrön whose publications enjoy widespread popularity.

New immigrants: South and Southeast Asia

Immigration from South and Southeast Asia was virtually nonexistent until the passage of the Hart-Celler Act; since the 1970s, immigration from traditionally Theravada Buddhist countries has increased dramatically. As we saw in previous chapters, Buddhism had all but died out in India long before the beginning of the colonial period. Subsequently Sri Lanka, Burma, and Thailand became centers for Pali-based Theravada Buddhism across the region. During the late colonial period, a nationalist movement arose in Sri Lanka, led in part by Theravada Buddhists including Anagarika Dharmapala. Despite Dharmapala's appearance at the World's Parliament of Religions, no institutional form of Sri Lankan Buddhism existed in the United States until the 1960s. In 1964, a Sri Lankan monk named Madihe Pannasiha Mahanayaka Thera visited Washington, DC, and met with members of the Sri Lankan embassy, delivering a dharma talk. Following this event, he decided to establish a temple in the United States. Returning to Sri Lanka, lay organizations helped him raise funds, and in 1966, along with another monk named Bope Vinitha, he opened the Washington Buddhist Vihara (Cadge 2005, 25). Other Sri Lankan temples followed throughout the 1970s, often being established by lay followers with the help of monastics in cities across the nation.

Temples, churches, and monasteries

Buddhist buildings, temples, and monasteries are known by a variety of names often depending on their cultural context. *Vihara* is a Sanskrit term originally used to refer to the dwelling place of monastics during a rainy season retreat, thus coming to mean "monastery." In Thailand, *wat* literally refers to the sacred space or shrine room within a *vihara*, though it is commonly understood to refer to a temple as a whole. In Japanese Buddhism, one may find the terms *dojo* (place of the dharma) and *zendo* (place of Zen) being used to refer to specific rooms or structures within a larger temple complex—and temples themselves are usually designated by the term *ji*. As we have seen, early Japanese Buddhist immigrants began calling their temples "churches" in the process of adapting to American religious norms. All of this reflects the complexity of nomenclature across Buddhist traditions and the various strategies Buddhist have employed to translate their traditions into American culture.

The region composed of Burma, Thailand, Laos, Cambodia, and Vietnam has a rich, complex, and interrelated history. Various empires and kingdoms from each of these modern nations had control over greater or lesser parts of the peninsula leading up to the colonial period, during which the region became known as Indochina. The French desired to control the region over and against British-dominated India. Thailand (then Siam) had a more stable government at the time, and acted as a noncolonized buffer state between the French-controlled eastern half of the peninsula and the British-dominated western half, which included Burma. The United States had long had political relations with Thailand; famously, the king of Siam offered to send elephants to the United States as beasts of burden, an offer President Lincoln politely declined in 1861. Indochina in general was the site of international struggle during World War II with various countries being occupied by both the Allied and Axis powers and Japan. Following the war, colonial forces withdrew and the region entered into a protracted period of upheaval. The post-colonial government in Burma was overthrown by a military coup in the early 1960s, and a military junta ran the country until the 2010s, inhibiting international relations and per-petrating a number of human rights violations. Thailand suffered a number of attempts to overthrow the government as well as small communist uprisings. Despite continued destabilization since the 1970s, Thailand and the United States have been strong inter-national and economic partners allowing for an exchange of cultures.

All of these events had some impact on the development of US Buddhism heightened by immigration law reforms in the mid-1960s. In addition to the Washington Buddhist Vihara, the late 1960s also saw the beginnings of US Thai Theravada Buddhism with the establishment of the Buddhist Study Center in New York (Cadge 2005, 26). By the early 1970s, Thai American organizations were establishing temples in other cities, including Los Angeles, Denver, Chicago, and Washington, DC. The general pattern for the establishment of these communities in many ways mirrors the earlier Japanese American pattern: lay followers would begin to host services in local homes or rented spaces; committees were organized to raise funds and make connections with monastic institutions in Thailand; and eventually monks would come to the United States and buildings would be purchased or constructed for the new temples. Thai Theravada communities in the United States are generally affiliated with the mainstream monastic branches in Thailand, either the Mahanikaya Council of Thai Bhikkhus or the Dhammayut Order. Whereas these communities were originally established to serve the needs of Thai immigrant communities, we should not assume that they are isolated or exclusionary. Theravada monks from various lineages and countries have often taught across sectarian or ethnic lines. By the late 1970s, American-born converts were taking monastic ordination; Scott Joseph DuPrez was the first to take full Theravada monastic vows in the United State in 1979 (Cadge 2005, 32).

Vietnamese began resisting French colonial rule well before World War II, during which the country was a pawn between Allied and Japanese forces serving as a staging ground for troop movements and exploited for natural resources. Anticolonial resistance was led by Ho Chi Minh (1890–1969) and others, and the French left the country, divided into north and south. The United States began offering military aid in the mid-1950s and eventually deployed troops to what was at first described by the US government as a civil war; however, it was also clearly evident that US involvement in the conflict was part of the anticommunist containment strategy, and it was believed that communist success in Vietnam would have a domino effect throughout the region. Over the course of the 1960s, US involvement increased and became increasingly unpopular, in many ways defining the era. By decade's end, it was clear that the war was un-winnable and that the US government and military leaders had been misleading the American public regarding operations, military involvement in neighboring Laos and Cambodia, and various war crimes. The United States formally began withdrawing troops from South Vietnam in 1973, and by 1975 the southern capital of Saigon fell leading to the reunification of a now communist state.

Immense human suffering across the region followed the war. Border disputes between neighboring countries erupted into open conflict; civil wars toppled existing governments; communist leader Pol Pot (1925–1998) and the Khmer Rouge came to power in Cambodia leading to both war with Vietnam and the holocaust of the killing fields, leaving several million dead. These tragedies displaced millions of people, leading to a refugee crises in the 1980s. Since 1975, more than a million refugees from Southeast Asia have settled in the United States.

Nebraska Buddhism

FIGURE 12 *Chùa An-Lac Buddhist Community, Lincoln, Nebraska. (Photo courtesy Michael Bruntz.)*

Lincoln, Nebraska, was designated by the US Office of Refugee Resettlement as a relocation city, and meatpacking plants across Nebraska and Kansas recruited refugees and other Southeast Asian immigrants for dangerous meatpacking work. Thus, through the 1980s and 1990s, Buddhism was established in the Great Plains. After raising financial capital, Vietnamese and Laotian meatpacking workers were able to leave their jobs and resettle in larger urban areas such as Lincoln and establish growing Buddhist communities serving the needs of second-generation Asian American Buddhists. Scholarship on US Buddhism has historically focused on the coasts—Los Angeles, San Francisco, New England. Midwest and Plains Buddhist communities are a potentially rich research site.[1]

This phase of immigration differs significantly from early-twentieth-century immigration from China or Japan in two respects. First, in an effort to mitigate the large influx of refugees to the United States, the government enacted a policy that scattered immigrants across the nation, often pairing them with host families. Thus, initially, refugees settled in disparate parts of the country rather than being restricted to major port cities (Chuong and Ta 2003). This had the effect of creating smaller pockets of refugee communities for several years before persons had the freedom or capital to move about the country, reconnect with extended families, and create new Asian American communities. Unlike Thai or Sri Lankan communities, many refugee communities had no ties with Asian Buddhist institutions (where they still existed) and lacked significant capital to establish their own Buddhist communities. As a result, it was not uncommon for Cambodian or Lao Buddhists to attend services at Thai or Sri Lankan Theravada Buddhist communities. Despite cultural or language difference, community was created by the Pali-based Buddhist services and modes of practice (Cadge 2005, 27).

Secondly, while the Asian American experience post-1965 has certainly not been without racist incident, late-twentieth-century immigrants and refugees entered an America distinctly different than that of their late-nineteenth-century predecessors. Whereas earlier immigrants faced significant obstacles to assimilation and widespread racial discrimination, by the 1970s America was on its way to becoming a more open and tolerant culture. Moreover, the very fact of increased immigration post-1965 allowed for an explosion of demographic diversity that did not exist a century before. Finally, as we will see, non-Asian American interest in Buddhism, building off the Zen boom, was much more pervasive and mainstream by the 1980s.

As we will see in Chapter 6, Vietnam is an exception to the generally Theravada Southeast Asia rule. Vietnamese culture has had more direct contact with China than the rest of the peninsula, and as a result Vietnamese Buddhism leans more toward Mahayana. Thus, whereas some refugees were able to find community in Theravada temples of other ethnic groups, Vietnamese Mahayana Buddhists affiliated either with pan-ethnic Mahayana groups, especially of Chinese origin, or created their own communities. The Berkeley Buddhist Monastery, an affiliate of the Dharma Realm Buddhist Association, is an example of the former where services are held in English, Mandarin, Cantonese, and Vietnamese. Several Vietnamese Buddhist associations have developed, including the Unified Buddhist Church, an organization founded by popular Thien (Zen) Buddhist monk Thich Nhat Hanh.

New pilgrims

From the 1960s on, as the United States became increasingly involved in foreign affairs, a generation of Americans born during and after World War II grew up in a climate of increased awareness and interest in Asian cultures. Political stability—or military or economic assistance from the United States—in various parts of Asia allowed for increased travel, tourism, and volunteerism abroad. Some served in World War II, like Robert Aitken who first encountered Zen Buddhism while a Japanese prisoner of war. Others travelled to Asia during the Zen boom of the 1950s and 1960s, such as Gary Snyder. Still others took advantage of the outward-facing social climate of the 1960s to volunteer abroad as Jack Kornfield (b. 1945) did; after graduating from Dartmouth College in 1967, Kornfield joined the Peace Corps and traveled to Thailand.

Like Kornfield, many other Americans sought opportunities to travel to Asia, including Joseph Goldstein (b. 1944), Sharon Salzberg (b. 1952), and Ruth Denison (1922–2015), each of whom began their Buddhist training in Asia.

Samatha and *vipasyana* are a pair of meditation practices of particular import in the Theravada tradition. *Samatha* is a form of mental serenity associated with rarified meditation practice. *Vipasyana* (more familiar in its Pali form *vipassana*), literally "insight," is the direct awareness of impermanence, suffering, and no-self one attains in meditation practice. For some, *samatha* is a prerequisite for *vipasyana* while many modern teachers, particularly in the United States, have focused on *vipasyana* by itself.

Those who traveled to Asia generally drew from a cluster of teachers and related approaches to Buddhist practice. The Burmese monk Mahasi Sayadaw (1904–1982) popularized a meditation practice that dispensed with many forms of classical Buddhist practice, including rituals and chanting as well as preliminary practice of *samatha* meditation, and focused instead on *vipasyana* or insight meditation (Chapter 5). S. N. Goenka (1924–2013), who studied in Burma but propagated his teachings in India, used a similar approach. In addition to removing elements of classical Buddhism, he removed the label of Buddhism altogether and initiated meditation programs divorced entirely from the Buddhist tradition. On the other end of this spectrum in Thailand; in addition to the mainline monastic orders, a revivalist movement called the Thai Forest Tradition had developed in the twentieth century, which sought to restore high standards of monastic practice to the Buddhist community. Many young Americans, like Kornfield, studied in the Thai Forest Tradition from teachers such as the popular and influential monk Ajahn Chah (1918–1992) as well as Burmese teachers including Sayadaw. There are a great number of overlaps between these teachers and their approaches; most importantly it should be noted that their focus was a Theravada-derived *vipasyana*-based meditation practice that was adapted from its monastic context for application to lay life (Fronsdal 1998).

After returning to the United States, Kornfield and Goldstein met in Shambhala International's recently opened Naropa University in Boulder, Colorado, in 1974. There they discovered affinities in one another's approaches to Buddhist practice and, together with Salzberg and Jacqueline Mandell, founded the Insight Meditation Society in Barre, Massachusetts, in 1975. Kornfield would later be one of the founders of Spirit Rock Meditation Center in northern California (Cadge 2005, 29ff; Prebish 1999, 39–40). Together, their retreats, writings, and public lectures have helped popularize the insight meditation movement in the United States (Chapter 5).

On the one hand, there are remarkable similarities between the US Buddhist landscapes of the early and late twentieth century. At the beginning of the century, small communities of Asian immigrants began to establish Buddhist communities while an intellectual and religious interest in Buddhism on the part of the non-Asian population led to occasional overlaps, conversions, and even ordinations. Following the Hart-Celler Act, small populations of Asian immigrants and refugees began establishing Buddhist communities and attracting the interest of non-Asian Americans. On the other hand, there is a distinct difference between the two eras, namely the widespread proliferation and adoption of Buddhism on the part of non-Asian Americans. The sudden spread, popularity, and acceptance of Buddhism during the 1960s and 1970s is arguably the result of shifting cultural currents, notably the "rapidly changing times and increasing turmoil brought on by mounting tension, urban uprisings, and the Vietnam War" (Iwamura 2010, 64) that caused many to immerse themselves in emotional, spiritual, and artistic pursuits. In this climate, there was a general willingness to embrace Asian religious and spiritual traditions, such as the Transcendental Meditation movement of the Maharishi Mahesh Yogi, popularized and mainstreamed by their celebrity followers such as The Beatles and actress Mia Farrow. Such mainstream acceptance is a marked departure from early-twentieth-century Asian exclusion and discriminatory laws. Coupled with a rapid increase in Asian immigration following 1965, the proliferation and diversification of the US Buddhist landscape is a natural consequence.

Paralellism

As new immigrant communities were founded and non-Asian Americans became increasingly interested in Buddhist practice, it would be only a matter of time before their interests converged, much in the way the young Beat poets had encountered the Berkeley Buddhist Temple's study group in the 1950s. Unlike the 1950s, however, by the 1970s and 1980s, there was a much wider diversity of Buddhist traditions in the United States, spread out across greater geographic regions. Thus, whereas earlier potential converts may have had only one or two Buddhist options to choose from, and only if they were fortunate enough to live in a part of the country that already had a Buddhist community, by the end of the twentieth century, Buddhist centers could be found in all fifty states and virtually all forms of Asian Buddhism have some presence in the United States (Figure 1, Introduction).

The convergence of immigrant-based Buddhists and American-born converts has led to what Numrich has called "parallel congregations." Based on ethnographic fieldwork in Chicago and Los Angeles, Numrich notes that Sri Lankan and Thai Theravada communities originally established to meet the needs of immigrant groups over time attracted the attention and interest of predominately white American sympathizers and converts. These converts tended to be attracted to Theravada communities, in part, because of a widespread belief that Pali-based Theravada Buddhism is closest to what the historical Buddha himself taught (Numrich 1996, 119). As a consequence of this interest, monks in these communities began offering meditation instruction to the new converts. To the extent that these communities were established to meet the larger social and cultural needs of specific immigrant populations, they necessarily hosted so-called cultural events, ceremonies, celebrations, and rituals that were mainly attended by members of the immigrant group. The white converts, by contrast, tended only to attend the meditation classes, thus giving rise to ostensibly two congregations in one community.

More recent scholarship has complicated this picture. As Cadge (Bielefeldt et al. 2001; Cadge 2005) and Hickey (2010) have noted, Numrich's fieldwork was conducted in the early 1990s and is thus now nearly thirty years old. Hickey specifically questions whether or not these parallel congregations will remain parallel, will converge into a single community, or diverge entirely. Noting that native-born children of immigrants are often more acculturated than their parents, she suggests that second and later generations of Asian American Buddhists may have interests more in line with white convert Americans; conversely, as converts age, have their own children, and face end-of-life decisions, there may be a deepening interest in ritually marking rites of passage such as marriages, births, and funerals. Indeed, Cadge's fieldwork suggests that the distinction between these parallel congregations may not be as strong as observed thirty years ago. Moreover, using the Buddhist Churches of America as a case study, Spencer's work suggest that there are multiple ways in which a multiethnic community may converge and develop over time (Spencer 2014). Arguably, Shunryu Suzuki may represent a case of parallel congregations that diverged into two distinct communities. While initially Suzuki was sent to the United States to minister to the needs of a Japanese American Zen Buddhist community, his meditation-focused white convert students had divergent needs and interests. These differing interests led to a split in the community resulting in what are arguably two traditions of Zen in America (Asai and Williams 1999, 20).

The maturation of US Buddhism

US Buddhism is both relatively new and well established. While some traditions have been on US soil since the late nineteenth century, many were established only in the last generation or two. However, despite the "newness" of these communities, it is also fair to say that many have become quite well established, allowing them to be well rooted, well connected to broader cultural currents, and provide a type of stability that will no doubt allow for longevity.

When they were first established during the Zen boom of the 1960s and 1970s, there was no way of knowing whether Zen Buddhist lineages and communities founded by Maezumi, Suzuki, and others would have any lasting influence. Writing in the late 1970s, Prebish described these and other groups as "flashy, opaquely exotic, and hip" (Prebish 1979, 51). Such characterizations have not abated. In a 2001 critique of "Boomer Buddhism"—which arguably overlaps but is not coextensive with the communities described by Prebish—Prothero dismissed this brand of Buddhism as "all too often shallow and small. It soothes rather than upsets, smoothing out the palpable friction between Buddhist practice and the banalities of contemporary American life, cajoling even the Dalai Lama to direct his great mind to small American preoccupations like 'The Art of Happiness'" (Prothero 2001). Despite such dismissals, or despite elements of these lineages that tend toward the faddish, such traditions are now quite large and well established, serving multiple generations of Buddhist students. In the case of the San Francisco Zen Center, as we saw in the previous chapter, their related organizations include training centers and businesses in the San Francisco Bay Area, and Suzuki's disciples have spread Soto Zen Buddhism across the country in potentially hundreds of small Zen centers.

A seemingly natural consequence of growth is internal conflict or controversy, to which US Buddhist traditions have not been immune. One recurring issue facing many US Buddhist communities has been the abuse of power by senior teachers vis-à-vis their students.

Shortly before his death in 1971, Suzuki named Richard Zentatsu Baker (b. 1936) his successor who was installed as the abbot of the San Francisco Zen Center. It was primarily due to Baker's efforts that the community expanded as much as it did, including the establishment of training centers and related businesses. However, following allegations that he was having an affair with a Zen Center financial benefactor's wife, Baker resigned as abbot, a crisis that caused several institutional changes within the community, including the adoption of new by-laws to manage "power differentials" between teachers and students (Coleman 2001, 167–168; Mitchell 2008, 142). Such allegations have been leveled at other Zen Buddhist teachers, sometimes with far-reaching consequences for US Zen Buddhist communities writ large, as was the case with Eido Shimano (b. 1932). Shimano traveled to Hawai'i in 1960, where he stayed as a guest of Robert Aitken and his wife, Anne Hopkins Aitken, and assisted them with their nascent Diamond Buddhist Sangha. Eventually, the two men would have a falling-out, and by 1965 Shimano had moved to New York where he was installed as the head teacher of the Zen Studies Society and abbot of Dai Bosatsu Zendo Kongoji monastery. Around the time of Aitken's death in 2010, his decades of written correspondence were archived at the University of Hawai'i. Amid these letters were hints of improper behavior by Shimano during his time in Hawai'i, and over time other former students came forward, attesting to decades of improper behavior and accusations of sexual misconduct. Shimano resigned from his post in 2011, and the scandal became mainstream media news (Oppenheimer 2010).[2]

The establishment of Vajradhatu was similarly plagued by the unethical conduct of its founder Chögyam Trungpa and his successor Ösel Tendzin (born Thomas Frederick Rich, 1943–1990). Chögyam Trungpa advocated a teaching style colloquially known as "crazy wisdom," which involved acting in erratic ways not expected of a wise teacher as part of a skillful attempt at undoing students' attachments to dualistic notions of right and wrong. Such behavior included drinking, smoking, wearing fine clothes, driving expensive cars, and having sex with students, behavior that proved problematic for the community. Ösel Tendzin followed in his teacher's footsteps, engaged in sexual relationships with both male and female students, and contracted the HIV virus, infecting two of his students (Dart 1989). Remarkably, whereas movements founded by charismatic leaders generally do not survive such large-scale and public scandals, Vajradhatu weathered this particular storm, reorganizing and emerging in the 1990s as Shambhala International (Eldershaw 2007, 75). It remains one of the largest and most influential Buddhist traditions in North America today (Chapter 7).

Skillful means

Upaya, especially in the form of *upayakausalya* and translated as "skillful means," refers to the pedagogical efficacy of the Buddha and advanced bodhisattvas—specifically, their ability to teach others in such a way as to most effectively lead them to awakening. *Upaya* also explains contradictions in the Buddhist teachings by suggesting that some are merely provisional and may be discarded once one is further along the path.

Sexual scandals are not the only difficulties Buddhists have had as they settle into American life. Often, troubles are the result of cross-cultural and legal misunderstandings. For example, Japanese Buddhist temples tend to be hereditary organizations run by the temple's head priest and passed on to the eldest son. In the United States, Buddhist communities are generally recognized as religious nonprofits run by lay members elected to boards of trustees who both own the temple property and effectively hire priests as employees. Japanese priests serving in American temples have been known to be confused or even offended at the American arrangements, causing difficulty or hurt feelings in the broader community (Kashima 1977, 69). In the Theravada tradition, monks are generally prohibited from owning property, which, in the US context, can create confusion as to who owns or runs an American temple or monastery, leading at times to splits in the community (Cadge 2005, 27). During the 1996 US presidential campaign, Fo Guang Shah's Los Angeles-based Hsi Lai Temple found itself in the middle of a political scandal. After hosting a fundraising luncheon attended by then vice president Al Gore, the temple raised $55,000 to contribute to the Democratic National Committee, later revealed to be temple funds in violation of campaign finance laws resulting in Senate hearings and convictions of Hsi Lai Temple members. News reports of the time mirrored earlier generations' xenophobic portrayals of immigrant Buddhists and highlights "the confusing ways Americans juggle courtesy, good will, political support, and money" (Seager 1999, 164).

These cross-cultural issues reflect both processes of translating Asian and Buddhist customs into an American context as well as the growing pains of new religious communities. Fundamentally, they reflect the various ways that US Buddhist traditions are coming into contact with American culture at large, negotiating a space in which to propagate and practice the Buddhist teachings.

A Vesak/Hanamatsuri celebration

In May 2008 the Buddhist Council of Northern California, the Institute of Buddhist Studies, and the Buddhist Churches of America's Center for Buddhist Education cosponsored "Buddha Day": a Vesak celebration to honor the birth of the historical Buddha, called *hanamatsuri* in Japanese. The celebration was held at the Jodo Shinshu Center in Berkeley, the recently opened flagship building for the Buddhist Churches of America. Representatives were invited from nine different communities across the San Francisco Bay Area, representing no less than eight different ethnicities and seven different practice traditions.

The ceremony began with the chanting of a Shin Buddhist text by then BCA Bishop Koshin Ogui. Thai monks from Wat Buddhanusorn of Fremont, California, led all assembled in the recitation of the three refuges and five precepts. A meditation led by Blanche Hartman Roshi of the San Francisco Zen Center was bookended by chanting led by Rev. Thich Tu-Luc of the Vietnamese Dharma Center of Hayward and Su Won Sunim of Yeo Lai Korean Temple of San Francisco. The Vietnamese contingent had brought with them two dozen school children who sang a version of the three refuges in English. Following the keynote dharma message by Venerable Heng Sure of the Berkeley Buddhist Monastery, the lay members of the Oakland Cambodian Buddhist Temple performed devotional chanting. Ayya Tathaaloka Bhikkhuni, founder of the Dhammadharini Vihara of Fremont, led a moving *metta* meditation and visualization before the Theravada contingent of Sinhala, Thai, and Cambodian monks bestowed a blessing on all those in attendance. The service concluded with the Japanese Buddhist practice of pouring sweet tea over an image of the Buddha.

Heng Sure began his dharma message by asking the audience what location on earth and time in history had the highest number of different Buddhist lineages coexisting simultaneously. His answer: Northern California, which boasts over forty-two different types of Buddhism. "Four times as many that existed at Dunhuang during the Tang Dynasty!" he declared, a claim hard to argue with while surrounded by two hundred lay and ordained Buddhists from such varied backgrounds all participating in and sharing their respective practice and ritual traditions.

As we have seen over the previous three chapters, this diversity is not an accident of history but the result of ongoing transnational movements and discourses stretching back to the colonial era in Asia. Contemporary US Buddhism is the result of these movements and discourses. From the colonial project that sought to define the Asian other as distinct from the Occident self, thus highlighting an exotic and mystical East, to Transcendentalists' open rejection of Victorian culture, there has been a consistent interest in Asian religions, including Buddhism. This originally purely intellectual interest developed simultaneously with the movement of Chinese and Japanese immigrants to the United States who brought Buddhism with them and established the first Buddhist communities on American soil. It was not long before these communities attracted the attention of non-Asian American seekers, and their interests would converge and diverge in numerous ways throughout most of the twentieth century. Social and political forces well beyond the scope of any one tradition have had profound impacts on US Buddhists—from the internment experience to the counterculture. These movements have brought Buddhists together in ways both unique to the modern American era as well as characteristic of an increasingly globalized and interconnected world.

As Diana Eck has argued, diversity is the fact of difference. Pluralism, by contrast, "is the engagement that creates a common society from all that diversity" (2006). We can see evidence of both in US Buddhism. To the extent that there is a multiplicity of Buddhist traditions in the United States, we see the fact of difference. But events such as Buddha Day attest to the ways in which these communities actively engage with one another. While there has certainly been divergence and even at times mutual isolation, examples of US Buddhists coming together to share the dharma, share resources, or solidarity abound. More than this, however, US Buddhists have actively engaged the broader American culture, through political activity, artistic production, and interreligious and cross-cultural exchange.

DISCUSSION QUESTIONS

1. Discuss the intent of the Hart-Celler Act and its actual consequences to immigration movements in the late twentieth century. What impact did this immigration law have on US Buddhism?

2. How did the establishment of early-twentieth-century Buddhist communities compare with the establishment of Buddhist communities following the 1965 immigration reform act? How were they different?

3. As Buddhist communities grew and matured in the United States, what were some of the developmental challenges they faced in relation to the transmission of teachings or interfacing with mainstream culture and politics?

SUGGESTIONS FOR FURTHER READING

Cadge, Wendy. 2005. *Heartwood: The First Generation of Theravada Buddhism in America*. Chicago: University of Chicago Press.

Mitchell, Scott A., and Natalie E. F. Quli, eds. 2015. *Buddhism Beyond Borders: New Perspectives on Buddhism in the United States*. Albany: State University of New York Press.

Numrich, Paul David. 1996. *Old Wisdom in the New World: Americanization in Two Immigrant Theravada Buddhist Temples*. Knoxville: University of Tennessee Press.

Numrich, Paul David, ed. 2008. *North American Buddhists in Social Context*. Boston: Brill.

Prebish, Charles S. 1999. *Luminous Passage: The Practice and Study of Buddhism in America*. Berkeley: University of California Press.

Prebish, Charles S., and Kenneth Tanaka, eds. 1998. *The Faces of Buddhism in America*. Berkeley: University of California Press.

Williams, Duncan Ryûken, and Christopher S. Queen, eds. 1999. *American Buddhism: Methods and Findings in Recent Scholarship*. Richmond, Surrey: Curzon.

PART TWO

Traditions

FIGURE 13 *Garden of One Thousand Buddhas, Arlee, Montana. (Photo courtesy Michael Friedman.)*

5

Theravada traditions

Chapter summary and outline

Following immigration reforms in the 1960s and refugee crises after the fall of Saigon in 1975, Theravada Buddhism saw substantial growth, with traditions from Sri Lanka, Burma, Cambodia, Laos, and Thailand all well represented. Increased interest in Buddhism and Asia more generally led to non-Asian American involvement in these traditions and the establishment of new communities. In addition to detailing this diverse set of Buddhist communities, this chapter also discusses the increasing popularity of mindfulness meditation and efforts to rebuild the Theravada female monastic community.

Introduction: Three vignettes

On a usually quiet side-street in south Berkeley, California, every Sunday morning Wat Mongkolratanaram opens its gates to the neighborhood and hosts Thai brunch; lay members of the community sell homemade Thai food to raise money for the temple, which is listed on Yelp, under restaurants, where it has favorable reviews. What the locals and college students might overlook, however, are the trio of monks in a shine room behind the main temple who are giving a dhamma talk. Meanwhile, on the other side of the country, in a large sparse room in Cambridge, Massachusetts, two dozen or so people sit on meditation cushions or in upright chairs, eyes closed, silently meditating. While there are Buddha images in the room and the lay teacher leading the session may give a talk, some in attendance would not consider themselves to be Buddhist at all but rather engage in the practice for personal reasons. And in a maximum security prison in Donaldson, Alabama, a group of convicted murderers participate in a ten-day, silent *vipassana* meditation retreat hosted in a gym converted into a practice space for just this purpose. The event is not without some controversy; all references to Buddhism must be downplayed to avoid the presumption of a state-sponsorship of religion or upsetting local Christian groups. At the end of the retreat, the prisoners report a deepening awareness of their own suffering and suffering they caused others, and the prison administrators report a decreased level of inmate violence (Kukura et al. 2008).

These three vignettes reflect the diverse array of contexts in which US Theravada Buddhism finds itself, a diverse set of origins in both Asia and the United States and a plurality of practices and orientations. To put it plainly, there is no such thing as Theravada Buddhism in the singular—let alone a single strand of the tradition in the United States—rather there are multiple traditions sharing multiple influences, flowing in sometimes disparate directions. Whereas these traditions have multiple origins in different parts of Buddhist Asia and have manifested themselves in locally specific ways in the United States, they share a common history and set of influences that express themselves in refugee communities, meditation retreats, and forest monasteries.

In the following chapter, we will begin with a short overview of the historical development of Theravada Buddhism and its central doctrines and practices both for monastics and laypersons. Because the history of US Theravada Buddhism is inextricably bound up with immigration movements, especially those following the 1965 Hart-Celler Act (Chapter 4), and US engagements with various southeast Asian countries, especially military engagement in Vietnam, it is worth examining country-specific expressions of US Theravada Buddhism. The reader is encouraged to consult the back matter for more information on specific schools and terms used in this chapter. And because the Theravada Buddhist tradition is based on the Pali-language canon, we will follow suit, using Pali terms in place of Sanskrit.

Overview of Theravada Buddhist history and practice

Historical origins

Religions, in some sense, constantly grapple with the conservative impulse to maintain tradition and the progressive necessity of adapting tradition to suit constantly chang-ing historical and cultural circumstances. Theravada Buddhism maintains tradition, in part, by tracing its origins to the mainstream schools of Indian Buddhism. Following the death of the Buddha, as the *sangha* developed both a canon of teachings and commentarial literature on those teachings, disagreements about the nature of enlight-enment, the path of practice, and other doctrinal points emerged that would lead to the development of what were, essentially, different philosophical schools within the tradition. Followers of these different schools were unified by adherence to a single set of monastic rules, the *vinaya*, and as long as all monks followed the same rules, philosophical disagreements could be put aside. Over time such disagreements arose about the *vinaya* itself, and thus emerged discrete monastic traditions, or *nikayas*, including the Sthaviranikaya, Sanskrit for "school of the elders," which in Pali is ren-dered Theravada (Gethin 1998, 52–53). It is by tracing its origins to this school, and the Pali canon, that modern Theravada makes the claim that its teachings are closest to that of the historical Buddha himself. However, while the Pali canon is certainly a very early recension of the Buddha's teachings, "the fact remains that the Pali canon can-not simply be taken as the last authority on questions of early Buddhism; quite clearly the traditions found in other sources may be of a similar or even earlier date" (Gethin 2001, 11).

Moreover, to assume that Theravada has remained unchanged and in a state of virtual stasis over the last two thousand years ignores historical complexity. As early as the third century BCE, Indian monks arrived in Sri Lanka, creating a network of exchange with the Indian *sangha* that lasted for centuries. At the same time, Buddhism expanded outside India and spread across Southeast Asia and Indonesia. This expansion included the full range of the Buddhist tradition—including Mahayana and later tantric developments—that competed with various mainstream schools and traditions. Various kingdoms and empires, large and small, ruled the area; the Srivijaya empire based in Sumatra influenced the region for centuries before giving way to a Khmer empire that controlled much of present-day Cambodia, Laos, southern Vietnam, and parts of Thailand. An empire based in Pagan, central Burma, created a network of Buddhist exchange with Sri Lanka. These kingdoms often gave imperial support to the *sangha* and as often purged non-mainstream traditions in efforts to consolidate power or forge national identity. It is in this way, over the course of millennia of competitive strands and multiple interpretations, that what we now think of as Theravada came to be the dominant form of Buddhism across South and Southeast Asia in the precolonial period.

Modes of practice

To begin, it is important to understand the basic social structure that supports Theravada Buddhist practice, the *sangha*. Whereas in its modern and especially American usage, the term *sangha* has come to denote the whole of the Buddhist community, originally the term was more narrowly focused on just the community of monks and nuns (*bhikkhu* and *bhikkhuni*). In canonical texts, laypersons are routinely described as taking refuge, that is putting their faith in or taking guidance from, the Three Jewels of the Buddha, the Dhamma, and the Sangha, where it was assumed that to take refuge in the *sangha* meant to put one's trust in the monastic community whose job it was to uphold the teachings of the Buddha (Numrich 1998, 149). When the term *sangha* is applied to all Buddhists, it can be qualified to refer to one of four categories of persons: monks, nuns, laymen, and laywomen. Thus we can speak of the monastic *sangha* as opposed to the lay *sangha*. Monastic roles are explicitly detailed in the *vinaya*, which not only lists a specific number of rules to be followed (227 for monks, 311 for nuns), but also procedures for how to become ordained and for dealing with transgressions. The *vinaya*, in theory, regulates all aspects of personal and communal life for the *sangha*.

Pali for "path," *magga* (Sanskrit, *marga*) refers to the path, course, or directions left by the Buddha for his followers to travel from suffering to awakening. *Magga* thus forms a central metaphor in Buddhism—a religion that provides a map, as it were, toward nirvana.

Generally speaking, Buddhism employs a metaphor of path (*magga*) to describe the progressive process of awakening—that is, one starts somewhere, is transformed along the way, and ends up someplace different. For Theravada Buddhism, one normative explication of this path can be found in Buddhaghosa's monumental fifth-century CE text, the *Visuddhimagga* (*Path of Purification*). This text is a useful starting point for a conversation about what constitutes Theravada monastic practice. The *Visuddhimagga* is divided into three sections covering trainings in morality, concentration, and wisdom. The first two chapters dealing with morality are focused on the *vinaya* precepts, which set the standard for proper monastic behavior and lay the foundation for meditation practice, the subject of the next eleven chapters. Through meditation practice, then, one develops wisdom. This tripartite schema for describing the Buddhist path recalls the Eightfold Path which can also be divided into essentially the same three parts. After its composition, the *Visuddhimagga* became a foundational text for many strands of Theravada across Buddhist Asia. We must keep in mind, however, that its "contents strictly concern the life of a monk. Though enlivened by some anecdotes by way of examples, they are fairly austere and afford few glimpses of devotional sentiment or popular practice. It is above all a handbook for meditators" (Gombrich 1988, 153).

For the Buddha, the ideal path toward the goal of awakening was to leave behind the life of a householder and enter into the life of a monastic, devoting oneself entirely to the path of practice without distraction. What, then, of the laity? Given that not everyone, either in premodern classical Buddhism or the modern world, is cut out for monastic life, what is the path of practice for householders?

For monastics, the path can be divided into morality (based on the *vinaya*), concentration, and wisdom. For the laity, the path is less comprehensive but clearly defined and divided into charitable giving (*dana*), morality, and meditation. Whereas charitable giving can be understood as merely making material donations of food or shelter to a monastic, it is also reflective of a more general attitude of generosity and the transfer of karmic merit such that all beings can benefit from good works (Gethin 1998, 109). Morality is defined by lay precepts: "(1) to refrain from harming living creatures, (2) to refrain from taking what is not given, (3) to refrain from sexual misconduct, (4) to refrain from false speech, (5) to refrain from intoxicants that cause heedlessness" (Gethin 1998, 110). Finally, meditation in this context is not merely the practice of seated meditation; rather, it is, in part, the arousal of faith or confidence in the Three Jewels engendered by the act of making offerings, prostrations before monks or Buddha images and relics, and the chanting or recitation of Buddhist texts, acts collectively referred to as *puja*. These acts are meditative in the broader sense of the word, and can lead to a calming of the mind that is a precursor for deeper levels of awareness and insight.

Generally translated as "meditative absorption," *jhana* (Sanskrit, *dhyana*) refers to a mental state characterized by a complete withdrawal from external sensory input brought about by single-minded concentration on a physical or mental object. Whereas this state is not an enduring insight into the true nature of reality, it does require a level of mental and meditative ability that is arguably a foundation for sustained practice.

Meditation, especially as it is practiced by committed monastics, is extensively detailed in both canonical and commentarial literature. It would be a mistake to reduce this literature down to a single practice, but in the interest of space, it is worth focusing on one form of meditation that has had enormous influence in the United States, the practice of *samatha* and *vipassana* meditation. Following along with the metaphor of path, after the requisite moral training, one begins with calming the mind. Calming the mind, through *samatha* meditation, leads to *samadhi*, a type of one-pointedness of concentration, which itself can lead to meditative absorption, *jhana*, characterized by a withdraw from external sensory input and complete absorption in concentration. *Samadhi* and *jhana* are not ends in themselves but merely preliminary stages along a path toward a deeper insight into the nature of reality. This insight can be attained through *vipassna* or insight meditation. And it perhaps goes without saying that the extent to which preliminarily stages are necessary for later stages has been the subject of much debate over the course of Buddhist history. Whereas some have argued that insight into the true nature of the mind and reality is possible through *vipassana* alone and that *samatha* is unnecessary—and *jhana* is actually dangerous without proper training or guidance—others have argued that *vipassana* is impossible without *samatha* (Gethin 2001, 344–350; cf Braun 2015).

We should be cautious here about reinforcing a normative vision of what constitutes proper Buddhist practice. While meditation has certainly played an important role in the history of the tradition, so have a host of other practices including social engagement, scholarly exegesis, and philosophical analysis. Indeed, the *Visuddhimagga* is a monumental text, over 800 pages in English translation, hardly the work of one who had not thought deeply about the path of practice. In some ways, the privileging of meditation practice over and against other forms of practice is highlighted by a distinction that is drawn between "forest-dwelling monks" and "village monks," a distinction that points toward two modes of both practice and relationships with the lay community. In pre-colonial Buddhist Asia, while forest-dwelling monks lived at a considerable remove from society in isolated monasteries and hermitages, village monks were located within urban areas or at the edge of villages where they had more direct interaction with laypersons. In this role, Buddhist temples were not mere religious institutions but were also schools and health clinics, and monks often served as political advisors to the ruling class. Rhetorically, these roles were looked down upon by forest-dwelling monks who saw them as necessarily distracting from the deeper call toward awakening. The forest monk could claim to be single-mindedly focused on the pursuit of awakening to the exclusion of the secular world. However, we should be on guard against naive idealizations of the forest and condescension toward the village. At times, the forest was seen as a place of heterodox views, a location where monks not only removed themselves from society but rejected its norms entirely, engaging in cultic practices that might have been contrary to orthodox Buddhist positions. Furthermore, such forest traditions, over time, were as institutionalized as any form of Buddhism. These two trends then should be seen as just that, trends, points along a spectrum of practice and polemical discourses that varied greatly from time to time and place to place (Robinson and Johnson 1997, 162–165; Gombrich 1988, 156–157).

The two sides of the *sangha*, monastic and lay, form a symbiotic relationship wherein the laity supports renunciants in exchange for spiritual merit. And a monastic *sangha*, even one at considerable remove from the village, cannot survive without the material support of the laity. Within this context, a variety of practices and approaches to the path have developed across various Theravada Buddhist countries, almost all of which have been imported into the United States. For many immigrant and refugee communities, Theravada Buddhism was established by the laity with an eye toward maintaining both the monastic tradition and cultural customs. Many of these communities follow a similar pattern: a small lay movement rents space and invites a monk from Asia or a larger US-based Buddhist community to lead services or give teachings; eventually funds are raised to purchase or build dedicated space for religious services and monastic quarters (as monks are not allowed to cohabit with laypersons); and a free-standing Buddhist community is established. In other instances, American-born travelers in the latter half of the twentieth century encountered Buddhist practices in Asia before returning with them to establish Buddhist centers focused almost exclusively on meditation. In what follows, we will discuss the specifics of how each thread of Theravada found its way into the United States, noting distinctions and overlaps.

US Theravada traditions of Sri Lanka and Burma
Historical Sri Lanka-Burma connection

Since Buddhism's introduction from India in the third century, Sri Lanka has had a complex relationship with Buddhism's homeland, alternately viewed as a location of doctrinal authority and ultimately corrupted by later developments. As Indian Buddhism was developing, it was exported into Burma[1] and the rest of Southeast Asia in all its forms. When promoted as a state religion in various Burmese kingdoms, latter Mahayana and tantric developments were often purged by importing Sri Lankan texts and monastic traditions. As Buddhism died out in India, and in times of monastic decline in Sri Lanka, the Sinhalese *sangha* in turn reached out to the Burmese, thus creating a network of Buddhist exchange between the island nation and Southeast Asian mainland.

By the colonial era, of course, the two nations were heading in rather different directions. Sri Lanka had been the site of various attempts at colonial control for centuries, first by the Portuguese, and later the Dutch and the British. Occupying colonial forces had not only stripped Buddhist institutions of political patronage but had also displaced Buddhist monastics from their traditional roles as teachers, doctors, and authority figures for the laity. Thus, by the nineteenth century, Sri Lankan Theravada Buddhism was politically weakened, preparing the ground for the revivalist movements covered in Chapter 2. Burma had a slightly different experience with colonialism. The British did not control Burma until well into the nineteenth century, and when the country came under British rule, Buddhist institutions were allowed to govern themselves. Despite a lack of active suppression, colonial educational and other institutions displaced Buddhist versions of them, resulting in a similar pattern of revivalist and nationalist sentiment among the Burmese Buddhist monastic community. And when the British attempted to ban political gatherings, many lay people became temporarily ordained in order to speak out against colonial rule during Buddhist gatherings (Robinson and Johnson 1997, 150–151). At the same time, efforts to revitalize the Buddhist *sangha* led reformers to institute new forms of Buddhist practice and establish new meditation centers (cf Schober 2006).

Sri Lankan traditions

The first Sri Lankan Theravada community in the United States was established in 1966 in Washington, DC, following the visit of a Sri Lankan monk named Madihe Pannasiha Mahanayaka Thera who noted that there was great interest in Buddhism in the United States but no Theravada institutional presence. Back in Sri Lanka, he worked with the Sasana Sevaka Society, a lay Buddhist organization, to help raise funds for a US temple. Bope Vinitha, a Sri Lankan monk who had spent several years studying at Harvard University, was asked to direct the temple. He arrived in 1966, and the Washington Buddhist Vihara was established. Within a few years, the *vihara* was able to purchase a new, dedicated building, and Bope Vinitha was joined by other Sri Lankan monks while ministering to a diverse community of Sinhala, Thai, Bangladeshi, Burmese, and white-American members (Cadge 2005, 24–25; Prebish 1999, 37–38). In 1968, Henepola Gunaratana arrived in the United States to assist with the *vihara*. Together with long-time student Matthew Flickstein, he established the Bhavana Society in 1982; though the project took several years to raise funds and purchase space, eventually a monastery and meditation retreat center was established in rural West Virginia. In addition to his work with the Bhavana Society, through his public teachings and travels and numerous books, such as *Mindfulness in Plain English*, Gunaratana has become quite influential beyond either the Sri Lankan or Theravada communities.

On the other side of the country, in the early 1970s, two Sri Lankan lay organizations laid the groundwork for what would become the Buddhist Vihara of Los Angeles. While the Sri Lankan Association of Southern California was concerned more broadly with enhancing Sinhala social and cultural networks, the Sri Lankan-American Buddha Dhamma Society was more narrowly focused on promoting Buddhism in the United States (Numrich 1996, 1-2). Social gatherings at the former led to the establishment by the latter of a fully functioning *vihara* in the mid-1970s. Wapola Piyananda was the first abbot of the new community, which served both Sri Lankan as well as Southeast Asian Theravada Buddhists more generally. However, within a year of its establishment, a schism developed in the community between the monks and various groups of laypersons over *vihara* management; the schism led to the establishment of a new community, the Dharma Vijaya Buddhist Vihara (Numrich 1996, 20–23; cf Cadge 2005).

The Buddhist Vihara of Los Angeles reflects the above-mentioned model for establishing a US Buddhist community; instigated by a local lay group, a monk is invited and funds are raised for a dedicated space. The schism represents another way new Buddhist communities have been established as well as some of the challenges in creating Buddhist communities in a new country. On the other hand, the Bhavana Society reflects a different type of Theravada community, one derived from a Sri Lankan tradition but established in cooperation with a multi-ethnic base. While some communities are large with charismatic and prolific writers as head teachers, as is the case with Henepola Gunaratana, other communities are small, relatively isolated, and still run out of homes in residential neighborhoods. We should also guard against equating the total number of Sri Lankan Americans with Sri Lankan Buddhists; many communities are multiethnic and not all Sri Lankan Americans identify as Buddhist. As a result, it can be difficult to gauge the exact number of Sri Lankan-derived Theravada Buddhist communities in the United States.

Burmese traditions

It is important to note that the modern country of Burma encompasses several dozen distinct ethnic groups and roughly a hundred different languages. Minority ethnic groups have fared better or worse compared to the majority, and ongoing political and international border disputes have caused various refugee movements to neighboring Southeast Asian nations and the United States. The United States has only tracked Burmese immigrants and refugees since the mid-1970s, meaning many who originally came from Burma, but passed through another country on their way to the United States may not be included in government statistics. At present, the Burmese American population is relatively small compared to other immigrant groups from the same region (Cadge 2005, 20) with large increases in population following times of turmoil. Burma gained independence from British rule in 1948, but in a 1962 coup d'état, a military junta seized control of the government and instituted a tightly controlled, one-party socialist government that lasted, more or less, until open elections were held in 2010. The military's oppressive government has led to mass protests over the last fifty years, which in turn led to violent crackdowns by the government as well as general economic impoverishment and human rights violations. The 8888 Uprising of 1988 was one of the largest and saw Aung San Suu Kyi (b. 1945) become a political leader and advocate for change, work that eventually led her to winning a Nobel Peace Prize. Further protests broke out in the mid-2000s which, like protests in the past, were organized in part by politically active Buddhist monks. These protests led to the release of Aung San Suu Kyi, a reformed constitution, and open elections. Whereas the country has endeavored to hold to promised reforms and work closely with international agencies, change has been slow and interethnic fighting continues, particularly between Muslim minorities and nationalist Buddhists.

Due to these ongoing crises, many Burmese come to the United States as refugees who necessarily have a more difficult time establishing religious communities due to smaller and more disparate populations with less financial resources or ties to organized communities in their country of origin. For Burmese Buddhists, historically this situation has led many to attend services at Theravada communities of other Southeast Asian groups, notably Thai Theravada Buddhists. However, since the early 1980s, more temples have been established, especially in the San Francisco Bay Area, Los Angeles, and Washington, DC (Cadge 2005, 31).

Despite the relative lack of scholarly studies on Burmese immigrant communities (Cheah 2011), one form of Burmese Buddhist practice has had a large impact on US Buddhism more generally, a trend that can be traced to Mahasi Sayadaw (1904-1982).

During the brief period of time between independence and the military overthrow of the government, Burma's prime minister promoted Buddhism and the reestablishment of Buddhist institutions. In this effort, he opened a meditation center in Rangoon and asked Mahasi Sayadaw to be its chief instructor. Originally from Mandalay, Mahasi Sayadaw traced his practice tradition back to a reclusive monk several generations before and taught a form of *vipassana* meditation. "Mahasi's method of meditation equated mindfulness with a precise noting of fleeting mental and physical events, pursued relentlessly until it produced certain physiological and psychological reactions that were identified with the stages of insight knowledge as set out in *The Path of Purification*" (Robinson and Johnson 1997, 153). In this regard, Mahasi Sayadaw was similar to other mid-century Buddhist reformers, such as his fellow countryman U Ba Khin (1899–1971), who opened his own meditation center in Rangoon. Notably, both of their centers were open to laypersons, members of a growing middle class who wanted to learn Buddhist meditation (cf Braun 2013).

As we will see later in this chapter, since the 1970s, there has been a growing insight meditation movement in the United States promulgated by Jack Kornfield, Ruth Denison, and others who studied in Asia. While this movement diverges from the Burmese tradition, it is hard to imagine its existence without it. In addition to being trained by Burmese teachers, in the movement's formative years, Mahasi Sayadaw and other Burmese monks were invited to the United States to speak and teach at nascent insight meditation groups. Incidentally, while touring the country, Mahasi Sayadaw spent time working with Burmese Buddhists, leaving two monks, U Silananda and U Keletha, to help establish temples in California and elsewhere (Cadge 2005, 31).

S. N. Goenka and meditation de-religionized

S. N. Goenka (1924–2013), born in Burma to Indian parents, after studying with U Ba Khin, moved to India in 1969 where he began teaching *vipassana* on his own. Both Joseph Goldstein and Sharon Salzberg studied at Goenka retreats in the 1970s, and arguably the insight meditation movement is as indebted to his approach as it is to the "Mahasi method" (Cadge 2005, 35; Prebish 1999, 150). Goenka's approach mirrors Mahasi's; however, he was adamant that he was not teaching a religion but, rather, a mental training. "The Buddha never taught a sectarian religion; he taught Dhamma—the way to liberation—which is universal."[2] Goenka courses are ten-day silent residential retreats led by lay students and recorded talks by Goenka. Their format is essentially the same in all centers across the world; thus, the Goenka method is unique in that, rather than accommodating or assimilating to local cultural contexts, it actually resists assimilation. For Goenka, the Buddha's teachings are universally true and therefore need no adaptation.

In some respects, then, Goenka retreats might not be "religious" at all but more a reflection of a secularized Buddhist practice as we will explore in more detail in Chapter 8. However, despite rhetoric that deemphasizes religion while emphasizing the psychological benefits of meditation, Goenka retreats retain both the presence of the Buddha (a religious figure) and an overall format derived from a specific Theravada Buddhist tradition. Thus, following Cadge's lead, we can trace Goenka's tradition to a lineage with roots in a traditionally Theravada Buddhist country (Cadge 2005, 23). Regardless of whether it should be labeled Theravada or not, it is clear that Goenka has played an important role in US Buddhism by establishing more than a dozen centers and influencing other traditions. The program at the Donaldson State Prison mentioned at the outset of this chapter is a Goenka retreat.

US Theravada traditions of Cambodia and Laos

The Khmer empire ruled over present-day Cambodia, Laos, and parts of Thailand and Vietnam from roughly the ninth to fifteenth centuries. Like other Southeast Asian cultures of the time, it inherited a mixture of Indian and Indonesian cultures, including Buddhism, Brahmanism, and local animist cults. Over time, Buddhism became the state-supported religion promulgated throughout the region. It was during the twelfth century that the massive temple complex of Angkor Wat was constructed, reflecting the scope and influence of the Khmer empire. However, over the next two centuries, the empire declined in power, obscured by both Burmese and Thai empires, before French colonialists began taking control of the peninsula (Robinson and Johnson 1997, 143–144). By this time, however, a trend of relating religion and kingship had been well established, leading to both state sponsorship of Buddhist institutions and Buddhist rituals in support of the state, some of which remain in practice to the present (Gyallay-Pap 2006).

Colonialism and World War II were devastating for the region. Cambodia, Laos, and Vietnam were pawns between European Allied powers and the Japanese during the war. In the immediate aftermath, no longer able to maintain their colonies, European withdrawal led to communist revolutions and US military interventions. Cambodia and Laos were pulled into the conflict between the United States and Vietnam, and by the fall of Saigon in 1975, the government of Laos had been overthrown by communist forces, and the Khmer Rouge had come to power in Cambodia. While the state undercut the authority of Buddhism and monastic institutions saw a sharp decline under communist rule in Laos, in Cambodia the Khmer Rouge targeted monks as enemies of the state, executing them in the killing fields. Large numbers of Cambodian, Laotian, and Vietnamese refugees began arriving in the United States in the mid- to late-1980s. Like Burmese refugees mentioned earlier, these new refugees also lacked financial resources to establish new Buddhist communities, and monastic institutions in Southeast Asia had largely been destroyed. Consequently, early on, many attended services of Thai Theravada communities; since the late 1990s, however, there has been a growth in both Khmer and Lao Theravada Buddhist temples across the United States.

Whereas other Asian immigrant communities have tended to settle in large metropolitan areas or port cities, refugees were often required to settle in disparate parts of the country. As a result, while the greater Los Angeles area still boasts the largest

FIGURE 14 *Glory Cambodian Buddhist Temple, Lowell, Massachusetts.*

concentration of Buddhists in the United States, one can find both small and large Theravada Buddhist communities in the Midwest and along the Gulf Coast (cf Wilson 2015). These communities often begin with lay support, in rented spaces, before growing large enough to purchase or construct dedicated temples. Situated in historically conservative and predominately Christian communities, negotiating local laws and customs can be challenging. At times, zoning restrictions have hampered the establishment of new communities while at others, local communities have welcomed the new diversity.

We may estimate, based on studies conducted by Cadge (2005) and Bankston and Hildalgo (2008), among others, that there are hundreds of thousands of Lao and Khmer Buddhists residing in North America. Despite these large numbers, these traditions have received relatively little scholarly attention. It is undoubtedly true that in many ways they serve a diverse set of religious, social, and cultural needs for displaced populations. Van Esterik's (1999) detailed accounting of Lao rituals points to the crucial role Buddhist institutions and traditional customs play in maintaining Lao identity in the face of refugee displacement, flight, and resettlement. Notably, this study is now nearly twenty years old, and it is perhaps the "newness" of Khmer and Lao traditions that is one reason for lack of scholarly attention. Of course, newness is relative; to the extent these communities have now been on American soil for over three decades and given birth to a native-born generation that has itself come of age, Theravada traditions from Cambodia and Laos represent a rich area of study that remains open, potentially changing how we conceptualize US Buddhism more generally.

US Theravada traditions of Thailand

Beginning in the thirteenth century, the Khmer empire gradually declined, allowing for Thai city-states to grow into first the Sukhothai and later Ayutthaya kingdoms, providing stability in the region as a bulwark against colonial aggression, supporting Theravada Buddhism, and eventually turning into the modern nation-state of Thailand. In the fourteenth century, Theravada was established as the state religion, setting a precedent that lasts to the present. During the reign of King Mongkut, who was an ordained monk before he was king, Thailand began the process of modernization during a time of increased pressure toward Westernization and trade with colonial nations. In response to these pressures, Mongkut instituted a number of cultural and political reforms, including a monastic reform movement that gave rise to a new order of monks, the Dhammayuttika Nikaya. Thai Buddhism can then be organized into two distinct monastic lineages with the Maha Nikaya being the second and larger of the two. Both lineages are overseen by the Supreme Sangha Council and the Supreme Patriarch (*Sangharaja*), a political appointee charged with overseeing the monastic community, highlighting the close relationship between Buddhism and the state in modern Thailand (Robinson and Johnson 1997, 152–153; cf Skilling 2006).[3] Both the Dhammayuttika Nikaya and Maha Nikaya lineages have established networks of temples across the United States, represented by the Dhammayut Council of the USA and Council of Thai Bhikkhus, respectively.

Thai Theravada Buddhism was well positioned to establish a foothold in the United States following passage of the Hart-Celler Act. "Inflation was high, and job opportunities and professional mobility low in Thailand at the time; factors that led many Thai professionals to decide to migrate to the United States" (Cadge and Sangdhanoo 2005, 10). Additionally, many Thai women married US servicemen stationed in Southeast Asia at the time. Thus, by the mid-1970s, tens of thousands of Thai immigrants had arrived in the United States. As a result of the relative stability and strong state support of the Thai *sangha* over the previous centuries, Thai monastic institutions were in a position to easily support overseas efforts to spread Buddhism. The first US temple (*wat*) was established as the New York Buddhist Study Center by both Thai immigrants and American-born Buddhists; incorporated in 1965, the center was not fully functional until a monk was invited in 1973. Thai immigrants in Los Angeles organized the Thai-American Buddhist Association in 1970, inviting the monk Phrakhru Vajirathammasophon from Thailand to teach and perform services. The following year, a group of Thai monks arrived, the lay community began organizing funds, and in 1972, the construction of a Thai-style temple was begun. Officially dedicated in 1979, Wat Phra Chetuphon, otherwise known as Wat Thai LA, has grown to be the largest Thai temple in the United States (Cadge 2005; Cadge and Sangdhanoo 2005; Numrich 1996).

From 1970 until the early 2000s, nearly a hundred Thai Buddhist temples have been established in twenty-nine states. While most are in large states such as California or Texas, temples can also be found in Arkansas, Nevada, New Jersey, and Utah. Most communities were established in the same manner as those of other immigrant groups; lay persons come together, raise funds, invite monks, and construct new spaces. Some communities, located near US military bases, were established by the wives of US servicemen who wished to create spaces for Thai cultural and religious events. As we saw with the Dharma Vijaya Buddhist Vihara earlier, differences in opinion within a community can lead to schisms that result in the establishment of new temples (Cadge and Sangdhanoo 2005, 18-19; cf Perreira 2004).

That many Thai Theravada temples were established with Thai cultural customs and holidays in mind speaks to the variety of functions these communities serve. Many non-Thai Americans interested in learning more about Buddhism have been attracted to these communities as well, creating opportunities for converts to learn Buddhist meditation and other practices. This interest has created, in some instances, the emergence of what Numrich (1996) described as parallel congregations, an issue addressed in Chapter 4. It is important to note, however, that in addition to serving the needs of both Thai and white Americans, many Thai Theravada temples serve the needs of

FIGURE 15 *Wat Mongkolratanaram, The Thai Buddhist Temple, Berkeley, California. (Photo by author.)*

diverse populations of Buddhists, including other Southeast Asian ethnicities. Wat Buddhanusorn, in Fremont, California, dedicated a new temple building in the late 1990s and serves a community not just of Thai Americans, but Lao, Vietnamese, and Khmer Buddhists as well. The San Francisco Bay Area is well known for its religious diversity, and the monks at Wat Buddhanusorn participate in local interreligious organizations with other US Buddhists, Muslims, Hindus, and Christians. Behind the temple's altar is a painting commissioned by a local Thai artist of various celestial Buddhist realms and this world, including an image of the Golden Gate Bridge, "a visual icon of the two-way traffic of influence and interaction constitutive of Buddhism in America" (Eck 1999, ix).

Forest traditions

As discussed earlier, a rhetorical distinction between village and forest monks exists within the Theravada tradition. In Thailand, an explicit forest tradition has developed and become a major force in modern Thai Buddhism. The forest tradition developed as part and parcel of broader cultural reforms and in response to the pressures of colonialism. Whereas the tradition plays on the distinctiveness of a community at a remove from urban centers and secular affairs, the modern forest tradition has played a key role in extending Thai Buddhist orthodoxy and forging a Thai Buddhist national identity. This is made possible by forest monasteries being locations not just of monastic practice but of outreach to the laity who learn Buddhist doctrine and engage in Buddhist meditation taught by forest monks. This outreach to the laity has continued to the present, attracting both Thai Buddhists and pilgrims from the world over. Over the past few decades, the Thai forest tradition has become much more visible in the United States; two California monasteries are illustrative examples of the tradition.

Located outside Valley Center northeast of San Diego, Metta Forest Monastery was established in 1991 by, among others, Ajahn Suwat Suvaco (1919–2001), who helped establish several monasteries in the United States, and Thanissaro Bhikkhu (born Geoffrey DeGraff, 1949). There are currently ten monks in full-time residence at the monastery, which also allows lay visitors to come for overnight retreats. After its foundation, Thanissaro Bhikkhu was appointed abbot of the monastery; he is also the first non-Thai monk to be a recognized preceptor in the Dhammayuttika Nikaya. In his public life outside the monastery, Thanissaro Bhikkhu is a prolific author, an important voice for US Buddhists beyond the Thai Forest Tradition.

Arguably, the most well-known teacher in the Thai Forest Tradition is Ajahn Chah (1918–1992) who was not only instrumental in the forest tradition's revival in Thailand but was responsible for opening monasteries abroad through an extensive network of both Thai and non-Thai students. In the early 1980s, one of his disciples, Ajahn Sumedho (born Robert Jackman, 1934) began receiving requests for teachings from Buddhists in California. By the decade's end, a small group of students had organized a community that would become Abhayagiri Monastery. In 1995, 120 acres of land

FIGURE 16 *Shrine room at Abhayagiri Buddhist Monastery, Redwood Valley, California. (Photo courtesy Christopher Taylor.)*

were gifted by the City of Ten Thousand Buddhas (Chapter 6) for the establishment of the monastery. Since then, the acreage has expanded as has the number of residents which includes both novice and fully ordained monks as well as lay men and women. The current abbot is Ajahn Pasanno (born Reed Perry, 1949), a disciple of Ajahn Chah.

Both monasteries allow for laypersons to visit, stay overnight, engage in *puja*, and learn meditation practices. Unlike other centers, such as those in the Goenka tradition that only operate for short periods, neither monastery can be seen as a "retreat center." They are full-time monasteries. Visitors are allowed to come either for long or short periods throughout the year; however, they are required to keep, in addition to the five lay precepts, three additional lay precepts, to abstain from eating past noon, engaging in singing or dancing or wearing perfumes, and resting on high or luxurious beds. Both monasteries operate fully on a donation basis as it is believed that the dhamma should be given freely as a gift.

It is worth noting that monasticism, and its requisite celibacy, has not been historically popular in the United States which, religiously, has been so influenced by Protestant Christianity. That a monastic Buddhist tradition not only survives in the United States but has attracted a growing following runs counter to this trend. While it is tempting to view this as a resistance to adaptation in that the tradition has not eschewed celibate monasticism, it is worth noting that the forest tradition has, historically, always had a space for lay practice. It is the ability of this tradition to hold to somewhat classical monastic rules while catering to lay interests that may account for its success in a cultural context unaccustomed to monastic practice.

The insight meditation movement

As discussed in previous chapters, the Zen boom of the 1950s and subsequent interest in Asian cultures in the 1960s, combined with volunteer and tourism opportunities, allowed a significant number of Americans to seek out Buddhism in the United States and travel to encounter Buddhism in its Asian contexts. Some, such as the aforementioned Ajahn Sumedho, discovered the forest tradition and committed to the life of a monastic. Ruth Denison, Jack Kornfield, Joseph Goldstein, and Sharon Salzberg all spent time in Burma, Thailand, and India in the 1960s and 1970s, learning meditation practices from Ajahn Chah, Mahasi Sayadaw, U Ba Khin, and S. N. Goenka, among others. While Kornfield briefly ordained as a monk, most returned to the United States as laypersons, often with the implicit or explicit desire to adapt Buddhist teachings to an American cultural milieu that has not, generally speaking, seen celibate monasticism in a favorable light (Prebish 1999, 150).

Following an encounter at Naropa University in Boulder, Colorado, Goldstein and Kornfield, along with Salzberg and Jacqueline Mandell, established the Insight Meditation Society (IMS) in 1975. The following year, they purchased a mansion and seventy-five acres of land in Barre, Massachusetts, outside Boston, and began leading intensive meditation retreats, generally lasting ten days, similar in format to the Goenka method. Early on, the center's teachers "concerned themselves with … what it meant to take the Buddhist tradition, steeped in the imagery and metaphor of Asia, to try and find its unchanging essence, and then to express that essence in the imagery of a new time and place" (Cadge 2005, 30). Despite this attempt to adapt the teachings to an American context, connections with Asia were maintained; Ajahn Chah, Mahasi Sayadaw, and even the Dalai Lama visited the center in its formative years. On the other side of the country, Kornfield, Sylvia Boorstein, and others established a West Coast *vipassana* tradition that eventually led to the purchasing of 410 acres of land in Woodacre, California, north of San Francisco, for what would become Spirit Rock Meditation Center. Whereas IMS, at least initially, tended to be rooted in the Theravada and Burmese traditions, the Spirit Rock community was influenced by other spiritual traditions and Western psychology (Gleig 2012b, 132). All the while, the founders of these centers began their long and prolific writing and teaching careers, releasing a number of books, distributing their lectures and teachings on audio tapes and later CDs and the Internet, and going on numerous teaching tours across the country.

By the end of the century, there were roughly 250 insight meditation centers across the country (Cadge 2005, 22). However, it is difficult to know the movement's scope of influence because centers can operate independently from any national organization and are not connected to a monastic tradition with ties to Asia. Thus, unlike

Ruth Denison (1922–2015)

FIGURE 17 *Ruth Denison, 1922–2015. (Photo courtesy Dagmar Schultz.)*

Following World War II, Ruth Denison emigrated from Germany to the United States where she met her husband, Henry. Together, they traveled widely, and in the 1960s spent time in Asia where she became a student of U Ba Khin in Burma. There she became a *vipassana* teacher in the lineage Ledi Sayadaw, and she was authorized by U Ba Khin to teach the dhamma in the West. She founded the *vipassana* center Dhamma Dena in Joshua Tree, California, where she led the first all-female meditation retreat. While her approach to teaching was in many ways consistent with her teachers, she also incorporated chanting, movement, and dance into her practice. Having taught at the Insight Meditation Society and Spirit Rock, and founding *vipassana* centers in many US locations and her native Germany, she left an indelible mark on the insight meditation movement and US Buddhism.

"congregational" religious communities, it is challenging to ascertain specific numbers of adherents. This is complicated by the fact that the tradition makes no requirement of exclusive membership (i.e., one can participate in the practice without claiming an explicit Buddhist identity). Many who attend insight meditation centers may not even think of themselves as Buddhist and might be thought of as "Buddhist sympathizers" or "night-stand Buddhists," those with an interest in Buddhist teachings and practices and who may not, for whatever reason, self-identify as Buddhists (Tweed 2002).

Regardless of the exact number of Buddhists (or non-Buddhists) in the insight meditation movement, it is clear that its centers and affiliated teachers have been responsible for training and educating a generation of *vipassana* teachers who in turn have spread a model of practice well suited to a particular segment of the US population, historically a predominately middle- to upper-class white demographic (Fronsdal 1998, 178). Generally speaking, rather than foregrounding the monastic *sangha*, insight meditation centers hold short retreats or meditation classes around a nine-to-five work week thus allowing those with the time and desire to devote themselves to meditation practice to do so.

It has been argued that by foregoing a monastic *sangha* model, the insight meditation tradition is inherently more democratic in nature, allowing for lay members to assume leadership roles, and even work against patriarchal hierarchies (Tanaka 1998; cf Simmer-Brown 2002); though, as we will see in Chapter 10, this by no means guarantees gender equality. Scholarship focused on these communities has tended to reinforce a false binary between these predominately white convert groups and Asian American communities, noting their innovative practices over and against "traditional" or "conservative" Asian practices (Coleman 2001; Seager 1999). There is in fact a deep affinity and continuity between these two streams of the Theravada tradition. As noted earlier, many of the founders of the insight movement trained in Burma, others (such as Kornfield) ordained as monks, and the two traditions have historically shared resources and teachers. And, of course, insight meditation is hardly the sole purview of white converts—it has been practiced across the Theravada Buddhist tradition by monastics and laity alike both in the United States and its Asian homelands.

Theravada and the mindfulness movement

Twin cultural discourses have given rise to the diversity of US Theravada Buddhist traditions outlined here. On the one hand, colonialism and the disruptions of war and cultural upheaval throughout the twentieth century in part led to various Asian Buddhist reform movements that shaped Theravada traditions and were brought to the United States by immigrants and refugees after 1965. On the other hand, a simultaneous increase in US political and military involvement in the region as well as a general interest in Asian cultures allowed for American-born seekers to travel to Buddhist cultures and bring traditions back with them. These discursive streams should not be read as separate, parallel, or mutually exclusive; rather, they converge and diverge in a variety of ways, giving rise to different configurations of Buddhist practice. In the United States, trends include: patterns of assimilation as Buddhists make adjustments to the tradition to fit American cultural norms; patterns of resistance as Buddhists attempt to maintain monastic institutions or cultural practices; the recreation of cultural customs in displaced communities to strengthen communal identity; and complete revisions to the tradition to suit lay-focused practice models. These trends have given rise to a plethora of approaches to the practice of US Theravada Buddhism, and in some cases have moved beyond the confines of Theravada Buddhism altogether.

Theravada has also converged with the discourse of psychology. Given that many prominent teachers in the insight meditation movement are also trained therapists, it is perhaps not surprising that this convergence has led to therapeutic applications of Buddhist practice that diverge from their strictly speaking religious purposes. Since the late 1970s and early 1980s, researchers have been studying the benefits of Buddhist meditation in clinical settings and proponents have been teaching meditation practices in an increasingly wide array of nonreligious contexts (Chapter 8). Best known in this regard is Jon Kabat-Zinn, a scientist who began testing the effects of mindfulness meditation at the University of Massachusetts Medical School in the late 1970s. Whereas Kabat-Zinn's Buddhist training was from a variety of traditions, not just Theravada, his Mindfulness Based Stress Reduction program, its off-shoots, and related programs, are indebted to his experiences in the insight meditation community. As mindfulness meditation has moved beyond a specifically Theravada context, Theravada Buddhists have expressed concerns about their uses and lack of an explicitly ethical framework that would inform a traditional approach. Much of these debates are ongoing and are having a significant impact on public Buddhist discourses of late. It is difficult to know how these discourses will shape the future of US Theravada Buddhism. Writing at the end of last century, Kraft noted:

> Any living religion or vital social movement changes constantly. Today, the Dalai Lama is widely regarded as the quintessence of engaged Buddhism, while a figure such as Jon Kabat-Zinn, who uses meditation techniques in pain-relief therapy, seems to occupy a more marginal position. Yet one can also imagine the reverse, say twenty years from now: the movement for Tibetan autonomy fails, the succession of Dalai Lamas is disrupted, and Buddhism becomes a force in Western culture through its impact on psychology and medicine (Kraft 2000, 486).

Whereas it may be difficult to know how Theravada-inspired mindfulness practices will shape both Buddhism and American culture in the decades to come, secular applications of mindfulness have already made a significant impact (see Wilson 2014).

A note on *bhikkhuni* ordination

As discussed in Chapter 1, the monastic *sangha* originally included both monks and nuns. In premodern Buddhist Asia, *vinaya* traditions split into several lineages, of which the Theravada *vinaya* is one of three surviving traditions. In Theravada countries, between the eleventh and thirteenth centuries, the lineage of nuns (*bhikkhuni*) died out completely and was never revived. (The cases of Mahayana and Vajrayana are slightly different, see Chapter 7.) Arguments against reviving the nuns order generally focus on the process by which a woman becomes a nun; namely, she must be ordained in the presence of a cohort of other nuns, and since the lineage died out, there are no existing nuns to ordain new ones.

Over the last half-century, several parallel movements have begun in both Buddhist Asia and the West directed toward reinstating the order of nuns, a global discourse in which US Buddhists have participated in the following ways. First, US Buddhism has been influenced by feminist and progressive political discourses that are, broadly speaking, directed toward social justice, equality, and human rights concerns. This discourse has joined Asian feminist discourses regarding the status of women in Buddhism. Secondly, there has been a considerably large number of women ordained in various Asian Theravada contexts and the West—some of whom involved or were initiated by North American Buddhists—though these ordinations are not universally recognized across all Theravada institutions. Third, US Buddhist organizations have been established to support *bhikkhuni*, advocate for change, and connect with international networks such as the Sakyadhita International Association of Buddhist Women, which coordinates women's activities around the globe (Mrozik 2013; Salgado 2004; Tomalin 2006; Tsomo 2002).

In conversation about how the term *sangha* historically was restricted to the monastic *sangha*, Numrich has stated that "the establishment of traditional Theravada Buddhism in any country depends on the establishment of the order of monks there" (1998, 149). To the extent that Americans are generally suspicious of celibate monasticism (reflecting a Protestant bias), establishing a US monastic *sangha* has been difficult. On the face of it, an inherently gender-unequal *sangha* may be a further hindrance to monastic projects as it directly counters a general American fondness for fairness and equality. Regardless of how *bhikkhuni* ordination is resolved in its Asian contexts, in its US contexts, it must to be understood within its cultural milieu that is both generally suspicious of monasticism and indebted to feminist discourses.

Finally, whereas *bhikkhuni* ordination has received somewhat more attention in Theravada traditions than Mahayana or Vajrayana, the reader should not assume that a tradition's gender equality can be measured solely by a woman's ability to become a nun or that non-Theravada traditions have a better track record in regards to gender discrimination. The opposite is in fact true, and each tradition must be understood on its own terms.

DISCUSSION QUESTIONS

1. Discursively, how did forest and village approaches to Buddhism critique one another? What were considered the drawbacks of village life and the dangers of the forest?

2. Religions often resist change while adapting to cultural and historical circumstances. Discuss some of the changes Theravada Buddhism has undergone as it has taken root in the United States. What are some traditions it has retained?

3. Discuss the many roles and functions of a Buddhist community beyond the purely religious. What are some cultural functions religion plays? Where is the line between religion and culture?

SUGGESTIONS FOR FURTHER READING

Braun, Erik. 2013. *The Birth of Insight: Meditation, Modern Buddhism, and the Burmese Monk Ledi Sayadaw.* Chicago: University of Chicago Press.

Cadge, Wendy. 2005. *Heartwood: The First Generation of Theravada Buddhism in America.* Chicago: University of Chicago Press.

Cheah, Joseph. 2011. *Race and Religion in American Buddhism: White Supremacy and Immigrant Adaptation.* New York: Oxford University Press.

Gethin, Rupert. 2001. *The Buddhist Path to Awakening.* Oxford: Oneworld.

Gleig, Ann. 2012. "Wedding the Personal and Impersonal in West Coast Vipassana: A Dialogical Encounter between Buddhism and Psychotherapy." *Journal of Global Buddhism* 13: 129–146.

Gombrich, Richard F. 1988. *Theravāda Buddhism: A Social History from Ancient Benares to Modern Colombo.* New York: Routledge.

6

Mahayana traditions

Chapter summary and outline

Mahayana Buddhism has the longest history in the United States, beginning with Chinese and Japanese immigrants in the late nineteenth century. Buddhists from both mainland China and Taiwan, Korea, and Vietnam benefited from 1960s immigration reforms, building new communities and adding to the rich diversity of US Buddhism. Non-Asian American involvement followed from the 1950s through the 1990s with the establishment of new communities, including Zen lineages and SGI-USA. US Mahayana communities are well rooted in the United States with multiple connections to pan-Pacific networks of Buddhist exchange.

Introduction: Three vignettes

On a spring Sunday morning, a children's program at the Zen Mountain Monastery of the Mountains and Rivers Order in upstate New York celebrates the birthday of the Buddha. A dozen or so children join their parents in the meditation hall where they chant the *Heart Sutra*, ritually pour sweet tea over a statue of the Buddha, and later perform an original song written for the occasion. In a strip mall in Boise, next door to a hair salon, is the Idaho chapter of Soka Gakkai International. On a Tuesday night, a small group of Nichiren Buddhists gather before an altar with a *gohonzon*, a placard with the title of the *Lotus Sutra* in traditional Japanese script. Following thirty minutes of chanting, they sit silently praying for world peace before sharing with one another the benefits Buddhist practice has brought them. A resident of Oakland, California, purchased a small Buddha statue at a local hardware store and installed it on a street corner that normally attracted prostitutes, drug dealers, and illegal garbage dumping. Within a few months, the dumping and crime stop, local Buddhists construct a shrine around the statue and begin holding services in the street every morning. Neighbors stop the city from removing the statue, and crime drops in a one-block radius around the make-shift shrine where Buddhists continue to make prostrations and hope for better rebirths in the Buddha Amitabha's Pure Land (Figure 18).[1]

FIGURE 18 *Pháp Duyên Tự, street corner Buddha shrine, Oakland, California. (Photo by author.)*

Originating in India more than two thousand years ago and spreading throughout Asia, today Mahayana Buddhism is most often associated with the cultures of China, Japan, Korea, and Vietnam. Mahayana traditions came to the United States as early as the late nineteenth century and have had a long and profound impact on the broader cultural landscape. Changing political relations with China and immigration reforms in the 1960s led to the diversification of US Mahayana traditions with an influx of immigrants and refugees. Whereas some traditions easily track to country-of-origin and a more-or-less homogenous ethnic character, this is by no means the only way Mahayana Buddhist communities find expression in the United States.

In the previous chapter, we noted how religions alternate between the conservative pull toward tradition and the progressive necessity of adjusting to current cultural and historical circumstances. This is true for Mahayana Buddhism as well; however, here we will also highlight a balance between the convergence of disparate practices and doctrines into syncretic schools and lineages, on the one hand, and rigid sectarianism on the other. The tendency toward syncretism is pronounced in the case of Chinese Buddhism, and to the extent that Chinese Buddhism has had a large influence on how Mahayana Buddhism developed across East Asia, and by extension the United States, following a brief overview of core Mahayana doctrines and practices, we will examine some Chinese schools and lineages. From there, we will take a somewhat chronological approach to US Mahayana Buddhist traditions, beginning with Japanese schools established at the end of the nineteenth century and further developments through the end of the twentieth, followed by an overview of Chinese, Korean, and Vietnamese traditions. We will conclude with a consideration of the relatively new Nichiren Buddhist movement, Soka Gakkai International. The reader is referred to the back matter for more information on specific schools and terms used in this chapter.

Two final points: first, whereas "Zen" has become the de facto term of choice in the United States, it is a Japanese term that refers to a tradition that originated in China as Chan, and is known as Sŏn in Korea and Thien in Vietnam. When referencing these country-specific traditions, I will refer to them in their original language. Second, despite being treated in a separate chapter, it is important to recognize the vital role tantric Buddhism has played in Mahayana Buddhism (Chapter 7). Virtually all of the Buddhist traditions discussed in this chapter owe some debt to practices developed in so-called esoteric schools.

Overview of Mahayana Buddhist history and practice

Historical and doctrinal foundations

As discussed in Chapter 1, the early mainstream schools of Indic Buddhism comprised a large body of commentarial literature called *Abhidharma*. While the unnamed authors of some texts concerned themselves with systematizing the teachings of the Buddha, others concerned themselves with the nature of reality broken down into discrete dharmas (where "dharma" refers not to the teachings but a rather atomistic unit of phenomenal matter). Others focused on reconciling a seeming paradox in the teachings—if everything is impermanent, what persists not only from incarnation to incarnation but from moment to moment?—a paradox that led some to posit that there must be some basic element, some dharma, that has an essence. This stance seemed in direct conflict with the Buddha's teaching of *anatman* (no-self), and rival schools of thought emerged that argued for *sunyata*, or the emptiness of all dharmas. The case was made that all fundamental elements of existence are devoid, that is empty, of all individual and inherent existence; things exist not only in *relation* to other things but *because* of other things. Other texts refocused the goal of the Buddhist path from the *arhat* to the bodhisattva, conceived as one who not only aspired for awakening but also aspired for both full Buddhahood and to help alleviate the suffering of other sentient beings. This idealization of the bodhisattva and of Buddhahood was combined with preexisting Buddhist cosmologies that posited the existence of multiple world systems in which celestial and cosmic Buddhas and bodhisattvas currently existed. These cosmic forces could be called upon as intercessors in this world during times of strife or could be communed with through deep and complex visualization rituals and meditative states. Thus, new texts, and indeed a whole new body of literature codified not in a vernacular Indic language but in Sanskrit and purporting to be the word of the Buddha, began proliferating in Northwest India, signaling the beginning of a new school of thought, the Mahayana (Harrison 1995; Robinson and Johnson 1997; Williams 2009).

Buddhavacana

Literally the word or voice of the Buddha, *buddhavacana* refers to teachings delivered by Sakyamuni Buddha. However, this term can also refer to those teachings that are in accord with awakening regardless of whether they were spoken by the historical Buddha or not. Thus, over time, *buddhavacana* has been used to authenticate teachings delivered by the Buddha's disciples and later generations of monks as well as celestial Buddhas and bodhisattvas.

Within this context of developing texts, ideas, and practices, new Buddhist schools emerged, such as Madhyamaka and Yogacara, and articulated by such philosopher-monks as Nagarjuna, Asanga, and Vasubandhu. Nagarjuna was especially important in clarifying *sunyata* (emptiness) as well as advancing the notion of "two truths." According to this doctrine, reality as it is, free of our conceptualizations or the subject-object dichotomy we impose upon it (sometimes known as *tathata* or "suchness") is ultimate truth. Provisional truth is the world as we ordinarily experience it, defined by discriminative thinking, which gives rise to attachment and suffering (Robinson and Johnson 1997, 86–90). The relationship between these two truths has been described by the rather poetic metaphor of the finger pointing to the moon: conventional truth (the finger) merely points toward the ultimate (the moon), and one should not mistake the former for the later. Yogacara thinkers built on *sunyata* and two-truths thinking in their examination of consciousness—what is consciousness, how does it function, and what is its relationship to Buddhism's ultimate concern, the path to awakening. In this pursuit, Yogacara developed a complex system of eight consciousnesses: six accounting for the interaction between our senses and the external world, a seventh (*manas*), which incorrectly constructs a sense of self out of the first six, and an eighth, the *alayavijñaya*, or storehouse consciousness. It is in the *alayavijñaya* that karmic seeds are planted, thus accounting for the sense of continuity we perceive moment to moment and across incarnations without relying on an immutable soul or essence. This eighth consciousness was in turn linked to the *tathagatagarbha*. *Tathagatagarbha* can be translated at the womb (*gharbha*) of the *tathagata* (an epithet for the Buddha) and has been understood as the innate possibility within sentient beings for enlightenment (what has come to be known as Buddhanature), a vein of thought that would have a sizable influence in later East Asian Buddhism (Masaaki 2005; Williams 2009, 103-104).

This complex of thoughts, texts, practices, and related schools coalesced into something recognizably and self-consciously Mahayana—the "great vehicle"—in the centuries around the beginning of the Common Era. Indian Mahayana spread across South and Southeast Asia; however, over time, the mainstream schools and later Theravada would come to dominate the region. In East Asia, Mahayana would flourish where it has been the dominant form of Buddhism for nearly two millennia.

Buddhism comes to China

As early as the first century of the Common Era, Buddhist monastics began following merchants through Central Asia along the Silk Road where they established large monastic complexes in desert oases and began the process of translating texts, and by extension Buddhism, into Chinese languages. Within a century or two, Buddhism began to have a widespread impact on Chinese religious culture. Of course, Buddhism neither entered China all at once nor as a single, coherent religious system. And virtually all forms of Indic Buddhism and their associated texts and practices came to China over several centuries. Meanwhile, Chinese monks began making pilgrimages to India over land as well as sea voyages to Southeast Asia and Indonesia, bringing new texts and teachings back with them. This array of approaches to Buddhist practice would be further influenced by Vajrayana developments in the seventh and eighth centuries. Because of the sheer volume of these teachings, texts, and practices, Chinese Buddhists began to systematize and organize them if for no other reason than to make sense of it all. This systematization was codified into a Chinese Buddhist canon and led to the development of specific lineages and sectarian schools. To the extent that Chinese Buddhism has had a large influence across East Asia, a rough understanding can aid our discussion of Mahayana Buddhism as practiced today (Ch'en 1964; Zürcher 2007).

In the interest of space, of course, we cannot do justice here to the whole of Chinese Buddhist history. We will focus our attention on three schools due to their direct impact on later traditions that would be exported to the United States; however, these three schools are hardly exhaustive of all Chinese Buddhist sects or lineages. Virtually the whole of Indic Buddhism found its way into China, allowing for the creation of Chinese corollaries to Madhyamaka, Yogacara, and mainstream schools as well as the importation of a *vinaya* tradition distinct from the Theravada *vinaya* found in South Asia. We should also guard against the assumption that Chinese Buddhist sectarianism is in any way similar to, say, Protestant Christian denominationalism. Whereas some Chinese Buddhist schools had rather strict lineage-based identities, others were "schools" in name only, philosophical movements or practices that were folded into more well-defined lineages. Huayan and Pure Land thought might best be seen in this light to the extent that the metaphysics of universal interdependence articulated in Huayan and the cosmologies and devotional practices advanced in Pure Land are found in nearly all other forms of Chinese Buddhism.

Tiantai

One of the clearest examples of how Chinese Buddhists both systematized the Indic tradition and created a new, native tradition is Tiantai, articulated by the monk Zhiyi (538–597). Zhiyi organized the Buddha's teaching career into five periods. First was a short period of time immediately following his enlightenment when the Buddha taught the *Avatamsaka Sutra*; serving as the basis for the Huayan, the *Avatamsaka* or *Flower Adornment Sutra* is massive in scope, detailing the interconnection of literally everything in the cosmos as well as a specific bodhisattva path of practice. Deemed too complex and difficult to understand, the Buddha then spent a period of several years teaching the foundational Four Noble Truths and dependent origination (*pratityasamutpada*) as contained in the *Agamas*, a collection of mainstream Indic texts similar to but distinct from the Pali sutras. The next two stages of the Buddha's teaching career were devoted to basic Mahayana doctrines and the teachings contained in *prajñaparamita* texts. Finally, at the end of his life, he taught the *Mahaparinirvana* and *Lotus Sutras.* Thus, the *Lotus Sutra* was taken to be the ultimate teaching of the Buddha wherein he details that all previous teachings are provisional, culminating in the "one vehicle" of the Mahayana, as best explained in the parable of the burning house.

The Tiantai approach had the benefit of organizing a wide and disparate set of teachings, texts, and practices into a coherent whole. Within Tiantai, one finds focused study on philosophic texts as well as meditation and esoteric practices, a blending of Huayan and Pure Land cosmologies with *vinaya* study. In Japan, known as Tendai, the school became the dominant and most influential school for several centuries. At the monastic complex on Mt. Hiei, Tendai monks generally specialized in one area of the overall system, becoming great intellectuals and exegetes, accomplished meditation masters, esoteric practitioners, or devoted themselves to Pure Land practices (Chappell 1987; Donner 1987).

The parable of the burning house

In the third chapter of the *Lotus Sutra*, the Buddha tells a parable. Imagine a very wealthy man who has many sons all living in a fine home. One day, the home catches fire, and the father narrowly escapes. His children, however, are so engrossed in play, attached to their amusements, that they do not even notice the house burning around them. The father, knowing that they will be killed by the fire, then conspires to tell the children that if they leave the house, he will give each of them fine sheep, deer, and ox carts. The children are excited about receiving new gifts and rush out of the house. Now safe, the children ask for their gifts. The father has none, of course, except for one single very large and luxurious cart for all the children which they enjoy together.

The parable teaches, first, the doctrine of *upaya* or skillful means, that Buddhas and advanced bodhisattvas tailor the dharma to suit the specific needs of individual suffering beings. Thus what looks like a lie (the promise of individual gifts) turns out to be an expedient device to save the children from mortal danger. Second, the single cart the father gifts to his children symbolizes the Mahayana itself with the presumption that what appear to be divergent teachings are really expedient devices used by the Buddha to draw practitioners closer to the ultimate teachings of the Mahayana.

Pure Land

Early Buddhist cosmology posited the existence of multiple world systems and realms of rebirth that were inhabited by various classifications of sentient beings, some with super-mundane powers. These cosmologies developed to include multiple Buddha fields of influence, wherein cosmic Buddhas in other dimensions or space-times existed either to benefit beings in this world or as locations to journey to in meditative states or post-mortem. There are an infinite number of Buddhas in their associated Buddha fields, but one particular Buddha emerged as the focus of specific rituals and devotion, the Buddha Amitabha (sometimes Amitayus), the Buddha of Infinite Light, who is said to live in the Pure Land of Sukhavati (lit. "ultimate bliss"), that lies to the west of our world. Amitabha appears in a number of texts and is the central figure of three specific sutras, the *Longer* and the *Shorter Sukhavativyuha Sutras* and the *Visualization Sutra*. In the first two, his origins, the contours of his land, and associated ritual practices are detailed, including a specific practice of reciting his name for rebirth in Sukhavati where one can easily attain Buddhahood. The *Visualization Sutra* includes portions of a larger Buddhist narrative revolving around an Indian king, Bimbisara, and the Buddha's adversary, Devadatta; this sutra details a visualization ritual that allows one to be in the presence of Amitabha in this life.

Pure Land soteriology became intertwined with the notion of the disappearance of the true dharma (*saddharmavipralopa*). In early Buddhist thought, it was assumed that all traces of the teachings need to vanish before the next Buddha appears to renew them. In later East Asian traditions, this disappearance was presumed to happen slowly over the course of several thousand years during which both access to the true teachings and persons' natural proclivities for practicing the dharma will decline (Nattier 1991). For those Buddhists who believed that they were already living in the age of declining dharma (C. *mofa*; J. *mappo*), practices that were easier than the stringent requirements of monastic life became foregrounded. Devotion to Amitabha Buddha played a key role here as merely reciting the Buddha's name was a practice that anyone could do and would have great karmic benefit. While Pure Land movements, such as the White Lotus Society, emerged from time to time in China, Pure Land thought and practice was generally infused within other traditions, including Tiantai and Chan (Sharf 2002). In Japan, former Tendai monks would establish distinct schools of Pure Land in the thirteenth century.

Chan

Chan is the translation of the Sanskrit term *dhyana* (P: *jhana*), which is often rendered simply "meditation" in English. The school is indigenous to China and traces its foundation to the (semi-mythical) figure of Bodhidharma who brought the teachings from India probably in the fifth century. By the early Tang Dynasty (618–907), the tradition was well established and constructing elaborate lineages going back to a disciple of the Buddha, Mahakasyapa, and the Buddha himself (Cole 2009; McRae 2003). A famous story recounts how the Buddha, about to deliver a teaching, silently held aloft a single flower; only Mahakasyapa smiled, knowingly. This story points to a central feature of the tradition, the "mind-to-mind" transmission of Buddhist teachings existing outside the canon proper. This "dharma transmission" from teacher to disciple has two consequences. First, the notion that a direct and sudden experience of awakening might be had beyond doctrinal study or textual exegesis has given rise to a particularly iconoclastic rhetoric within Chan and later Zen writing. One finds a seemingly inexhaustible supply of sarcastic monks whose behavior flies in the face of social decorum. We should, of course, not mistake narrative accounts of monks rejecting social norms for everyday practice. More often, one finds Chan monks engaged in serious study, poring over texts, writing commentaries, and engaging in highly ritualized behavior, including ritualized meditation practices (Leighton 2008). It is with meditation that Chan is popularly associated, a practice that requires a level of serious commitment not usually associated with those who reject all authority and structure and, historically, conducted within a monastic context where one would be expected to follow complex rules and codes of conduct.

The Sanskrit form of *jhana* (Chapter 5), *dhyana* is usually translated as meditation in English. The meditative states of advanced practitioners came to be viewed as necessary for the attainment of awakening and were propagated in China where they became foregrounded in the Chan school. Chan is the Chinese rendering of the Sanskrit *dhyana*.

Second, dharma transmission codifies a teacher-student relationship that forms the basis of formalized lineages. Chan teachers are teachers insofar as they have received dharma transmission, and to the extent that it is presumed to be the same experience of awakening as the one experienced by the Buddha and Mahakasyapa, one's connection to a lineage carries with it substantial meaning and weight. The creation of lineages, in turn, allows for Chan to veer toward the sectarian, where mountain temples and monastic complexes are defined as belonging to specific sectarian lineages over and against rival schools. For our purposes of the traditional "five houses and seven schools" of Chan in China, two lineages are most relevant: Linji and Chaodong known as Rinzai and Soto respectively in Japan.

US Pure Land and Zen traditions of Japan

Japan inherited Chinese Buddhism via Korea as early as the third century, though the official introduction of the tradition came in 552 when the king of Korea sent a delegation to the Japanese capital, then in Nara. Whereas a half-dozen sects proliferated over the ensuing centuries, two dominated, Tendai and Shingon (Chapter 7). Japan was destabilized during the Kamakura period (1185–1333) as the capital shifted, and a *shogun*, or military commander, took control of the government. During this period, several former Tendai monks established new schools of Buddhism that juxtaposed themselves against the powerful Tendai sect as providing more direct paths toward awakening or having practices more suited to those living in the age of declining dharma (*mappo*). Thus, Pure Land, Zen, and Nichiren Buddhism would come to eclipse the older schools in scope and influence across Japan up to the modern period. Unlike their corollaries in China (where they existed), these schools became increasingly sectarian in nature, a sectarianism that was enforced by the Tokugawa *shogun* in the seventeenth century. Finally, a defining feature of one tradition—the lack of fully ordained monastics in the Pure Land Jodo Shinshu school—would become the norm for all schools under the Meiji-era reforms at the end of the nineteenth century.

US Pure Land traditions

The Japanese Pure Land tradition is divided into two major sects, the Jodoshu and Jodo Shinshu, each of which has dozens of sub-schools. In the United States,

Japanese Pure Land is predominately represented by the Buddhist Churches of America (BCA), an overseas branch of a major denomination of Jodo Shinshu head-quartered in Kyoto, Japan. The history of the BCA has been well covered in Chapter 3 and necessitates only a brief overview here. In 1899, Japanese immigrants solicited the Honganji temple to send priests and missionaries to the Americas, in part to counter the work of Christian missionaries who had had some success converting early Japanese immigrants. That same year, the North American Buddhist Mission was founded, an umbrella organization that saw the establishment of temples along the west coast of the United States as well as in parts of Canada. The organization grew considerably up until the start of World War II when Japanese Americans were forcibly interred for the duration of the war. Despite what could have been a dev-astating setback, the community reorganized in the camps and saw an exponential growth in the immediate postwar years. This growth was fueled, in part, by the coming together of Japanese Americans who felt an understandable desire to cre-ate a community of practice safe from the overt hostility of the dominant culture. This tendency toward ethnic exclusivity, however, should not be mistaken for dis-engagement with the broader culture; there were explicit attempts to reach out to non-Japanese Americans which led to interactions between US Shin Buddhists and Beat Generation poets and writers in the 1950s (Ama 2011; Kashima 1977).

As a Pure Land school, Jodo Shinshu practice in the United States has focused on the recitation of the name of the Buddha Amitabha (Amida), known as the *nen-butsu*. Early on, the tradition adopted an overtly congregational style of practice in response to overarching social pressure to blend in to American Christian religious norms. In recent decades, the community has made attempts to overcome both the stereotype of ethnic exclusivity and "church-like" practices; non-Japanese members have taken on increasingly active roles within the community, and some local churches have begun offering meditation classes or self-consciously blending Pure Land and Zen practices. As a congregational organization, assessing the number of US Jodo Shinshu Buddhists is somewhat more straightforward than other Buddhist schools. At present, there are over sixty temples and fellowships affiliated with the BCA across the con-tinental United States with an estimated membership of fifteen to twenty thousand (Mitchell 2010; Spencer 2014).

Whereas the BCA is the largest Japanese Pure Land community in the United States, it is by no means the only community. The BCA was established in San Francisco several years after a community was founded in Hawai'i, which, at the time, was still an independent country. The Hawai'ian and mainland organiza-tions have a relationship but remain separate organizations. Similarly, when first established, the BCA oversaw temples in Canada which, following World War II, became affiliated under a separate organization, which was renamed the Jodo Shinshu Buddhist Temples of Canada in 2005. And finally, both Jodoshu and other Jodo Shinshu organizations are present in North America and have thus far been understudied.

US Zen traditions

The two main lineages of Zen in Japan, Rinzai and Soto, were established by Eisai (1141–1215) and Dogen (1200–1253), respectively, in the twelfth and thirteenth centuries.[2] Despite their great popularity in the United States, neither lineage was as large or influential in Japan as the Pure Land traditions until the modern era when Zen Buddhist scholars and apologists, such as D. T. Suzuki, began promoting Zen Buddhism both within Japan and the West (Amstutz 1997). Zen Buddhism in the United States begins roughly at the same time as Pure Land Buddhism as one tradition among many brought by Japanese immigrants. The pre-World War II history of these communities mirrors in many ways the history of the BCA. Many remain active to this day, serving both Japanese and non-Japanese members and maintaining strong ties with Japanese Zen Buddhist organizations. For example, established in Los Angeles in 1922, the Zenshuji Soto Mission serves as the North American headquarters of Soto Zen Buddhism with oversight from the two main Soto Zen temples in Japan, Eiheiji and Sojiji (Asai and Williams 1999).

As was mentioned in Chapter 3, something of a Zen boom occurred in the 1950s and 1960s, during which time two streams of US Zen Buddhism diverged, one serving primarily the needs of Japanese Americans, the other attracting the attention of primarily white American converts. Scholarship on these two streams has been bound up with highly charged racial discourses that have obscured both their characteristics (modes of practice, history, institutional organization, and so forth) and their interrelation by treating them as wholly separate and ignoring cross-development (Chapter 9). For our present purposes, we will follow the Zen lead of identifying lineage and note that whereas large Japanese institutions have a presence in North America, such as the Soto Mission, other lineages have branched off from the Japanese mainstream, established by mid-century charismatic figures such as Robert Aitken, Shunryu Suzuki, and Taizan Maezumi.

A somewhat new Zen lineage calling itself Sanbokyodan and self-consciously blending both Rinzai and Soto Zen practices was formally established in Japan in 1954 by Hakuun Yasutani and his disciple Koun Yamada (Sharf 1995a). This lineage was brought to the United States by Robert Aitken who, with his wife Anne, founded the Honolulu Diamond Sangha in 1959. Aitken first learned of Buddhism while a prisoner of war during World War II, traveled extensively in the postwar years, and studied with, among others, Nyogen Senzaki, Soen Nakagawa, Yasutani, and Yamada, from whom Aitken received authorization to teach and train his own students. Institutional differences marked the Diamond Sangha's relationship with the larger Sanbokyodan organization, differences that were heightened following Yamada's death in 1989. Thus, the organization, which has affiliate centers across the United States and the world, has always been somewhat independent of the Japanese leadership, an independence formalized in the mid-1990s. Aitken's work with the Diamond Sangha and his publications, his students and their affiliated organizations, and the writings of Yasutani's other well-known student Philip Kapleau, are largely responsible for ushering in the Zen boom of the 1950s and 1960s. This influence has only recently gained serious scholarly study (see Baroni 2012), at times overshadowed by their association with Sanbokyodan and the more recent scandals surrounding Eido Shimano (Chapters 4 and 11).

Maezumi was trained in the Soto lineage and assigned to the Los Angeles Soto Zen Mission in 1956. However, he also received Rinzai training and studied with Yasutani in the 1960s. In 1967, along with non-Japanese American students, he opened the Los Angeles Zen Center, which, like Shunryu Suzuki's San Francisco Zen Center, diverged in focus from the Japanese American community that preceded it. Unlike Suzuki, Maezumi's approach reflected his interests in both Soto and Rinzai, expressed as an emphasis on both sitting meditation and the study of *koan*. Maezumi had a large number of students who in turn spread his lineage of Zen across the United States, at times creating wholly new schools, such as the Mountains and Rivers Order of John Daido Loori, mentioned at the outset of this chapter. Describing itself as "Western Zen,"[3] the Order explicitly distances itself from the Japanese tradition in an attempt to create a new form of Zen Buddhism in the United States. Suzuki and the San Francisco lineage sit somewhere between these two streams. On the one hand, like Mountains and Rivers, the community orients itself closer to a non-Japanese American demographic; on the other, institutionally the community retains close connections both with the Soto Mission in North America and Zen training centers in Japan.

In some sense, then, these lineages have branched off from an explicitly Japanese Zen Buddhist tradition. To call these lineages wholly independent, however, overlooks the interconnection they have had with Japanese and Japanese American Zen Buddhism. In the abstract, this includes the widely influential writing of various teachers, both Japanese and American; in the concrete, it includes the reality that many American-born teachers have studied extensively in Japan and many Japanese-born teachers have served in so-called convert communities. Perhaps best symbolizing the coming together of these divergent streams is the building of a new training center in northern California, Tenpyozan, a project led by Gengo Akiba (b. 1943). Raised in Japan and trained at Eiheiji, Akiba first visited the United States in 1983 where he studied at the San Francisco Zen Center and Tassajara Zen Mountain Center. After a chance meeting with the owners of a local Japanese restaurant and jazz club, Yoshi's, he established a new Zen temple in Oakland, California, and was eventually appointed head of the North American Soto mission. Tenpyozan is an attempt to create a new training center open to all members of the broader Soto Zen Buddhist community, regardless of lineage (Tebbe n.d.).

Lineages such as these are of course but a hint of a much wider and complex US Zen Buddhist landscape. In part because of the ability of Zen teachers to appoint dharma heirs who may then go on to open new centers without direct institutional oversight, small Zen groups and store-front meditation centers have proliferated across the United States since the 1970s. Some have come and gone while others have affiliated with larger organizations. Still others remain independent, resisting any particular institutional authority altogether.

US Chan/Pure Land traditions of China and Taiwan

Whereas Chinese immigrants first arrived in the United States in the 1850s, the community's establishment and growth was hindered by exclusionary and racist immigration and citizenship laws that were rescinded in the mid-twentieth century. Thus, the current make-up of Chinese-derived US Buddhist communities is indebted to immigration reform and changing US-China relations from the 1950s to the present, as was discussed in Chapter 4. The communist revolution and subsequent establishment of the nationalist Chinese government in Taiwan have had profound implications on the development of modern Chinese Buddhism. Owing in part to the rapid economic development and urbanization of the Republic of China in Taiwan, four transnational Buddhist organizations have come to prominence since the 1960s: Dharma Drum Mountain, Fo Guang Shan, the Tzu Chi Foundation, and Chung Tai Shan (Chandler 2005; Huang 2005). All four organizations have some presence in the United States, a result both of a large influx of Chinese and Taiwanese immigrants since the 1970s and the outreach efforts of these organizations. And while these groups may have originally served primarily a Chinese American demographic, each has made significant contributions to and has relations with larger Buddhist networks and communities. Whereas, the founders of Dharma Drum and Fo Guang Shan both come from a Chan lineage, these communities represent a syncretic blend of Chinese Buddhist practices, including Pure Land; and, importantly, each have some focus on what has come to be called "humanistic Buddhism."

Humanistic Buddhism, for the founders of these traditions, is variously understood as an interpretation of traditional Buddhist teachings that both make Buddhism practical in this life as well as being directed toward specific humanitarian efforts such as disaster relief and philanthropic support for health care and education. At times, this is expressed as the creation of a pure land on earth, with the assumption that through charitable work the suffering of sentient beings in this world can be transformed into the idyllic and perfected world of a Buddha. For the founder of the Tzu Chi Foundation, the nun Cheng Yen (b. 1937), this has meant the establishment of a hospital and nursing collage in Taiwan and aid work following natural disasters in Taiwan, mainland China, and Southeast Asia.

Fo Guang Shan, which shares this humanitarian outlook, is the largest of these organizations in the United States. Established by the Linji Chan monk Hsing Yun (b. 1927) in 1967 in Taiwan, the organization grew quickly and began expanding oversees (Chandler 2004). After visiting the United States in the mid-1970s, construction began on what would become the largest Chinese Buddhist temple in the western hemisphere; Hsi Lai Temple, dedicated in 1988, now serves as the North American headquarters of Fo Guang Shan and oversaw the establishment of the University of the West in 1994 (Lin 1999).

Dharma Drum Mountain was established by Sheng Yen (1930–2009) who took over leadership of the Chung-Hwa Institute of Buddhist Culture and Nung Chan Monastery in Taiwan following his master's death in 1977. The organization grew rapidly under his guidance, and construction of Dharma Drum Mountain began in 1993. The site now includes a complex of monasteries and the Dharma Drum Buddhist College. From the 1970s until his death, Sheng Yen actively promoted Buddhism around the world, opening dozens of centers in the United States, including a large retreat center in upstate New York.

Also in upstate New York is Chuang Yen Monastery—boasting the largest indoor Buddha statue in the United States (Figure 19)—established by the Buddhist Association of the United States (BAUS) founded by C. T. Shan. Born in mainland China, Shan immigrated to the New York area with his family in 1951, where he became a successful businessman allowing him the resources to fund Buddhist organizations beginning with the Temple of Enlightenment, founded in the Bronx, New York, in 1964. The BAUS is based primarily in the New York area and serves a predominately Chinese American population; however, recently, the Theravada monk Bhikkhu Bodhi (b. Jeffrey

FIGURE 19 *Chuang Yen Monastery, Carmel, New York. (Photo courtesy V. T. Polywoda.)*

Block, 1944) was nominated president of the organization and has led seminars on *Abhidharma* literature.

The BAUS is an example of a Chinese-derived tradition that is supported, in part, by the Chinese American community with little to no connection with mainland Chinese Buddhist organizations. The Dharma Realm Buddhist Association (DRBA) is similar. Established in 1959 by the Chan master Hsuan Hua, the community was initially supported by Chinese American Buddhists but quickly embraced non-Chinese Americans who were interested in studying Buddhism. The community expanded, grew, established centers and temples across North America, and eventually built the City of Ten Thousand Buddhas in Ukiah, California, one of the largest monastic communities in the Western world.

Chinese American Buddhist communities reflect the diversity of the Chinese American community, which is hardly homogenous, reflecting not only different languages and cultural norms from China proper but also the broader Chinese diaspora including Taiwan, Hong Kong, Burma, Indonesia, and elsewhere, to say nothing of socioeconomic class divisions. The US Buddhist communities that have grown from these populations have engaged the broader culture in a variety of ways, from successful outreach programs to connections with larger, transnational Buddhist networks to the establishment of Buddhist educational centers such as the University of the West or Dharma Realm Buddhist University. Many of these communities are forward-facing and progressive; indeed, as Chen (2008, 159) notes, Taiwanese immigrants have cast Buddhism as a modern, rational, and scientific religion and have converted to Buddhism to be seen as more American (i.e., more modern and scientific) than Taiwanese American Christians, a move that reflects the internal diversity of Chinese American experiences, the community's engagement with broader US religious discourses, and cuts across the stereotype of immigrant Buddhists as mere traditionalists (cf Quli and Mitchell 2015).

US Mahayana traditions of Korea

When Buddhism came to Korea from China in the fourth century CE, Korean rulers almost immediately adopted it as the state religion. As was true elsewhere, a large diversity of Buddhist traditions and schools were imported to the peninsula, and with state sponsorship, Buddhism thrived. Attempts at reconciling sectarian differences or constructing new lineages were carried out over the course of many centuries, with the Sŏn tradition remaining one of the more influential schools. When Japan annexed the country in 1910, the occupying government forced Buddhist institutions to conform to a Soto Zen style of organization, most importantly the requirement that Buddhist monks give up their vows of celibacy as had become the norm in Japan. In response to these pressures, the various strands of Korean Buddhism organized themselves in 1935 as the Chogye Order in an attempt to preserve the native Korean Buddhist tradition. The Chogye Order brought together different Korean Buddhist schools; however, it is essentially Sŏn in orientation and remains the primary school of Buddhism greatly outnumbering smaller schools and sects.

Korean American history is almost as long as Japanese American history with the first Korean immigrants arriving in Hawai'i as plantation workers a few decades after the Japanese, around the 1910s. However, due to immigration restrictions and the conflicts leading up to and including World War II and the Korean War, the number of Korean immigrants was virtually nil until the passage of the Hart-Celler Act in 1965. Since the 1970s, the number of Korean Americans has increased dramatically; however, the large majority of Korean Americans are Christian—some 70 percent to 80 percent (Suh 2004, 3)—making Korean American Buddhists a minority within a minority.

The majority of Korean American Buddhist temples are affiliated with the Chogye Order, headquartered in Seoul, South Korea. Whereas Chogye can be seen as conservative and tightly controlled at its highest levels, individual temple membership is purely voluntary; thus, while local temples may have a desire to preserve Korean Buddhist traditions and customs through their affiliation, there is often little direct oversight affording communities some autonomy (Kim 2008, 165). In the United States, most temples are located in large metropolitan areas with correspondingly large Korean American populations; whereas some were established directly by the Chogye Order, others were established independently. Generally speaking, these temples, headed by a monastic who may have been sent from Seoul to serve for any number of years, serve the needs of primarily immigrant communities and their descendants, orienting themselves around regular worship services, holidays, and social functions.

In addition to temples with a direct and ongoing connection to Korea, there are other Korean-derived communities established by quasi-independent and charismatic teachers, such as Samu Sunim (b. 1941) and Seung Sahn (1927–2004). Born Sam-Woo Kim, Samu immigrated to Montreal, Quebec, in the late 1960s, and established a Sŏn temple in Toronto, Ontario, some years later. Following the establishment of several more centers in Ann Arbor, Michigan, Chicago, Mexico City, and elsewhere, Samu's organization grew into the Buddhist Society for Compassionate Wisdom. The community trains non-monastics in meditation, serves both Korean-speaking and non-Korean members, and orients itself as a modern revision of the essential truths of Mahayana Buddhism. Similarly, Seung Sahn migrated to the United States in 1972 and began teaching out of his apartment in Providence, Rhode Island. His popularity grew rapidly, and within a few short years, he not only opened the Providence Zen Center but also founded a new tradition, the Kwan Um School of Zen. By the century's end, the school had dozens of practice centers across the United States and Europe while maintaining a headquarters in Rhode Island. Seung Sahn's tradition combines meditation training with other Sŏn and Pure Land practices such as sutra chanting and prostrations. Not exclusively monastic in orientation, the community trains lay leaders in an adapted monastic style and has contributed to a growing US Zen Buddhist discourse over the last several decades (Yu 1988).

These traditions represent but a small slice of a much wider field of US Korean Buddhist traditions, some of which are not affiliated with Chogye or charismatic leaders. More research on Korean Buddhism in general is needed, a field that has just begun to open in the last few decades (see Buswell 2005).

US Mahayana traditions of Vietnam

Because of its proximity to Southeast Asia, there is a significant Theravada presence in Vietnam; however, because Buddhism developed here at a time when it was controlled by China, Chinese Buddhism in general, and Tiantai in particular, have been extremely influential. Following several reform movements during the colonial era, the South Vietnamese government unified all existing denominations under a single order during the war with the United States. This order was ostensibly Thien in orientation, though in practice, like Tiantai, it combined Chan-style meditation with Pure Land and even Theravada and esoteric practices. Following the fall of Saigon in 1975, a large influx of Vietnamese refugees found their way to the United States; whereas the majority of refugees eventually settled in major metropolitan areas, the US government settled many in disparate parts of the country. There they have made new communities and established networks of loosely affiliated Buddhist organizations that in many ways mirror the organizations and experiences of Burmese, Lao, and Cambodian traditions as discussed in Chapter 5. Together, these communities largely define the Vietnamese American Buddhist experience. However, we should pause here and say a word about the Vietnamese Buddhist monk, Thich Nhat Hanh.

Despite not being a US resident, Thich Nhat Hanh has had a rather large influence in the United States. Born in 1926, he was ordained as a monk in a Thien lineage in 1949. Through the 1960s, he traveled widely, studied and lectured at US universities, and worked with various nonviolent political movements in Vietnam, work that led him to both being nominated for the Nobel Peace Prize in 1967 and to be denied reentry to Vietnam by the government in 1973. Since that time he has lived in exile at the Plum Village community he established in Southern France, has authored dozens of extremely popular books, and established the Order of Interbeing and the Unified Buddhist Church (UBC). The UBC in the United States is an umbrella organization overseeing virtually all of Thich Nhat Hanh's other organizations including several monasteries and retreat centers and the publishing company Parallax Press. Thich Nhat Hanh's popularity goes well beyond the Vietnamese community, and, generally speaking, scholars have assumed his work to be of primary interest to English-speaking converts or dismissed it as more in line with New Age philosophy than Buddhism (Nguyen and Barber 1998; Pepper 2012). However, this attitude overlooks the fact that some affiliated communities cater to the needs of both Vietnamese Americans and white Americans, and some centers are the result of interethnic cooperation, such as the Magnolia Grove Monastery in Mississippi, founded by Vietnamese immigrants with the support of white converts (cf Le 2009).

By the turn of the twenty-first century, the majority of Vietnamese American Buddhist communities were similar in nature to the communities of other Southeast Asian Buddhists. Largely established by local communities and lay groups in individuals' homes or store-front shops, a monastic is invited to lead services and give teachings. Services and practices include social and cultural events, as well as teaching and training in Buddhist practices including meditation, sutra chanting, and Pure Land Buddhist devotion (some of which can be seen in the Oakland street-corner shrine noted in the opening of this chapter). Overtime, such communities may grow large enough to build dedicated spaces or larger residential halls; and they may or may not be connected to translocal networks of Vietnamese Buddhist associations. Most of these have no official connection to any organizations in Vietnam owing to the fact that the first generation of immigrants and refugees were unable to return to their homeland until the normalization of US-Vietnamese relations by President Bill Clinton in 1995.

Nichiren Shoshu and SGI-USA

As we saw earlier, the Kamakura era in Japan was one of great social turmoil during which several Buddhist thinkers began challenging the dominant forms of Buddhism of their day. One monk, Nichiren (1185–1333) became convinced of the supreme efficacy of the *Lotus Sutra*, an interpretation of the Buddhist path somewhat consistent with Tendai doctrine. Nichiren, however, was highly critical of Tendai, which he believed had become corrupted, and was convinced that recitation of the *Lotus Sutra* (in the form of *nam-myoho-renge-kyo*) was the most appropriate practice for people living in the age of declining dharma. He worked aggressively to promote his teachings, employing an evangelistic style of propagation known as *shakubuku*, activity that found him often in trouble with the ruling powers (Hammond and Machacek 1999; Hurst 1998).

The community he founded split into several denominations, including Nichiren Shoshu. It was in this school that an educational reform movement, known as the "value creation society," was established in the 1930s by Tsunesaburo Makiguchi and Josei Toda. During the war, the two men ran afoul of the Japanese imperial government for, among other things, challenging the divine authority of the emperor; Makiguchi died in prison, but his student, Toda, reinvigorated their group in the postwar years, named it Soka Gakkai, and began to aggressively promote Nichiren Buddhism. For decades, the lay movement remained in an uneasy relationship with the established Nichiren Shoshu with the latter certainly benefiting from the former's aggressive recruitment campaigns.

Whereas Nichiren Buddhism was one of several Japanese traditions imported to the United States in the early twentieth century, it was not well represented until the postwar years when both Nichiren Shoshu generally and Soka Gakkai specifically began to actively propagate the tradition. Japanese women who had married US servicemen stationed in Asia during the Allied occupation of Japan and the Korean

War brought the tradition back to the United States with them. In 1960, the third and very charismatic president of Soka Gakkai, Daisaku Ikeda (b. 1928), visited the United States and encouraged these women to become US citizens, engage the broader culture, and begin organizing Nichiren activities. Over the course of the 1960s and 1970s, Soka Gakkai and Nichiren Shoshu began active outreach programs across North America which resulted in the community's rapid growth (Geekie 2008).

This growth was made possible by a number of factors including the general popularity of Buddhism at the time and the often aggressive proselytization of Soka Gakkai members; however, we should not overlook the overall message of Soka Gakkai and Ikeda. The central practice of Nichiren Buddhism is the recitation of *nam-myoho-renge-kyo*, which is said to be powerfully transformative not only religiously but in everyday affairs; Soka Gakkai members regularly attribute this-worldly benefits to their practice, including health and emotional as well as professional and personal successes. This, combined with the group's focus on world peace, social justice, and a generally progressive political orientation, no doubt contributed to the Soka Gakkai's success in the confusion and uncertainty of the postwar and Cold War years. Importantly, this growth has not been restricted to a single ethnic group as we have seen in other traditions; Soka Gakkai is perhaps the most ethnically and culturally diverse form of US Buddhism, attracting Asian, African, Latino/a, and white Americans alike.

Soka Gakkai's rise, however, has not been without controversy. Its initial introduction to the United States coincided with other new religious movements, some of which were dangerous cults that met disastrous ends (Chapter 7). Soka Gakkai's conversion techniques have been criticized in both Japanese and American press as overly aggressive and even militaristic. Such negative publicity did not sit well with the larger Nichiren Shoshu organization, which was already at odds with the lay movement. Combined with disagreements over doctrinal interpretation and ritual authority, the organizations formally split in 1991. Renaming itself Soka Gakkai International (SGI), its American branch, SGI-USA, remains a robust lay-lead organization while pulling back from the aggressive proselytization of an earlier era.

Such controversies, and scholarly attitudes dismissing new religious movements, have contributed to a distinct lack of scholarship on Nichiren Shoshu and SGI-USA. This is unfortunate. While SGI may be properly understood as a new religious movement owing to its foundation less than a century ago, it is situated within the larger stream of Nichiren Buddhism that is itself part of a larger stream of Tendai specifically, Mahayana generally. Responsible scholarship should attend to documenting all forms of a religious tradition without passing normative judgments about the rightness or wrongness of theological truth claims. This is not to suggest that studies of SGI should be uncritical; quite the contrary. Objective scholarship could provide valuable insight into how a lay organization is able to maintain long-term stability and weather the storms of institutional change and scandal without a recognized clerical body or priestly class, something that makes SGI rather unique among Buddhist schools. Indeed, it is this lack of a monastic tradition within SGI that stands in such contrast to our usual expectations of what Buddhism looks like that contributes to scholarly disinterest. Studies of Buddhism, whether in the United States or elsewhere, that overcome a privileging of monastic practice reveal the domestic, lay, and family-oriented practices of the tradition that are just as important in passing Buddhism down generation to generation as dharma transmission and monastic authority.

Mahayana in US religious history

The above overview reveals the long and complex history of US Mahayana Buddhist traditions in relation to both domestic and international cultural currents and historical events (counter-cultural interest, changing immigration laws, the Chinese communist revolution, the US war with Vietnam). US Mahayana Buddhism manifests itself in long-standing, well organized and national communities fully embedded in the American religious landscape; transnational organizations connected to missionary Asian Buddhist organizations; native traditions self-consciously distancing themselves from their Asian predecessors; and new religious movements dedicated to humanitarian aid and peace work.

Apart from the innumerable smaller communities and strands of traditions not covered in this chapter, one other issue remains: the intersection of race and Buddhist identity. To be sure, this is an issue that is relevant to all forms of US Buddhism, but it takes on some additional import in the Mahayana traditions for several reasons. First, from a historical perspective, owing to its long presence in the United States, Mahayana traditions afford us a glimpse into the ways in which religious communities are racialized in the United States and the effect this has on community development. We need look no further than the experience of Japanese Buddhists as an example: beginning as communities facing profound pressure to "blend in" and adopt congregational styles of practice and to deemphasize their Japanese ethnic identity, to being forcibly interred during the war in the interest of national security, to remaining trapped under the stereotype of an "ethnic fortress" (Tanaka 1999), these communities reveal the complex ways immigrant groups negotiate race and religion in the United States. Second, because US Zen Buddhist communities effectively split along racial lines in the 1950s and 1960s, two streams of the tradition emerged that are regularly cast in ethnic roles both in the scholarly and popular literature (Chapter 10). And, finally, this discourse of "two Buddhisms" divided into "Asian" and "white" has obscured research on other American Buddhists of color, especially African Americans and Hispanic Americans. The aforementioned lack of scholarship on SGI-USA is relevant here to the extent that this community has attracted a disproportionate number of Americans of color as compared to other convert groups, a subject well deserving of future research.

In many respects, the diversity—and attendant challenges of that diversity—of US Mahayana Buddhist traditions is a reflection of US culture more generally. The broader cultural discourses surrounding race, religion, and nationality are the ground upon which these traditions have been built and, over the last century and a half, matured.

Far from being exhaustive, this chapter is but the tip of a much larger field of study waiting to be explored.

DISCUSSION QUESTIONS

1. On what basis are teachings considered to be the word of the Buddha and thus included in the Buddhist canon?
2. How did the Zen boom affect the development of US Zen Buddhist traditions and lineages?
3. What does a study of US Mahayana Buddhist history reveal about the intersections of race and religion in US religious history more generally?

SUGGESTIONS FOR FURTHER READING

Coleman, James William. 2001. *The New Buddhism: The Western Transformation of an Ancient Tradition.* New York: Oxford University Press.

Harrison, Paul. 1995. "Searching for the Origins of the Mahāyāna: What Are We Looking For?" *The Eastern Buddhist*, n.s., 28, No. 1: 48–69.

Learman, Linda, ed. 2005. *Buddhist Missionaries in the Era of Globalization.* Honolulu: University of Hawai'i Press.

Mitchell, Scott A., and Natalie E. F. Quli, eds. 2015. *Buddhism beyond Borders: New Perspectives on Buddhism in the United States.* Albany: State University of New York Press.

Prebish, Charles S., and Kenneth Tanaka, eds. 1998. *The Faces of Buddhism in America.* Berkeley: University of California Press.

Suh, Sharon A. 2004. *Being Buddhist in a Christian World: Gender and Community in a Korean American Temple.* Seattle: University of Washington Press.

Williams, Paul. 2009. *Mahāyāna Buddhism: The Doctrinal Foundations.* London; New York: Routledge.

7

Vajrayana traditions

Chapter summary and outline

Japanese esoteric Buddhism arrived in the United States at the turn of the twenti-eth century. This tradition was joined by the Tibetan tradition following the Chinese occupation of Tibet in 1950. While these traditions are numerically small in the United States, they hold an outsized presence owing in no small part to the widespread popu-larity of the 14th Dalai Lama. In addition to providing an overview of both Japanese and Tibetan esoteric traditions, attention is paid to new religious movements and their relationship to established Buddhist schools.

Introduction: Three vignettes

For ten days in July 2011, the 14th Dalai Lama performed a complex initiation ritual known as the Kalachakra Tantra in Washington, DC. Whereas most tantric rituals of this sort are more intimate affairs transferring ritual knowledge from teacher to student, the Kalachakra for World Peace was conducted at the Verizon Center sports arena before an audience of thousands (Figure 20). While purporting to cleanse the world of negativity, if nothing else, the event brought a wide array of Buddhists into the nation's capital, filling the neighborhood around the arena with monks and nuns from virtually all Buddhist schools (Mowe 2011). In the foothills of Appalachia, a group of men and women gather every Sunday morning at the Shambhala Center where a non-monastic lay teacher leads a two-hour *samatha* meditation session. Some meditators have come for the first time; others have been attending for well over a decade. Some do not consider themselves Buddhists while others fully embrace the panoply of Tibetan-derived practices and training sessions the center offers (McKinley 2014). Over the course of Memorial Day weekend in late May, the Shinnyo-en school of Japanese Buddhism sponsors a lantern-floating ceremony in Honolulu, Hawai'i. Since its beginning in 1998, this has become a deeply embedded part of Hawai'ian public life, attracting tens of thousands of participants, many of whom are oblivious to the ritual's Buddhist origins as they set votive candles out into the ocean, remembering their lost relatives and ancestors, and hoping for peace in the future (Montrose 2014).

FIGURE 20 *The 14th Dalai Lama performing the Kalachakra for World Peace, Washington, DC, 2011.*

Thus, Vajrayana Buddhism finds expression in the United States. Emerging within Indian Mahayana Buddhism, beginning in the sixth century of the Common Era, Vajrayana is centered on a genre of texts (tantra) and their associated ritual practices. These practices were infused within the larger spread of Buddhism outside India and are particularly important in the development of Tibetan Buddhism and many forms of East Asian Buddhism. Vajrayana is perhaps best understood as a specific set of practices or an approach to the Buddhist path, founded on core Mahayana doctrines, cosmologies, and soteriologies, and not, properly speaking, a distinct school. Most Vajrayana Buddhists would see themselves as such, articulating Vajrayana as part of a tripartite path of practice beginning with so-called hinayana, moving through the exoteric practices of the Mahayana, and culminating in the esoteric practices contained in tantric texts. Nevertheless, it can be instructive to separate out Vajrayana traditions for several reasons, the least of which is that this schema has become somewhat widespread in modern popular and academic literature. More importantly for our purposes, focusing on Vajrayana apart from Mahayana will allow us to examine the unique experiences of Tibetan Buddhism in the United States on the one hand, and to shed some light on little-studied non-Tibetan esoteric (*mikkyo*) schools, on the other, especially Japanese Shingon.[1]

Following an overview of Vajrayana history and practice, we will begin with Japanese Shingon; from there, the bulk of this chapter will focus on numerous Tibetan Buddhist lineages in the United States. Tibetan Buddhism has become extremely popular and highly visible in the mainstream media over the past several decades, a popularity made in no small part by both the Dalai Lama and Shambhala International, a Tibetan-derived lineage founded in North America in the 1970s. This popularity represents a different mode of development for US Buddhism, one that has happened without a large immigrant base as we saw in previous chapters. The reader is once again referred to the back matter for more information on specific schools and terms used in this chapter.

Overview of Vajrayana Buddhist history and practice

From Mahayana to Vajrayana

Vajrayana Buddhism finds its origins within Mahayana at the intersection of ongoing Indian Buddhist discourses and broader religious developments beginning in the sixth century of the Common Era. Prior to this time, the Gupta Empire (320–550) had brought a level of unity and prosperity to the Indian subcontinent from which Buddhism benefited greatly, allowing for the development of large monastic complexes and universities, such as Nalanda. By the end of the Gupta period, however, other religious movements began to appear, including the cult of Shiva, which competed with Buddhist institutions for patronage. Within this context, both inside and outside Buddhist institutions, a large complex of religious practices began to develop based on texts called tantra. Referring to the ordering of things, tantras are essentially ritual manuals, laying out a specific path toward awakening that would have both a profound impact on Buddhism as well as representing the final development of the tradition in India before Buddhism vanished from its homeland. Thus, as Gethin notes, Vajrayana Buddhism is

> a particular approach to the practice of the Buddhist path occurring within the general Mahayana philosophical framework, as set out by the Madhyamaka and Yogacara, and giving special emphasis to the idea of the equivalence of nirvana and samsara. (Gethin 1998, 268)

As mentioned in the previous chapter, according to the two-truths doctrine, the ultimate truth is that of suchness (*tathata*), the world as it is free of our discriminative thinking. Texts such as the *Heart Sutra* implied a fundamental relationship, an equivalence between, awakening and *samsara*. This equivalence—our inability to see the world in its true suchness—is the result of our discriminative thinking, the result, as it were, of faulty perceptions. The solution offered was to clarify and purify one's perceptions and behaviors in order to see through dualistic thinking or the false separation of subjective self and objective other.

Within this context, a nexus of ideas and practices developed within Mahayana Buddhism that was related to the broader Indian tantric movement. This movement was popularized in part by tantric masters—male yogi and female yogini—who engaged in ecstatic rituals meant to clarify subtle energies in the body and enter into union with various divinities and manifestations of the transcendent. Overtly transgressive in nature, such as performing rituals in unclean spaces with lower-caste persons, such rituals were intended to cut across discriminative thinking by calling into question moral and religious dualisms such as right and wrong or sacred

Transgressive practice

For better or worse, as a result of their rich visual imagery and symbolism that often plays on sexual tropes such as the merging of female and male energies, tantra has picked up connotations of the exotic and sexual in the modern West. It is important, however, to keep in mind first that whereas a tantric text may contain sexual imagery, we should not assume that these texts were to be taken literally; after all, they are *esoteric* in nature, and their true meaning can be known only in practice with a qualified teacher. Somewhat more importantly, we should guard against the tendency of judging sexual activity through our own cultural lens and instead be attentive to the culturally constructed nature of sexual expression and gender relationships across cultures and religious traditions.

and profane. Tantric adepts directly competed with Buddhists for royal patronage (Robinson and Johnson 1997, 119), and over time these practices and their resonance with preexisting Mahayana doctrines became incorporated into Buddhism itself as a specific path—Vajrayana, literally the diamond-like thunderbolt vehicle (Davidson 2002; Bjerken 2005). While far too complex to be detailed here, a few points regarding the nature of the path, specific ritual practices, and, importantly, the teacher-student relationship will help lay the foundation for our later discussions of US Vajrayana traditions.

Ritual and power

Tantric texts are often highly abbreviated, containing only the bare outlines of a ritual or how to construct a *mandala*; a teacher is required to fill in the blanks for properly conducting the ritual. Moreover, such texts and rituals are presumed to have a deeper (or esoteric) meaning that can only be explicated by one's teacher. Thus, the guru (or lama) becomes of paramount importance in the tradition not only as the person from whom esoteric knowledge is learned but as a lineage holder, passing on this essential wisdom generation to generation. Lineages, as we saw in the previous chapter, are important in many Mahayana schools; for the Vajrayana, it becomes doubly important as a guru necessarily has specialized (and potentially powerfully dangerous) ritual knowledge existing outside the texts. As a result, over the centuries, various gurus, lamas, and incarnations of past teachers have played pivotal roles in the development of the tradition.

Knowledge is passed from teacher to student through initiation or empowerment rituals, *abhiseka*. *Abhiseka* means "consecration" and can refer both to the consecration of a king as well as the Buddha himself. In *abhiseka* rituals, an initiand is given instruction on how to correctly perform specific ritual practices, each of which are intended to clarify or purify actions of the body, speech, and mind, thus allowing the practitioner to overcome the three afflictions of greed, hatred, and ignorance and transcend the *samsara*/nirvana dualism. *Mudra* are associated with bodily acts; iconographically represented in Buddhist art by various hand gestures, *mudra* include bodily postures more generally symbolizing various qualities or aspects of enlightenment. *Mantra* and *dharani* are repeated phrases found throughout Mahayana and tantric texts, phrases that are often syntactically meaningless but reflect sacred syllabaries used to purify verbal acts. Mental acts are clarified via complex visualization meditations wherein the practitioner may mentally come to identify oneself with either a specific Buddha or an aspect of awakening and are often associated with *mandala*.

A *mandala* is a visual representation of the sacred realm. Set out in complex geometric patterns of various shapes and concentric circles, a tantric practitioner may enter into a *mandala* either literally—through constructing one as part of an *abhiseka* ritual—or mentally by visualizing its construction. In the process, one comes to identify with various aspects of awakening represented by the celestial and cosmic persons that populate the *mandala*. These beings may be Buddhas, both the historical Buddha Sakyamuni as well as cosmic Buddhas such as Akshobhya and Amitabha; they may also be gods and goddesses, historical lamas, or embodiments of wisdom and compassion. This pantheon of beings is based on preexisting Mahayana cosmology as well as *tathagatagarbha* literature and the three bodies of the Buddha theory advanced by Indian Mahayana Buddhists.

The three bodies of the Buddha were articulated in the centuries following the death of the historical Buddha in response to questions that arose regarding his nature and the nature of awakening. Briefly, the theory states that the Buddha has a physicality (*nirmanakaya*) that manifested as Siddhartha Gautama; he also has the power to create emanation bodies (*sambhogakaya*) or mind-made apparitions that account for the miraculous accounts of the Buddha being in two places at the same time or traveling to various heavenly realms to teach the dharma, accounts that can be found in some of the earliest Buddhist texts. This ability comes, in part, from the *Dharmakaya* or "truth body" of the Buddha, representing the fundamental ground of reality, again, true suchness, from which all Buddhas manifest. The Dharmakaya became an object of devotion itself in the development of Vajrayana Buddhism and plays an important role in East Asia. Finally, through visualizing oneself as being identical with various aspects of the Buddha or awakening in all its forms, the tantric practitioner is able to both cut across dualism and purify one's nature, shortcutting the process toward awakening.

Quite apart from any spiritual or religious benefits tantric practices may have, it is also clear that these practices are believed to be powerfully efficacious in the temporal realm. Tantric ritual specialists were called upon by kings and emperors to perform rituals in protection of the state; the seemingly endless cast of celestial deities, gods, and demons found in Vajrayana and Mahayana cosmologies could be called upon both to protect the dharma as well as wreck havoc on one's enemies. It was said that Japanese esoteric rituals were responsible for causing storms that fended off Mongol invaders in the thirteenth century The Kalachakra Tantra, mentioned in this chapter's outset, is performed for world peace, in part, precisely because it speaks of the dharma overcoming real-world military threats. This relationship between tantra and the powerful forces they engender reinforces the importance of finding a good teacher. It is the guru's responsibility to ensure that both proper ritual knowledge is conferred and the student is prepared for such knowledge and the power it carries.

Tantric practices were embedded within Buddhism as it spread across Asia. In Central and East Asia, esoteric practices were embedded within Buddhist traditions generally and distinct and explicitly esoteric schools were established. Indian Buddhism was imported into Tibet as early as the seventh century, and Vajrayana in particular thrived. Both the Japanese and Tibetan forms of the tradition have made their way to the United States, the subject for the remainder of the chapter.

US Vajrayana traditions of Japan

Shingon

By the early ninth century, Buddhism had already been well established in Japan, being imported via Korea several centuries earlier. Most of the major Chinese schools were imported as well as a range of texts and practices. Esoteric Buddhism became systematized largely as a result of Kukai (774–835) and Saicho (767–822) who established the esoteric schools of Shingon and Tendai (C. Tiantai), respectively. Following his travels to China in 804, Kukai brought to Japan the Shingon tradition, which has a dual focus on *mandala*-practice and textual analysis largely based on the *Mahavairocana Sutra*. The central object of devotion is the Dharmakaya Buddha Mahavairocana Tathagata, Dainichi Nyorai in Japanese. Kukai had a deep interest in the study of texts and was purportedly instrumental in the development of a native Japanese writing system. Moreover, Kukai himself has become an object of devotion—a fairly common occurrence in many Japanese Buddhists schools—and he is popularly referred to as Kobo Daishi. The Tendai school had an enormous impact on Japanese Buddhism generally (Chapter 6); however, there exists very little Tendai in North America whereas Shingon, on the other hand, has been in the United States for more than a century.[2]

Shingon Buddhism, like the Shin and Zen Buddhist traditions, was brought to the United States via Japanese immigration to Hawai'i and the West Coast in the early twentieth century. Its establishment in Hawai'i was the result of lay practitioners who, in one case, hoped to recreate a Japanese pilgrimage route on the island of Kauai and, in another case, claimed that devotion to Kobo Daishi had curative powers. The lack of priests or ministers in the early days led to the accusation that the Shingon tradition was unorthodox, prompting the Koyasan branch of Shingon to establish a mission in Honolulu in 1926. In 1909, a Koyasan priest traveled to California with the intent of establishing the tradition on the mainland; his efforts were hampered due to health and economic circumstances, but by 1913 what would become known as the Koyasan Beikoku Betsuin was established in Los Angeles. Within two decades, both the mainland US and Hawai'ian branches were thriving, a period of prosperity impeded by the outbreak of World War II and Japanese American internment.

Whereas Shin Buddhist communities saw significant growth in the postwar years, and Zen Buddhist communities thrived and began attracting non-Japanese Americans, Shingon Buddhism has remained relatively small (and understudied) in the United States. Its small size is partly a consequence of immigration patterns; the majority of Japanese immigrants pre-World War II hailed from prefectures that were predominately Jodo Shinshu (Nishimura 2008, 91). Anti-Japanese sentiment leading up to the war created a situation wherein Shingon Buddhists were isolated from and generally ignored by non-Japanese Americans. By the 1980s, many communities had seen sharp declines in membership and even schisms that led to the closure of some temples

(Eastman 2009). It is worth noting, however, that this decline came at a time when another form of esoteric Buddhism—Tibetan—was on the rise. What accounts for the sudden popularity of one form of Vajrayana Buddhism while another has remained relatively obscured from mainstream discourse? Arguably, Tibetan Buddhism has been "exoticized" in the popular imagination over against the Shingon tradition which, like other Japanese American religious groups, adopted a largely Protestant Christian congregational style of practice in an attempt to become more American in its formative years. "The adaptation to mainstream Protestant norms is substantial enough … that even those Americans whose interests led them to investigate a wide variety of esoteric traditions did not find the Shingon tradition appealing enough to pursue" (Payne 2005, 111). We should be cautious here against assuming that merely because the tradition outwardly displays Protestant forms of worship that it has lost its esoteric focus; Shingon priests in the United States regularly perform tantric practices and rituals. Very little sustained research has been directed toward US Shingon Buddhism despite its century-long history.

Shinnyo-en

Even less research has been directed toward the Shingon offshoot Shinnyo-en—though this may be due to Shinnyo-en's status as a so-called new religious movement. Founded in 1936 and officially recognized as a religion in postwar Japan, the school was established by a Buddhist layman, Shinjo Ito and his wife Tomoji. Both came from nominally religious backgrounds and in the mid-1930s became interested in the teachings of the Shingon school and especially practices devoted to the deity Fudo Myo-o. While meditating in front of an image of Fudo Myo-o, Tomoji had a vision that her husband should dedicate his life to religious practice. Following this event, the couple formally established a new religious association and affiliated themselves with the Shingon temple Daigoji. Following World War II, as Japan adopted religious freedom laws, the organization changed its name to Shinnyo-en, "the garden of the Tathata (true reality)." This was a time when many religious movements, such as Soka Gakkai (Chapter 6) began proliferating in Japan, and Shinnyo-en saw significant growth through the latter half of the century (Cornille 2000, 25–28). Whereas the group is not significantly large in the United States, its influence should not be underestimated. In addition to funding academic chairs at major research universities such as the University of California, Berkeley, international arts and cultural shows, and being a major sponsor of a 2010 PBS documentary *The Buddha* (narrated by actor Richard Gere), Shinnyo-en also established the lantern-floating ceremony discussed at this chapter's opening.

    In the 1970s, Ito and his daughter visited Hawai'i, toured the USS Arizona Memorial at Pearl Harbor, and prayed for the dead on both sides of World War II. From this experience, they were not only inspired to establish Shinnyo-en on the islands but also decided to host an annual lantern-floating ceremony in Honolulu over the course of Memorial Day weekend (Figure 21). Floating lanterns as a way to pacify the spirits of

FIGURE 21 *Lantern-floating Shinnyo-en Memorial Day ceremony, Honolulu, Hawai'i. (Photo courtesy Victoria Montrose.)*

the dead is a fairly common and traditional Japanese ritual that, over the centuries, has become associated with the Buddhist ceremony of *obon* usually held in late summer, a ceremony Hawai'i's numerous Japanese Buddhist communities were celebrating long before Shinnyo-en's arrival. Shinnyo-en's lantern ceremony has eclipsed all other *obon*-style celebrations on the islands (Montrose 2014). Whereas this ceremony might be seen as Shinnyo-en's most public event, the community's central practice revolves around "*sesshin* training,"[3] a kind of one-on-one spiritual guidance where a Shinnyo-en medium assesses a practitioner's karmic needs via communication with the spirit world. In this process, one is encouraged to see through delusions and develop one's own inner "Buddha-spirit" (Shiramizu 1979).

Shinnyo-en maintains an affiliation with Daigoji while being an independent organization. This affiliation provides us with a direct, if largely institutional, connection with an established Vajrayana tradition. In practice, Shinnyo-en shares commonalities with other esoteric traditions as well. The group doctrinally justifies itself through an interpretation of the *Mahaparinirvana Sutra*, an important Mahayana text. During the *sesshin* training, practitioners are encouraged to move past the three afflictions of greed, hatred, and ignorance while discovering their inner "Buddha-spirit," essentially Buddhanature. Shinnyo-en's mediums in service to this end are said to commune with the spirit world, and it is here that we find some divergence from what might be

considered more traditional forms of Vajrayana—and indeed general—Buddhist practice, a divergence that contributes to its being labeled a new religious movement. As
Winfield (2014) has noted, however, such a label may have outlived its usefulness. The
study of new religious movements (NRMs) has been hampered by an academic field
that delegitimizes NRMs by privileging established, institutional forms of religion on
the one hand, and the popular association of these groups with often dangerous cults,
on the other (see insert). Dismissing new Buddhist movements such as Shinnyo-en,
and NRMs more generally, as cults precludes the possibility of taking them seriously
on their own terms (Hubbard 1998); it limits our understanding of the diversity of
approaches to religious practice and institutional development that are of concern to
all religious scholars (Chryssides and Zeller 2014); and it allows us to overlook what
are potentially fruitful areas of research. As mentioned, while still small in number in
the United States, Shinnyo-en has a substantial amount of capital and media influence
that, quite apart from anything else, is worth academic study (cf Nobutaka 2012).

Cults and new religious movements

In the late 1950s, Jim Jones founded a new church, the People's Temple of the
Disciples of Christ. Two decades later, he led his nearly one thousand followers in a
mass suicide at their commune in northwestern Guyana. In 1993, federal and state
authorities raided a Branch Davidian compound in Waco, Texas, where self-described
prophet David Koresh was suspected of weapons violations and abusing his followers. A fire during the raid led to the deaths of nearly one hundred of his followers and
Koresh himself. In 1995, members of the Japanese new religious movement Aum
Shinrikyo, which blends Buddhist, Hindu, and millennialist Christian ideas, released
deadly sarin gas on several Tokyo subway lines. The attack resulted in a dozen deaths,
and Aum Shinrikyo has since been listed as a terrorist organization.

    To these, one could easily add a longer list of cults that have, over the last half-
century, caused death and harm to their followers. It is because of such events that
the word "cult" has become a pejorative term used to discredit related groups and
contributed to the continued marginalization of scholarly studies of new religious
movements in more established academic disciplines.

US Vajrayana traditions of Tibet

Historical background

Narrative accounts of Buddhism's introduction to Tibet, as well as several important
historical events, reveal much about the specific character of the Tibetan Buddhist
tradition. Buddhism was first promulgated in Tibet by Songtsen Gampo and his two
Buddhist wives in the mid-sixth century. During his reign, Tibet began the process of

becoming a major power in Central Asia. A century later, the emperor Trhi Songdetsen further expanded the kingdom, exerting considerable influence over the Silk Road and capturing the large Buddhist complex at Dunhuang. It was during this period that the first Tibetan monastery, Samye, was opened. Santaraksita, a scholar from the Indian Buddhist monastery Nalanda, was invited to oversee the construction of Samye; however, a series of natural disasters and civil unrest forced him to leave the country. Another Indian monk, the tantric master Padmasambhava, was called upon to conquer and subdue the local Tibetan demons. As the tradition continued to develop, it received influence from China as well as India, exemplified by a great debate held in the late eight century. The debate centered around a classic Mahayana distinction between a sudden or gradual approach to awakening, with the former characterized by a sudden and penetrating insight into reality (often followed by a gradual path of deeper cultivation) and the latter characterized by a slow process of deepening awareness. Following a period of Buddhist decline and persecution, the tradition was reestablished in the eleventh century when what would become some of the foundational Tibetan schools and monasteries opened and the Tibetan canon took shape. By the fourteenth century, the canon was more or less complete having translated a large collection of Indic Sanskrit texts into Tibetan and divided into Mahayana sutras, tantric texts, and the Mulasarvastivada *vinaya*, on the one hand, and commentaries and treatises, on the other. Thus, the Tibetan canon represents the third major Buddhist canon in addition to the Pali canon of the Theravada tradition and the Chinese canon used throughout East Asian (Robinson and Johnson 1997, 271–285; Kapstein 2000).

Over the successive centuries, several schools and lineages developed, four of which will be relevant for our discussion below. The earliest was the Nyingma which traces its origins back to Padmasambhava. The Kagyu school is based on the teachings of eminent Tibetan and Indian masters including Gampopa, Milarapa, Marpa, and, ultimately, Naropa. The head of one Kagyu sub-school, the Karma Kagyu, is known as the Karmapa, a teacher said to be the reincarnation of a former lama (*tulku*). Conversely, the Sakya school, established in 1073, is headed by a lineage of married yogins who pass leadership from father to son or uncle to nephew. The most recently established Gelug school traces its origins to Tsongpa in the fourteenth century and, since the sixteenth century, has been led by the Dalai Lamas.

Since the Yuan Dynasty (1271–1368), the relationship between Tibet and China has been complicated. From the point of view of the People's Republic of China, it was during this period that the Mongol Emperor Kublai Khan incorporated Tibet into China. Chinese emperors in successive dynasties have had a close relationship with the rulers of Tibet, often officially recognizing political and religious leaders. From the Tibetan point of view, however, this relationship is best understood as a "priest-patron" one, a relationship that has no corollary in modern, Western conceptions of the nation-state. Put simply, Tibet viewed itself as an independent territory or kingdom that provided the ruling Chinese government with spiritual or karmic benefits in exchange for political or economic support. By the colonial period, this relationship was in many ways rather informal and something of a nonissue, at least for the Chinese who were, at the time, far more concerned about the growing threat of European colonial interests. By the dawn of twentieth century, of course, all this would change as the republican government of China was overthrown by the Maoist communist revolution that emphatically claimed Tibet as having always been an integral part of China. By 1950, communist forces had invaded Tibet, and following an uprising in 1959, celebrated as Tibetan Uprising Day, tens of thousands of Tibetans fled their homeland. In diaspora, the Tibetan people have attempted to rebuild a sense of identity and nationality without a nation, and it is in this context that Tibetan Buddhism has come to the United States.

The popularity and influence of Tibetan Buddhism

The practice of recognizing either reincarnations of important lamas or incarnations of deities is an important part of Tibetan Buddhism, especially in those schools headed by a reincarnate lama, such as the Karma Kagyu and the Gelug. It was in this context that the position of the Dalai Lama developed. The head of the Gelug school is considered to be an incarnation of the bodhisattva of compassion, Avalokitesvara, and it was the third *tulku* of this lineage who was first given the title Dalai Lama by the Mongolian king Altan Khan in 1578. Since that time, the Dalai Lamas have been the spiritual head of the Gelug school as well as the political rulers of Tibet—or at least those areas of Tibet

FIGURE 22 *President Barack Obama meets with the 14th Dalai Lama at the White House, 2010. (Getty Images.)*

under the control of the capital at Lhasa. During the reign of the 13th Dalai Lama, who declared Tibet an independent country in 1913, China asserted its sovereignty over Tibet, something of a nonissue over the course of two world wars and the communist revolution. The 14th Dalai Lama, Tenzin Gyatso, inherited this ambiguous situation, was formally enthroned as ruler of Tibet in 1950, and attempted to maintain Tibetan independence until the 1959 uprising when he fled into India where, in Dharamsala, a government in exile has existed ever since.

Since then, the Dalai Lama has remained steadfastly committed to a nonviolent response to the Chinese occupation of Tibet, a response that earned him the Nobel Peace Prize in 1989. This commitment, in the face of a rather large humanitarian crisis that threatens Tibetan culture, provides one reason for the Dalai Lama's popularity which, since the 1980s, has grown exponentially. The Dalai Lama's personal popularity dovetails with the rising popularity of Tibetan Buddhism—fueled in part by the release of several successful Hollywood films in the 1990s and celebrity support of the free Tibet movement—as well as an increase in the academic study of the tradition, which has helped to preserve Tibetan texts, arts, and culture in the face of Chinese occupation (Seager 1999, 119–123). As the Dalai Lama has continued to travel the United States, giving public talks and being hosted by political and cultural leaders, he has virtually become not only the face of Tibet but the face of Buddhism itself—a popularity both deserved and somewhat problematic. It is problematic for the same reason any one leader's popularity is problematic, namely, it obscures complexity and nuance. To put it plainly, regardless of the persuasiveness of his message and his effectiveness as a political leader, Buddhism is larger than any one man, even a man as important as the Dalai Lama.

To be sure, the Dalai Lama has led a remarkable life and has done much to promote the cause of his people, playing no small role in preserving an entire culture without a homeland. His articulation of a specifically Buddhist approach to peace is also noteworthy (Gyatso 1999; King 2005, 195–198). However, we must guard against the urge to presume that the Dalai Lama is universally beloved by Buddhists or that he holds the same position as, say, the pope for Catholics as an infallible intercessor between humanity and the divine. The Dalai Lama speaks for the Tibetan people in general as a political leader (a position he abdicated in 2011); but he speaks as a doctrinal authority for only one school of Tibetan Buddhism, the Gelug. And even in this role he has his critics.

A consistent source of criticism has come from the so-called Dorje Shugden controversy. Dorje Shugden is a dharma protector, a common figure in Mahayana and Vajrayana cosmologies who, prior to the twentieth century was a relatively minor figure in the overall Tibetan pantheon, believed to be responsible for creating discord or destruction against those who blended teachings from different schools. Beginning in the 1930s, he was promoted by some in the Gelug school not as an evil spirit but as an enlightened being. The 13th Dalai Lama had put some restrictions on practices devoted to Shugden, and in the mid-1970s the 14th Dalai Lama began discouraging Shugden devotion largely on the grounds that he was a divisive figure in the face of the

FIGURE 23 *Members of the Shugden Community protest religious intolerance as the Dalai Lama attends an event in New York, 2015. (Getty Images.)*

Tibetan people's larger problems with China. Over the ensuing decades, the controversy was fiercely debated within Tibetan circles while being largely unknown outside the community. In 1996, the Dalai Lama decreed that Shugden was an evil spirit and a threat to the Tibetan people, a pronouncement that Shugden's supporters took as nothing less than religious persecution. In addition to ongoing demonstrations against the Dalai Lama and the Gelug school (Figure 23), several groups broke off including the New Kadampa Tradition (NKT) founded by a Gelug monk, Kelsang Gyatso, in 1991. Based in the United Kingdom, the NKT has centers around the world including several dozen in the United States. Apart from this institutional presence, NKT members and nonmembers regularly engage in debate, especially online, attracting wider attention to the ongoing controversy (Chandler 2015; Williams 1996).[4]

The incredible popularity of the Dalai Lama and Tibetan Buddhism also obscures the relatively small number of Tibetans residing in the United States. The bulk of scholarship on US Tibetan Buddhism has focused almost exclusively on meditation centers, many of which were established by a Tibetan monk or lama with substantial financial support from non-Tibetan converts (Seager 1999; Lavine 1998), which points to the economic realities of practicing Buddhism in the United States. In premodern Tibet, lay Buddhists relied on monastics for both spiritual teaching as well as karmic merit; in exchange, monastics relied on the laity as a means of economic support. As Tibet was essentially governed by a monastic institution, monks were naturally in a position of leadership vis-à-vis the lay population. In the United States, both lay and monastic

Tibetan Buddhists are part of the larger, global Tibetan diaspora—that is, refugees—who are often at an economic disadvantage. Monastics must find a way of providing for themselves, and lay Tibetans generally have limited financial resources. This contrasts with sympathizers and converts who necessarily have the means to support burgeoning meditation centers but may not be as inclined to support traditionally lay Buddhist practices. Lay Tibetan Buddhists, meanwhile, may focus their energies on maintaining Tibetan traditions writ large and celebrating major holidays such as Losar (New Years) or commemorating Tibetan Uprising Day (Mullen 2001, 2006). While scholarship has tended to focus more on the meditation centers and activities of well-known teachers or monks, it has been slow to recognize the practices of lay Tibetans.

US Tibetan Buddhist traditions

All four main branches of Tibetan Buddhism have some presence in the United States. Beginning in the 1950s, a small number of Tibetan and Kalmyk (see insert) refugees began emigrating to the United States, followed by larger numbers of immigrants following the Chinese invasion of Tibet and coinciding with a rising interest in Tibetan Buddhism through the 1970s and 1980s. Many Tibetan lamas and monks established training centers, monasteries, and other organizations at this time which have grown, diversified, and spread considerably over the ensuing decades.

Republic of Kalmykia

Kalmykia is an autonomous republic in the Russian Federation, lying on the coast of the Caspian Sea, north of Georgia, historically settled by descendants of Mongolian groups spread across Central Asia. The region has been predominately Buddhist for several centuries with strong cultural ties to Tibet.

Geshe Ngawang Wangyal arrived in the United States in 1955 as part of a Kalmyk refugee group escaping then-communist Russia. Having trained in a Tibetan monastery since the age of six, Wangyal helped to establish the Tibetan Buddhist Learning Center in 1958 in New Jersey (Urubshurow 2013). He invited a number of Tibetan teachers to the center and also attracted the attention of non-Tibetan converts, including Robert Thurman who eventually traveled to India, received ordination from the Dalai Lama, and became a great supporter of the Tibetan cause. The center works with both the Tibetan and Kalmyk communities while providing an important hub of scholastic and educational resources for the Gelug school in North America. Gelug is also represented in the United States by the work of Lama Thubten Zopa who, together with his late teacher Lama Thubten Yeshe, established The Foundation for the Preservation of the Mahayana Tradition (FPMT) in Nepal in 1975. Currently headquartered in Portland, Oregon, the FPMT oversees dozens of training and meditation centers around the

world as well as Maitripa College, also in Portland, that began offering degree programs in Buddhist studies in 2006. Of course, in addition to these centers is the US
residence of the Dalai Lama in Ithaca, New York, Namgyal Monastery, which houses
a residential monastery, educational programs, a study center, and other programs
(Prebish 1999, 40–42).

Rivaling the scale of the US Gelug tradition is a Nyingma network of retreat centers
and temples established by Tarthang Tulku Rinpoche who arrived in the United States
in 1968. Within a decade, Tarthang Tulku had founded the Nyingma Meditation Center,
Dharma Publishing, and the Nyingma Institute, all in Berkeley, California. Roughly a hundred miles north of San Francisco, the organization has also constructed the Copper
Mountain Mandala, Odiyan Retreat Center, and the Ratna Ling Retreat Center, a collection of traditional Tibetan-style buildings and stupas in the midst of the forest overlooking the Pacific Ocean open to both monastics and short-term meditation retreats.
The Tibetan Aid Project raises funds and awareness of and for the preservation of
Tibetan and Buddhist culture. Tarthang Tulku is also responsible for bringing specific
Tibetan teachings to the United States, including *kum nye*—a type of movement-
based meditation—as well as helping to popularize *dzogchen* practice.

Dzogchen, literally the "great perfection," is a meditation technique representing
the highest form of practice in the Nyingma tradition. In the United States, it has been
popularized beyond both this one school and monastic contexts by various Tibetan
teachers, including Tarthang Tulku and Sogyal Rinpoche, as well as Lama Surya Das.
Surya Das (b. Jeffery Miller, 1950) traveled to India and Nepal in the 1970s where he
studied with various Hindu, *vipasyana*, and Tibetan teachers. A Hindu guru gave him
his name, and in the 1980s he began studying at a Nyingma retreat center in France,
eventually becoming a lama in the *dzogchen* tradition. He founded the Dzogchen
Foundation, currently headquartered outside Austin, Texas, in 1991. A prolific author
and engaging speaker, Surya Das has contributed greatly to the ongoing discourse
regarding the development of Buddhism in the United States, advancing something of
a non-sectarian version of Tibetan-influenced Buddhism (Prebish 1999, 44).

While sometimes overshadowed by the Shambhala movement that derives in part
from the same lineage, the Kagyu school, and especially the Karma Kagyu lineage,
has a growing presence in North America. The head of this lineage, a reincarnate lama
known as the Karmapa, is currently disputed. Two men, Ogyen Trinley Dorje and Trinley
Thaye Dorje, born in 1985 and 1983 respectively, are recognized as the Karmapa, and
whereas a sizable minority of Karma Kagyu-affiliated monasteries and centers recognize the latter, Ogyen Trinley Dorje is more recognized, especially in North America. His
official representative in the United States is Dzogchen Ponlop Rinpoche (b. 1965) who,
being young and charismatic, has become a popular figure in the United States through
his talks and books, such as *Mind Beyond Death* (2007) and *Rebel Buddha* (2010), as
well as engagement through social media.

The US Sakya tradition is perhaps not as large as other Tibetan schools but has
had a significant impact on the academic study of Tibetan Buddhism due to Deshung
Rinpoche who arrived at the University of Washington, Seattle, in 1960. Invited by

Turrell Wylie, who is responsible for creating a transliteration scheme for rendering Tibetan into Latin characters, Deshung Rinpoche's stay in the United States coincided with an extremely productive period of academic research on Buddhism and Tibet (Prebish 1999, 42).[5] He also helped to establish a Sakya Monastery in Seattle, and another center in Cambridge, Massachusetts. Sakya is also represented in the United States by networks of meditation and retreat centers, both large and small.

Tibetan Buddhism has become extremely popular among non-Tibetans in the United States in part due to the general interest in Asian religions and cultures that has only increased since the 1960s. Unlike US Buddhist traditions that were established first by a large immigrant base and then attracted the attention of non-Asian Americans, US Tibetan Buddhist traditions have grown over the last several decades without a large immigrant base. Thus, when surveying the landscape of US Tibetan Buddhist traditions, one finds networks of meditation and retreat centers, educational organizations, and academic projects directed toward preserving Tibetan culture, and monastic institutions catering to both Tibetan exiles and non-Tibetan converts. Major centers can be found in the Pacific Northwest, upstate New York and the surrounding areas, as well as the Southwest. Some centers are more explicitly focused on preserving traditional Tibetan arts, culture, and religion; others have significant cross-over with growing secular meditation movements (Chapter 8). As the tradition grows and develops in its new locale, it faces challenges in adapting centuries-old traditions to American norms, adaptations that can lead to wholly new articulations.

Shambhala International

Shambhala International occupies a unique space relative to Vajrayana/Tibetan Buddhism and the broader North American Buddhist landscape. Its placement here is to note its historical relationship to more classically defined Tibetan Buddhist traditions while highlighting the ways in which it has diverged from those roots.

Chögyam Trungpa (1939–1987), Shambhala International's founder, was born in Tibet and recognized as the eleventh incarnation of the Trungpa line of lamas in the Kagyu school. He was also interested in the *rimé* movement which sought to overcome sectarian differences among the Tibetan schools, and he was trained in the Nyingma tradition. Like the Dalai Lama, he fled Tibet in 1959 and settled in India where he continued his education. By the early 1960s, he had traveled to the United Kingdom where he studied at Oxford and, following a car accident, gave up his monastic vows, established meditation centers, and began teaching non-Tibetans. His decision to quit the monastic life was inspired, in part, by his desire to cut against Westerners' preconceptions about exotic guru figures, a teaching style called "crazy wisdom," loosely based on the Tibetan concept of *yeshe chölwa*. Chögyam Trungpa's popularity increased, and by 1970 he was invited to the United States where he traveled extensively and eventually founded a new Buddhist organization called Vajradhatu, headquartered in Boulder, Colorado, in 1973. The following year, also in Boulder, he founded Naropa

University, a small liberal arts college. He invited several Beat Generation poets and avant garde artists—including Allen Ginsberg, Anne Waldman, John Cage and Diane di Prima—to establish an arts program there, what eventually became the Jack Kerouac School of Disembodied Poetics. In 1983, Gampo Abbey in Nova Scotia, Canada, was opened—the community's first monastic center in North America. In 1987, Chögyam Trungpa moved the international headquarters of the organization there, shortly before his death (Prebish 1999, 44–45).

His connection to the arts, as well as being a lineage holder in two different Tibetan schools, speaks to Chögyam Trungpa's style of Buddhist training. Whereas his approach certainly included Tibetan forms of meditation—as well as tantric initiations and empowerments—he also self-consciously constructed a mode of practice that borrowed heavily from a diverse set of Buddhist and artistic influences. Known as Shambhala Training, the practice is intended to create an enlightened society through the cultivation of the self in both the spiritual and worldly realms, incorporating a wide range of Tibetan Buddhist practices as well as Japanese archery and flower arrangement (*ikebana*), dance and poetry, and even psychotherapy (Midal 2004). Fundamentally, it can be viewed as a modern interpretation of traditional Buddhist practice, a convergence of Tibetan approaches with modern Western culture, a convergence that ultimately diverged into a wholly new lineage.

This divergence was, in part, the direct result of Chögyam Trungpa's crazy wisdom approach and the aftermath of his death. Through the 1970s and early 1980s, Vajradhatu grew rapidly, establishing centers across North America. Whereas members held Chögyam Trungpa in high regard and were fiercely loyal to him, local centers had a fair amount of autonomy from any centralized authority, an organizational structure that would prove beneficial. New religious movements that are founded by a charismatic leader often do not survive the death of that leader; and in this case, the controversies surrounding both Chögyam's and his successor's behavior and death could have been disastrous for the community. However, the decentralized structure of Vajradhatu was instrumental in allowing local communities to survive the loss of a charismatic leader (Eldershaw 2007). Vajradhatu was reorganized into Shambhala International and reached out to high lamas in the Kagyu tradition who legitimated Chögyam Trungpa's son, Sakyong Mipham, to be the head of the organization. By 2000, Sakyong Mipham had begun referring to the community as a new Buddhist lineage.

Shambhala International presents us with a rather eclectic blending of traditional and modern, Tibetan and non-Tibetan approaches to Buddhism. Despite this eclecticism, it is hard to overstate how widely influential the community has been in popularizing Buddhism in North America. His questionable teaching style aside, Chögyam Trungpa's books, including *Cutting through Spiritual Materialism* (1973), remain popular with many US Buddhists, regardless of their lineage or community. Moreover, through various publication ventures, including the magazines *Shambhala Sun* (now *Lion's Roar*) and *Buddhadharma: The Practitioner's Quarterly*, Shambhala has been a major contributor to the US Buddhist public discourse. And, finally, through the work and writing of popular teachers, a Shambhala approach to Buddhist practice has had widespread influence across North America, perhaps best illustrated by the work of Pema Chödrön.

Pema Chödrön, born Deirdre Blomfield-Brown in 1936, grew up on the East Coast but went to college at the University of California, Berkeley, during the 1960s. Following several personal crises, she spent time pursuing different religious and spiritual paths before being introduced to Buddhism and Chögyam Trungpa. By 1974 she had taken the novice vows of a nun, and by 1981 she was fully ordained as a *bhiksuni*, making her perhaps one of the first American women to be ordained in a Tibetan tradition. She remained apart or above the scandals surrounding her teacher through the 1980s and 1990s while traveling, speaking, and writing prolifically. By the beginning of the twenty-first century, she had become something of a brand in herself, with over a dozen best-selling books and a busy travel and teaching schedule. She is currently the resident teacher of Gampo Abbey (Haas 2013, 117ff; Koppedrayer 2002).

As mentioned in previous chapters, Buddhist monastic rules are codified in the *vinaya*, which at present is represented in three distinct traditions and their associated texts. Whereas the Theravada *vinaya* remains the standard in South and Southeast Asia, the Dharmaguptaka and Mulasarvastivada were exported into Central and East Asia. The *bhiksuni* lineage eventually died out in Theravada contexts; it is possible that it was never established in Tibet (Wilson 2012c, 264); but in East Asia, a lineage of *bhiksuni* has persisted, following the Dharmaguptaka *vinaya*. Establishing a new line of Mulasarvastivada nuns in Tibet has been difficult, to say the least, due to the requirement that a cohort of living nuns is needed to ordain new ones (Trinlae 2010). Pema Chödrön's ordination was made possible because she ordained as a Dharmaguptaka nun, a now common—though hardly universally accepted—solution to the problem of ordaining new *bhiksuni*. Since her ordination, other women have been similarly ordained, thus forwarding the cause of reinvigorating the female monastic line within Tibetan Buddhism.

Vajrayana and new religious movements

Vajrayana Buddhism has come to the United States primarily through Japanese immigration and the Tibetan diaspora, and in its Tibetan form has enjoyed widespread popularity. This popularity is the result of several factors, not the least of which is the ability of charismatic teachers to adapt traditions to a new cultural context and, arguably, the exotic appeal of Tibetan Buddhism and culture. The juxtaposition between Shinnyo-en and Shambhala International in this context provides a useful starting point for a conversation on new religious movements and the study of North American religions. New religious movements are largely glossed over or ignored completely within established academic disciplines, such as Buddhist studies, owing to their charismatic founders' divergences from traditional approaches and rearticulation of practices and doctrines in the service of an adaptation to or a rejection of modernity. In short, new religious movements are defined both by their vintage, their newness, and their own rejection of tradition.

Of course, newness, adaptation, and charisma are as likely to emerge within established religions as they are to come from outside. Michael Roach, an American-born Buddhist teacher ordained in the Gelug school, for example, has used his charisma to establish a new community in the deserts of Arizona. And whereas he was legitimated by the tradition for a time, revelations that he had violated monastic rules by marrying one of his students led the Dalai Lama to prevent him from teaching in Dharamsala. Eventually he and his wife divorced, and she married another student of Roach's who subsequently died of dehydration while meditating outside Roach's retreat center (Kaufman 2008; Santos 2012). That such tragedies are too often a common feature of new religious movements supports the argument that by treating them within the context of mainstream or established religions only serves to legitimate leaders who may be taking advantage of their followers.

It is worth noting, then, that scholarship on Shambhala International has tended to unproblematically include the community within the larger scope of US Tibetan Buddhism (Prebish 1999; Seager 1999) despite the fact that the group is new—newer in fact than many other Buddhist new religious movements—self-consciously adapts traditional practice to suit modern needs, and was founded by a charismatic leader whose actions caused harm within the community. This inclusion of Shambhala International into the category of Tibetan Buddhism normalizes the community, providing it a type of legitimation. To be clear, including Shambhala International within the larger scope of Vajrayana Buddhism should *not* be problematic; there is a clear continuity of practice and doctrine between Shambhala and its antecedents in Tibet, Vajrayana, and Mahayana. The characterization of Shambhala International as a normative part of Tibetan Buddhism while other new movements are excluded should raise in our minds questions about the categories we employ, the choices scholars make, to include some and exclude others from the broader categories of religion and Buddhism. Indeed, the question of what "counts" as a new religion or an established religion may not be as important as taking note of where the line is being drawn, who is drawing it, and based on what criteria.

DISCUSSION QUESTIONS

1. What accounts for the lack of scholarly research of popular interest in Japanese forms of esoteric Buddhism such as Shingon?

2. Despite the small number of ethnic Tibetans in the United States, Tibetan forms of Buddhism have become extremely popular and visible. Discuss the reasons for this popularity.

3. What defines a new religious movement? And how might new religious movements be legitimated as a natural outgrowth of an establish religion, on the one hand, or as a divergent cult on the other?

SUGGESTIONS FOR FURTHER READING

Chandler, Jeannine. 2015. "Invoking the Dharma Protector: Western Involvement in the Dorje Shugden Controversy." In *Buddhism beyond Borders*, ed. Scott A. Mitchell and Natalie E. F. Quli, 75–91. Albany: State University of New York Press.

Davidson, Ronald M. 2002. *Indian Esoteric Buddhism: A Social History of the Tantric Movement*. New York: Columbia University Press.

Kapstein, Matthew. 2000. *The Tibetan Assimilation of Buddhism: Conversion, Contestation, and Memory*. New York: Oxford University Press.

Payne, Richard K. 2005. "Hiding in Plain Sight: The Invisibility of the Shingon Mission to the United States." In *Buddhist Missionaries in the Era of Globalization*, ed. Linda Learman, 101–122. Honolulu: University of Hawai'i Press.

Payne, Richard K, ed. 2006. *Tantric Buddhism in East Asia*. Boston: Wisdom Publications.

Sperling, Elliot. 2004. "The Tibet-China Conflict: History and Polemics." *Policy Studies* 7.

Trinlae, Bhikṣuṇī Lozang. 2010. "The Mūlasarvāstivāda Bhikṣuṇī Has the Horns of a Rabbit: Why the Master's Tools Will Never Reconstruct the Master's House." *The Journal of Buddhist Ethics* 17: 311–331.

Wedemeyer, Christian K. 2013. *Making Sense of Tantric Buddhism: History, Semiology, and Transgression in the Indian Traditions*. New York: Columbia University Press.

8

Postmodern horizons?

Chapter summary and outline

The coming together of such a wide diversity of Buddhist communities, intermingling with American culture at large, has created opportunities for critical examination of received traditions and experimentation, manifesting in: non- and pan-sectarian Buddhist communities; Buddhist practices deployed into secular spaces; and online and virtual Buddhist practice and community. These streams overlap with established communities while signaling the emergence of potentially new traditions.

Introduction: From the modern to the postmodern
Non- and pan-sectarian Buddhist communities
Secularism and secular Buddhism
Online practice and online dissent
    Online practice
    Online dissent
Looking back, moving forward
Discussion questions
Suggestions for further reading

Introduction: From the modern to the postmodern

In 1543, Copernicus redrew the solar system, displacing the earth from its center. The geocentric solar system was an expression of a broader premodern European Christian cosmology that claimed the earth as being at the center of a universe divinely created primarily for human ends where the Church acted as intercessor between humanity and divinity, between the secular and the sacred. Copernicus' displacement of the earth, then, was reflective of a larger displacement of religion in the modern era, the rise of scientific rationalism, and secular nation states (Chapter 2). The premodern, geocentric worldview is a grand narrative or meta-narrative, a way of explaining the universe both on the macro- and micro-levels from the cosmic and sacred to the ordinary and everyday. This geocentric worldview was displaced by a heliocentric one—the modern. In many ways, however, the modern view is also a meta-narrative, or rather, a series of meta-narratives, grounded in scientific rationalism that sought to explain the world largely in reference to empirically provable natural law. This methodology, originally trained on the external physical world, was eventually used to study humanity itself through, first, the biological sciences (e.g., Darwin's *Origin of Species*) and later history and the social sciences. Eventually, a blind appeal to scientific rationalism and natural law itself became critiqued, giving rise to the postmodern, an era in which meta-narratives—including narratives about human progress and history—have come to be seen as arbitrary, as much a product of human invention as premodern myths. Postmodernity, then, can be defined as the critical rejection of grand narratives that seek to organize human knowledge and experience by relying on a single system or heuristic to account for everything while at the same time culturally and historically relativizing truth claims and ethical values.

One reason for the development of postmodern sensibilities is the awareness of difference. Grand narratives held sway in premodern cultures owing their relative isolation from one another. The modern period, and with it colonialism and later globalization, brought cultures into contact with one another, highlighting cultural difference and relativity. One response to cultural difference was a tendency toward perennialism, an attempt to reconcile difference by the imposition of sameness. This tendency eventually gave way to an acceptance and even celebration of diversity that has become a hallmark of pluralism in the United States. Of course, pluralism itself can be contested: how do we live with difference? How do we engage religious practice when there are competing traditions? What are appropriate articulations or interpretations of one's tradition for a contemporary context? And these questions often give rise to different modes of religious practice and the formation of new religious communities.

In this chapter, we will explore some potential future trajectories of the US Buddhist tradition as it responds to diversity and the postmodern condition. Such responses include: the formation of non-sectarian and pan-sectarian Buddhist communities; an engagement with secularism and embrace of nonreligious forms of spiritual practice; the application of Buddhist practices to psychotherapeutic ends; and the extension of these discourses and communities into online and virtual worlds. Whereas the preceding three chapters dealt with modern US Buddhist communities classically defined, and whereas Chapter 12 will examine Buddhist modernism as a discursive and methodological frame, our focus here will be on those communities of practice that, while informed by modern trends, at times self-identify as "postmodern" (Gleig 2014), or even "post-Buddhist" (cf McMahan 2002)—a signal of something new. These potential Buddhist horizons, potentially new traditions or mere passing fads, both exist within and transcend classically defined Buddhist schools. Thus, a focus on them apart from the tripartite division of Theravada-Mahayana-Vajrayana will help illuminate their unique characteristics.

Non- and pan-sectarian Buddhist communities

One response to the reality of cultural and religious diversity is a tendency toward universalism or perennialism. Nineteenth-century movements such as Theosophy sought to reconcile differences between religious traditions by claiming an underlying, metaphysical and ahistorical truth that unified apparent differences. Others laid the blame for diversity within Buddhism to sectarian divisions of one sort or another, and throughout the twentieth century we find numerous examples of pan-sectarian Buddhist groups. Such organizations generally appeal to the possibility that there lies at the heart of the Buddha's teachings some essential core that has been obscured by cultural adaptations over the centuries and argue for a return to this essence while minimizing what are thought to be surface-level differences. Such arguments can be made in the face of larger, political concerns, such as those we saw in Chapter 3 with second-generation Japanese American Buddhist youth groups who wanted to distance themselves from the sectarian organizations of their parents during World War II internment. Pan-sectarian orientations can also be woven into sectarian schools. Shambhala International is arguably sectarian to the extent that is a clearly defined Buddhist lineage; at the same time, however, its practices are derived from a variety of Buddhist traditions thus giving it a pan-sectarian feel. More recently, other groups, communities, and loosely defined movements have situated themselves as expressly pan- or non-sectarian, thus filling a niche in the US Buddhist landscape.

Examples of such communities include the Buddhist Peace Fellowship, of which more will be said in Chapter 11. Begun in 1978 in Hawai'i by, among others, Robert

FIGURE 24 *Robert Baker Aitken, 1917–2010. (Photo courtesy Robin Scanlon.)*

Aitken (Figure 24), Anne Hopkins Aitken, and Ryo Imamura, the founders were originally concerned about nuclear proliferation and American militarism. Over the course of the 1980s, the organization relocated to Berkeley, California, opened dozens of chapters across North America, and engaged in a wide array of largely progressive political activities from antiwar and antinuclear weapons protests to prison outreach and support to those living with HIV/AIDS. Whereas most of the founders were from Mahayana Buddhist traditions, the community was inspired by a wide range of Buddhist thinkers and perspectives and came to embrace a diversity of practice traditions. The Buddhist Peace Fellowship is part of a global socially engaged Buddhist movement that sees engagement with political and environmental suffering as a form of practice in itself, and is inspired by Buddhist activists such as Thich Nhat Hanh and Sulak Sivaraksa.

The Oakland, California, East Bay Meditation Center (EBMC) is another example of a pan-sectarian community responding to larger, social and political trends. Many so-called convert communities, especially in the Zen, Insight Meditation, and convert-Tibetan traditions, have attracted a largely white, middle-class demographic. Buddhism, however, appeals to a much wider cross-section of the population, and some Buddhists from historically marginalized populations (women, people of color, LGBTQI) have felt out of place in communities founded or led by predominately middle-class white Americans. Responding to these concerns, a group of San Francisco-based Buddhists came together in the early 2000s to create a new community with the express purpose of being a safe practice space for diverse populations of Buddhist traditions, ethnicities, abilities, genders and sexual identities. Many of the EBMC's teachers come from the Spirit Rock community—and Jack Kornfield is listed as a teacher on the community's website—though it is by no means a purely Theravada or insight meditation-based community. Teachers come from Zen, Shambhala, and Tibetan practice traditions unified by the shared desire for inclusivity. One way this manifests is exemplified by the Alphabet Sangha, a *vipasyana* sitting group for LGBTQI Buddhists that regularly meets at the EBMC. Whereas the San Francisco Bay Area is home to a number of gay and lesbian Buddhist groups and meditation centers, JD Doyle, one of the Alphabet Sangha's founders, was frustrated by these groups' general lack of diversity. Together with Larry Yang, she established the LGBTQI group to be "more reflective of the racial, sexual, and gender diversity of the queer community in Oakland … an intentionality to move beyond the heterogeneous white, middle-class demographic that characterized other LGBTQI *sanghas* in the Bay Area" (Gleig 2012a, 205). We will spend more time discussing LGBTQI Buddhism generally in Chapter 11; for now, it is worth noting that queer theory is one way in which US Buddhists critique the received tradition of Buddhism and Buddhist institutions, here perceived as being exclusive of (and therefore causing suffering to) a segment of the population. In response, then, the EBMC manifests as a pan-sectarian or non-sectarian community in juxtaposition to classically defined Buddhist schools of practice.

A final example of a non-sectarian Buddhist movement is Against the Stream, founded by Noah Levine. Son of Buddhist and spiritual teachers Stephan and Ondrea Levine, Levine was deeply troubled in his youth, abusing drugs and alcohol, and spending several years incarcerated. By the early 2000s, he had left that part of his life behind while embracing the *vipasyana* -based meditation practices he learned from Jack Kornfield, Ajahn Amaro, and his father, also a meditation instructor, establishing his Los Angeles-based meditation center in 2008. The community has a large network of related organizations across North America, connected via the Internet and united by an interest in both Buddhist meditation practices and punk or alternative rock and subaltern cultures and movements. By explicitly connecting his recovery from substance abuse as well as overcoming violent and destructive behavior to his

Hardcore dharma

FIGURE 25 *Brad Warner, b. 1964. (Photo from Doubtboy/Wikimedia Commons/ CC-BY-SA-3.0)*

Noah Levine is one of several North American Buddhist teachers who have infused their practice with a punk rock ethos. Another well-known teacher is Brad Warner, born in 1964 in Ohio. As a teenager and young man, Warner played bass for the punk bands Zero Defex and Dementia 13 while studying Zen before moving to Japan in the 1990s where he ordained as a priest in the Soto Zen Buddhist tradition. Author of several books, including *Hardcore Zen: Punk Rock, Monster Movies & the Truth About Reality* (2003) and *Sex, Sin, and Zen: A Buddhist Exploration of Sex from Celibacy to Polyamory and Everything in Between* (2010), Warner has maintained a popular blog since 2006 and contributed essays to the softcore pornographic website Suicide Girls.

meditation practice, Levine makes plain the connection between Buddhist practice and psychotherapeutic practice. Unlike mindfulness-based secular therapies we will see later in this chapter, the Against the Stream community can still be read as essentially Buddhist in orientation as their stated objective is "to make the teachings of the Buddha available to all who are interested," while being in the process of "founding a new tradition, one inspired and influenced by all the wisdom and compassion teachings of all of the Buddhist traditions."[1] Though Levine was trained in the *vipasyana* tradition, Against the Stream self-consciously distances itself from other insight meditation communities as well as Theravada while pushing the boundaries of Buddhism itself by incorporating the language of recovery programs, psychotherapy, and punk rock culture (cf Schedneck 2014).

The East Bay Meditation Center and Against the Stream are both heavily indebted to the *vipasyana* meditation movement more generally and Spirit Rock Meditation Center specifically. As such, they could arguably be seen as part of a continuum of practice traditions within the broader category of Theravada. However, they also embrace practices and teachers from a variety of lineages and traditions and self-consciously refrain from aligning themselves with a traditionally defined Theravada or Mahayana community. At the very least, their divergence from classically defined schools complicates traditional sectarian divisions. That both communities are heavily indebted to the *vipasyana* meditation movement, however, brings us to our next topic of consideration: the spread of mindfulness practices outside of Buddhism proper.

Secularism and secular Buddhism

As Taylor (2011) and others have noted, the term "secular," despite its ubiquity in contemporary public discourse, has a long and complicated history that reveals its shifting set of meanings. Originally from the Latin, "secular" referred to "this century," roughly meaning, concerning current events and times. In premodern Christian Europe, the term was meant to juxtapose mundane and sacred time: mundane time referred to the world we live in on a daily basis, immanent and secular; sacred time was transcendent, divine, and the purview of the Church. Moving forward through the Enlightenment up to the present day, areas of social and cultural life that used to be the domain of the Church gradually shifted over to the domain of the secular, the most obvious example of which would be the clear separation of church and state (i.e., religion and politics) encoded in the First Amendment to the US Constitution. In common discourse, secular then most often refers to the nonreligious, which in the American case can refer to both matters of the public and the state (as opposed to the private and the personal) as well as an orientation that seeks to either diminish religion's importance or invalidate its truth claims in their entirety, as is the case with the so-called new atheists such as Richard Dawkins and Sam Harris. (Harris, it should be noted, has been largely forgiving of Buddhist meditation while being highly critical of Buddhism-as-religion, best seen in his 2014 book *Waking Up: A Guide to Spirituality Without Religion*).

What were once solely Buddhist/religious practices have, over the last few decades, slowly begun to shift from the religious to the secular—the clearest example of which has been the deployment of meditation practices into secular settings. Since the latter half of the twentieth century, many prominent teachers in the insight meditation movement (Chapter 5) have also been licensed therapists and psychologists. This convergence of interests—the spiritual and the psychological—has led some to explore the possibility of using Buddhist-derived meditation techniques in psychotherapeutic contexts, with mindfulness meditation and the work of Jon Kabat-Zinn being perhaps the most well known. Kabat-Zinn's mindfulness-based stress reduction program borrows from both meditation retreat and group therapy models; programs are generally conducted over an eight-week period where participants meet regularly and do the practices on their own while directing their mindfulness practice to managing chronic pain and reducing stress (Gilpin 2008). Thus, the program is exclusively therapeutic in nature, having moved entirely from the religious to the secular (Wilson 2014). While the specifics of each program may vary, most in one way or another refer back to Kabat-Zinn's (or other related researcher's) work and view mindfulness as "a way of being in which one is highly aware and focused on the reality of the present moment, accepting and acknowledging it, without getting caught up in the thoughts that are about the situation or emotional reactions to the situation" (Bush 2011, 188).

Whereas Kabat-Zinn's program was originally designed to be used for chronic pain management and stress reduction, since the 1980s the popularity of mindfulness and its application to other contexts has grown exponentially (Williams and Kabat-Zinn 2011). The deployment of mindfulness into secular settings dovetails with larger modernist discourses that tout the physical and emotional benefits of meditation, supported by scientific study, a discourse that has been especially important in the development of US Buddhism (Chapter 12). Apart from hospitals and clinical settings, mindfulness programs can now be found in corporate and business settings, prisons and the military, and public schools. A number of organizations in the United States, Canada, the United Kingdom, and elsewhere have begun promoting mindfulness practices in schools, including the Mindfulness in Schools Project, Mindful Schools, and the Inner Kids Program. Oakland-based Mindful Schools, for example, offers professional training—"to teach children how to focus, manage their emotions, handle their stress, and resolve conflicts"—in-class instruction, and other resources to support mindfulness in education and sees itself on the forefront of integrating mindfulness into education.[2] Whereas by and large these organizations have taken great care to distance themselves from Buddhism by suggesting that mindfulness is a universal practice or that the practice has been sufficiently secularized, other promoters of secular mindfulness blur the boundary between its religious and nonreligious senses, with some making the claim that inserting mindfulness into public spaces is a kind of "stealth Buddhism," a way to bring the Buddha's teachings to a new cultural context without the overtly religious aspects of the tradition (Brown 2015). There may be legal consequences to this rhetorical strategy of linking and simultaneously distancing an educational program from its historically Buddhist roots given the United States' separation of church and state. If court cases involving the use of Transcendental Meditation or yoga in US public schools are any indication, tracing a link between mindfulness and Buddhism may be enough to bring a suit against these programs by those who see the practice as inextricably bound up with religion and therefore inappropriate in a public school (Chananie 1982).[3]

The critique of mindfulness in public schools on the basis of a First Amendment violation has only just begun to receive much attention; other critiques have been much more well articulated over the past several years. And whereas some commentators have viewed these critiques as polarizing—with the assumption that people are either wholly and uncritically supportive of mindfulness and its benefits or wholly and too-critically against mindfulness—the debate has nevertheless been far-reaching, nuanced, and thoughtful. Whereas neuroscientists, therapists, and the scientific community have found mindfulness and meditation to be both a useful tool in treating a range of cognitive disorders and a fascinating subject of research for helping us better understand neuro-processes, Buddhists, scholars, and activists have argued for both a more substantive ethical awareness as well as a deeper appreciation of the social and cultural contexts in which these practices are enacted. Whereas a twenty-first-century American woman, married with children and working a full-time job and a first-century Buddhist monk may be engaged in a similar or even identical practice, we cannot assume that this practice has the same meaning for these two persons, even if the practice—and its consequent neurological processes—appear identical (McMahan 2015b). Social and cultural location shapes meaning; if nothing else, it determines the uses to which such practices are put (religious versus therapeutic) and the values we ascribe to them. This is what is meant by "corporatist spirituality" (Payne 2014), the argument that once mindfulness becomes stripped of anything overtly religious, it may be embedded in a different context (e.g., the corporate world of business) where it can be used to serve the interests of this new context, primarily a practice one can adopt to be a happier, healthier, and more productive worker (cf Purser and Loy 2013). Such critiques seek not to discredit the project of secular mindfulness practices (nor to discredit their benefits) but to examine the specific ways in which Buddhism is adapted to and shaped by its North American cultural contexts.

Wilson (2014) has argued that mindfulness' ability to transcend the confines of religion and become an acceptable mode of practice is one way that Buddhism has adapted itself to an American cultural milieu, something Buddhism always does as it moves from culture to culture. This may be true; however, it is worth noting that mindfulness practices are often decontextualized to the point where their association with Buddhism is completely removed, raising the question of whether or not "Buddhism" will survive this process of adaptation. Moreover, the process of deploying a Buddhist term into non-Buddhist contexts is certainly not new; the proliferation of "Mindfulness and the Art of ..." books one finds today on Amazon.com was preceded by a wealth of "Zen and the Art of ..." books in bookstores in the 1980s (Yamada 2009). In other words, it is difficult to know whether the proliferation of mindfulness in North American culture today is a harbinger of Buddhist things to come or is merely a passing fad.

Nevertheless, if mindfulness-based practices have been thoroughly secularized, does this necessarily mean that Buddhism has been secularized? One straight-forward example of secular Buddhism would be the appropriately named Secular Buddhist Association which seeks to promote a "natural, pragmatic approach to early Buddhist teachings and practice." The organization, which began as an online podcast, has gained support from Buddhist teacher and scholar Stephan Batchelor, well known for his books *Buddhism without Beliefs* and *Confessions of a Buddhist Atheist*. Batchelor's oeuvre essentially makes the claim that the Buddha taught a path to awakening that can be achieved without relying on belief or faith in super-natural states or mythologies, including reincarnation, celestial beings, or rote ritual. The Secular Buddhist Association makes use of a similar logic in claiming that secular Buddhism "has no dependency on assertions not in evidence, it is based solely on that which can be verified in the natural world," and that since reincarnation has not been scientifically proven, "like the claims of other religions which cannot be verified by any known means, can be set aside."[4]

Advocates of a secular approach to Buddhist practice make the claim that this approach speaks to the particular needs of the modern West, thus it can be read as an outgrowth of Buddhist modernism while simultaneously critiquing modernity and returning to the origins of Buddhism. Higgins (2012), for example, notes that Buddhist modernism arose in the colonial era, in part, as a way to deflect European Christian missionary work in Asia. He argues that in the process of modernizing, traditional authority structures remained to carry on the tradition in the contemporary world, and these structures, in particular the patriarchal hegemony of male monastics, are funda-mentally incongruent with the contemporary modern West. Secular Buddhism, in turn, "leans toward … a discourse and set of practices in aid of full human flourishing, one that disavows superhuman agencies and supernatural processes" (111). This is made possible, in part, by returning to the original teachings of the Buddha,which Higgins claims have been obscured by later commentaries and orthodoxy. Batchelor echoes these themes. He notes that "traditional Buddhism"—which for him means any form of Buddhism that "operates within the soteriological worldview of ancient India" (2012, 89)—is separated from us by a cultural gap so wide that it is anathema to the contem-porary West. Not even "Buddhist modernism" can overcome this divide, and we are thus in need of something new, a "Buddhism 2.0." This new Buddhism will be better able to fit the time in which we now live, our own secular age. Batchelor notes that the British National Health Service has begun offering mindfulness practices, hence what was once the purview of religion has shifted to the arena of the state, a move he clearly believes to be a good one since we no longer live in ancient India. He critiques later generations of Buddhists as having wrongly asserted that they have preserved, intact, the original teachings of the Buddha; ironically, however, he and other secular-ists seem to be attempting to recover the original teachings of the Buddha by focusing solely on the Pali canon. Batchelor writes

I need to be alert to the tendency of falling into the very trap that I am critiquing. The more I am seduced by the force of my own arguments, the more I am tempted to imagine that my secular version of Buddhism is what the Buddha originally taught, which the traditional schools have either lost sight of or distorted. This would be a mistake; for it is impossible to read the historical Buddha's mind in order to know what he "really" meant or intended. At the same time, each generation has the right and duty to re-interpret the teachings that it has inherited. (Batchelor 2012, 90)

The quest for origins

Does it matter whether or not we can know what the historical Buddha *really* taught? Does "history" mean the same thing in classical Buddhism and the contemporary West? Recall from Chapter 1 that biographies of the Buddha go out of their way to note that Sakyamuni was not the first Buddha but simply the latest in a long line of Buddhas stretching back innumerable eons. The assumption that religions have historical founders is a decidedly recent and arguably Protestant one. Largely in response to Enlightenment-era rational empiricism that challenged the validity of religious truth claims, Christian thinkers began using scientific methods to explore Christian history by searching for empirical evidence supportive of Biblical stories. A correlation was then made between historical fact and religious truth. Once this way of framing religion became normalized, it was applied to other world religions—Buddhism is a religion; religions have founders; the founder of Buddhism is the historical Buddha. Identifying which teachings are of the historical Buddha is then used as a means to legitimize these teachings for a modern, Western context. However, until the modern period, this was rarely the concern of Buddhists themselves who would have had a wholly different understanding of their tradition and its relationship to history. We need to be attentive, then, to the ways in which our own cultural assumptions frame our understanding of different religions and cultures.

As we will see, this critique of being able to know what the Buddha "really" meant while at the same time suggesting that there is some truth to be found in the Pali canon that is relevant today is a complicated and contested argument. Nevertheless, it is precisely this type of rejection of modernity and reappropriation of tradition that lies at the heart of the postmodern critique outlined above. And while it is difficult to assess from this vantage point whether or not the Secular Buddhist Association is a fully functioning community or a loose association of like-minded individuals who happen to be engaged in a particular secular discourse via an Internet discussion site, it is worth noting the following. First, the Secular Buddhist Association was founded by Ted Meissner, who is based in Minnesota, with teachers coming from across the United States and Canada; Batchelor is based in the United Kingdom; and Higgins is based in Australia, thus suggesting that the secular Buddhist discourse is one of concern across the Anglophone West while directing our attention to ways in which the Internet creates translocal and global discourse. Which brings us to our second point: online communities have become increasingly relevant in the development of US Buddhism, and in some cases such online community-building has measurable effects offline, as we will see in the following section.

Online practice and online dissent

Strictly speaking, the Internet is merely a collection of networked computers (both massive server farms in remote locations and the smart phone in your bag) and the information (everything from bank statements to pictures of cats) residing on and between those computers. Defining what the Internet is, however, may not be as important as recognizing how we talk *about* the Internet, especially as to how this reveals its importance in the development of US Buddhism. In general, it may be fair to say that we talk about the Internet either as a tool or as a location. As a tool, we might say that we *use* email or chat or social network messaging for the purpose of communication; and as a communication tool, its texts (blogs, podcasts, websites, and so forth) function much in the same way as books, print media, radio, and television (Chapter 9). Second, we refer to the Internet as a location. We *visit* a website, say, or "surf the net." The sense of location is reinforced by the common assumption that people behave differently on the Internet than they do in the "real world" or "meatspace." Since the emergence of usenet groups and text-only chat rooms more than three decades ago, people have discussed the importance of netiquette, the idea that one should have good manners in online spaces. And the more recent concerns about online bullying, trolls, and other forms of harassment often betray the sense that "people are different" online.

Both of these senses, of course, imply a fundamental distinction between online and offline, a sense that there is some demarcation between the virtual world of the Internet and the reality of meatspace. Slater (2002) and others, however, have long noted that this distinction is arbitrary and that we should pay more attention to where the line is drawn (and who is drawing it) rather than the line itself. For example, depositing a check into your bank account, whether via a real person or a smart phone, is irrelevant; these are merely two ways of telling the same networked system to move a value of money from one account to another. Bullying did not manifest with the invention of the Internet but rather bullies employ the Internet as a new tool in their arsenal. Leaving aside the philosophical debate about the "realness" of the Internet (or meatspace, for that matter), it is clear that US Buddhists, like Buddhists the world over, have been both using and practicing on the Internet since its inception (Hubbard 1995; Prebish 1999). In short, US Buddhist practice—and whole communities—extend from the real world of meatspace to the virtual worlds of online spaces and the Internet, from community-building to the construction of new communities to engaging in discourses of dissent.

Online practice

One of the clearest examples of community-building on the Internet may be found in the Buddhist Geeks, a podcast founded in 2007 by former Naropa University students Vincent Horn, Ryan Oelke, and Gwen Bell. Buddhist Geeks was started with the explicit purpose of having conversations about the intersection of Buddhist practice and twenty-first-century culture, especially as it related to Generation X and millennial Buddhists who they believed were not well represented in mainstream Buddhist media. Over time, it became clear that their podcast was more than merely a show and was becoming a movement; in 2011 they hosted the first Buddhist Geeks conference which attracted over a hundred participants and some mainstream media attention. Buddhist Geeks employs discourses that perpetuate while critique modernist approaches to Buddhist practice. On the one hand, the show replicates modern fascination with science and technology and hopes to reimagine Buddhism for contemporary Western audiences; on the other hand, to the extent it represents a primarily younger demographic, the Buddhist Geeks podcast also openly critiques Baby Boomer generation Buddhists who helped popularize current mainstream modern Buddhist rhetoric (Gleig 2014). Regardless of how well Buddhist Geeks' hosts and guests are able to distance themselves from earlier generations or are merely replicating existing modernist discourses, what is clear is that Horn and his colleagues manifested a real-world community by mobilizing online connections. This use of the Internet is not unique to the Buddhist Geeks (or Buddhists themselves); for example, a long-running Twitter hashtag, #OMCru or online meditation crew, was used as a means of connecting solitary Buddhists via the Internet. By coordinating practice periods, Buddhists at a distance from one another would use the hashtag as a means of signaling the beginning and end of a meditation period without being in the same physical location, thereby creating a virtual and temporary community. (The hashtag seems to have fallen into disuse and is most often, as of this writing, associated with a Twitter account selling a meditation timer app for smart phones.)

The #OMCru hashtag represents one way that Buddhists use Internet technology to connect online while practicing in the real world. Taking this to the next logical step is the case of Buddhist meditation centers in the virtual world of Second Life (Figure 26). Second Life is, in some respects, a massive multiplayer online role-playing game; however, unlike other games of this genre like World of Warcraft, Second Life has no end goal or in-game system of rewards and quests. Rather, Second Life is a virtual world filled with user-generated virtual content. Participants create a virtual likeness of themselves, an avatar, which is free to move about the world and collect in-game money which can then be used to purchase upgrades in clothing or build in-game artifacts including buildings and whole cities. Buddhists moved into Second Life early on, constructed temples, practice spaces, and meditation centers where participants can engage in Buddhist rituals, listen to dharma talks, and meditate. Researchers have recently taken this new practice seriously, using Second Life as an anthropological field site and have begun

FIGURE 26 *Yordie Sands' Zen Garden inside Second Life.*

to examine what it means to practice Buddhism online. For some, the motivation may be to connect with others, especially when one is at a distance from any real-world Buddhist community. For others, it is a natural extension of their Buddhist practice, another landscape in which to engage with the teachings of the Buddha and the distinction between real world and virtual world is meaningless (Connelly 2012; Grieve 2015).

Merely using technology in the service of Buddhist practice may not be particularly remarkable; religion has always mediated, and as we will see in the next chapter, mediation changes how religion is practiced. However, new media technologies make possible not only new modes of communication but new virtual worlds, worlds that shape Buddhist practice and community formation in ways that we are only now beginning to appreciate (Grieve and Veidlinger 2015). Had Buddhist Geeks, for example, remained a podcast, the show could effectively be read as text, as another example of Buddhist media akin to a print magazine. However, at some point the show developed into something more—a community, one that exists primarily via online communication rather than the real world. It is worth noting that this movement aligns itself with younger Buddhists and overlaps in interesting ways with postmodern technoscience, hybrid and even cyborg discourses pointing toward potential future vistas for Buddhist practice and community.

Online dissent

Whereas Twitter hashtags and Second Life may not be particularly pervasive activities across the US Buddhist landscape, generally engaging in online communication almost certainly is. There are, at present, literally thousands of US-based Buddhist bloggers and website owners inclusive of real-world communities and solo practition- ers, to say nothing of Buddhist groups making use of larger social networks such as Facebook, all of which extend real-world Buddhist activity to the online realm. These online communication spaces, in turn, often function as a platform for Buddhist dis- courses of dissent.

Consider, as a beginning, David Chapman who has critiqued—on his personal blog, in Buddhist Geeks podcast episodes and conferences—what he labels "Consensus Buddhism," a particular kind of approach to Buddhist practice popularized by largely white American converts in the 1960s and 1970s and aligned predominately with the insight meditation and Zen movements. Consensus Buddhism finds expression in mainstream Buddhist media—magazines such as *Tricycle: The Buddhist Review*, *Shambhala Sun*, and their related online and publishing projects—which cater to this same demographic (Padgett 2000). The term "consensus," for Chapman, refers to a general lack of debate or critique within these forms of Buddhism which, in an effort at inclusion where everyone feels comfortable, dissent from normative points of view is actively discouraged. This rhetorical move then imposes a type of hegemony of Buddhist understanding that silences divergent viewpoints and is actually exclusive rather than inclusive. By discouraging alternate points of view, Consensus Buddhism then stifles creative adaptions or innovations to practice to the extent that they diverge from mainstream Buddhist normative understandings (Chapman 2011; Gleig 2014, 24).

Another version of this critique is the even broader category of "x-Buddhism" which has been the subject of analysis by the contributors to the blog "Speculative Non-Buddhism." Founded in 2011 by Buddhist scholar Glenn Wallis and later joined by several other Buddhist thinkers, contributors seek to critically analyze the ideological underpinnings of x-Buddhism, a term that refers to virtually all forms of Buddhism from the historical to the contemporary—"from *a* (atheist) through *m* (Mahayana) to *z* (Zen)" (Wallis 2012a). The project intends to focus its attention on the "x" rather than the "Buddhism" in order to reveal how the various strands of the tradition are culturally and historically specific—even and especially those forms in the contempor- ary world. Popular US Buddhist teachers such as Ken McLeod and Brad Warner are regularly challenged on their assumptions, and even the widely respected Thich Nhat Hanh has been the subject of critique. It is worth drawing our attention here to a series of posts that critique Batchelor and the Secular Buddhist Association wherein Wallis raises several concerns about (especially Batchelor's) secular turn. Whereas secular- ism, as we've seen, can refer to many things, Batchelor renders it as simply referring to the times in which we now live and suggests that the historical Buddha's original teachings—stripped of anything that may have been later added to the canon—can speak directly to the human condition in the present. Wallis notes that this is essen- tially an article of faith; if the soteriological worldview of ancient India infuses all later forms of Buddhism, surely that same worldview was at work in the Buddha's mind as he taught the dharma. According to Wallis, for Batchelor and other secular Buddhists, "The dharma is unconditioned. It is not the product of any century, particularly not of that century in which its creator (discoverer?) lived. It is timeless" (Wallis 2012b). There is no way to empirically prove the claim that the dharma is ahistorical or acultural (i.e., "not the product of any century") because we have no direct access to the teachings of the Buddha apart from the historically and culturally created tradition that followed him and passed the dharma down to us in the present. Because our understandings of the world are necessarily culturally constructed, we can only conclude that either the Buddha's teachings were also culturally constructed or that his teachings are akin to the law of gravity—something that is true regardless of whether or not we believe it or are even aware that such a law has been expressed. Thus, there is something deeply ironic about an interpretation of Buddhism that rejects ancient cultural world views while postulating that teachings first promulgated in the ancient world remain relevant two-and-a-half thousand years later.

The Speculative Non-Buddhism blog was extremely active for several years with posts regularly generating hundreds of comments and topics being picked up across the Buddhist web. It should be mentioned that much of this conversation was intentionally antagonistic, and the blog received more critique about its methods than its arguments. By 2014, Wallis had stopped posting regularly, but the overall project has continued in other forums, blogs, and websites as well as both the online journal *non + x* and a book-length collection of essays, *Cruel Theory | Sublime Practice*.

Blogs have long been a tool to critique the status quo, something the Angry Asian Buddhist has been doing since 2008. Writing under the name "arunlikhati," this anonymous blogger began writing about Asian American Buddhists on a blog called "Dharma Folk" before beginning a stand-alone blog to address issues of Asian American Buddhist representation. Whereas Chapman's critique against Consensus Buddhism merely hinted at issues of race and racism, for arunlikhati these become foregrounded. His (or perhaps her)[5] central critique has been that mainstream Buddhist media has generally marginalized Asian American Buddhists who have both been primarily responsible for bringing Buddhism to the United States and outnumber non-Asians significantly. That magazines such as *Tricycle*, *Shambhala Sun*, and others routinely publish articles primarily by white Americans marginalizes the contributions of Asian Americans. For a period of time between 2008 and 2012, arunlikhati was extremely active and engaged in discourses and debates on a number of websites eventually being profiled on *Tricycle's* own blog where he drew a connection between the "perpetual foreigner" stereotype and the representation of Asian American Buddhists in mainstream Buddhist discourses:

people tell us that we are different. For example, people ask me where I'm from, and I tell them. And then they ask, "Where are you really from?" I say, "What do you mean by that?" And they're always telling me, "You look Chinese," or "You look Japanese." I am a fourth generation San Franciscan! Why would these people ask me that when these very people might be first generation San Franciscans? ... There's a tendency in the Buddhist community to associate American with white, and immigrant with Asian.[6]

As we will see in the following chapters, the issue of who "represents" US Buddhism is not to be taken lightly. According to an oft-quoted Pew Forum survey on religion in the United States, white American Buddhists outnumber Asian American Buddhists by 53 percent to 32 percent (Lugo 2008). The survey has been the subject of critique by both US Buddhists and Buddhist scholars who noted its many limitations regarding how it counted Buddhists. First, by conducting the survey only in the continental United States, it missed Buddhists in Hawai'i, the state with the largest per capita Buddhist population. Moreover, the telephone survey was only available in English and Spanish, thus overlooking Asian Americans who may speak any one of a dozen different languages and are also practicing Buddhists. Thus, the survey grossly undercounted Asian American Buddhists, effectively rendering them invisible. A subsequent survey on Asian American religion more generally found that the original numbers were incorrect, that the demographic split should be upwards of 69 percent Asian American (Lugo and Cooperman 2012). Interestingly, two years earlier, using US Census data and simple math, arunlikhati estimated that 62 percent of American Buddhists are Asian.[7]

Looking back, moving forward

Modern Buddhism was forged in the colonial contexts of Asia. It was here that Buddhist reformers made explicit attempts to adapt the tradition, revitalize it, and make it relevant in the turbulent times of the early modern period. These were the Buddhisms that found their way into North America, as an intellectual object of study for Western consumption, carried along with immigrants making new homes, and shared with seekers and pilgrims throughout the twentieth century. As a result, there is a tremendous diversity and pluralism of Buddhist traditions, lineages, and communities in the United States at present, a plethora of approaches that has become embedded within the larger diversity of American religion and culture. Such diversity is a challenge. Cultural relativism raises questions about how to live, how to engage religious practice, and how to be moral in the seeming absence of absolute values or norms. It may also be an opportunity for experimentation, a space in which the old can be critiqued in favor of the new—new forms of religious community and approaches to practice can be tested, adopted, and abandoned.

The topics under consideration in this chapter thus represent both potentially new articulations of the Buddhist tradition that may (or may not) manifest as wholly new traditions as well as developmental issues facing Buddhists as they navigate the intersection of modernity, secularity, American culture, and Buddhist history. Some of these movements will have staying power, will continue to gain momentum, and become the established traditions of the future. Others will be absorbed into already existing Buddhist lineages or even broader secular discourses, mere apparitions in a larger historical narrative. Still others will vanish completely as media and communication technologies change or become displaced by the next new thing.

Beneath these trends and fads, however, are perhaps more fundamental questions about who we are as persons of different ethnic, gender, and sexual identities, who must live together both in Buddhist communities and in the culture at large. The preceding chapters discussing broad historical trends (part one) and rough outlines of US Buddhist traditions (part two) thus provide us with the foundation for the road ahead, an exploration of these more fundamental questions.

DISCUSSION QUESTIONS

1. Discuss how a pan- or non-sectarian Buddhist tradition is different from a classically defined Buddhist lineage. How is it the same?
2. How might Buddhist practice be transformed by its enactment in online spaces or in virtual worlds? How might Buddhism be transformed by its enactment in secular spaces?
3. How have Buddhists used the Internet to challenge and critique mainstream discourses about Buddhism, religion, race, and representation?

SUGGESTIONS FOR FURTHER READING

Batchelor, Stephen. 2012. "A Secular Buddhism." *Journal of Global Buddhism.* 13: 87–107.

Gleig, Ann. 2014. "From Buddhist Hippies to Buddhist Geeks: The Emergence of Buddhist Postmodernism?" *Journal of Global Buddhism.* 13: 129–146.

Grieve, Gregory P., and Daniel M. Veidlinger, eds. 2015. *Buddhism, the Internet, and Digital Media: The Pixel in the Lotus.* New York: Routledge.

Schedneck, Brooke. 2014. "Noah Levine: Punk Rocker and Buddhist Meditation Teacher." In *Buddhists: Understanding Buddhism Through the Lives of Practitioners*, ed. Todd Lewis, 107–114. West Sussex: Wiley Blackwell.

Taylor, Charles. 2011. "Western Secularity." In *Rethinking Secularism*, ed. Craig J. Calhoun, Mark Juergensmeyer, and Jonathan VanAntwerpen, ix, 311. New York: Oxford University Press.

Wilson, Jeff. 2014. *Mindful America: The Mutual Transformation of Buddhist Meditation and American Culture.* New York: Oxford University Press.

PART THREE

Frames

FIGURE 27 *Kathina preparations at the American Buddhist Seminary, Sacramento, California. (Photo courtesy Natalie Quli.)*

9

Buddhist medias: Art, practice, and representation

Chapter summary and outline

Religion is necessarily mediated. In ritual and practice, in communicating ideas and expressing selves, Buddhists employ a range of media from texts to music to fashion and, in the contemporary world, art, film, popular music and literature. The convergence of Buddhism and Western culture has allowed for new Buddhist media expressions as well as the potential for Buddhist arts to filter into not-Buddhist spaces drawing our attention to genre and category—what is Buddhist art? Attention is also given to cultural appropriation and the commercialization of Buddhist media.

Introduction: The Jamba *thangka*

Jamba Juice, a California-based fruit-juice smoothie franchise, began marketing a new line of products called "Enlightened Smoothies" in 2003. The marketing campaign included colorful posters in the style of Tibetan *thangka* paintings. *Thangka* are religious art. Depictions of the cosmic realm replete with various celestial deities, Buddhas, and bodhisattvas, *thangka* paintings are related to *mandala* (Chapter 7), visualization aids used during tantric meditation practice with a central deity as the object of focus, an embodiment of awakening. The Jamba Juice posters mimicked the style of *thangka* while removing any overtly religious imagery and replaced the central deity with a smoothie cup with the company's logo. The company commissioned the artwork from a Tibetan artist living in the United States who agreed to do the work as part of a broader, personal project of preserving traditional arts in diaspora.

The Jamba-*thangka* serves as a useful frame for the following discussion of Buddhist art, media, and the commercialization of Buddhism in the United States. Buddhism, as all religions are, is necessarily mediated through visual and performance art, literature, music, and dance, mediation that generally occurs within the contexts of ritual and practice. In practice, Buddhists employ a wide range of media from sacred texts to specific dress to objects (bells, incense) used during rituals or meditation, all of which carry with them specific meanings within these religious contexts. All of these media, uses, and meanings have been brought to the United States with Buddhism and Buddhists where they have developed and adapted to their local cultural contexts, often intersecting with broader American cultural and religious trends.

Clearly, Buddhist media and its constitutive elements can easily transcend the boundaries of "religion" and seep into the culture at large either intentionally or through the processes of appropriation. Once released from their original context, their meanings are recontextualized. In the case of the *thangka*, a media form in service to explicitly religious ends has been transformed, in the Enlightened Smoothie, to a media form in service to explicitly commercial ends. And the Jamba-*thangka* is hardly alone; North American media is rife with examples of originally Buddhist or Asian imagery and icons being appropriated into new and unusual contexts, often with much controversy. Shields explores one such controversy surrounding a Victoria Secret's bikini adorned with Tibetan Buddhist iconography; many critics were offended because the product displayed a clear lack of sensitivity, born out of ignorance, for non-Western religions (Shields 2011, 85). While it is tempting to follow the thread of critique and offense and deconstruct the rightness or wrongness of both sides' arguments, here we will instead focus our attention on the process of boundary construction and maintenance.

The Jamba-*thangka* and the Buddha bikini draw our attention to a dichotomy between *Buddhist media* and *not-Buddhist media*. Whereas we may be able to describe the intentions and meanings of both categories, where exactly is the line that separates them? At what point did the *thangka* painting stop being Buddhist and become commercial? In this chapter, our hope is not to definitively answer this question but rather provide some framework for how one might begin to answer the question. That is, by exploring what we mean by the terms art and media, practice and ritual, we can draw closer to the systems of meaning implicit in both categories of Buddhist and not-Buddhist media. Examining these systems of meaning, we can unpack the underlying set of assumptions and cultural biases at play in the appropriation or commercialization of Buddhist imagery in not-Buddhist spaces. Ultimately, a focus on boundary maintenance reveals the underlying set of assumptions regarding authenticity and authority—what counts as *authentic* Buddhism and who gets to decide—that undergird our acceptance or rejection of pop-cultural representations of Buddhists and Buddhism.

Buddhist media, Buddhist practice

Mediating Buddhism

What does it mean to say that Buddhism is mediated? What is media? While we might commonly associate the word "media" with specific types—television and film, magazines and newspapers, the Internet, and so on—media refers to all of the ways in which persons communicate ideas. Language itself is a type of media, whether that communication happens verbally and in person or via the shorthand of text messages and Emoji. Of course, as should be obvious by the reference to Emoji, there is a relationship between media technologies, how messages are transmitted, and what those messages mean. This is the heart of what Marshall McLuhan meant when he famously wrote that the "media is the message" (McLuhan 1964), namely, there is a symbiotic relationship between the various forms of media and how their transmitted messages are received. Orally transmitted messages, for example, might be said to reinforce small-group and tribal relationships because they are necessarily transmitted to small audiences of usually in-group members. Broadcast media, by contrast, destabilizes small-group connections by reaching larger audiences who are then able to imagine alternate possibilities beyond their immediate and local circumstances. At the same time, broadcast media also tends to be disseminated in a top-down, one-way fashion, communicating ideas from content producers to content consumers. By contrast, Internet media is necessarily decentralized, allowing large numbers of individuals to become both content consumers and producers and communicate ideas directly (Veidlinger 2015, 4).

Specifically, religious media is made possible because of larger media technologies and structures. Prior to the adoption of moveable type in fifteenth-century Europe, the Christian Bible was produced by hand, allowing for the development of the illuminated manuscript as a specific Christian art form. The printing press not only made possible the widespread dissemination of the Bible but displaced this earlier art form in the process of ushering in a new media industry—the printed book. In this way, religious art is both an extension of and influence upon nonreligious media and media technologies.

Media—specifically as it relates to sacred texts—plays an important role in Buddhist history. The Buddha's teachings were passed on orally for about four centuries following his death. This oral tradition is why the texts take the form they do and necessitated specialists and specific practices to ensure proper transmission. "The oral transmission of the [canon] was aided by mnemonic features such as repetition, formulae, meter, and numbered lists, and was entrusted to specially trained monks [who] were divided into several groups ... responsible for the retention of a different part of the canon" (Veidlinger 2006, 2). It is far easier to remember repetitive verse and numbered lists (the four noble truths, the eightfold path) than complicated prose (such as the style of writing you're reading right now); and distributing parts of the whole collection to a larger number of persons ensures that the whole canon will be memorized for later generations. At some point, however, Buddhists began writing down the teachings. This did not wholly displace either the memorization or recitation of Buddhist texts—indeed, monastics continue to recite the canon up to the present day—but it did give rise to new forms of religious practice. Written texts as embodiments of the teachings became objects of devotion themselves, stored in *stupa* much like relics of the historic Buddha, carried in processionals on important holidays or during the consecration ceremonies of kings, and venerated during *puja* rites. Early Buddhist communities may have had libraries full of texts, but these texts may not have been read in the way that we think of reading today; instead, they were sacred objects to be revered, whereas the teachings contained in them lived in the minds of the monks who memorized them (Veidlinger 2006). Developments in media technology then can give rise to new forms of religious practice.

Practicing Buddhism

That Buddhist texts written on palm leaves and stored in Southeast Asian Buddhist temple libraries were themselves objects of devotion brings us to another set of questions: what do we mean by the terms practice and ritual? Throughout this book, we have generally glossed over this question by merely referring to various *types* of Buddhist practice—devotional, sutra recitation, meditation, and so on. In this way, we have followed a long-standing academic approach to the study of Buddhism that sees the religion's practice as a series of trainings (*yoga*) or disciplines aimed at moving one along the path toward awakening. "Such a view of Buddhist practice," writes Bielefeldt, "has been widespread not only in our academic literature but in the contemporary popular understanding of the religion, where the question, do you practice? is very often almost synonymous with do you meditate? ... Put this way, the great majority of Buddhists throughout history have never practiced their religion" (2005, 231). Historically, the practice of meditation has been the purview of only a very small class of monks committed to this one practice above all others, and the equation of "Buddhist practice" with "Buddhist meditation" obscures the wider array of practices in which Buddhists have engaged. Moreover, the assumption that Buddhists *should* meditate is, as Bielefeldt notes (ibid.), an inherently theological one, one that reflects the other sense of "practice" as the opposite of "theory." In other words, what Buddhists should do *in theory* is meditate; what they actually do *in practice* is something wholly different. Whether it is our responsibility to judge proper Buddhist behavior is, here, irrelevant. For now, let us note that a related term, ritual, may also refer to the wide array of practices listed earlier. Devotional practices, sutra recitation, and even meditation itself have all been highly ritualized by Buddhists across history despite the fact that many in the modern world have come to understand ritual as "scripted and stylized" activity and the "very antithesis of meditation" (Sharf 2005, 260). Whereas we may be tempted to dismiss ritual as merely scripted or performative and therefore secondary to some deeper or more authentic expression of religious feeling, it is worth noting that it is often through the performance of ritual that persons *learn* how to be religious in the first place, what Bell refers to as the "ritualized body" (Bell 1992; cf Campbell 2011). That is, the performance of ritual is in many ways similar to the performance of music, a learned set of skills and behaviors that can be "read" in one sense but truly appreciated only in practice (Sharf 2005).

Theology and praxis

More than merely referencing the study of god, theology refers to the *prescriptive* study of religious theory and doctrine, sometimes called a normative understanding of religion, often conducted by a scholar who is a practitioner of the tradition. This can be contrasted with a *descriptive* study or analysis of religion, often conducted by a scholar of religion who may not have any religious commitments whatsoever.

The use of the term theology is not unproblematic in a Buddhist context. The discipline of theology makes use of Christian structures of thought and categories that may be wholly irrelevant to Buddhism. Payne (2012b) has suggested "Buddhist praxis" as a more appropriate term to describe the critical self-reflection Buddhists engage in that gives shape to the religion's self-understanding of both theory and doctrine.

Regardless of how we define ritual and its relationship to practice, the fact remains that during ritual/practice media is employed. Returning to the case of *thangka* painting and *mandala*, a *mandala* is itself a type of media, a mode of transmitting or communicating a certain type of information. The construction of a *mandala* as part of a larger ritual ceremony then makes that media necessarily religious. The process of transmitting the Buddha's teachings orally through the recitation of canonical texts was also a way of mediating the religion. The recitation of texts is an essential Buddhist practice found in virtually all Buddhist cultures across Asia and the West. This recitation may take the form of formally reciting parts or all of the canon as is the case with reciting the *vinaya* in *pratimoksa* ceremonies. In Vajrayana contexts, the recitation of *dharani* and *mantra* is another form of mediation/practice. Reciting the *nenbutsu* in the form of "namo Amida Butsu" or the *Lotus Sutra* title in the form of *"nam-myoho-renge-kyo"* in Japanese Buddhist contexts is yet another form of mediation/practice. In Chapter 7, we saw that Chögyam Trungpa included Japanese flower arrangement (*ikebana*) as part of a broader practice program where an explicit connection was drawn between the refined ascetics of a specific art form and the process of cultivating an awakened mind. Finally, even in the course of practicing silent meditation such as *zazen* or *vipasyana*, media is employed; whether it is a bell to signal the beginning and ending of a session or formal robes or other clothing worn for the occasion, practice is mediated.

Buddhist (and not-Buddhist) media and art

How might we define the category of Buddhist media? Where is the line between Buddhist art and not-Buddhist art? *Ikebana*, or Japanese flower arrangement, is generally considered an art form that might *also* have a Buddhist sentiment. Nevertheless, *ikebana* can and has been appreciated on a purely aesthetic level, as an art form *apart from* its connections to Buddhism. Similarly, whereas they may be used in formal religious practice, *thangka* paintings and tapestries are also visually and aesthetically pleasing, appreciable on their artistic merits apart from their religious function. The chanting and recitation of the Buddhist canon can be the subject of a musicologist's study, appreciated for its musicality apart from the literal meaning or doctrinal significance of the words being uttered. Indeed, entire music theories have been constructed in China and Japan for the sole purpose of properly performing such recitations—music theories that in turn were put to use in nonreligious contexts such as Chinese opera or Japanese *noh*. Thus, whereas we can note the religious uses to which media and art are put, we can also take note of the ways in which such media may be appreciated on its own terms apart from any expressly religious function. Some examples from Buddhism's long history in the United States will illuminate the various ways, both religious and nonreligious, that Buddhist media and art have found expression.

Since Buddhism first came to the attention of interested Western sympathizers, a key aspect of this interest was artistic. Nineteenth-century European impressionists were inspired by Japanese woodblock prints, exemplified by the International Exposition of 1867 in Paris, which featured a Japanese pavilion with a notable arts collection. French artists such as Odilon Redon and Paul Ranson had depicted the Buddha or Buddhist imagery in their work around the turn of the century. At the same time, American intellectuals and philosophers also had begun to embrace Buddhism, discuss Buddhist philosophy, or import Buddhist art, as we discussed in Chapter 2. In 1878, art historian and philosopher Ernest Fenollosa (1853–1908) traveled to Japan where he taught at the Imperial University in Tokyo; during his time there, he became increasingly interested in Japanese art and worked with the imperial government to identify and save Japanese Buddhist artwork that had been damaged or destroyed during Buddhism's persecution in the early years of the Meiji Restoration. While in Japan, Fenollosa amassed a sizable personal collection of Japanese and Buddhist art which he would later gift to the Boston Fine Arts Museum. His work and lectures were an influence on his colleague Arthur Wesley Dow whose own art pedagogy influenced early-twentieth-century artists such as Georgia O'Keeffe and Max Weber. Fenollosa's writings and lectures led to his being selected to choose the Japanese art for display at the World's Columbia Exposition in Chicago in 1893. Such exhibits allowed for the dissemination of Buddhist arts to the wider public while inspiring American artists (Tweed 1992, 111; Walker 2014). Thus, what had been expressly religious art or media in its Japanese context came to be appreciated for its purely aesthetic qualities in this new American intellectual context.

Concurrent with the events surrounding the World's Columbia Exposition and the World's Parliament of Religions was the beginning of Japanese immigration which brought its own varieties of Buddhist media and art to the United States. For Jodo Shinshu Buddhists, this included a range of ritual practices, chanting sutras, and the recitation of the Buddha's name; it also included music. Whereas devotional poems, hymns, and songs were a part of the tradition for centuries in Japan, on the US mainland and Hawai'i these traditions converged with Protestant Christian liturgies resulting in the creation of an American Buddhist song culture (Tanabe 1998; Wells 2002, 2003). By the early twentieth century, US Shin Buddhists were composing hymns—which they called *gatha*—in both Japanese and English, sometimes explicitly in the style of Christian hymns, though sometimes centuries-old Japanese poems merely set to modern music. This tradition has continued to the present, and the composition of devotional songs remains an important part of US Shin Buddhist practice today (Mitchell 2014a). In the Shin case, such music is generally only performed in a ritual context; other Buddhist music, however, finds expression both inside and outside the temple proper. Heng Sure, the abbot of the Berkeley Buddhist Monastery, is also a folk musician who has performed his Buddhist music in expressly religious contexts as well as for the general public, including the 2008 album *Paramita: American Buddhist Folk Songs*.

The Zen boom of the 1950s and 1960s was ushered in in part through the work of Beat Generation poets and artists as well as the avant garde. Some writers, such as Alan Ginsburg and Gary Snyder, self-identified as Buddhist and wrote poetry inspired by or as expressions of their Buddhist practice. Other writers, such as Jack Kerouac and William Boroughs, had more ambivalent relationships with Buddhism (with Kerouac referring to himself at turns as Buddhist and Catholic). However, novels such as *The Dharma Bums*—with its references to Buddhist poetry, bodhisattvas, and tantric practice—clearly employed Buddhism as a plot device. Composer John Cage is well known for being inspired by Buddhist ascetics; it has been said that his 1952 piece *4'33"*, which consists entirely of four-and-a-half minutes of silence, was inspired by his study of Zen Buddhism. Somewhat more recently, hip hop artists The Beastie Boys' 1994 album *Ill Communication* included two songs that sampled recordings of Tibetan Buddhist monks chanting. One, the instrumental "Shambala," is a reference to band member Adam Yauch's practice of Shambhala Buddhism; the other, "Bodhisattva Vow," is a more straightforward expression of a Buddhist sentiment—Yauch's desire to do Buddhist practice and act compassionately toward other living beings—and thus can be read as an explicitly "Buddhist song." However, unlike US Shin Buddhist *gatha*, the song does not function within a ritual context but rather in a commercial one. That is, regardless of the spiritual intention the songwriter had when composing it, *Ill Communication* is not religious music per se but commercial or popular music, joining a wide range of musical artists who are also Buddhist or make music inspired by Buddhism, such as Tina Turner, k.d. lang, Born I Music, and Ravenna Michalsen (Meade Sperry 2013).

Buddhist vows

Making vows is fairly common in Buddhist literature and practice. According to stories of the Buddha's past lives (*jataka*), in a previous incarnation, the Buddha-to-be made a vow before the Buddha Dipankara to become awakened, a vow that bore karmic fruit millennia later when he was born as Siddhartha Gautama. Other Buddhas and bodhisattvas are regularly seen making vows for their eventual awakening or to end sentient beings' suffering. And in many Mahayana Buddhist traditions, practitioners may formally take the bodhisattva vows as part of their practice or initiation into a lineage.

The existence of work that intersects religious and nonreligious realms calls into question genre categories or typologies, a topic raised by Beek (2015), among others. Noting that a body of literature has come to be explicitly labeled "Buddhist literature," Beek has sought to both identify instances of this literature as well as wrestle with the important question of how one defines such a genre in the first place. Drawing on Duff (2000), she suggests that Buddhist literature might be thought of as either work *about* Buddhism or work *of* Buddhism (Beek 2013). Work *about* Buddhism takes Buddhist concepts or themes as a central plot device or as an explicit concern of the work such as the Scottish novel *Buddha Da* (2003) about a Glasgow father who suddenly takes an interest in Buddhism, practices meditation, and attends Buddhist retreats. Work *of* Buddhism might be said to be infused with a Buddhist sentiment or take certain Buddhist understandings for granted while either not mentioning Buddhism per se or being about some other topic such as Charles Johnson's *Middle Passage* (1990), a novel about slavery in nineteenth-century America, written by a self-described Buddhist, and reflecting the Buddhist concept of interdependence. One might be tempted to create two separate categories of literature, Buddhist literature as opposed to Asian American literature, with the former explicitly foregrounding Buddhist themes and topics. However, keeping in mind the "about" versus "of" distinction, it is important to note how Buddhist elements are infused within or are taken for granted aspects of classically defined Asian American novels such as Amy Tan's *The Kitchen God's Wife* (1991). Where Asian American literature may not foreground Buddhism, "Buddhism is often a component … in the genre of Asian American literature" (Beek 2015, 137), which suggests that it, too, can be said to be *of* Buddhism, perhaps placing it within both genre categories.

Charles Johnson (b. 1948)

FIGURE 28 *Charles Johnson, b. 1948. (Photo courtesy Mary Randlett.)*

Born in Evanston, Illinois, Charles Johnson began his creative career as an illustrator and political cartoonist. His first published novel, *Faith and the Good Thing* (1974) followed several years of writing what he called "apprentice novels," including the acclaimed *Middle Passage*, first published in 1990. His 1982 novel *Oxherding Tale* blends the genres of slave narratives and philosophical fiction to explore issues of race and Eastern philosophy. The title is an allusion to a twelfth-century Zen Buddhist graphic narrative, the 10 Oxherding Pictures, symbolizing the quest for the true self which is, of course, ultimately illusory. Johnson's writings have become central to the burgeoning genre of Buddhist fiction, however it is defined, and he has lent his voice to numerous Buddhist magazines and media sources over the past several decades.

Beek's work joins a growing body of scholarship dedicated to the study of Buddhist literature and Buddhist influences on Western literature (Whalen-Bridge and Storhoff

2009, 2011; Normand and Winch 2013). There has been a concurrent interest in studies of Buddhist cinema, Buddhist-inspired or Buddhist-influenced movies, or analyses
of films from a Buddhist point of view (Green 2014; Whalen-Bridge and Storhoff 2014;
Suh 2015). Green (2014), for example, used a range of international films to illuminate Buddhist concepts or traditions such as the Japanese film *Departures* (2008)
to discuss Jodo Shinshu Buddhism or *Fight Club* (1999) to describe the Four Noble
Truths. The complex way in which Buddhism has been linked to violence in actions
movies such as *The Matrix* (1999) is examined by Anderson and Harper (2014). Suh
(2015) explores representations of Buddhism, race, and gender in contemporary films;
similarly, Mullen (2014) examines Orientalist and Romantic idealizations of Tibet and
Tibetan Buddhism in films such as *Little Buddha* (1993) and *Seven Years in Tibet* (1997).
These last two films take Buddhism as a central theme or focus and thus might be said
to be *about* Buddhism, examples of a "Buddhist film" genre. Other films that are not
expressly about Buddhism (and might not even be *of* Buddhism) are routinely labeled
as such, with *Groundhog Day* (1993) being a prime example. That such a wide variety
of films lend themselves so easily to either the Buddhist film label or a Buddhist critique raises again the question of genre boundaries and whether or not such categories are useful or relevant.

Leaving aside the question of how one defines such a genre category or whether it
is even necessary to do so, such work points toward the ways in which Buddhist icons
and ideas have been permeating the pop-culture landscape. Whalen-Bridge (2014)
notes that there have been dozens of Buddhist film festivals in the United States
since the beginning of the twenty-first century, and that since the 1990s, a plethora of Buddhist and Buddhist-influenced major motion pictures have been released.
Collectively, these films and festivals help to normalize Buddhist concepts and icons
in the popular culture, perhaps alluding to what Seager has labeled a "free-floating
Dharma discourse." Since the mid-twentieth century, an "eclectic, free-floating, book,
art, and culture-generated discourse about Buddhism and other Asian religions"
(Seager 2015, 115) has allowed Buddhist images and icons to become unmoored
from religious contexts, to be deployed into pop-cultural spaces (where they have
become known as *dharmaburgers*), and exert an influence on US culture writ large.
Seager points to several of the artists already discussed here, such as John Cage, as
well as more contemporary artists like Ernesto Pujol, Marina Abramovic, and Sanford
Biggers who all employ Buddhist imagery in their works of self-expression. Here,
Seager wants to make a distinction between "those Americans who use Dharma
images for religious practice in community and those who use them as vehicles for
artistic self-expression" (114), a distinction reminiscent of one made between Asian
American literature and Buddhist literature. Such a distinction, of course, merely
raises the question: in what way can we say that a Buddhist's use of dharma images
in the service of ritual practice is not *also* in the service of self-expression (Payne
2015, 225)? Regardless, the existence of such a free-floating dharma discourse may
help explain the spread and popularization of Buddhism in the United States, of which
more will be said later.

Coined by Josh Bartok and popularized by Rod Meade Sperry of the now defunct website *The Worst Horse*, a *dharmaburger* is any instance of Buddhist iconography or language being used in popular media or advertising.

Thus, for over a century, Buddhism has had some impact on US media and art, both explicitly Buddhist or otherwise. How Buddhist images and media function, what it signifies and means, varies depending on these contexts. However, our opening frame—the Jamba-*thangka*—reminds us that such images and media are no longer confined to either the realms of religion or artistic self-expression. Buddhist images and media function differently and take on a different set of meanings when recontextualized in the realms of commercialism, capitalism, and commodity fetishism (Faure 1998), a topic to which we will now turn.

Colonialism, appropriation, and representation

Neo-Orientalism

We would do well to pause and reflect on the not-unrelated issue of appropriation. Appropriation merely means the act of taking something for one's own use without permission from the owner or creator. Cultural appropriation is the process by which cultural products (art, music, fashion, and so forth) are removed from their original cultural contexts or communities and selectively and superficially redeployed in another (usually white or Western) cultural context. The claim of cultural appropriation often surfaces in popular discourse when music created within African American communities becomes coopted or repackaged for largely white audiences, whether the music in question is the Beach Boys' unattributed use of Chuck Berry's song "Sweet Little Sixteen" (1958) for their "Surfin' U.S.A." (1963) or Robin Thicke's "Blurred Lines" (2013) borrowing from Marvin Gaye's "Got To Give It Up" (1977). The assumption in these cases is that the white artists are benefiting (usually to the tune of large sums of money) not through their original work but by copying or appropriating the work of (usually) unattributed black artists. Whereas one might make the case that such cultural borrowing is but one way that cultures develop over time—for example, disparate cultural flows of European folk music converging with West African music which gave rise to slave music that in turn developed into Negro spirituals, the blues, and jazz—we would do well to pay critical attention to the history of power imbalances between cultural groups. Indeed, the logic of appropriation hinges on the logic of colonialism.

Colonialism was, on the one hand, merely the fact of European powers taking control of most of the globe, of setting up colonies, and governing all the persons in those colonies. Colonialism is also the process by which the West assumes ownership over the colonized culture writ large. This ownership is made possible, in part, by the rhetorical strategy of constructing two opposing cultural spheres—West and East or the Occident and the Orient—and rendering the latter in a subservient position in relation to the former. The Orient was presumed to be less culturally developed and in need of the civilizing influence of the Occident. Once tamed, cultural products such as artwork or religious texts can be removed from their original contexts and brought to European (and later American) universities, museums, and libraries where they can be studied and analyzed in isolation from their home cultures. Once understood by the Westerner, they can then be appreciated or used in this new context. European and American museums, for example, are replete with artwork from Asia that can be appreciated merely for its ascetic value now that it has been removed from its original religious or ritual contexts. This, too, can be read as an act of appropriation—or, perhaps, expropriation, where an object that belongs to one person is taken without permission by another. From this point of view, appropriation is not merely the by-product of a convergence of cultures but is, instead, the by-product of an unequal power relationship between colonizer and colonized in which the colonized is stripped of its agency and ownership over its culture. Thus, there is significant historical, political, and cultural weight behind the desire of those who wish to protect their culture from appropriation.

Postcolonial scholars such as Bartholomeusz (1998) have labeled the appropriation of Asian religious and spiritual practices into American popular culture as a type of neo-Orientalism, perpetuating the colonial dynamics between East and West of an earlier era. Iwamura explores how this dynamic is mediated in her *Virtual Orientalism* (2010) wherein she sketches a genealogy of hyper-real or idealized versions of Asians and Asian religious figures, what she terms the "Oriental Monk." This mediated icon reveals Western perceptions of the Orient, from the sinister and dangerous Fu Manchu of the early twentieth century to the submissive and sexual geisha in the postwar years to the benevolent and wise spiritual gurus up to the present. In its simplest narrative form, the Oriental Monk, who is in some way cut off from his own culture or community, imparts onto a young disciple specific spiritual trainings to be put into the service of resolving the student's personal conflicts. Thus, the wisdom of the East is detached from its original culture, decontextualized, and used by the West for divergent purposes. The Enlightened Smoothie advertisement thus works by trading on the notion that there is some special wisdom or practical value signified by the term "enlightened" and the associated Asian/Buddhist-inspired artwork. Importantly, Iwamura's Oriental Monk can be discerned in fictional characters as well as in media representations of real persons, such as D. T. Suzuki. Whatever we may learn from Suzuki's actual life or works, we can also separately analyze the way in which he was represented as a public figure in American media—especially in fashion magazines where we see the beginnings of a "Zen style" in American popular culture (Iwamura 2010, 32ff) defined by a refined aesthetic, Oriental art, traditional Japanese clothing, and so forth.

It may be tempting at this point to note that the deployment of mystical Asian characters or the appropriation of Buddhist imagery into advertising is somehow "not authentic," is something that happens in mainstream or popular culture, and is therefore irrelevant to the practice of Buddhism. However, we should be attentive to how such appropriations or representations are not always confined to commercial advertising campaigns but emerge within Buddhist contexts as well. Building off Iwamura's icon of the Oriental Monk, Mitchell (2014b) has noted the preponderance of another icon in popular culture, the "Tranquil Meditator," a figure who stands in for the supposed benefits of meditation in nonreligious contexts such as personal growth and health, or as a tool for calming the minds of action movie heroes (cf Anderson and Harper 2014). Importantly, this figure is as likely to show up in a summer blockbuster movie as on the cover of a Buddhist magazine or in an advertisement for a Buddhist meditation retreat. Thus, both Buddhists and not-Buddhists benefit from a larger cultural narrative about the benefits and value of Buddhist practices.

Representing Buddhism and Buddhists

Whereas the logic of appropriation and colonialism can help us examine instances of Buddhist icons or art being deployed in not-Buddhist and commercial spaces, it is worth noting that the subject of Iwamura's work is not objects but persons. Of course, "we must keep in mind that Iwamura draws a distinction between the real persons and the mediated 'hyperreal' images of those persons" (Mitchell 2012, 71). That is, her criticism of D. T. Suzuki, for example, is not of the man himself but of how his image has been constructed in media spaces and what that image reveals about American attitudes toward Asia and Asian religions. Such representations necessarily cannot fully or accurately represent real persons or whole communities. Real persons and communities in all their complexity and nuance cannot be reduced to an essentialized trope or stereotype. However, popular culture discourses may have an effect on how real persons and communities are perceived by the culture at large.

Wuthnow and Cadge (2004) found that a majority of Americans (55 percent) had had some contact with Buddhism, despite the very small number of Buddhists in the country. Moreover, most associate words such as "tolerant" or "peace loving" with the religion. Tweed suggests that it is useful here to contrast such findings with other minority religions, especially Islam, and compare their respective media representations. More often than not, Islam is represented in US media by the actions of a violent minority whereas Buddhism is represented, time and again, with "the solitary meditator, eyes half closed, sitting in [meditation]" (Tweed 2008b, 91). Anecdotally, Wuthnow relates how a Vietnamese-born monk in Houston, Texas, has had to adjust to the popularity of Buddhism in the United States. "In Vietnam … meditation was practiced mainly by monks and laity who took the monastic life very seriously; in the United States, people meditate casually because it makes them feel better" (2005, 93). This is not to suggest that media representations have a causal effect over popular perceptions; however, there is undoubtedly a relationship between Buddhism's popularity and mediated representations of Buddhism, for better or worse.

Conversely, one can also learn a great deal about cultural attitudes by what is *not* being represented. Iwamura (2010) and others have noted the distinct absence of Asian American Buddhists in North American media. Contributors to major Buddhist publications such as *Tricycle* and *Shambhala Sun* now (*Lion's Roar*) skew white and there is an often casual association between Buddhism and middle-class, white culture (Prothero 2001). The lack of Asian American voices suggests that Asian American Buddhists have been rendered invisible in mainstream discourses despite the fact that the majority of American Buddhists are of Asian descent (Chapter 8).

Buddhist responses to appropriation and representation

Responses by US Buddhists to the appropriation of Buddhist images into not-Buddhist contexts have been varied. On the one hand, there is a tendency—found in online discussion forums and blogs—to dismiss such appropriation as trivial, as something disconnected from actual Buddhist practice, and therefore not worthy of attention. On the other hand, there is the tendency to view such appropriation as simply wrong or, at the very least, insulting to practicing Buddhists. For example, it is common in many Buddhist cultures (indeed in most cultures around the globe) to view the feet and the floor as inherently unclean; therefore, one should always treat an image of the Buddha (or anything sacred) with respect by keeping it off the floor or above the level of one's waist. In 2012, the home decor store Bed Bath and Beyond briefly sold a toilet brush whose cover was decorated with images of the Buddha—a product that would necessarily be placed on the floor and beside something else generally considered unclean, the toilet. This was cause for much criticism and offense online.[1] Here, regardless of one's personal feeling about the relative cleanliness of different body parts or the sanctity of images, it is not hard to see how such a product would likely be insulting to someone.

Interestingly, in online debates regarding such products, in addition to those who take offense, one also find instances of Buddhists claiming that one should *not* be offended. Such arguments follow a predictable pattern of suggesting that since Buddhism teaches that one should not be attached, one should also let go of one's feelings of offense or insult. This is a strong argument to make, and one that is inherently theological, if we recall Bieldfeldt's distinction between practice and theory mentioned earlier, namely the idea that there is something Buddhists *should* do or a way in which Buddhists *should* behave (unattached) as opposed to how they are *in fact* behaving (being offended). In this case, it is important to recall that there is no unified code of ethics or behavior to which all Buddhists are bound (there are multiple canons with even more interpretations of those canonical texts); whereas the Buddha may have said that one should not be attached to certain ideas regarding the nature of the self, it does not follow that one should never express an emotion or feel insulted; and, perhaps most importantly, regardless of whatever we may believe the Buddha *intended* for us to do, that does not mean that commercial enterprises should attempt to benefit financially by producing products that necessarily insult (rightly or wrongly) large numbers of persons across the globe.

Shields (2010) provides some additional insight to these debates in his discussion of the Victoria Secret's Buddha bikini (mentioned earlier) and t-shirts sold by Abercrombie & Fitch with racially stereotyped images of the Buddha and Asians. He notes that the online complaints surrounding such products can be grouped together into several broad categories from the offense taken at advertisers' ignorance of other cultures to a concern about the commercialization of the Buddha image. These critiques suggest a type of ethical or moral stance, one that implies or asserts that such (mis)uses of the Buddha's image, such as placing it on a bikini, are morally wrong from a specifically Buddhist perspective. Shields notes that this is a somewhat misleading interpretation of Buddhist ethics which, generally speaking, places more emphasis on intentionality (ibid, 86). That is, when determining whether or not something is ethically correct in a Buddhist context, one must take into consideration the intentionality behind the act; if the intention of the Buddha bikini was merely to sell bikinis, and not to offend people, is it morally wrong?

Leaving aside the (specifically Buddhist) moral implications here, we can also reflect on what such appropriations and representations mean, what they *signify*, in the particular cultural context of North America. Whatever the intended message of Buddhism

FIGURE 29 *Jizo, Budai, and meditating elephant statues for sale at Pier One, El Cerrito, California. (Photo by author.)*

may or may not be, that message may be wholly lost on those who display Buddha statues in their homes and gardens (Figure 29). These uses of the Buddha image serve other purposes—signifiers of peace and tranquility (Eastman 2008). This dilution of the Buddhist tradition to a trite stereotype might be discouraging to some observers— such as Webster who acerbically comments "Put a Buddha on your mantelpiece to indicate to visitors that ... you may be dull and selfish, [but] you [have a] little counter-culture influence" (2012, 51). If nothing else, this is one result of a free-floating dharma discourse; if Buddha images are unmoored from their original contexts and assigned divergent meanings, it is perhaps inevitable that they would find a home in the consumer marketplace where they come to represent something different than what the tradition may have intended. And whereas we are not required to judge this divergence as purely counterproductive to an "authentic" Buddhist practice, it is worth our time to critically analyze such representations as they can reveal much about our own cultural attitudes toward Asia and Asian religions. Being offended about a toilet brush may not be the most worthwhile use of our time; however, it is arguable that the same complex of discourses that allow for the appropriation and representation of Buddhist *images* in not-Buddhist media also allows for the representation of Buddhist *persons*.

What is perhaps most at stake in discourses of appropriation and representation— of both Buddhism and Buddhists—is the question of authenticity and authority. What is a proper or correct representation or use of a Buddhist image? Who has the right to sell Buddhist images for not-Buddhist purposes? Who has the right to define and represent what Buddhism is in popular media? And what are the consequences of such decisions on real-world persons and communities?

Authenticity and authority

Let us recall the metaphor of the finger pointing to the moon (Chapter 6). This metaphor stands in for a complex set of Buddhist philosophical concepts including emptiness (*sunyata*), suchness (*tathata*), and the two truths doctrine. According to the two truths, ultimate truth, reality as it is, is suchness and emptiness. Everything is empty of inherent, independent essence; and reality exists just as it is, free of our conceptualizations of it. Conceptualizing the world, discriminating between our subjective selves and objective others places us in the realm of provisional truth, the world of discriminative thinking—which, of course, is a necessary condition of being un-awakened, of not being a Buddha.

The process of creating conceptual categories—such as "Buddhist media" and "not-Buddhist media"—is surely an example of discriminative thinking. It is an act of looking at the world and making decisions about categories of things. Like genres of film or music or art, we group things together that bear a family resemblance, come up with a list of qualities that define that resemblance, and then label the family with an identifying marker. Earlier, in our discussion of Buddhist literature and film, we saw examples of this; these things have the quality of Buddhist literature, these other things do not. This process of categorization should be evident in the ways in which we talk not just about Buddhist art but Buddhism more generally for "Buddhism" is itself a category, set off from "not-Buddhism." Buddhism-as-category has some significance, some system of signs and meanings, and when confronted with something that conflicts with this system of meanings, we reject it as not-Buddhism. Thus, while Buddhism has come to signify certain attributes like "peaceful" in the Western imagination, when confronted with examples of Buddhists not acting peaceful, we are forced to either declare those actions "not really Buddhist" or adjust our definition.

The intention here is not to argue for any one particular definition of Buddhism (or not-Buddhism for that matter); it is merely to call our attention to this process of boundary construction and its consequences. To the extent that Buddhism has burst onto the American pop-culture scene in a rather specific way—as a religion that does not require blind faith, engenders a calm equanimity of mind through meditation, is basically compatible with science and progressive values, and is more *spirituality* than *religion* (McMahan 2008, 4)—the category of Buddhism has acquired for better or worse a set of meanings that may or may not capture the religion in its fullness. While some may be tempted to discredit this set of qualities as not in line with some traditional or classical definition of Buddhism, another line of inquiry might be to examine the processes by which this set of meanings came into existence, was legitimated, and perpetuated. McMahan's (2008) work on Buddhist modernism is crucial in this regard as is Iwamura's (2010) for tracing the genealogy of pop-cultural icons who are the bearers of these tropes and stereotypes. It is through these processes that we come to know (or think we know) what constitutes some version of authentic Buddhism, what counts as an appropriate or inappropriate use of Buddhist media, art, and iconography.

Authenticity must be legitimated in some way, either through cultural inertia (the sense that things have always been thus) or the active force of authority. Authority comes in many forms, of course. The monastic sangha is one system of authority that has the explicit role of authenticating Buddhist belief and practice through the work of clarifying Buddhist doctrine in light of tradition. Scholars and academics, for better or worse, are often called upon to authenticate Buddhism, especially in Western media (Mitchell 2012). When new forms of Buddhist media and art emerge, regardless of whether they are judged authentic and by whom, we ought to keep in mind our collective responsibility in cocreating these new forms of Buddhist culture. As researches, practitioners, and consumers, we participate in cultural change and in many ways determine its trajectory.

While this process of boundary construction and maintenance has clear relevance for the study of Buddhist media, art, and practice, these same issues are at play in social categories as well. The consequences of determining whether or not a *person* counts or not as a member of a social group are notably higher than determining whether or not *The Matrix* counts as a Buddhist film. Because the stakes are higher, we should be attentive to both the processes of boundary construction and those who claim the authority to do so.

DISCUSSION QUESTIONS

1. What are some of the ways in which Buddhist practice is mediated?
2. How might you define a genre of Buddhist literature, film, or music? What would distinguish this genre from other related genres?
3. Why might some object to certain uses of a Buddha image such as on commercial products or in advertising?

SUGGESTIONS FOR FURTHER READING

Bielefeldt, Carl. 2005. "Practice." In *Critical Terms for the Study of Buddhism*, ed. Donald S. Lopez, 229–244. Chicago: The University of Chicago Press.

Iwamura, Jane. 2010. *Virtual Orientalism: Asian Religions and American Popular Culture*. New York: Oxford University Press.

Johnson, Charles. 1990. *Middle Passage*. New York: Atheneum.

Mitchell, Scott A. 2014. "The Tranquil Meditator: Representing Buddhism and Buddhists in US Popular Media." *Religion Compass* 8 (3): 81–89.

Shields, James Mark. 2011. "Sexuality, Blasphemy, and Iconoclasm in the Media Age." In *God in the Details: American Religion in Popular Culture*, ed. Eric Mazur and Kate McCarthy, 80–102. London: Routledge.

Suh, Sharon A. 2015. *Silver Screen Buddha: Buddhism in Asian and Western Film*. London: Bloomsbury Academic.

Whalen-Bridge, John, and Gary Storhoff, eds. 2009. *The Emergence of Buddhist American Literature*. New York: SUNY Press.

Whalen-Bridge, John, and Gary Storhoff, eds. 2014. *Buddhism and American Cinema*. New York: SUNY Press.

10

Buddhist identities: Race, gender, and sexuality

Chapter summary and outline

Social identity is constructed at the intersection of race, gender, sexual orientation, and, for US Buddhists, religion. This complex intersectional perspective is explored in relation to systems of power and privilege before being used as a frame for discussing the various ways in which US Buddhist history has been shaped by racial, feminist, and LGBTQI discourses in the broader culture. Finally, attention is paid to academic tropes that have perpetuated a racial binary in the study of Buddhism in the West.

Introduction: Defining whiteness
Defining identity
    Identity as social construction
    Identity and privilege
US Buddhist identities
    Racializing Buddhists
    Women, gender, and feminist theory
    LGBTQI Buddhists and queer theory
Power and privilege in US Buddhism
A note on two Buddhisms and the academy
Discussion questions
Suggestions for further reading

Introduction: Defining whiteness

In 1922, Takao Ozawa, born in Japan but living in California and Hawai'i for more than two decades, lost his bid for naturalization when the Supreme Court ruled that only "free whites" or those of "African nativity and descent" could apply for citizenship.[1] Ozawa did not merely argue that Japanese or Asians should be allowed to apply for citizenship; he argued that Japanese should be included in the category of "white." Ultimately, the Supreme Court ruled that Japanese—and by extension other Asian immigrants—were an "unassimilable race" and therefore not eligible for US citizenship. Such rulings played into ongoing anti-Japanese sentiment of the early twentieth century (Chapter 2). Eventually, this general feeling was coupled with a specific suspicion of Japanese Buddhists as the United States and Japan inched closer to war. The FBI, who had begun to track Japanese communities and community leaders, were especially focused on Buddhist temples, which the FBI believed were disseminating pro-Japanese propaganda and supporting Japan financially (Williams 2003, 256). Thus, through legal cases and government action, at the intersection of race and religion, a specifically Japanese American Buddhist identity began to form.

To the extent that Buddhist philosophy can be understood as non-essentialist—that is, through doctrines such as no-self (*anatman*) or emptiness (*sunyata*) it is presumed that there exists no essential self or ego to cling to, that one's sense of self must be critically engaged and deconstructed—it has been argued that there is an inherent contradiction between identity politics and Buddhist philosophy. In short, some might claim that, since Buddhists argue there is no self, discourses that foreground specifically racial, gendered, or sexual identities are at best unhelpful in the pursuit of awakening. Here, we will set aside this argument for two reasons. First, such an argument is inherently theological in nature. Recalling Bielefeldt's (2005) comments regarding practice versus theory in the previous chapter, the claim that Buddhists *should* behave one way or another based on some aspect of Buddhist doctrine (or, more to the point, a particularly narrow interpretation of Buddhist doctrine) is to make a claim that rests on the veracity of a religious truth claim and is therefore only valid if the underlying truth claim (the nonexistence of the self) is also true. Our intention in this chapter is not to engage in a theological discussion about the nature of the self; rather, it is to explore the various ways that race, gender, and sexual orientation have shaped Buddhist experiences in the United States.

Second, regardless of whether or not racial, gender, and sexual identities have any substantive reality to them, the fact of the matter is that persons are socialized to believe and to act as though they are real. In the example above, it made very little difference whether or not Japanese Buddhist immigrants were attached to any particularly "Japanese" or "Buddhist" identity or whether or not such identities are empty—the culture writ large, backed by governmental and social institutions, grafted onto those persons specific identities that were in turn used to justify forced incarceration for the duration of World War II. In the face of this historical fact, claiming that "identity is but an illusion" is rendered at best unhelpful, at worst condescending.

Therefore, to the extent that US Buddhists have been labeled and identified one way or another in specifically racial, gendered, and sexualized ways, and given our responsibility as scholars to research, critique, and analyze history and culture, it is worth spending some time exploring the ways in which these identities are shaped and expressed, the subject of the present chapter. We will focus on three key aspects of identity formation in the United States: race and ethnicity, gender, and sexual orientation. The intersection of these with a specific Buddhist identity will be linked to the development of US Buddhist histories and communities, from Asian American and immigrant experiences, to the important contributions of feminist and queer theorists. We will begin with a brief overview of how race, gender, sexual orientation, and privilege are used in current scholarship to provide a foundation for the following discussion.

Defining identity

Identity as social construction

While it might seem counterintuitive a century later that Ozawa could argue for his right to American citizenship by asking that an entire ethnic group be added to the category of "white persons," had he been successful, it certainly would not have been unprecedented. The nineteenth century saw widespread discrimination against Irish immigrants owing to their status as second-class citizens in the United Kingdom and the presumption, at the time, that whiteness was limited to those of Anglo-Saxon decent which necessarily excluded other European ethnicities. In this context, there was no reason to believe that the Irish, who themselves had been sold into slavery in the early days of North American British colonialism, should be automatically included in the category of "free white person." Nevertheless, over the subsequent centuries, the category of "white person" shifted and grew to include a wider array of European peoples. "Rather than a single, enduring definition of whiteness, we find multiple enlargements occurring against a backdrop of the black/white dichotomy" (Painter 2010, 201) revealing that "race is an idea, not a fact" (ibid, ix), a social construction not a biological reality.

While we presume there is some biological basis for the existence of racial categories, some relationship between persons' ancestry or physical characteristics and some essential nature, such biological definitions of race have long since been debunked by the biological sciences and linked inextricably, especially in the United States, with African slavery. That is, one reason the Irish were allowed to be classified as "white" was precisely because they were not sub-Saharan African. Nineteenth-century racial hierarchies presumed that African peoples were both culturally and biologically inferior to Europeans, thereby justifying their enslavement. Whereas ethnicity has at times been used in place of race, we should note that the terms function in largely similar ways. Both refer not to some natural or essential aspect of being but rather to a system of social codes or behaviors that are deployed to classify groups of persons in the body politic.

Institutional racism and prejudice

Institutional or systemic racism refers to systems that privilege one group while taking away or limiting the rights of another. Such systems can be legal systems (e.g., Jim Crow laws) or social institutions and processes (e.g., a university's legacy admissions policy). Institutional racism is not the same thing as individual prejudice. An institution can be racist regardless of the personal feelings of the individuals who make up the system; persons can benefit from the system even if they themselves have no personal or individual prejudice.

Omi and Winant (1986) use the term "racialization" to refer to the process of assigning meaning or signification to classes of persons based on presumed biological or physical differences. This is a process that necessarily takes time and is predicated on the micro-level of personal behavior or social customs and reinforced through macro-level cultural discourses and legal and social systems and institutions. The history of slave laws and, following the Civil War and post-war Reconstruction era, Jim Crow laws is the clearest example of this process. Such laws necessarily defined two races of persons and then privileged one (whites) while disenfranchising the other (blacks). Social customs that allowed whites to deny housing or jobs to blacks were reinforced by voter restriction laws that made it difficult to impossible for blacks to assert their political rights. And anti-miscegenation laws policed the boundaries between racial categories in the service of maintaining the supposed purity of the white race. A century later, having lived through generations of social customs and legal structures that reinforce this racial binary, we take the existence of racial categories such as white and black at face value, as though they are natural and normal, and not for what they are—the result of centuries of human history and behavior. Within this context, we come to see ourselves as "belonging" to one race or another, and assume that these categories have some fixed meaning. It is this presumption of fixedness that causes us to believe that the category of white includes some persons (Europeans) but not others (Japanese). Thus, whereas racial (and to a similar extent ethnic) categories often appear natural, they are in fact fluid and arbitrary and subject to endless configurations across history and within systems of power.

A critique of the naturalness of race or ethnicity can be equally applied to gender and sexual orientation. As de Beauvoir famously wrote in *The Second Sex* (1949), "one is not born a woman, one becomes a woman." This is to say that whereas there may be biological differences between human beings, the category of "woman" is a social construction, defined not merely in reference to biological sex but in reference to social and cultural modes of conduct. Contemporary US culture presumes that women "naturally" behave in feminine ways whereas men "naturally" behave in masculine ways, a gender binary that merely appears natural but, when compared to other times and cultures, is revealed to be arbitrary. Consider, for example, the Bugis people of Indonesia who have five gender categories. These five categories represent a spectrum of gender orientations from cisgender male to cisgender female, with *bissu* being a harmonious gender expression of the other four genders simultaneously. *Bissu* may also be intersex individuals born with both female and male genitalia, a phenomenon that undermines even our assumption of a biological distinction between female and male. That strict female/male binaries are only sometimes biological and that gender roles change over time and culture is evidence that these categories are not natural but are instead subject to the fluctuations of human history and culture, constructed within specific networks of power.

> By analogy with transgender, cisgender refers to those persons whose self-identity matches the biological sex and gender they were assigned at birth.

Butler further problematizes the biological basis of gender by critiquing the system of meanings assigned to the body via social and political processes. In *Gender Trouble* (1990), more than merely critiquing the ways in which the body politic creates and reinforces social norms around gender, Butler discloses the complex interrelationship between individual bodies, politics, gender, sex, and sexual orientation. Briefly, culture attempts to maintain normative standards of sex and sexual activity by rendering specific acts and persons as, in Douglas' words, pure or polluted (2005). Persons (e.g., gays, lesbians, intersex) and acts (e.g., homosexual acts, cross-dressing) are framed as unnatural, or transgressive—the "other"—a set of identities defined in large part by their being different from, other than, what is presumed to be normal and natural. Once rendered thus, these identities become the subject of both social scorn and regulation. Crucially, Butler introduces the concept of coherence—where one's gender identity and sexual orientation line up with the supposed appropriate physical body according to culturally normative standards. This coherence—of, say, a masculine gender paired with heterosexual desire residing in a physically male body—is assumed to be "natural" when it is in fact merely a coincidence, a coincidence that just happens to be more socially accepted than its alternatives.

Gender is performative. Persons are socialized to believe that certain acts are appropriate or inappropriate for different genders (boys don't cry, girls are emotional, men focus on careers, women raise children) or that certain kinds of desire and sexual behavior are correct or natural (heterosexual desire is "natural" because it results in childbirth). Our behavior often runs counter to these cultural narratives, and such behavior gets variously problematized and regulated. Aggressive men pursuing their careers are labeled effective leaders; aggressive women are called bitchy and their effectiveness as mothers called into question. Women professors are more likely to receive negative student evaluations (MacNell et al. 2014). Men are taught to never show emotion, even in the face of severe depression such as that caused by posttraumatic stress disorder. Homosexual behavior was regulated and even outlawed in many US states until such laws were deemed unconstitutional by the Supreme Court in 2003. The logic of same-sex marriage bans rests almost solely on procreation; heterosexual marriage is considered socially important because it results in children; therefore, same-sex marriage serves no purpose. This set of social behaviors, however, is easily transgressed. The existence of persons whose gender identity and physicality do not align, are not coherent, undermines the logic of coherence as a natural or essential aspect of humanity.

Obviously, these three markers are hardly the only ways in which persons' identity is constructed in the social realm. To this list, we might add other markers such as physical or mental ability, native language, country of origin, socioeconomic class, and, of course, religion. Nineteenth-century Japanese immigrants were identified as foreign, as un-American, both in terms of race *and* religion. Thus, it is the sum total of these various markers—and more—that cocreate our sense of who we are. Moreover, apart from merely taking note of how our selves are socially constructed, we can also use this knowledge as a way of critiquing specific types of exclusion, discrimination, and oppression. It is the creation of, say, a second sex that allows for the creation of gendered hiring practices which result in the exclusion of women from the work force or unequal payment policies.

Identity and privilege

Privilege has been a part of American social theory since at least the 1930s. In his *Black Reconstruction in America*, Du Bois reflected on the concept of a "public and psychological wage" given to poor whites by virtue of their race; that they were not subject to discriminatory Jim Crow laws, they were made to feel superior to poor blacks with whom they shared much in common—more in common than with wealthy whites—most notably the burden of being poor in the United States (Du Bois 2012). By the 1980s, largely as a result of Women's Studies and Black Feminism, the phrase "white privilege" had begun to find widespread acceptance among both academics and antiracist activists. Here, it refers to the systemic privileges and advantages white straight men generally have over and against persons of color, LGBTQI persons, and women. By systematic, we mean legal and cultural institutions that are easier to navigate or preference certain groups either explicitly or implicitly. Whereas privilege is operative in part because individuals willfully or unintentionally avoid deconstructing it, it is not the same as personal or individual bias or prejudice. "One reaps the benefits of membership in a dominant group *regardless* of whether one wants or intends to do so, and regardless of whether one is personally prejudiced toward non-dominant groups" (Hickey 2010, 3, emphasis in original).

McIntosh describes white privilege as "an invisible package of unearned assets that I can count on cashing in each day," assets that manifest as "special circumstances and conditions I experience that I did not earn but that I have been made to feel are mine by birth, by citizenship, and by virtue of being a conscientious law-abiding 'normal' person of goodwill" (2004). She goes on to describe nearly fifty such circumstances that, individually and cumulatively, make life generally easier for her as a white person when compared to the circumstances and experiences of persons of color who do not have these privileges. Examples include:

- I can turn on the television or open to the front page of the paper and see people of my race widely and positively represented.

- I can do well in a challenging situation without being called a credit to my race.

- I can worry about racism without being seen as self-interested or self-seeking.

- I can be late to a meeting without having the lateness reflect on my race.

- If I want to, I can be pretty sure of finding a publisher for this piece on white privilege.

Like institutional forms of racism (e.g., Jim Crow laws) white privilege is primarily a set of systematic advantages and entitlements bestowed on one group and kept from others. Unlike institutional racism, white privilege also refers to broader cultural norms and assumptions. In both cases, it is not individual choices or preferences that create systemic privileges or systems of discrimination; it is the repeated cultural practices that over time become normative, presumed to be natural. It is this normalcy that allows us to overlook or ignore privilege in the first place. "I did not see myself as racist because I was taught to recognize racism only in individual acts of meanness by members of my group, never in invisible systems conferring racial dominance on my group from birth" (McIntosh 2004).

Heteronormativity

Heteronormativity is the belief that heterosexual behaviors and identities are normal and natural and either ignores or actively works against accepting persons who do not fall into a strict gender or sexual orientation binary. Heteronormativity on a social or cultural scale, much like institutional racism, privileges one class of persons (cisgender heterosexual persons) and disenfranchises those who do not fit into these binary categories.

Individual identities cannot be reduced to a single or essential frame—race, say, or sexual identity. Rather, it is the intersection of race, gender, sexual orientation, and other social markers that contribute to our subjective experiences and are the object of interlocking legal systems of dominance and discrimination. Often, critical analyses of gender and race foreground the experiences of middle-class white women and black men, respectively, thus reducing the experiences of black women, for example, into one of these frames. An intersectional approach recognizes that the experience of being both a woman *and* black is greater than the sum of its parts (Crenshaw 1989, 140). An overly reductionist approach to understanding identity and privilege necessarily obscures the multidimensionality of subjective experience.

Crenshaw (2010) notes the complexities of conflicting agendas and legal systems that are ostensibly created to help marginalized populations. For example, she found discussion of domestic violence within minority communities often silenced because of a concern that such conversations would perpetuate the stereotype of aggressive back men; thus concerns for protecting and supporting one group (black men) came at the expense of helping another (black women). "The concept of political intersectionality highlights the fact that women of color are situated within at least two subordinated groups that frequently pursue conflicting political agendas" (Crenshaw 2010, 484). One must choose, as it were, which frame of analysis—gender or race—is more essential, a choice that elides and erases the experiences of women of color who are effectively reduced to *either* women *or* black. Such a tendency reproduces division where persons are forced to choose which community to call "home," which identity is of more importance. Intersectionality "requires that we first recognize that the organized identity groups in which we find ourselves are in fact coalitions, or at least potential coalitions waiting to be formed" (Crenshaw 2010, 489).

US Buddhist identities

Racializing Buddhists

Beginning in the mid-nineteenth century, as Chinese and later Japanese immigrants began arriving on the West Coast, anti-Asian discourses emerged which systematically excluded these workers from enjoying full participation in American public life. Jim Crow-era laws forged in the post-Reconstruction South were expanded across the United States and applied to "Mongolian" races, prohibiting interracial marriage, restricting voting rights and property ownership, denying citizenship, and culminating in the exclusion of Asian immigration. It was through the enactment of these laws and social structures that a racial category of "Asian" was constructed—or, to paraphrase Omi and Winant (2014), the making up of a people. Persons marked by this racial category were subject to the system of discrimination that disallowed them from participating fully in American public life. The establishment and maintenance of ethnically focused communities was a logical consequence (Hickey 2015, 44)—communities that often conformed to normative Protestant American religious structures. At the same time, as the twentieth century progressed and cultural attitudes changed, white American subcultures such as the Beat Generation had grown disillusioned with or critical of normative American culture and sought its opposite—often looking for it in romanticized idealizations of Asian cultures and spiritualities.

As Iwamura (2010) has noted, in the mid-twentieth century we see a shift in US media representations of Asians from the "yellow hoard"—representative of the political and military threat posed by an aggressive imperial Japan—to the geisha, representative of a passive "other" who serves erotic desire. Concomitant with the image of the geisha is the image of the Oriental Monk (Chapter 9), a mystical figure who serves not erotic but spiritual desire. Thus, the racialization of Asian American Buddhists has moved from being depicted as an "unassimilable" or even dangerous race (Kashima 1977) to a source of spiritual and psychological desire fulfillment. When grafted onto Buddhism, the consequences are such that those forms of the tradition that align with normative American traditions and values (as exemplified by many Japanese American communities) are not seen as exotic enough to be properly Buddhist (Payne 2005) and are glossed over by both potential converts and scholars alike (Quli 2009). Meanwhile, other traditions seemingly benefit from the trope of exotic spiritual other; Tibetan Buddhists have accused lamas of seeking out financial support from white converts to the neglect of the Tibetan diaspora community, for example (Mullen 2006), a situation that speaks both to the racialization of US Buddhists as well as class divisions within this community (Chapter 7).

US Buddhist experiences thus intersect with racial identities in a variety of ways; from the internment of Japanese Americans to the Angry Asian Buddhist (Chapter 8), from ethnically exclusive Asian refugee communities to Tibetan lamas seeking out white patrons. All of these and more serve as examples of specific racial or ethnic Buddhist identities. However, we need to be aware of the fact that race and ethnicity apply not only to Asian and Asian American Buddhists but to white Buddhists as well. Popular representations of US Buddhism that tend to highlight the cultural aspects of Asian American Buddhisms overlook the cultural aspects of white American Buddhisms. As Hickey notes, "European American converts are *also* 'ethnic Buddhists'" (2010, 14, emphasis in original). Individualism and progressivism are cultural values that shape how white Buddhist converts and their decedents engage Buddhist practice and form community.

Women, gender, and feminist theory

It would not be unfair to say that Buddhism has a problem with gender, one that may go back to the historical Buddha himself. It is said that he instituted the *bhiksuni* (nuns) *sangha* only reluctantly at the behest of his step-mother, Mahaprajapati, and his senior disciple Ananda. While recognizing that women were capable of attaining advanced spiritual levels, he also suggested that allowing women to ordain would shorten the length of the dharma in the world. Moreover, the monastic code for nuns is not only more exhaustive than it is for monks, but also necessarily puts nuns in a subordinate position vis-à-vis monks: nuns must treat all monks as their senior even in the case when a nun has been a monastic for a longer period of time; when confessing lapses of monastic rules, nuns must do so before monks; and nuns must be ordained in the presence of both nuns and monks (Robinson and Johnson 1997, 44ff). Modern apologists are quick to suggest that such stories and *vinaya* regulations are the result of ancient cultural contexts, or may even be apocryphal, made up by later generations of male Buddhists upholding strict gender norms. Indeed, so the argument goes, the Buddha was rather progressive for his day in even allowing women to ordain in the first place.

The naga girl and the *Lotus Sutra*

In the twelfth chapter of the *Lotus Sutra*, the Buddha declares that everyone may attain awakening, including women and animals. As a demonstration, an eight-year-old girl is shown quickly attaining awakening. Oft-cited as an example of gender equity in Buddhism, the girl in question is, in actuality, a *naga*, a type of mythical dragon or serpent. And before she becomes a Buddha, she transforms herself into a human male. Thus, far from being a straightforward representation of feminine spirituality, not only was the girl not a woman when she became a Buddha, she wasn't even human to begin with (Nattier 2009).

Whereas, the less-than-ideal beginnings of the female monastic *sangha* and inherently imbalanced nature of the *vinaya* should be the subject of critique, we should not use them as nothing more than evidence of a thoroughly sexist and misogynistic religion. A single-minded focus on (male) monastic practice often distracts from a full appreciation of womens' roles within Buddhism across its history. We might begin with the *Therigatha*, a collection of seventy-three poems by the female monastic disciples of the Buddha, including Mahaprajapati. These poems speak to the unique experiences of early Buddhist women and against the narrative that awakening is the exclusive purview of men. There are numerous examples of feminine spirituality in the tradition, both mythic and historic, including the transformation of the male bodhisattva Avalokitesvara to his female forms of Quan Yin and Kannon in China and Japan. The long history of the female monastic order in East Asia and contemporary Asian women leaders such as Cheng Yen, the founder of the Tzu Chi Foundation (Chapter 6), points to specific ways in which women engage Buddhism. Women's involvement has been a central feature of Buddhism's move to the West; the *Therigatha* was first translated into English by Carolyn Rhys Davids, for example, who was an influential part of the establishment of Buddhist studies as an academic discipline in the West. Women have played crucial roles in the spread of Buddhism into the United States: from Jane Imamura of the Berkeley Buddhist Temple (Chapter 2) to Ruth Denison (Chapter 5), from Mushim Ikeda to Pema Chödrön (Chapter 7).

Mushim Patricia Ikeda (b. 1954)

FIGURE 30 *Mushim Ikeda, b. 1954. (Photo courtesy Rivka Shapiro.)*

Born and raised in rural Ohio, Mushim Ikeda studied at Oberlin College and the University of Iowa with the intention of writing and teaching. In the early 1980s, however, she began studying and practicing Zen Buddhism, first in Ann Arbor, Michigan, and later across the United States and South Korea. Since the early 1990s, she has been a contributor to numerous Buddhist publications, including the Buddhist Peace Fellowship's *Turning Wheel* magazine. Currently a teacher at Oakland's East Bay Meditation Center, in addition to her work as a Buddhist leader and mindfulness meditation instructor, she is committed to engaged Buddhism, diversity training, and social transformation.

More than merely providing examples of the ways in which women have participated in Buddhist practice or history, scholars have also brought womanist and feminist scholarship into conversation with Buddhist philosophy and practice in important ways. Feminist and Buddhist thinker Rita Gross is perhaps most well known in this regard through her groundbreaking work *Buddhism After Patriarchy* (1993), which sought both to account for Buddhist women's history within the tradition and apply Buddhist thought to the deconstruction of sexist hierarchies within Buddhism. Other scholars, such as Anne Klein (2008), have sought to bring feminist theory into conversation with Buddhist philosophy, exploring the nonessentialist aspects of both.

Scholarship that focuses on convert groups has the tendency to obscure the experiences of Asian American Buddhists; similarly, scholarship that focuses on monastic practice overlooks the contribution of lay Buddhists generally and women Buddhists specifically. Arai's work on women Buddhists in Japan provides an important corrective to a scholarly narrative that privileges (largely male) monastics by foregrounding Buddhist practice and ritual at home (2011). In the United States, her work finds company in scholarship by Usuki and Suh who analyze the experiences of women Buddhists in the Buddhist Churches of America and the Los Angeles Korean temple Sa Chal (Usuki 2007; Suh 2004). Collectively, such work points to the gendered aspects of Buddhist practice; when scholarship focuses on one set of practices that have been enacted predominately by male members of the community, a distorted picture of Buddhism emerges, one that is enhanced by the inclusion of women's voices and experiences.

LGBTQI Buddhists and queer theory

Related to Buddhism's problem with gender is a problem with sex. This should not be surprising, after all, given the fact that the central problem of Buddhism is *duhkha* (suffering), and its cause is desire. "Sexual desire traps us; it renders us slaves to pleasure, slaves to our partners, slaves to the body itself … sex is vilified as the ultimate source of samsara, for it is what brought us all into our unhappy existence in the first place" (Gyatso 2005, 274). Accordingly, monastic *vinaya* regulations go to great length to describe inappropriate sexual behavior for monastics. However, we should not take this to mean that Buddhism has anything against specific sexual identities. "The principle question for Buddhism has not been one of heterosexuality vs. homosexuality but one of sexuality vs. celibacy" (Cabezón 1998, 30). A strict hetero-/homosexual binary obscures what is in fact a wide spectrum of sexual behavior, behavior that may have very little to do with whether or not one identifies as straight or gay. It is these behaviors (not the identity of the individual engaging in them) that are the subject of *vinaya* regulations. Thus, when we read that monks should not engage in specifically homosexual *behavior*, we should not read this as a condemnation of a homosexual *identity*. These are two different things.

However, one needs to be attentive to the fact that these monastic regulations are just that—rules for monks and nuns—and not necessarily applicable to the laity. In a very general sense, lay Buddhist ethics are defined by the five lay precepts that include the rather broad statement that one should refrain from sexual misconduct, a precept that has been interpreted variously in different cultures and times, determined more by local custom than monastic oversight. Thus, to understand Buddhist attitudes toward homosexuality, one would necessarily need to look beyond the *sangha* and to the larger sociocultural context in which Buddhism is embedded. In the specific case of the contemporary United States, homosexuality has come to refer both to a set of behaviors as well as a specific identity. Since the mid-twentieth century, persons who self-identify as gay and lesbian have increasingly advocated for equal legal treatment under the law, a discourse that emerged part and parcel with the civil rights and feminist movements.

LGBTQI

An acronym for Lesbian, Gay, Bisexual, Transgender, Queer, and Intersex used by persons who do not identify as heterosexual or cisgender especially in regards to civil rights activism.

Since the 1970s, LGBTQI persons have been a visible presence in many US Buddhist communities. More than that, several communities have been established exclusively for gay and lesbian Buddhists such as the Gay Buddhist Fellowship in San Francisco or the Lesbian Buddhist Sangha in Berkeley. While both communities are ostensibly pan-sectarian in character, they are closely related to the Zen Buddhist tradition. Based on field work at the Gay Buddhist Fellowship, Corless suggests that creating such communities can be profoundly important for young LGBTQI persons who have internalized homophobia, manifesting as a type of self-loathing that is the cause of high suicide rates among young gay men. Such groups explicitly link work to eradicate internalized homophobia with Buddhist liberative philosophies directed at ending suffering (2000, 271).

Much in the way that racial and gender identities are managed through legal systems, LGBTQI identities are similarly managed as evidenced by antisodomy laws and same-sex marriage bans. Whereas these laws have been deemed unconstitutional and whereas popular opinion has shifted rapidly in the last twenty years in support of LGBTQI equality, this is a recent development. An earlier era of US Buddhist history saw teachers from time to time denying the existence of gay persons in their communities or of warning that same-sex relationships are dangerous (Corless 2000, 272; Wilson 2012a, 33). The Buddhist Churches of America, however, appears to have been an early supporter of LGBTQI rights, and there is evidence that BCA ministers were performing same-sex weddings in California as early as 1976 (Wilson 2012a, 37), some thirty years before it became legal in the state. In 2008, *Star Trek* actor and gay rights advocate George Takei married his long-time partner Brad Altman in a ceremony officiated by BCA minister Rev. William Briones.

Whereas marriage equality has become a defining feature of the contemporary gay rights movement, it is important to note that other voices in the larger LGBTQI community have been critical of an exclusive focus on this one issue as it tends to overshadow other issues of economic, racial, and gender inequality. At the heart of this critique is the assertion that same-sex marriage, to the extent that is it modeled on heterosexual marriage, replicates heteronormative values; it cannot, therefore, critique heteronormative culture and threatens to disenfranchise those who do not feel comfortable in these normative categories. It is within this space that queer theorists have been active in pushing the boundaries of gender and sexual identities, arguing for the diversification and acceptance of a wider spectrum of human experience. Queer theory is:

[c]ommonly employed as an umbrella signifier for people with culturally marginal gender and sexual identities, queer emerged as an intellectual term to delineate a

distinct theoretical discourse—queer theory—that developed, in part, as a critique of gay, lesbian, and bisexual studies. Whereas gay, lesbian, and bisexual studies often advocate an essentialist model of sexuality, following the anti-foundational orientation of postmodern and poststructural thought, queer theory proposes a radical social constructivism. It disrupts all stable, binary, and fixed configurations of gender and sexual identity and claims rather that all gendered and sexual identities are discursively conditioned, contingent and ideologically motivated. (Gleig 2012a, 120)

Buddhist scholars and activists alike have begun to have fruitful dialogues between Buddhist thought and queer theory. Corless (2004), Hopkins (1997), and others have advocated that queer theory and Buddhist theory share a natural affinity to the extent that both seek to deconstruct notions of the self or essentialist identities. This work suggests a "queering" of Buddhism, or, to use Corless' term, a "queer dharmology," that moves past both Western tropes of homophobia and sexism as well as Asian and Buddhist hierarchies and patriarchy. As hopeful as this work is, however, Gleig's (2012a) ethnographic fieldwork suggests that LGBTQI Buddhists have tended to de-emphasize their queer identities in light of Buddhist concepts such as no-self and emptiness. It is partly in response to this "de-queering" of Buddhism that groups such as the Alphabet Sangha, discussed briefly in Chapter 8, have emerged. Begun within the already progressive East Bay Meditation Center in Oakland, California, the Alphabet Sangha's founders were critical of a heteronormative, white middle-class Buddhism that was inattentive to the unique experiences of LGBTQI Buddhists, especially those of lower socioeconomic standing and Buddhists of color.

In this way, a postmodern queer dharmology, to mix both Corless and Gleig, gestures toward a fuller understanding of intersectionality. Buddhist identities emerge within a complex matrix of religion, class, race, gender, and sexual identity, a full accounting of which is necessary to understand personal experience and recognize the ways in which larger systems of meaning are supportive of or undermine individual rights and thus are a cause of suffering.

Power and privilege in US Buddhism

Much has been said about democratization as a defining feature of US Buddhism. Generally speaking, the argument has been advanced that US Buddhists have leveled the playing field, so to speak, by giving laity access to practices that have historically been the purview of a monastic elite. Coupled with the inclusion of women in positions of leadership, one might assume that US Buddhism has well overcome issues of power and inequality endemic to other religious traditions (Tanaka 1998).

A note of caution is in order. Regardless of how many people may be engaged in meditation practice, we should not assume that this translates into a wholesale reversal of the types of hierarchy and patriarchy critiqued by Gross and others. Indeed, by all accounts men remain disproportionally represented in leadership roles in many US

Buddhist communities, and as we will discuss in the following chapter, there have been several high-profile cases of sexual abuse on the part of male leaders toward their female students. We should not assume that equal access to *practice* (e.g., lay people meditating) is equivalent to equal access to *power* (e.g., being in a position of leadership) (Mitchell 2008; cf Cadge 2004). And such inequality often intersects with race, gender, and sexual orientation.

Religion is not merely a matter of belief. Religion is also a matter of action, of what persons do, how they interact with other persons and engage the world. These engagements are necessarily embodied. Whether embodiment is a factor of ritual and practice (a meditating body) or the means by which beliefs are articulated (a particular person confessing belief or delivering a dharma talk), religion happens in bodies. And bodies are the subject of regulation and legislation. Anti-miscegenation laws, birth control laws, anti-sodomy laws, and so forth, all in one way or another regulate bodies marked in the social realm in specifically racial, gendered, and sexualized ways. A failure to appreciate the ways in which different bodies are defined in the body politic is a failure to appreciate the lived experiences of persons, regardless of the ultimate reality (or emptiness) of their identities. In short, the government is not concerned with *anatman* when it passes legislation.

Critical race, feminist, and queer theories have been embraced by a new generation of Buddhist social activists and provide the theoretical, philosophical, and ethical framework within which engaged Buddhists confront social and ecological suffering, the subject of the next chapter. Whereas we have chosen here to discuss the intersection of race, gender, sexuality, and religion, attention should be paid to a wider variety of identity markers including age, physical and mental ability, national origin, language, and socioeconomic class. Scholars and observers have only just begun to explore this interlocking set of identities and the roles they play in the formation of Buddhist communities and modes of practice. Class is perhaps the most obvious next step for research. Activists have already begun critiquing the standard US Buddhist practice model of the meditation retreat as one that privileges a certain class of Buddhists—those with the financial means to attend.[2] Even sessions that are offered for free may still take place at a distance from urban centers and necessarily require participants to be able to take time off from work. Given the widening economic divide in the United States, more sustained discussion around class and Buddhism may well surface in decades to come.

A note on two Buddhisms and the academy

Almost since the beginning of the serious academic study of US Buddhism, scholars have attempted to categorize the diversity of US Buddhist traditions; and since the 1990s, race has become a central feature of these taxonomies. In the 1970s, two foundational texts set the terms for the following several decades' worth of academic study: Layman's *Buddhism in America* (1976) and Prebish's *American*

Buddhism (1979). Both books noted that, at the time, US Buddhist communities could be reasonably divided into different categories; whereas race was not explicit in these categories, it was hard to miss the connection between Layman's "church-like" groups and predominately Asian American *sanghas* or between Prebish's new, charismatic, and flamboyant communities and the (at the time) recently established predominately convert *sanghas*.

Race became foregrounded in the 1990s, largely in response to an editorial in *Tricycle: The Buddhist Review* by then-editor Helen Tworkov who noted that the "spokespeople for Buddhism in America have been, almost exclusively, educated members of the white middle class." She went on to say that Asian American Buddhists had not yet "figured prominently in the development of something called American Buddhism" (1991, 4). Whether intentionally or not, this editorial both explicitly split US Buddhists into Asian and white communities and suggested that the former were not authentically American.

Several scholarly and popular articles followed, including Prebish's "Two Buddhisms Reconsidered" (1993), Nattier's "Visible and Invisible" (1995), and Numrich's "Two Buddhisms Further Considered" (2003). Each, in their own way, argued for different articulations of the typology and/or its continued relevance. There are, after all, different traditions of Buddhism in the United States that historically track, more or less, to spe-cific ethnic groups. Taxonomies or typologies that merely observe this are not, in them-selves, problematic. How these typologies are applied or the language that is used, however, may be problematic, such as in the case of Nattier's taxonomy that sought to focus on the methods by which Buddhism enters the United States—either imported by native-born Americans or exported from Asia via immigration. Unfortunately, her typology was burdened by her use of the term "baggage Buddhism" for immigrant groups, thus reinforcing the notion that cultural traditions are mere baggage that can be discarded in favor of some essential Buddhist identity, and that converts are not similarly weighed down by their own cultural baggage. Despite these and other limi-tations, Numrich nevertheless argued for the continued relevancy and usefulness of the two Buddhisms typology for, if nothing else, the distinction "highlights important majority/minority ethnic dynamics" in North America (2003, 65), a subject sorely in need of further study.

Hickey (2010; 2015) has provided some thoughtful and cogent criticism of the vari-ous taxonomies, importantly calling our attention to the way in which they trap com-munities in time and are thus unable to account for generational differences.[3] Both categories are so wide and internally diverse that at some point the only commonal-ity among different communities is ethnicity; put another way, in what specific ways are the Buddhist experiences of fourth-generation Japanese American Zen Buddhists similar to recent Burmese Theravada refugees such that they should be included in the same category? Moreover, typologies such as Nattier's are unable to account for "export"-like activity in "import" groups and vice versa. Similarly, as Masatsugu (2008) notes, studies that treat Asian and white/convert communities as mutually isolated overlook the ways in which both communities were in conversation and dialogue with one another historically and in the contemporary scene. And, finally, by rendering all US Buddhists as *either* Asian *or* white/convert, we create and reproduce a dichotomy that "obscures the presence of Buddhists who are neither, such as Latino/as, African Americans, Pacific Islanders, or people of mixed heritage" (Hickey 2015, 48; cf Quli 2009).

If the typology is so problematic, why have scholars been so attached to defending and refining it? One reason may have to do with the development of Buddhism in the West as a distinct sub-field of Buddhist Studies more generally—or, to borrow from Payne, the unloved stepchild of this broader academic field (2015, 217). Buddhist Studies has traditionally been done through area studies; scholars specialize in East Asia, say, or more narrowly on Japan. It would make sense, then, that one could become a specialist of Buddhism in North America akin to a specialist of Buddhism in East Asia. However, Buddhist Studies has historically been indifferent or even hostile to the study of Buddhisms outside Asia, which is privileged as Buddhism's ideal field site (Quli 2009, 3). Thus when Layman and Prebish were writing their foundational studies in the 1970s, their academic disciplines did not consider the subject a legitimate area of inquiry (Numrich 2008, 4; Prebish 1999). In this context, much work was necessary to justify the study of Buddhism in Western contexts, work that replicated an area studies approach, foregrounding what made Buddhism in the West distinctive from its predecessors. As a consequence, "American Buddhism" became rendered "as a monolithic geographic/cultural movement" (Wilson 2015, 23) eliding over its internal diversity, regional variation, and translocal connections and continuities with Asian Buddhisms.

This discussion is not meant to delegitimize the project of creating typologies of US Buddhism; nor is it intended to argue for or against one particular view point. Indeed, my aim here is not to suggest that we are wrong to employ the "two Buddhisms" typology or that it should be abandoned. Rather, this discussion is merely to situate the academic study of Buddhism within its proper historical and cultural context. As Hickey notes, "some of the *assumptions* underlying *taxonomies of American Buddhism* reflect unconscious white privilege" (Hickey 2015, 39, emphasis in original). This is not to say that scholars are racist; rather, drawing from MacIntosh's work covered earlier, privilege manifests as easily in academic communities as anywhere. As scholars, we are not immune from the larger forces of social history that often inform how we conduct our work, subtly, and at times unconsciously, influencing how we frame that which we study. Responsible scholarship necessarily takes self-reflection and self-criticism seriously, turning its critical faculties on itself from time to time to reveal shortcomings and blind spots. From this point of view, it is somewhat irrelevant whether or not there are two Buddhisms or three or four in the United States; here, it is merely enough to note the *implications* of these categories, who they include, who they exclude, what the typology reveals, and what it obscures. Indeed, all scholars should regularly ask themselves the most basic of research questions—does this methodology *work*? Is it helpful or does it get in the way?—and when the answer is in the negative, be open to new ways of approaching their subject.

DISCUSSION QUESTIONS

1. How does the legal construction and maintenance of racial categories disrupt our assumption that race is natural or biological?

2. What were the consequences to Buddhist community formation and practice as a result of discrimination against Japanese immigrants?

3. What are some of the ways feminists and queer theorists have been in conversation with Buddhist philosophy?

SUGGESTIONS FOR FURTHER READING

Adams, Sheridan, Mushim Ikeda-Nash, Jeff Kitzes, Margarita Loinaz, Choyin Rangdrol, Jessica Tan, and Larry Yang, eds. 2000. *Making the Invisible Visible: Healing Racism in Our Buddhist Communities*. Woodacre, CA: Spirit Rock.

Gleig, Ann. 2012. "Queering Buddhism or Buddhist De-Queering?" *Theology & Sexuality* 18 (3): 198–214.

Hickey, Wakoh Shannon. 2010. "Two Buddhisms, Three Buddhisms, and Racism." *Journal of Global Buddhism* 11: 1–25.

Kolmar, Wendy K., and Frances Bartkowski, eds. 2010. *Feminist Theory: A Reader*. 3rd ed. Boston: McGraw-Hill Higher Education.

Manuel, Zenju Earthlyn. 2015. *The Way of Tenderness: Awakening through Race, Sexuality, and Gender*. Boston: Wisdom Publications.

Numrich, Paul David. 2003. "Two Buddhisms Further Considered." *Contemporary Buddhism* 4 (1): 55–78.

Quli, Natalie E. 2009. "Western Self, Asian Other: Modernity, Authenticity, and Nostalgia for 'Tradition' in Buddhist Studies." *Journal of Buddhist Ethics* 16: 1–38.

11

Buddhist engagements: Confronting environmental and social suffering

Chapter summary and outline

Largely in response to political turmoil in Asia in the late twentieth century, and drawing from Western human rights and environmentalist discourses, the engaged Buddhist movement is global in scale with a sizable influence in the United States. Following an overview of the movement's history, attention is paid to environmental activism, peace work, restorative justice, and prison outreach. Analytical frames aimed at social suffering have also been used to address racial and gender inequality within Buddhist communities.

Introduction: Wisdom 2.0

Over the last decade, Silicon Valley technology companies such as Google, Facebook, and Twitter have increasingly embraced and begun offering courses in "spiritual technologies" like yoga and mindfulness meditation to their employees. Google's "Search Inside Yourself" course led by Chade-Meng Tan, a software-engineer-turned-resident-meditation instructor, teaches its employees to better manage their emotions and increase productivity. One cofounder of Twitter hosts meditation sessions at the company's San Francisco headquarters throughout the workday. Such initiatives are featured at a series of conferences called Wisdom 2.0 where technology workers are exposed to a wide array of techniques—many inspired from Buddhist teachings—on how to connect with their emotions, disconnect from distractions, and focus on both career and personal goals with the aim of making the world a better place. These programs have come at a time of soaring tech company profits, a profitability that has led to an influx of young tech workers to San Francisco which has displaced long-time residents. Frustrated by gentrification and the displacement of lower-income residents, the activist group Eviction Free San Francisco staged a protest at the 2014 Wisdom 2.0 conference to highlight the disconnect between the technology sector's claims of creating a better world and the reality of economic disparity in San Francisco. Protesters, especially those who were members of the East Bay Meditation Center and the Buddhist Peace Fellowship, were also concerned about the use of Buddhist-derived practices in this corporate environment and the supposed commercialization of mindfulness meditation divorced from any ethical framework (Corbyn 2014; Ream 2014; Shachtman 2013).

Regardless of where one stands on such issues as gentrification or the commercialization of religion, the Wisdom 2.0 protest highlights many of the themes under consideration in this chapter. First, it is an example of method—that is a specific way in which Buddhists have engaged perceived social suffering through direct action and nonviolent public protest. Second, it is an example of rhetorical strategies used by engaged Buddhists. In publications and online discourse following the protest, engaged Buddhists articulated a specific Buddhist critique both of the conference as well as what are perceived to be the underlying causes of social suffering—capitalist systems that perpetuate economic inequality. Whereas this critique is primarily directed toward sources of suffering outside the Buddhist community, it is also self-reflective, critiquing the ways in which Buddhist teachers have promoted mindfulness meditation and other practices in corporate environments, opening a space for Buddhists to reflect on their responsibility in perpetuating both the social institutions that cause suffering as well as the commercialization of religion. Thus, the Wisdom 2.0 protest highlights the ways in which engaged Buddhists seek to critically engage social systems of inequality while being self-reflective and self-critical. While hardly universally supported by all US Buddhists, engaged Buddhist movements have been and continue to be both a facet of US Buddhist practice and a subject of scholarly attention.

To be sure, socially engaged Buddhism is hardly an American or even Western phenomenon. It is a global movement "found throughout the Buddhist world East and West" (King 2012, 196). Nevertheless, it is also true that such movements are the result of a convergence of Buddhist and Western thought, emerging "in the context of a global conversation on human rights, distributive justice, and social progress" (Queen 2000, 1). This convergence has been the ground upon which Buddhists have engaged in antiwar and antinuclear proliferation protests; have articulated a Buddhist response to social and economic inequality; and have justified specific types of engagement such as nonviolent protest or chaplaincy work. Engaged Buddhism is thus both a mode of action or practice as well as a particular socially critical orientation or set of rhetorical discourses.

The purpose of the present chapter is not to offer a detailed engaged Buddhist ethic or a defense of any one particular engaged Buddhist approach to, paraphrasing Victoria, redeem the potential of engaged Buddhism by uncovering and critiquing all of the skeletons in its closet (2001, 89). Rather, the intent here is to highlight some of the ways in which US Buddhists have engaged particular environmental and social justice issues, both within and outside the *sangha*, movements that have dominated much US public Buddhist discourse and shaped the development of several US Buddhist communities. We will begin with a short overview of these movements' histories and doctrinal justifications. From there, we will examine several specific movements and engaged Buddhist causes such as climate change, restorative justice, and chaplaincy; and finally we will reflect on how this complex of engaged orientations has been used to self-critique injustices within Buddhist *sanghas*.

History and origins

One might say that modern engaged Buddhism begins in Asia—in India, Thailand, Tibet, and Vietnam. Throughout the twentieth century, activists across Asia began advocating for social change by making explicit appeals to Buddhist philosophy and ethics. In India, at the end of British colonial rule, B. R. Ambedkar (1891–1956) argued for an end to the caste system that disenfranchised untouchable classes such as the *dalit*. Toward the end of his life, Ambedkar formally converted to Buddhism along with nearly half a million of his followers, most of whom came from lower castes. In Thailand, Sulak Sivaraksa (b. 1933) has worked for social, economic, and environmental causes since the 1970s. An outspoken critic of government corruption, he has argued that foundational Buddhist principals can be a guide for social change while also arguing for the need to modernize the Buddhist *sangha* to be an effective voice for change on the world stage. Following the occupation of Tibet by People's Liberation Army in 1959, the Dalai Lama has spent much of the last half-century articulating a message of compassionate action rather than violence in response to the humanitarian crisis in his homeland. Finally, Thich Nhat Hanh is an heir to a long tradition of Buddhist activism in

FIGURE 31 *Thich Nhat Hanh, b. 1926. (Getty Images.)*

Vietnam, which began with resistance to French colonial rule and was reinvigorated in the mid-twentieth century as the war with the United States escalated. It was during this time that Thich Nhat Hanh first began using and popularizing the phrase "engaged Buddhism" (Hunt-Perry and Fine 2000). In works such as *Being Peace* (1987), he has articulated an approach to nonviolence and peace work that applies traditional Buddhist concepts and practices such as compassion and mindfulness in service of conflict resolution (King 2012, 199).

Figures such as Thich Nhat Hanh, the Dalai Lama, and Sulak Sivaraksa are the inspiration for American engaged Buddhist movements. Arguably, no organization has been as influential and central to the establishment of US engaged Buddhism as the Buddhist Peace Fellowship (BPF). In the late 1970s, Robert and Anne Aitken, Nelson Foster, and others met at the Aitken's home in Maui, Hawai'i, where a conversation about increased US military build-up and nuclear proliferation over the preceding decade led to questions of how Buddhists could or should respond. This, in turn, led to the establishment of what would become the BPF, a self-consciously nonsectarian, grass-roots organization dedicated to peace, environmentalism, feminism, and social justice. By the 1980s, dozens of chapters had been established across the United States, and an office was opened in Berkeley, California. Also at that time, a new Buddhist publishing house, Parallax Press, and several teaching tours brought Thich Nhat Hanh's works to a wider North American audience. This coincided with the expansion of the BPF's socially engaged network, which drew from a diverse set of leaders and teachers including, among others, Jack Kornfield, Al Bloom, Ryo Imamura, Joanna Macy, Taitetsu Unno, Alan Senauke, and Tova Green. During the first Gulf War (1990–1991), the BPF actively protested increased military involvement in the Middle East, and BPF chapters held meetings and protests in several states. Such work brought the group to some mainstream attention and allowed for even more growth through the end of the century (Simmer-Brown 2000). In the early 2000s, Senauke stepped down as director; Maia Duerr and Susan Moon led the organization through a few turbulent years before leadership was handed over to a new generation of Buddhist activists. Current codirectors Katie Loncke and Dawn Haney have reinvigorated the BPF, reimagining the *Turning Wheel* journal as an online multimedia platform and inaugurating several activist training and education projects that embed modern human rights discourses within Buddhist moral frameworks.[1]

The BPF is but one of several US engaged Buddhist organizations that focus on environmental activism, peace work, and restorative justice. Such organizations include, but are certainly not limited to, the following. Begun in 1982 with the opening of the Greyston Bakery in Yonkers, New York, Bernie Glassman's Zen Peacemakers Order has affiliates across North America and the world. The Greyston Foundation, building on experiences learned at its founding bakery, has built a network of conscious businesses and urban poverty reduction projects. The Zen Peacemakers Order is engaged in several international projects focused on ending international conflict, poverty and homelessness, and prison outreach. In this last category, they are affiliated with the Prison Mindfulness Institute, established in 1985 by Fleet Maull, which works with prisons and inmates across the country, distributing books and leading meditation courses. Apart from large networks of activist communities, both individuals and local communities participate in engaged Buddhist work, such as the environmental activism of poet Gary Snyder (Barnhill 2010) and retreats he has inspired at locations such as the Zen Mountain Monastery in New York. These organizations are joined in the United States by transnational groups such as Thich Nhat Hanh's Order of Interbeing, Sulak Sivaraksa's International Network of Engaged Buddhists, the Tzu Chi Foundation, and various Nichiren-derived organizations that are active world-wide and are devoted to world peace (Stone 2003).

At the risk of oversimplifying various engaged Buddhist strategies and discourses, contemporary engaged Buddhist thinkers and activists generally articulate their approach and justify their movements in one of several interrelated ways. First, extrapolating from Buddhist concepts such as interdependence and *tathagatagarbha* or Buddha-nature thought, some engaged Buddhists contend that we cannot view ourselves as isolated individuals but rather as part of a larger, interconnected whole. The notion of interconnectedness is then tied to an articulation of karma that stresses both its cause-and-effect and collective senses. That is, rather than viewing karma in a fatalistic or purely moral sense, engaged Buddhists seek to understand the complex causes and conditions that lead to the creation of social structures and their coincident problems. Karma is thus reframed from an individual or personal problem to a collective one; current social suffering is the result of collective action not an individual's past bad behavior. The proper response to our collective social ills is then based on several related, and often vaguely defined (Keown 2012, 216, 224), Buddhist values such as loving kindness, nonviolence, and compassion. Such values point toward both our capacity for empathy as well as specific modes of action expressed in terms of nonviolence or non-adversariality (King 2012, 209). Sometimes, such attitudes are linked explicitly to the bodhisattva path, here presumed to mean that a bodhisattva is one who foregoes personal liberation by first attending to the suffering of others. These last two points direct our attention to ways in which engaged Buddhists have articulated engagement *as* practice; that is, rather than viewing engaged activity as secondary to or the consequence of doing Buddhist practice proper, it is understood as a type of practice in itself. Ideally, engaged Buddhists encourage a balance between political or social activism and spiritual development wherein one's sense of inner peace or equanimity is extended outwardly into social justice work.

Engaged Buddhist values

In the Buddhist context, *ahimsa* (nonviolence) is mostly related to the precept against killing. *Maitri* (*metta* in Pali) is usually translated as "loving kindness" and refers to the wish for others' well-being. By comparison, *karuna*, or compassion, is the specific desire for others to be freed from suffering. These values often form the basis of an engaged Buddhist ethic.

These understandings of the Buddhist path are drawn from multiple sources covering the wide spectrum of Buddhist traditions from Theravada through Mahayana and Vajrayana. This eclecticism combined with obvious reinterpretations of Buddhist doctrine have contributed to criticisms against engaged Buddhist movements as essentially modern or thoroughly Western understandings of Buddhism inconsistent with traditional beliefs or practices. In premodern Buddhism, karma, for example, was often understood in punitive terms; persons born into less-than-ideal circumstances could be seen as suffering the results of past bad actions (Anālayo 2014; King 2012, 201). Whereas it might seem obvious to extend a generalized sense of empathy or compassion toward the natural world based on the Buddhist values listed, there is little evidence in canonical sources for something akin to an "environmental ethic," which suggests that such sentiments owe more to Western than Buddhist thought (Blum 2009; Keown 2012). Indeed, such values can be interpreted in any number of different ways, especially in a tradition that at times has valued the "home-leaver," one who leaves behind the comforts of society to dedicate himself or herself entirely to Buddhist monastic practice, suggesting that "Buddhism is about escaping samsara, not trying to fix it" (King 2012, 207).

Perhaps the most cogent critique of engaged Buddhism concerns the idealized presentation of the religion as progressive and nonviolent, a stereotype that is inconsistent with historical and contemporary realities. Rising Japanese Buddhist nationalism from the Meiji Restoration through World War II is now common knowledge (Sharf 1995b; Victoria 1997, 2001; cf Miyata 2002); it is also hardly uncommon across Buddhist history (Jerryson and Juergensmeyer 2010). Recent incidents of Buddhist nationalism and concomitant violence in Sri Lanka and Burma have made mainstream news in the United States, which, combined with sometimes conflicting or confusing ethical guidelines in canonical sources, makes it difficult to hold the view that Buddhism is necessarily and always pacifistic (Jenkins 2009). Whereas some may be wont to dismiss such activity as "not Buddhist," it is clear that such behavior was and is often expressed in Buddhist terms, realities that do not always line up with contemporary American progressive or liberal values with which Buddhism has become closely associated. This disconnect between idyllic views of a pacifist and compassionate Buddhism and the harsh realities of the world has led some to assert that

> Engaged Buddhism cannot expect to be taken seriously when it claims to be a movement dedicated to constructive and liberating change for both individual and society ... [W]ho but the naive will believe that Engaged Buddhism is the sole exception to the ongoing reality that national *self*-interest readily turns religions, *all* religions, into its willing and obedient servants, ever ready to condone state-sanctioned killing when called upon to do so? (Victoria 2001, 89, emphasis in original)

The less-than-perfect track record of Buddhist history vis-à-vis social justice and environmental ethics is joined by a concern that the movement is really more Western than Buddhist. Blum (2009) argues persuasively that interpretations of the dharma that are the foundation of a Buddhist environmental ethic are more indebted to American Transcendentalism than they are to traditional Buddhism. One can find a clear line of continuity between Emerson's and Thoreau's valorization of the wild, of nature, and their antinomian attitudes and post–World War II environmental Buddhists such as Gary Snyder. When one contrasts classical depictions of a world-renouncing (and nature-renouncing) Buddhism with the lofty embrace of the natural world of the high Sierras in Snyder's poetry, for example, or when reflecting on how such orientations give a type of sentience or agency to the natural world, Blum suggests that "we are no longer in the realm of Buddhism ... but in something of a Buddhist-inspired new American religion, one that appears to draw on the legacy of Emerson and Thoreau as much as Jizang and Dogen" (2009, 234). Nevertheless, Blum is quick to note the importance of such environmental movements, that they are necessary, needed, and to be valued. "Setting ecologically sound priorities toward the natural world that are not only very different from but at cross-purposes to someone else's exploitative priorities is reasonable, plausible, and ethical, but it need not be *religious* to have meaning and power" (ibid., emphasis in original).

Inarguably, contemporary engaged Buddhist movements are the result of a convergence of modernity and traditionalism, Eastern and Western thought, emerging within specific contexts and often in response to particular social and ecological crises, representing one strategy of adaptation that allows Buddhism to remain relevant in its modern American context. Engaged Buddhists should, no doubt, be honest about Buddhism's past and present failings and imperfections; this does not mean that they cannot also, perhaps simultaneously, attend to social and environmental suffering.

Environmental engagement

Engaged Buddhists must address the causes and effects of human-created global climate change if for no other reason than because all persons need to address current ecological crisis. Certainly engaged Buddhists do not need to address climate change *as Buddhists*; nevertheless, many have done so, articulating specific responses or strategies to address a wide range of ecological dilemmas. For example, Blum's comments about the American Transcendentalist influence on environmentally engaged Buddhism were inspired by "eco-monks" in Thailand who have devised a wide array of strategies for confronting environmental problems and deforestation in Thailand. One strategy to curb deforestation is to ordain trees as monks thus conferring upon them the same respect given to human monastics (Darlington 2003, 2009; King 2012).

In North America, environmentally engaged Buddhism takes many forms. Often, based on a generalized sense of empathy or respect for the natural world, environmental engagement may simply be a concern for animal welfare. Whereas many Buddhist traditions in East Asia have long advocated for a strict vegetarianism, this has hardly been the norm throughout Buddhist history. In the West, vegetarianism has become popular in some Buddhist circles both because of this general concern for suffering sentient beings as well as a concern for the larger agricultural system that produces meat and is in many ways not sustainable (Kaza 2010, 46). At times, this concern for animal welfare is expressed through traditional Buddhist rituals such as the release of animals (Williams 1997), a common practice in many parts of Buddhist Asia of ritually freeing animals intended for slaughter. At Gampo Abbey in Nova Scotia, for example, Buddhist residents annually buy a batch of lobsters from local fishermen and release them back into the wild (Verchery 2007).

Other small-scale acts of environmental engagement may be undertaken by a single *sangha* or community. Since its establishment in 1979 by Taizan Maezumi, the Zen Mountain Center has always worked hard to ensure that its activities are not impactful to the delicate ecosystem of the San Jacinto Mountains. Beginning in the 1990s, the center has initiated several environmental programs and hired a forester to oversee their future building development plans (Yamauchi 1997). In 2015, the Buddhist Churches of America passed an "EcoSangha" resolution, initiating a nation-wide campaign to help local temples become more environmentally friendly through reducing resource consumption, recycling, and composting (Castro 2015).

Environmental engagement can also take the form of direct action protest. In the late 1980s, a small, locally owned logging company in Northern California was taken over by a larger, national corporation; in short order, the new owners reversed more than a century of sustainable forestry with clear-cutting of Pacific Coast redwoods, a policy that threatened local ecosystems. Local environmental activist groups were joined by Zen Buddhists calling themselves "ecosattvas," extending the bodhisattva vow to save all beings to the redwoods. Here, activism took the shape of nonviolent protests to stop clear-cutting; the Buddhists joined in by engaging in seated meditation, the chanting of sutras, and generating "a field of loving-kindness" (Kaza 2000, 159). Such direct action protests continue to the present. For several years, activists in both the United States and Canada have been protesting the construction and extension of the Keystone Oil pipeline, intended to transport crude oil across North America. The pipeline system has been critiqued both because it has a high rupture rate resulting in ecologically disastrous oil spills and because it perpetuates reliance on fossil fuels. Buddhists have joined protesters, including a large protest at TransCanada offices in Houston, Texas, in 2013 (Thomas 2013). In September 2014, more than 300,000 people participated in the People's Climate March in New York in advance of the UN Climate Summit. The march was intended to highlight the growing concern many Americans have about global climate change and the sense that world political leaders are doing little to address ecological problems. Hundreds of Buddhists from dozens of different communities participated in the event, including Shin Buddhist priest T. Kenjitsu Nakagaki, Buddhist journalist and activist Joshua Eaton, and bhiksuni Ayya Santussika of Karuna Buddhist Vihara (Eaton 2014; Fisher 2014b).

Whereas direct action protests are certainly one way to address ecological problems, engaged Buddhists have also worked at providing an "analysis of social structures and [the] creation of new alternatives" to our current ways of being in the world (Kaza 2000, 170)—the articulation of Buddhist approaches to or critiques of the systemic causes of ecological crises. Kaza (2010) has argued that the root causes of environmental problems are consumerism and overconsumption. Global systems of capitalism and the consumption of consumer goods and resources often results in pollution, deforestation, and human-created climate change. After noting traditional Western critiques of consumerism—such as the Puritan critique that argues that goods should only serve practical ends and not be objects of desire in themselves or the Marxist critique that focuses on how capitalist systems exploit workers—Kaza offers suggestions for a specific Buddhist critique of consumerism and overconsumption. Rooted in classical formulations of the Buddhist path beginning with desire as the cause of suffering, she argues for a Buddhist critique "that consumerism facilitates the formation of a false identity, promotes harm to other living beings, and impels clinging and attachment" (49). The formation of a false identity—or, more precisely, the deconstruction of a false notion of the self or the ego—is the crux of the Buddhist path. Dake takes up this issue in his critique of forms of (particularly Western) Buddhism that seem to reify the self rather than undertaking a deep examination of the problem of attachment (2010, 78). This analysis may run counter to a distinctively American preoccupation with optimism and individual self-sufficiency, suggesting a radical approach to engagement that undercuts often uncritically accepted Western values (Payne 2010, 7).

Such analyses of social structures are clearly not limited to human beings' impact on the environment but are linked to both capitalist structures and other social systems that cause not just environmental suffering but social suffering as well, a subject to which we will now turn.

Social engagement

Modern engaged Buddhists have begun to rearticulate such concepts as interdependence and karma in decidedly social terms. That is, as discussed earlier, rather than viewing karma as merely individual or personal—an explanation of how *my* past actions have led to *my* current lot in life—it is seen as collective, having social implications in a global web of interconnectivity. This perspective is brought to bear in an analysis of social systems wherein engaged Buddhists seek to understand the systemic roots of suffering. This may mean revealing inherent inequality or violence in economic or social institutions and then articulating specifically Buddhist responses or solutions. Social engagement may also mean deepening one's sense of compassion or empathy (often expressed as loving-kindness) toward those who are suffering and, rather than seeking to protest or overturn social systems, merely attend to and help to alleviate suffering. The following examples of various organizations, movements, and activists are hardly exhaustive but are meant to gesture toward the breadth and depth of US Buddhist engagements.

Peace work

Explicit in its name—the Buddhist *Peace* Fellowship—a central concern of both the BPF and other engaged Buddhist movements is peace work. The genesis of the BPF was in response to US military actions around the globe, and members have actively protested both wars in Iraq and militarism over the past three decades (Simmer-Brown 2000). They have hardly been alone in their antiwar and peace work activities. In 1977, two American-born converted monks, Heng Sure and Heng Ch'ua, engaged in a pilgrimage from Los Angeles to the City of Ten Thousand Buddhas, some 800 hundred miles north, taking three steps and a bow, as a public display of peace. Such activity—walking meditation, chanting, bowing, and so forth—is a common way that Buddhists engage in antiwar protests. The Nichiren school Nipponzan Myohoji Renge-kyo regularly engages in such walks for peace, in their case carrying small drums and chanting the *Lotus Sutra*. Whereas they are based in Japan, the organization has a global presence, constructing "peace pagodas" across the globe (Figure 32) (Green 2000).

Following the terrorist attacks of September 11, 2001, and US military engagements in Afghanistan and Iraq, engaged Buddhists have continued their opposition to war. This has included nonviolent protest. Antiwar Buddhists joined massive protests against the invasion of Iraq in 2003 in San Francisco, for example. That same year, Maia Duerr of the BPF took part in an act of civil disobedience, shutting down Westover Air Force Base in Chicopee, Massachusetts.[2] Since revisioning its newsletter as *Turning Wheel Media*, the BPF has posted numerous antiwar essays on its website and included reflections on the suffering caused by rising military engagement in its social activist curricula.

FIGURE 32 *Buddhist Peace Pagoda, Leverett, Massachusetts. (Photo courtesy Laura Bittner.)*

In *Being Peace*, Thich Nhat Hanh wrote that "[t]here is a lot of anger, frustration, and misunderstanding in the peace movement . . . It cannot fulfill the path we expect from [it]. A fresh way of being peace, of doing peace is needed" (1987, 81–82). He went on to note that this was why it was so important to do Buddhist practice; for Thich Nhat Hanh, Buddhist practice can engender a sense of inner peace that can then be put into service of peace work in the world. Engaging in explicit Buddhist acts such as meditation or chanting while also participating in public protest seems to serve two functions. First, there is the presumption that external, social violence is the result, in part, of inner states of mind. Thus, by engendering a peaceful state of mind, Buddhist meditation during a protest is intended to facilitate peaceful and nonviolent action. Second, and related to this, public displays of Buddhism such as meditating at a protest rally serve the (largely symbolic) function of demonstrating an alternative to violence and aggression, the very thing being protested (King 2012, 199).

Social justice causes

Such antiwar protest strategies have been applied to other contexts. At times, this is framed as "bearing witness" to social injustice, historic or contemporary. Bernie Glassman of the Zen Peacemakers Order began leading bearing witness retreats to

Dissenting opinions

FIGURE 33 *Members of the Buddhist Peace Fellowship protesting outside the White House, 2015. (Photo courtesy Katie Loncke.)*

In May 2014, a conference was held in Washington, DC, organized in part by William Aitken of SGI-USA and Bhikkhu Bodhi of Buddhist Global Relief. Delegates from a diverse array of US Buddhist traditions discussed climate change and racial justice and met with representatives from US State Department and the White House.

At the conclusion of the conference, a group led by members of the Buddhist Peace Fellowship carried three banners to the White House, one of which read "US Militarism Breeds Violence, Not Safety: I vow to work for peace and freedom." The sentiment was intended as a critique of US military engagements, not of the military itself.

Zen teacher Brad Warner (Chapter 8), who was not present, critiqued the action on his blog, stating that "We Buddhists only get to be nice, soft, peace-loving wimps (let's please be honest about that) because other people are willing to put themselves in harm's way to protect us." His critique was met with counterarguments from the BPF, other Buddhist teachers, and spilled over across several blogs and Facebook pages.

It is important to note here that US Buddhist do not always see eye-to-eye on political issues or specific actions, and despite the widespread engaged Buddhist movement, there are dissenting opinions and Buddhists who identify with many points along the political spectrum.[3]

the Auschwitz concentration camp in Poland in 1996. Doing Buddhist practice at the site of genocide is a way of connecting with those parts of our history where we were at our most disconnected, an attempt to both recognize and remember this historic truth as well as heal from it. Others have led similar bearing witness retreats in the United States, including, Taigen Daniel Leighton who led a meditation session at a Transatlantic Slave Trade memorial in Richmond, Virginia (Wilson 2012b, 187–217). Smaller-scale acts of public meditation have taken place in New York City subway stations as a means of juxtaposing the calm repose of mindfulness meditation with the frenetic reality of urban life.[4]

Public displays of meditation have become an important part of the Buddhist response to growing economic inequality and the emergence of the Occupy Movement. Following the global economic collapse in 2008 and the presumption that those who caused widespread poverty—investment banks—were effectively left blameless, a group of protestors set up a camp in New York City's Zuccotti Park near Wall Street in late 2011. Rallying under the slogan "We are the 99%"—a reference to the belief that 1 percent of the population holds an outsized share of the country's wealth—the movement quickly spread across the United States and the world. In New York, members of the Shambhala-derived Interdependence Project held mindfulness meditation training sessions at Zuccotti Park. In Oakland, California, the movement caught on and dovetailed with existing protest movements dedicated to economic equality and an end to police brutality. An Occupy camp was set up in the plaza adjacent to Oakland's City Hall where members of the Buddhist Peace Fellowship engaged the crowd with meditation as well as folding one thousand paper cranes for peace.[5]

A view of karma as collective, an articulation of Buddhist compassionate responses to social suffering, and a critical examination of social systems have become an increasingly important part of engaged Buddhist activism, which has been extended to issues of racial inequality. Racial tensions have been exacerbated over the past several years as a result of highly publicized acts of police violence resulting in the deaths of unarmed young black men and women, often caught on cell phone video, including Sandra Bland, Oscar Grant, Trayvon Martin, Mike Brown, Eric Garner, and Walter Scott. In addition to providing sustained analysis of social systems mentioned earlier—in this case focused on issues of institutional racism and the justice system—engaged Buddhists have also contributed to the critical discourse around police violence and the militarization of local police forces. In late 2014, a protest was organized in Oakland against police violence, and members of the BPF participated by sitting in meditation at the entrance of a police conference venue. "We used the peacefulness of our sitting meditation posture to interrupt the flow of foot traffic ... Buddhist monks from the Nipponzan Myohoji temple in Bainbridge Island, Washington offered meditative drumming and chants in what was otherwise a markedly silent protest" (Haney 2014).

Prison and chaplaincy work

An important contribution of the BPF and other engaged Buddhist networks has been the articulation of a Buddhist response to systemic inequality and institutional racism. For example, several essays posted to *Turning Wheel* deal with rising US prison populations and how this disproportionately affects the poor and persons of color. In addition to detailing such institutional structures that allow for injustice and inequality to persist, these essays also articulate a specific Buddhist response to such suffering, generally through the lens of compassion and empathy (Crooms 2013).

Such reflections are tied to specific outreach programs. Several engaged Buddhist organizations work within prisons, bringing both general Buddhist teachings as well as meditation practice to inmates—what might be collectively referred to as "prison dharma." Mentioned earlier, Fleet Maull, a student of Chögyam Trungpa and incarcerated under drug charges in the 1980s, has established several prison outreach programs and heads a network of prison ministry organizations, many of which are connected to other engaged Buddhist groups such as the Zen Peacemakers Order. Many of these programs offer mindfulness-based stress reduction programs or meditation intensives such as those featured at the opening of Chapter 5. At times, inmates must "go it alone," such as in the case of Jarvis Masters, on death row at San Quentin Prison in California. Masters practices in a Tibetan tradition of Buddhism largely on his own, having to modify *abhiseka* rituals to suit his specific needs. Oftentimes, the work of connecting the dharma with prisoners is facilitated through prison chaplains, a generally recognized figure within the prison system who may work as a go-between inmates and the outside world. Whereas most prison chaplains are Christian, increasingly Buddhist chaplaincy has emerged as an important vocation and means of expressing Buddhist compassionate action across North America (Kassor 2009).

Chaplains, of course, serve in a wide range of institutions from prisons to universities to hospitals and hospices to the military. Chaplaincy work can be seen as a type of engagement that takes seriously the call to end suffering without necessarily engaging in large-scale, public protest or activism. Indeed, many Buddhist chaplains are not interested in overturning the status quo necessarily but are instead focused on confronting suffering where it is, whether through working with those suffering from terminal illnesses such as cancer or AIDS or connecting with inmates and those in the military. Over the last decade, as Buddhist chaplaincy has emerged as a viable career path, a number of training and educational programs have begun offering advanced degrees in Buddhist chaplaincy, including Harvard Divinity School, Naropa University, University of the West, and the Institute of Buddhist Studies. Not only do these programs prepare Buddhist chaplains for careers of religious service and spiritual care, they also connect Buddhists with larger US networks of chaplaincy and religious professionals such as the Association of Professional Chaplains, thus allowing for Buddhism to further enter the North American mainstream. Finally, in addition to their work as chaplains, they have also contributed to a growing body of literature on the subject of Buddhist spiritual care, including such books as *The Arts of Contemplative Care*.

Engaging the *sangha*

It is perhaps inevitable that an engaged Buddhist discourse that seeks to reveal the ways in which social institutions perpetuate inequality or injustice and thus create suffering would eventually turn on the *sangha* itself. Buddhist communities, regardless of their intentions or basis in any particular religious tradition, are human-made communities subject to the same failings as any social institution. The history of US Buddhism is not without incidents of discrimination and inequality; and as focused as engaged Buddhists have been on relieving social suffering generally, they have also made explicit attempts to relieve suffering within their own communities.

An acknowledgment of inequality within Buddhist institutions takes many forms, perhaps the most central being: an awareness of race, gender, sexual, or class inequality and various attempts to resolve attendant issues; gender parity particularly in regards to female monastic ordination and women's leadership and confronting abuses of power and sexual abuse.

As we saw in the previous chapter, race has played a central role in the development of US Buddhism and Buddhist identity. While divisions between the so-called two Buddhisms persist and are in need of critical examination, it is also true that divisions persist within *sanghas* where Buddhists of color in particular have expressed feelings of marginalization. An important booklet distributed to predominately white communities around the turn of the twenty-first century collected personal experiences of many Buddhists of color who expressed their frustration at being excluded from Buddhist communities and discourses. One contributor wrote

> The idea of "invitation" is so crucial when approaching communities outside of the perceived mainstream. "Invitation" has very important cultural meaning and significance. Often, people who have been marginalized (whether due to race, orientation, class or other disenfranchisement) experience rejection, at best, and often abuse when walking into a space uninvited. Many of us have learned and been conditioned, not to go where the invitation is not explicitly given. Even when there is consent for inclusion, if it is silent, the consent is not experienced by those who need to be included. (Adams et al. 2000, 29)

Teachers such as Mushim Ikeda have spoken about the need for diverse *sanghas* as well as offered trainings on how to reconcile such differences. Other teachers such as angel Kyodo williams, have created sitting groups for persons of color within established communities. Still others have branched off to create new communities, such as the East Bay Meditation Center and the Alphabet Sangha (Chapter 8).

It is important to note that inequality may also manifest in terms of socioeconomic class or access to teachings, practices, or retreats. Whereas some Buddhists believe that the dharma should be freely given and operate their centers on a purely donation basis, such as the Thai Forest Monasteries (Chapter 5), other Buddhist centers require some form of payment, albeit purely as a donation, in line with traditional notions of supporting Buddhist institutions through charity (dana), a position that may be an economic necessity in the North American context. On the other hand, there are certainly some Buddhist teachers who both charge for access to teachings as well as trademark their approaches as is the case with Denis Genpo Merzel. A student of Taizan Maezumi, Merzel's trademarked approach to Zen practice, called "Big Mind," is a convergence of Zen practice and psychotherapy that promises enlightenment in this moment. His approach has been criticized by other US Zen Buddhist teachers, such as Brad Warner, both on the basis of its divergence from a traditional Zen approach and its high cost. Apart from a generalized sense that the dharma should be freely given, the deeper concern here is that if the teachings are only available to those who can afford it then the dharma becomes something of value only to the wealthy, thus perpetuating economic inequality and its concomitant social ill-effects. Even in those cases where meditation retreats or training sessions are free of charge, the very act of traveling great distances, taking time off from work, or negotiating family responsibilities can be significant burdens, suggesting that such retreats are open only to those of economic privilege.

Basic solutions to economic inequality are two-fold. On the one hand, there are Buddhists and communities that recognize that not all persons can attend expensive or distant retreats and have, therefore, begun reformulating meditation practice as something anyone can do, "in the world," at home or even at work. On the other hand, others have called into question the meditation-centric approach to Buddhist practice, noting that the privileging of one type of Buddhist practice above all others is in itself problematic. As we have touched on in previous chapters, feminist scholarship has directed attention to the ways in which a preference for meditation obscures Buddhist practices devoted to home and family, creating a hierarchy of approaches. If practice is reframed from something that must be done on a meditation cushion (regardless of whether it is in the home or in a retreat center) and is understood instead as a range of approaches from textual study to chanting to art to dana to puja to keeping moral precepts—in short, to the vast range of traditionally defined practices in Buddhist Asia—an important step has already been taken to alleviate inequality.

A further form of inequality in the sangha of concern to engaged Buddhists is of course gender inequality, which manifests in several ways. First, as has been discussed in previous chapters, the lineage of female monastics, bhiksuni, vanished in some parts of Buddhist Asia, and various attempts to restart the community have been hampered by more conservative voices. Whereas bhiksuni lineages have been reestablished in Sri Lanka and elsewhere across Southeast Asia and the West, and whereas the nun's order has been revitalized in the Tibetan traditions—events made possible in no small part by female monastics from Mahayana lineages in East Asia—resistance to these communities continues. Those who deny the legitimacy of the bhiksuni sangha generally do so based on vinaya regulations that state that a woman must be ordained before a cohort of other nuns to be valid. Because the first nuns to be ordained in these new lineages were ordained by nuns from *different* lineages, critics contend that they cannot be seen as valid ordinations in the Theravada or Mulasarvastivada *vinaya* traditions. It should be obvious here, however, that this legal interpretation of the *vinaya* presents the Buddhist community with no solution to the problem and effectively closes the door to *bhiksuni* ordination.

US engaged Buddhists have participated in this global discourse in a number of ways. Scholar-practitioner nuns such as Karma Lekshe Tsomo and organizations such as the Sakyadhita International Association of Buddhist Women have brought sustained focus to this issue, including hosting the 2007 International Congress on Buddhist Women's Role in the Sangha in Hamburg, Germany. This event was focused primarily on the establishment of the *bhiksuni* lineage in Tibetan contexts, though its import to other traditions was clear. At the conclusion of the event, the Dalai Lama gave his general support of the nun's order; however, he could not unilaterally endorse the movement without support of other Tibetan Buddhist leaders. (Since then, several concrete steps have been taken to restore the nun's order.) That US Buddhists participate in debates regarding *bhiksuni* ordination, however, has been cause for some to claim that Westerners are attempting to assert undue influence on Asian Buddhist communities, part of a critique against engaged Buddhism as something essentially "Western" and therefore not authentically "Buddhist." Anticipating this critique, Bhiksuni Lozang Trinlae has argued that as there is no way to appease conservative voices who have argued for the invalidity of *bhiksuni* ordinations, the only solution is to look outside Buddhist *vinaya* and ethical guidelines (Trinlae 2010). Regardless of the success or failure of these efforts, the debate has highlighted the inherent gender hierarchy within the Buddhist monastic institutions, which privilege male monastics and suggests that women can be full participants and leaders in the community in ways other than as monastics.

Regrettably, little sustained research has been directed toward the question of how women serve their US Buddhist communities in non-monastic positions. What research has been done along with anecdotal evidence, however, suggests that there are a disproportionate number of male meditation teachers and leaders across the US Buddhist landscape despite the fact that women make up the majority of community members (Cadge 2004; Suh 2004; Usuki 2007). Whereas there are a number of prominent women in US Buddhist history—such as Pema Chödrön, Ruth Denison, Blanche Hartman, angel Kyodo williams, Mushim Ikeda, Maia Duerr, and so forth[6]—they remain a minority compared with a longer list of men who serve as the heads of organizations. And as we noted in the previous chapter, while working to overcome this disparity is clearly important, installing "token women" as public leaders will not *ipso facto* end sexism; a deeper conversation about respecting women, regardless of their role or place within the *sangha*, is of equal importance.

Such a conversation about the need to respect all persons within the *sangha* is not at all unrelated to the growing concern among US Buddhists about various abuses of power, most importantly in regards to sexual abuse by prominent Buddhist leaders. In the late twentieth century, revelations of abuse of power and sexual scandals came to light in the San Francisco Zen Center community and Shambhala International (Chapter 4). More recently allegations of sexual abuse have been brought against Zen teachers Joshu Sasaki, Eido Shimano, and Genpo Merzel, all of whom were asked to resign their positions as abbots of their communities for decades of extramarital affairs or sexual assault against female students. By 2015, not only had such events attracted mainstream news media attention—with articles about Shimano being published by the New York *Times* and *The Atlantic*—but Buddhist media was coming to terms with the problem as well with the magazine *Buddhadharma* devoting an entire issue to "Confronting Abuse of Power." In her opening editorial, Tynette Deveaux notes that "We took our time getting to the issue of abuse in Buddhist sanghas—perhaps too long … Somehow, many of us thought Buddhism would be different" from other religious communities where similar abuse has occurred (2014, 7).

Sexual assault has little to nothing to do with sex; it is about power, and in the gender dynamic under consideration here, it is also about misogyny, the assumption that women are inferior and need to be controlled. Reflecting on the tendency of Buddhist bloggers to focus on supposed "romantic" relationships between these teachers and the women they assaulted, Buddhist activist Daniel Fisher wrote bluntly that "[s]exual assault is not a kind of flirtation. It has nothing to do with romance or even lust per se; it has to do with violence and domination. Furthermore, it's a criminal act." Quoting Buddhist teacher Joan Halifax, he goes on to write

> Every time one of these scandals breaks, we talk about the power differential, appropriate relationships between teachers and students, and everything else but misogyny. We don't want to believe that it has crept into Buddhism and our individual communities, I think. We want to believe we're better than that. But the practice [Halifax] asks us to undertake here—"compassion that is clear and brave, liberating and just"—is essential. It won't be easy work, but it will be work that benefits all beings, and, in the end, isn't that why we're all practicing? (Fisher 2013)

Converging approaches to Buddhist praxis

Charles Prebish is well known for coining the term "scholar practitioner" to refer to those Buddhists who are both committed to Buddhist practice and to the scholarly, academic study of Buddhism (1999). Inhabiting these sometimes very different worlds can be a difficult task. For some, being a scholar necessarily means that one should not also be an advocate, that one must have proper distance from that which one studies (cf Reader 2008). Practitioners, on the other hand, may have an antinomian distrust of academic authority or hold the view that true Buddhist practice happens in the meditation hall, not the library. It may be naive to believe that much has changed since Prebish first noted this divide; nevertheless, and in no small part thanks to his own work, scholar-practitioners are more open and accepted in both worlds. The convergence of these approaches to the study and practice of Buddhism has indelibly altered the course of both.

Engaged Buddhists similarly inhabit multiple worlds. On the one hand, as devoted Buddhists, they may feel compelled to practice, to being self-critical, to engage their chosen paths, a choice that may lead them away from the world. On the other hand, they are also compelled to hear the cries of the world (to evoke the bodhisattva Avalokitesvara) and to act compassionately in service to other sentient beings. As their inspiration comes from both Buddhist and non-Buddhist, Asian and Western sources, they inhabit the worlds of classical Buddhist thought and modern discourses of human rights or environmentalism. They are as likely to be inspired by Buddhist figures as they are by Mohandas Gandhi or Martin Luther King, Jr.

The convergence of these approaches has been celebrated by an initial wave of engaged Buddhists as potentially a transformative moment in the history of Buddhism with some going so far as to call it the fourth turning of the wheel of the dharma (Queen 2000). Less activist-minded scholars and practitioners alike have been critical of this view, noting that engaged Buddhism is a particularly modernist (re)interpretation of classical Buddhist thought in light of progressive Western values. Of course, to the extent that scholar-practitioners are now contributing their voices, lending both critical acumen and passionate commitment, the task of articulating Buddhist ethics in the contemporary age is maturing and developing apace with the suffering the movement hopes to alleviate. Regardless of whether engaged Buddhism is little more than modernist trope, the fact remains that it has become an indelible aspect of how US Buddhists continue to make Buddhism relevant in its new home.

DISCUSSION QUESTIONS

1. What specific Buddhist values or beliefs have informed the creation of an engaged Buddhist ethic? How have modern interpreters reframed traditional Buddhist doctrines?

2. What are some causes that US Buddhists have been particularly concerned with protesting or critiquing?

3. How has a feminist critique of the centrality of meditation informed Buddhist engagements within the sangha?

SUGGESTIONS FOR FURTHER READING

King, Sallie B. 2005. *Being Benevolence: The Social Ethics of Engaged Buddhism.* Honolulu: University of Hawai'i Press.

————. 2012. "Socially Engaged Buddhism." In *Buddhism in the Modern World*, ed. David L. McMahan, 195–213. New York: Routledge.

Payne, Richard K, ed. 2010. *How Much is Enough?: Buddhism, Consumerism, and the Human Environment*. Somerville, MA: Wisdom Publications.

Queen, Christopher S., ed. 2000. *Engaged Buddhism in the West*. Boston: Wisdom Publications.

Queen, Christopher S., Charles S. Prebish, and Damien Keown, eds. 2003. *Action Dharma: New Studies in Engaged Buddhism*. New York: RoutledgeCurzon.

Tucker, Mary Evelyn, and Duncan Ryûken Williams, eds. 1997. *Buddhism and Ecology: The Interconnection of Dharma and Deeds*. Cambridge: Harvard University Press.

Victoria, Brian Daizen. 2001. "Engaged Buddhism: A Skeleton in the Closet?" *Journal of Global Buddhism* 2: 72–91.

12

Buddhist modernities: US Buddhism in its global context

Chapter summary and outline

US Buddhism is the result of modernist discourses made possible through the apparatuses of globalization. This concluding chapter reexamines topics under discussion in light of Buddhist modernism and globalization, twin theories of increasing importance to Buddhist studies. It was a thoroughly modern Buddhism that found its way into North American contexts, and it is this Buddhism that continues to adapt and change as it spreads across the globe via networks of trade, travel, and telecommunications.

Introduction: Measuring compassion

Over the past several years, Stanford University scientists have been studying the neurological effects of compassion meditation. Working in Stanford's Center for Compassion and Altruism Research and Education, a program that was funded in part with a donation from the Dalai Lama, neuroscientist Brian Knutson, in collaboration with Thupten Jinpa, has been asking men and women to lay down in an fMRI machine to measure the centers of the brain that are activated by compassion meditation, especially the Tibetan practice of *tonglen*. The hope is to "predict … the parts of the brain related to anticipation of pleasure and pain, as well as those related to self-similarity and readiness to act, [that may] be activated during the exercise of compassion, and may differ between adepts and novices."[1] The control group, the novices, is comprised of Stanford University students. The adapts are Tibetan monks and nuns, part of a global diaspora that followed the Chinese takeover of Tibet. Knutson's larger body of scientific research has investigated changes in the brain related to pleasure and pain that may have an impact in our decision-making processes. Thupten Jinpa is a Tibetan ex-patriot currently living in Montreal, Québec, author of several books on Tibetan Buddhism, and has been a translator of the Dalai Lama's work since 1985.

Literally "giving and taking," *tonglen* is a meditation practice whereby, as the meditator inhales, he or she imagines all the suffering of all sentient beings entering the meditator's body; on the exhale, the meditator images all his or her happiness and merit entering the bodies of all sentient beings.

The "monk study" is made possible by the intersection of Buddhism, modernity, and globalization. Advances in scientific technology such as fMRI machines have allowed researchers unprecedented access to neurological processes. A science-centered approach to understanding humanity has attracted the attention of Buddhists who, like the Dalai Lama, have invested in such studies now focused on Buddhist practice itself. Such projects are successful in part because of global networks of communication and mobility that allow for Tibetan monks and nuns to travel to California to have their brains scanned by fMRI machines in the first place. As Marilyn Ivy writes, remarking on the complex set of historical events that led to the establishment of a Nipponzan Myohoji Renge-kyo peace pagoda in Massachusetts: "to the extent that we can even talk about Buddhism as an ism, to that extent we are already talking about a modern object. Modernity, then, is the very ground and possibility of Buddhism itself. And Buddhism … is also an inescapable constituent of what can be imagined as modernity" (Ivy 2005, 312).

What does it mean to suggest that modernity is the "ground and possibility of Buddhism"? Surely something that may be recognizable as the Buddhist religion existed in premodern contexts; nevertheless, the emergence of Buddhism-as-religion, where "religion" has a set of specific meanings recognizable to contemporary readers, was the result of colonialism, Western imaginings, and Asian nationalism. We cannot understand the contours and characteristics of Buddhism in the United States without also attending to the discourses of modernity that have made it possible. What's more, as Ivy suggests, we cannot understand modernity without taking into consideration Buddhism's place within it as a constitutive element. Further, globalization is also a constitutive element of modernity. That is, through the collective effects of colonialism, nationalism, capitalism, and technology, the world has become evermore connected, persons and whole religions evermore mobile, allowing for the spread of modern Buddhism from its ancestral homes in Asia to all parts of the globe.

In this final chapter, we will begin with an overview of contemporary theories of modernity and globalization that have become an increasingly integral part of Buddhist studies. Modernity, on the one hand, can be understood variously as a set of discursive narratives and characteristics applied to Buddhism and deployed by Buddhists, both in the East and the West. Globalization, on the other hand, can be seen as both the mechanisms by which persons and ideas are spread across the globe and enacted in specific locales as well as the emergence of global collective identities linking once disparate persons. In a very real sense, we have spent most of this book discussing, indirectly, both modernity and globalization; this chapter will make this connection explicit. In short, we will examine the specific ways in which US Buddhists have been shaped by the discursive frame of modernity and the forces of globalization.

Buddhist modernism

Whereas modernism—and the related terms modern and modernity—mean several different but related things across academic disciplines, in the case of Buddhist studies, Buddhist modernism refers to a set of discourses emerging at the intersection of Western and Asian responses to the modern era, beginning in the late 1800s and, according to some, continuing to the present.

Modernity's temporal attributes are more than its relationship to a particular time period; it is also the relationship between the modern and its antecedent, the traditional. That is, more than merely referencing a particular epoch, modernity in important ways references modern people's sense of leaving a particular past and entering into a new time. Hallmarks of this new time are the abandonment of myth and superstition and the concomitant embrace of scientific rationalism; a widespread faith in humanity's progress from a less civilized or less developed past toward an ever-increasingly efficient economy and well-developed culture; and a deepening focus on the individual expressed through individual human rights and personal spiritual or psychological development. This complex of attitudes that define the modern and differentiate it from the traditional are in many respects the products of the European Enlightenment, the Industrial Revolution, and the Romantic's rejection of their totalizing effect over European culture. And it should go without saying that this complex of orientations has been exported from Europe first through colonialism and later via global capitalism (Bechert 1984; Habermas 1985; McMahan 2008).

To suggest that modernity spread from Europe and was applied to the colonies suggests that modernity is an essentially Western phenomenon. This overly reductionist point of view can be critiqued as an *acultural* model of modernity wherein the presumption is that all cultures will eventually become *modern like us* (Taylor 2001). The acultural model of modernity overlooks the ways in which "different communities, nations, and religious groups selectively adopt and adapt elements of Western modernity, combining them in unique ways with local concepts and practices … There are, in effect, multiple modernities: ways of being modern that creatively blend elements of indigenous cultures with the globalizing forces of modernity" (McMahan 2015a, 182). Multiple modernities is, what Taylor labels a *cultural* model of modernity, one that "rejects the idea of modernity as a value-neutral operation. It takes seriously the diversity of cultures both past and present" (Quli and Mitchell 2015, 200).

In nineteenth-century Asia, for example, we find an array of Buddhist reform and revival movements reacting in similar but distinct ways to colonization thus giving rise to locally specific varieties of Buddhist modernism. In colonial Ceylon, now Sri Lanka, Portuguese, Dutch, and British colonialists and Christian missionaries had destabilized local Buddhist institutions in a variety of ways. The colonial government did not recognize the authority of the Buddhist *sangha*, which was then left without the precolonial state support it had once enjoyed. Missionaries evangelized to the people and set up Christian schools, which provided an education compatible with the colonial government thus creating a financial incentive to upwardly mobile Sinhalese to attend these new schools, which in turn weakened popular support for the Buddhist *sangha*. In response, Sinhala Buddhist nationalists such as Anagarika Dharmapala (Chapter 2) appropriated specific Western tropes such as rationalism and a rejection of superstition to argue for the superiority of Buddhism over Christianity. The very existence of a "nationalist" movement, of course, is only possible in this modern context, which argued against a particular form of Western modernity while establishing its own brand of Buddhist modernism, what Gombrich and Obeyesekere (1988) call "Protestant Buddhism" to highlight its connection to this specific rejection of (protest against) British imperialism (cf Almond 1988; Blackburn 2010).

Protestant Buddhism emerged as one response to European colonialism. However, it is important to note that modernity, and how it affected various cultures and Buddhisms in colonial Asia, is necessarily complex, requiring nuance that accounts for "the heterogeneity of interests within those communities called 'Europe' and 'the Orient' as they encountered each other" (Hallisey 1995, 33). The Kingdom of Siam, now Thailand, for example, was never directly controlled by a colonial power; nevertheless, the development of modern Thai Buddhism, a new monastic lineage or *nikaya*, the development of the forest tradition, meditation training aimed at the laity, and so forth, were all in some way a response to and a negotiation with modernity. Such reform movements mirror and parallel developments in other parts of Southeast Asia, such as Burma where Buddhist teachers began popularizing meditation practices among the laity and the rising middle class (Braun 2013). Like Thailand, while Japan was never colonized, since opening trade relations with the United State in the

1850s it has actively engaged the West, sending delegations to European universities and importing elements of Western culture. During the Meiji Restoration, Buddhist institutions reacted to these changes first by being the subject of harsh criticism and later being appropriated into the modern zeitgeist as the very soul of Japanese culture (Sharf 1995b). Once reimagined, Buddhism could present itself as an alternative to Christianity; following their experiences at the World's Parliament of Religions in 1893, Japanese Buddhist intellectuals claimed that European and American interest in Buddhism was proof of its superiority to Christianity and a religion fit for a rising international power.

From these examples, it should be clear when Buddhist modernism begins—the mid- to late-nineteenth century (cf Lopez 2002, *x*)—but when does it end? When does the modern end and give way to the postmodern, or even more simply, the contemporary, the now? The challenge in answering that question comes from the fact that modernity has two meanings: "modernity as a historical epoch and modernity as demarcating a relationship to temporality not limited by particular chronological boundaries" (Ivy 2005, 313; cf Osborne 1995). That is, modernity is both a reference to a specific period of time as well as a set of discursive narratives or defining characteristics.

Characteristics of the modern; the modern as narrative

Without losing sight of this distinction, we can nevertheless reasonably agree on some general defining features of Buddhist modernism. McMahan has suggested three "cultural processes that are largely a product of modernity" and have thus come to define Buddhist modernism: detraditionalization, demythologization, and psychologization (2008, 42).

The modern impulse toward reason and secularization has elevated personal insight and experience over centralized or communal authority, and this tendency has resulted in the detraditionalization of Buddhism. Religious institutional authority has traditionally rested within recognized figures—an ecclesiastic class of monastics or priests—that has set the standard for orthodoxy and orthopraxy. Following the Enlightenment that emphasized empirical reasoning and the Romantic period that emphasized personal subjective experience, religion in the modern era has tended to place authority more in the realm of the individual than in institutional bodies. "Detraditionalization embodies the modernist tendency to elevate reason, experience, and intuition over tradition and to assert the freedom to reject, adopt, or reinterpret traditional beliefs and practices on the basis of individual evaluation" (McMahan 2008, 43). Buddhism converges well with this impulse to the extent that there exists within the tradition hints of what may be interpreted as an individual appeal to reason; a prime example that has been used by modern interpreters is the *Kalama Sutta*, which has been read as endorsing freedom of choice and personal investigation of religious truth claims rather than a type of blind faith (64–65).

The *Kalama Sutta*

According to the *Kalama Sutta*, the Buddha was approached by a group of people known as the Kalamas who had heard other teachers, brahmins, and wandering ascetics (*sramana*) teach divergent views. They wanted to know which teachings were true. In response, the Buddha said, in effect, do not rely on traditions or scripture, do not follow someone simply because he claims to be a teacher, but when you know some practices lead to harm, you should abandon them; when you know other practices are beneficial, you should adopt them.

Taken out of context, this advice has been used by contemporary interpreters to suggest that the Buddha was advancing a specifically modern skeptical rationalism; that is, rather than merely following what has come before, new ideas should be investigated and judged against one's individual experience. The claim is then made that Buddhism advocates an individualistic and scientific approach to spirituality.

It is important to contextualize this *sutta*. The intended audience, of course, was not the general reader or modern practitioner; it was the monastic community that was competing against other contemporary religious groups of the day. The question posed by the Kalamas is really a question about what distinguishes the Buddha's teachings from these other groups—why choose him over some other teacher? The advice to judge these teachings as either being beneficial or harmful was not given without guidelines; specifically, one should make these judgments by checking them against a person who has already put them into practice, a wise person. It is only then that one should either accept or reject any particular practice.

Finally, it is worth noting that the *sutta* ends with the Kalamas declaring that they have taken refuge in the Buddha and his *sangha* and will follow him as lay disciples.

Following from this is a reframing of traditional mythologies, the process of demythologization, "of attempting to extract—or more accurately, to reconstruct—meanings that will be viable within the context of modern worldviews from teachings embedded in ancient worldviews" (McMahan 2008, 46). The paradigmatic example of this trend is the recasting of the Buddhist round of rebirth (*samsara*) not as literal realms into which one is reborn but as symbolic representations of various psychological or emotional states. Thus, the realm of hungry ghosts is read not as a literal state one may befall postmortem but rather a representation of persons so consumed by greed and desire that they can never be satisfied. This is not to suggest that premodern Buddhists were not interested in what we now think of as psychology or subjective experience; rather, it is merely to note that the rich mythologies and cosmologies would have been taken for granted as literal by Buddhists in earlier eras. "For traditional Himalayan Buddhists, the world is alive not only with awakened beings but also countless ghosts, spirits, demons, and protector deities" (McMahan 2008, 55; cf Faure 2004, 15). Demythologization by modern Buddhists has been affected by the rise of Western psychology more generally and, arguably, is an important factor in understanding how Buddhism became so popular in the West (cf Payne 2012a).

Building from the reinterpretation of classical Buddhist mythologies and cosmologies as psychological states, the psychologization of Buddhism refers to the process of interpreting Buddhist doctrines and practices as reflective of inner states of mind or as a type of spiritual therapy in itself. Psychologization is a by-product of the Enlightenment and Romantic periods, which first undermined religious authority through empirical reason and then sought individual and personal liberation and inspiration from the natural world in ecstatic experience. In this process, as traditional religious behaviors and superstitions were rendered irrational and ineffective, they became reframed as reflections of persons' inner states of mind—the subject of psychology, not religion. When Western thought and Buddhism converged, both Buddhist practices and iconography became reframed as mere symbol; the complex of Buddhas, bodhisattvas, and both benevolent and wrathful deities reduced to symbolic metaphor.

Whereas the psychologization of Buddhism may be read as a departure from traditional interpretations, it is also clearly one way that Buddhism has been so well received in the West. By rendering this pantheon of celestial beings as nothing more than symbol, they are effectively neutralized, no longer a threat to the dominant monotheism of Western Christianity. Perhaps more importantly, once neutered, Buddhist modernists are free to recast the tradition and its rituals not as religion per se but as "spiritual technology," as a set of practices and therapies aimed at healing one's psychology rather than leading one away from *samsara*. This shift, perhaps, has enabled Buddhism to be surprisingly well received in its American contexts despite being a foreign religion with a mythology and soteriology contrary to normative Christianity.

It is tempting to view the traditional and the modern as diametrically opposed; however, McMahan is clear that these traits exist on a continuum of Buddhist orientations that, while demarcating the modern from the traditional, suggests their (inter)relationship, rhetorical strategies that bear a family resemblance. In this way, it may be more helpful to view Buddhist modernism as a set of narrative discourses designed to define and interpret the religion in juxtaposition with both modernism and traditionalism. For example, in embracing the "new" and rejecting specific elements of the "old," Buddhist reformers in post-Meiji Japan were able to inculcate themselves within the new imperial government by arguing against traditional Buddhism whose institutions were thought to be corrupt and out of step with modern (largely Western) forms of science and political institutions. Other modern Buddhists may subtly or overtly embrace tradition in a rejection of modernity such as Theravada teachers who criticize psychologization and highlight the spiritual efficacy of deep meditation states such as *jhana*. Whereas this critique may seem "traditional," it is only possible in a modern context where the presumption of a psychologized Buddhism exists in the first place (Braun 2015; Quli 2008). Moreover, the application of the labels "modern" and "traditional" to specific Buddhist traditions is uneven and culturally arbitrary. What is modern in the United States may be rendered traditional in Asia (Quli and Mitchell 2015). From this point of view, modernity is more a hermeneutic than an absolute set of characteristics applied evenly across Buddhist traditions.

Modernity as hermeneutic

To say that modernity is a hermeneutic—that is, a method or theory of interpretation— is to highlight not the definition of the modern but rather to focus on how it is applied to its subject. In other words, the labels "modern" and "traditional" are applied by Buddhist teachers or practitioners to various practices and doctrinal interpretations as a way to define the tradition as either in step or out of touch with the contemporary world. Conversely, modernity is a label used by scholars to define and characterize Buddhist traditions and to normalize them as either consistent with or as departures from traditional or classical forms. Finally, these interpretations and definitions are evaluated variously as innovations or aberrations.

Following on McMahan, let us consider these labels of traditional and modern as lying on a continuum (see Figure 34). The horizontal axis—which has some relation to, but is not equivalent with, time moving from the historical Buddha to the present— measures these discourses qualitatively from the very traditional to the very modern. The vertical axis then represents the evaluative judgment of these discourses as either positive or negative. Both scholars and Buddhists then render this continuum of discursive narratives as essentially good or bad.

We can read a historical figure such as Dharmapala as a modern reformer who reduced one set of modernist discourses—in his case, the forces of colonialism—as negative and was critical of some forms of traditional Buddhism that were ineffective in the face of foreign influence, while valorizing other modernist tropes such as scientific rationalism in service of Sinhala nationalism. Thus, while arguing against some

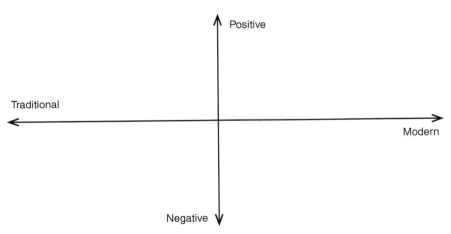

FIGURE 34 *Modernity as hermeneutic.*

aspects of both the traditional and the modern, Dharmapala constructs a version of Buddhism that appropriates other aspects of both the traditional and the modern, a nuanced vision of Buddhism made possible wholly because of modernity.

For a more contemporary example, consider Australian Buddhist teacher Winton Higgins who argues, in part, that Buddhist modernism is a "fraught mix of ancestral Buddhism and modern discursive practices [that] initially arose to deflect Western colonialism's Christianizing mission in Asia, and provided a bridge for missionary Buddhism's entry into the West" (2012, 111). This version of Buddhist modernism is a "compromise" insofar as it embraced the secularism and rationality of the West without ever letting go of the central authority and patriarchy of monasticism, which has not only disenfranchised women but proved a stumbling block for Buddhism's acceptance in many Western contexts. Suffice to say, Higgins' definition of modernity is somewhat narrowly focused on responses to Westernization (and his definition of Buddhism seems narrowly focused on the Theravada tradition and the continued centrality of monasticism). Thus, he deploys the Buddhist modernism hermeneutic to criticize certain aspects of modernity and their sources (the West) as well as certain aspects of tradition (patriarchal monastic authority). His solution is to argue for a "secular Buddhism." Of course, in arguing for secularity, he is arguing for a decidedly modern approach to religion; thus while remaining critical of some aspects of modernity, he embraces others. As discussed in Chapter 8, Batchelor has made a similar case for secularism, and in his case argues for a return to the original teachings of the Buddha; here, tradition—the ultimate tradition residing solely in the Buddha himself—is championed, while all tradition between the Buddha and the present is discarded, and a secular Buddhism is advanced (see Figure 35).

This discursive move plays itself out time and again and is deployed variously by Buddhist teachers. Some embrace modernity wholeheartedly, such as Chögyam Trungpa who unapologetically reframed the traditional realms of rebirth as psychological

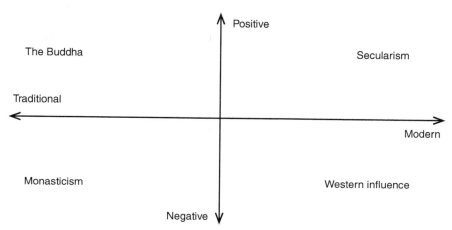

FIGURE 35 *Employing the hermeneutic of Buddhist modernity.*

states (McMahan 2008, 45) and happily married Tibetan practice with Western psy-chotherapeutic models. Others follow the logic of Batchelor and Higgins in that they reject some aspects of the traditional (sometimes referred to as "cultural") Buddhism, embrace the historical Buddha, and package it for Western consumption. Noah Levine's *Against the Stream* (Chapter 9), for example, rejects "traditional Buddhism" as being "in an awful state of degradation, corruption and delusion" and self-consciously con-structs a community founded on a demythologized reading of the Pali canon.[2] The British-born Theravada monk Ajahn Brahm, widely known and respected in the United States both for his numerous books and his support for reviving the *bhiksuni* order, often refers to himself as a traditionalist; indeed, being a monastic rather than lay teacher is one marker of traditionalism. Nevertheless, one could read his rejection of monastic authority that has prevented *bhiksuni* ordination and his championing of pro-gressive values as essentially modern approaches (Fisher 2014a).

Arguably, there is more than a little academic snobbery implicit in much scholarly writing on the subject of modern Buddhism. Scholars are quick to point out when mod-ernist interpretations diverge from the tradition or are infected, as it were, by Western discourses. As discussed in the previous chapter, some have dismissed engaged Buddhism precisely on the grounds that it is a movement predicated more on Western thought or American Transcendentalism than on anything particularly Buddhist, trad-itionally defined. Quli (2009) argues compellingly that much of this scholarly disdain for the modern can be traced to what anthropologists describe as "salvage studies." In effect, building on Said's critique of Orientalism, salvage studies are motivated by nostalgia to preserve ancient cultures and civilizations from the corrupting influences of the modern West. As a consequence, any form of contemporary culture/religion that has obvious influences from the West is rendered as a degenerative form of a once pure tradition; or, put into the hermeneutic advanced here, modernity is bad and tradition is good. In this view, the East/West dichotomy is unproblematically grafted onto the traditional/modern dichotomy, which then reinforces the notion that the West is modern, the East is traditional. Salvage studies then seeks to reclaim whatever was lost in the exchange between East and West, a move with several consequences, fore-most among them being the unquestioned assumption that "real" Buddhism lies in the traditional past; therefore, the proper subject of study for Buddhist scholars is not the contemporary scene, let alone the West, but ancient Asia (Quli 2009, 19).

Buddhist globalization

In important ways, modernity and colonialism laid the foundation on which our cur-rent age of globalization rests. It is fair to say that various parts of the world have experienced globalization at different times over the long course of human history. Often these periods follow the establishment of large empires that give rise to relative stability and peace thus allowing for the free flow of persons and cultural exchange. So-called *pax Romana* or *pax Mongolica* are such examples. The Mongol Empire, at its height in the late thirteenth century, was the largest continuous empire in human history, uniting virtually all of Asia and allowing for trade from Eastern Europe to Beijing. As a result of the political stability created by vast empires, culture spreads across large territories creating a sense of shared identity and purpose.

What differentiates these historical empires from our current globalized age is largely a matter of scale and of time. Of scale, whereas the Mongol Empire may have covered more than twelve million square miles, arguably the entire planet at present feels some degree of globalization. Of time, even though those twelve million square miles were connected, it took Marco Polo twenty-four years to travel from Venice to Beijing and back. Beginning in the nineteenth century, communication and transportation technology improved rapidly, with railroads and steamships allowing for persons and materials to be transported great distances in relatively short periods of time. Moving through the twentieth century, modernity's space-time compression (Tweed 2012, 38) continues apace with the development of commercial jet airliners, satellite television, and the Internet. This ease of access is not merely about movement but also about the ability of once disparate peoples to create a shared sense of identity and purpose. It may have been *possible* for Marco Polo to travel to Beijing, but Italy and China were still worlds apart. In the nineteenth century, Henry Steel Olcott (Chapter 2) was easily able to communicate with—and identify with—Buddhists in colonial Ceylon well before he was traveling the world several times over on steamships. A century later, defenders and critics of Dorje Shugden create solidarity and engage in dissent in real time via the Internet regardless of their physical location on the planet (Chandler 2015).

Printing presses, jet travel, books and magazines, television and the Internet are all made possible by the driving force behind modernism and globalization: capitalism. The modern world was forged in the Industrial Revolution, which was a consequence of colonialism, which itself was as much about the acquisition of new territory as it was about securing trade routes. As colonial empires slowly gave way to modern nation states, persons have been less interested in directly controlling foreign cultures; what remains, of course, is controlling trade. Thus, even though the British Empire no longer directly governs a fifth of all persons around the globe, persons are still connected through global systems of commerce. This economic imperative contributes to the development of new technologies to move capital, protect trade agreements, and connect persons, all of which gives rise to our current globalized age.

Globalization was thus initially theorized not in terms of religion but in terms of economics. In the latter half of the twentieth century, as a result of the liberal economic models of the Reagan and Thatcher administrations in the United States and United Kingdom, global corporations extended their reach and strengthened international trade agreements. Whereas these policies arguably had the effect, in the United States, of moving factory and manufacturing jobs overseas, others have critiqued them for their cultural consequences, namely, the global spread of Western culture, or the "McDonaldization" of global culture (Ritzer 2007). It is not particularly remarkable that McDonald's, an exemplar of capitalism, can be successful in communist China; it is remarkable that McDonald's brings with it Western cultural tropes such as the celebration of children's birthdays that then become a part of Chinese culture (Watson 2006). Of course, global corporations also need to be attentive to local contexts, well demonstrated in a scene from Quentin Tarantino's 1994 film *Pulp Fiction* when Vincent Vega (John Travolta) reflects on the differences between Europe and America. McDonald's cannot sell a "Quarter Pounder with cheese" in a country that follows the metric system; thus, in France, it is sold as the "Royale with Cheese."

While seemingly insignificant, the Royale with Cheese is an example of "glocalization," a reflection of the ways in which global corporations and globalized culture are always locally enacted. Rather than viewing globalization as merely the tendency toward a global, homogenous culture, it is more helpful to understand how the global is enacted in the local, the relationship between the universal and the particular (Beyer 2006; cf Robertson 1992). We saw an example of the global-local enactment of Buddhism in the Shinnyo-en lantern floating ritual in Chapter 7. Whereas floating lanterns in celebration of *obon* was not uncommon in Hawai'i, the Shinnyo-en version was first conceptualized by Japanese Buddhists who hoped to establish a local version of the ceremony. Thus, "the Shinnyo-en Lantern Floating was the result of an international decision to create a local ritual institution and in this way can be seen to mirror the glocalizing activities of global corporations to which the term first applied" (Montrose 2014, 179).

By creating a local ritual with global significance—one that is literally broadcast worldwide via satellite television and the Internet—Shinnyo-en creates a global Buddhist imaginary. Appadurai has postulated the existence of *imagined worlds* populated by the "historically situated imaginations of persons and groups spread around the globe" (1996, 33). These imagined worlds are made possible by interlocking global cultural systems: (1) ethnoscapes; (2) mediascapes; (3) technoscapes; (4) financescapes; and (5) ideoscapes. These five *-scapes* represent the landscapes in which persons, ideas, and artifacts traverse the globe and constitute shared collective subjectivities and identities that define in many ways the worlds we inhabit. Shinnyo-en Buddhists collectively identify as such regardless of their physical location in part due to their ability to "participate" in these global rituals and discourses. Appadurai does not focus on religion as such; arguably, religion infuses multiple *-scapes* from Tibetan Buddhists in diaspora (ethnoscape) moving from nation to nation (technoscape) to the dissemination (mediascape) of religious doctrines (ideoscape) all of which is made possible due to funding (financescape). Thus, Buddhism can be read as both discursive subject and translocative object in the globalized world.

To call Buddhism a discursive subject of the globalized world is to call our attention to what sociologists refer to as communicative function systems. Societies are composed of recursive, self-referential communicative systems that demarcate specific social institutions and modes of belonging—economic institutions, say, or the institutions of higher education or science or politics (Beyer 2006, 80). Modern global societies are defined by these interlocking systems of meaning that have spread across the globe. This is not to say that every society functions the same way or enacts politics in the same way, but to the extent that specific social and political systems have come to define what it means to be a "modern nation-state," these systems have been extended globally. Religion is one such system, one that seeks to define itself in contradistinction from other systems—think the separation of church and state—a communicative discourse that claims that religion is in some way fundamentally different from some other discourse—secular politics, for example. These discourses become highly specialized with Buddhism being a subset of the larger category of religion. A global Buddhist discourse, then, is one that is directed toward the project of defining what it means to be Buddhist, to do Buddhist practice, and to distinguish this from other religious and social realms in the multiple contexts of the modern world (Beyer 2006).

As a translocative object, Buddhism—this communicative discourse—moves about the planet embodied in persons, carried as artifacts, and articulated in ideas. This is to borrow from Tweed's (2008a) theory of religion that highlights religion's capacity for movement, its ability to easily transcend geopolitical boundaries and be transformed in the process. This movement is necessarily a consequence of religion's relationship to larger social and cultural forces and is seen in the movement of refugees, artwork and artifacts, and ideas in books or on the Internet flowing across the globe. These persons, artifacts, and ideas come to signify Buddhism in specific ways in relation to larger discursive fields. To paraphrase Beyer (2006, 59), South Asian immigrants and refugees to the United States carry with them something that they may or may not explicitly call "Buddhism"; but in their new American homes, they will be encouraged to imagine their religion as just that—one religion among many in a pluralistic, secular society. This encouragement comes from interactions and interrelationships with other social systems that define (and regulate) religion in the American context. Once defined as "Buddhism," these forms may then be carried off back to their original Asian contexts, furthering the processes of globalization (see also Tweed 2009; Vásquez 2009; Vásquez and Marquardt 2003).

From this example, it should be clear that globalization is not simply a unidirectional movement of persons, artifacts, and ideas from the developed to the developing world; nor is globalization confined to the large and ambiguous cultural spheres of "the East" and "the West." Rather, global culture flows in multiple directions and between multiple cultural centers and actors. Iwabuchi (2002), for example, has argued that large Japanese communication and entertainment networks have been creating and distributing cultural products across Asia for some decades now, creating a parallel system of cultural communication that competes for Asian consumers directly with Western entertainment corporations such as Disney and NewsCorp. These cultural products have also found their way into Western markets; the popularity of Japanese *anime* and *manga* in the United States is but one example of a global network flowing from East to West. Globalization then should not be used synonymously with Westernization; it may be more appropriate to note the multidirectionality of global cultural flows that explains, in part, Buddhism's influence on contemporary American culture. Thus, the sources of global culture may come from anywhere, putting down roots in new localities before being picked up once more by global networks. That is to say, "globalization is at the same time the universalization of the particular and the particularization of the universal" (Beyer 2006, 24).

If one extreme end of globalization is the homogenization of world cultures; hyper-local expression may be the other. Wilson (2012b; 2015) argues that US Buddhism is best understood not as a homogenous singularity but as enacted within eight specific cultural regions within the United States. Hawai'i, the West Coast, and the

Ekoji Temple

FIGURE 36 *Ekoji Buddhist Temple, Richmond, Virginia. (Photo courtesy Jeff Wilson.)*

Buddhism in Richmond, Virginia, is locally specific. Former Buddhist Churches of America Bishop Takashi Tsuji desired to spread Shin Buddhism in the South and established the Ekoji Temple in 1985. Unlike other large urban centers, there is no critical mass of either Asian immigrants or non-Asian converts. Therefore, several distinct Buddhist groups have come together to share resources in this one building. Unlike Buddhists in San Francisco or New York whose religious identity would hardly be out of the ordinary, in the South, Buddhists are religious minorities who may feel compelled to hide their religious identity from coworkers or even family members. These local conditions reflect translocal concerns—immigration patterns, the missionary activity of the temple's founder—thus demonstrating the local-translocal nature of globalization.

Northeast benefit from large metropolitan centers that both draw immigrant populations as well as upwardly mobile white Americans who may convert to Buddhism, resulting in relatively diverse Buddhist populations in locations such as Honolulu, Los Angeles, or upstate New York. Whereas there are fewer per capita Buddhists in the Mountain States and the Plains, each of these areas is a draw for particular communities (Williams and Wright 2015). The Midwest is perhaps best known for the Buddhists of Chicago and other large urban areas. The Southwest and the South remain particularly understudied despite the existence of Buddhist communities along the Gulf Coast, in large urban areas, and the deserts of Arizona and New Mexico. These regions are locally distinct and shape the formation and development of the Buddhist communities that take root within them.

Buddhism—as persons, ideas, and artifacts—is swept up in global cultural flows. Returning to the opening vignette, the "monk study," here we see ostensibly Buddhist practices and orientations largely revolving around compassion and happiness becoming the object of a scientific study with arguably non-Buddhist potential. The monks' presence in the United States is made possible in part by the structures of globalization. The interest in Buddhism on the part of the researchers is made possible by modernist discourses about the utility of science as well as Buddhism as a religion with spiritual technologies that can be studied empirically. This aspect of modernity—scientific rationalism—is a discursive realm Buddhists engage with in various ways in different cultural locations. Modernity and globalization are related in that they have a similar genesis (industrialization, capitalism, colonialism); for our present purposes, it may be useful to view modernity as discursive and globalization as operative. Modernity is the subject, a collection of rhetorical or hermeneutic strategies; globalization is the system or means by which these discourses spread across cultures via networks of trade, travel, and telecommunications.

US Buddhism in its global context

US Buddhism is the result of modernist discourses made possible through the apparatuses of globalization. The self-conscious discursive move from the realm of the traditional to the modern was made in the nineteenth-century Western world largely as a consequence of cultural developments dating to the Enlightenment. As we saw in Chapter 2, a defining feature of the era was a turn away from both the mythology and authority of religious institutions to an embrace of empirical reason and rationality. This embrace of reason would in turn lead to the scientific revolution that had a destabilizing effect on European Christianity in many ways; among them was the rise of secular nation states that sought to cleave religious institutions from modern political systems. Detraditionalization as discussed earlier relocated sources of authority from classically defined religious authority to the realm of the individual who was then able to engage religious doctrine rationally to determine its validity or

utility. Contemporary "secular Buddhists" (Chapter 8) and the seemingly easy marriage between Buddhism and science (Lopez 2008) are exemplars of a detraditional-
ized, modern Buddhism.

The Enlightenment coincided with the expansion of European colonialism, especially into the New World where the American colonies would become the testing
ground for new, rationalist political philosophies. Abstract notions of the separation
of church and state, for example, would become political realities codified by the First
Amendment to the US Constitution—a wholly new mode of social organization that
was extended into the Asian colonies. It was in these contexts that various Asian
Buddhist nationalist movements emerged in response to European colonialism, direct or indirect. Such movements highlight both the adoption of Western sociopolitical
modes as well as responses to the forces of Western hegemony.

Modernity—and Buddhism, religion, and so forth—are all types of meta-narratives,
explanations of history, the cosmos, and humanity. One such meta-narrative was
on display in the "white city" at Chicago's World's Fair in 1893 (Chapter 2), which
organized human history into progressively more civilized cultures beginning with
indigenous peoples and culminating with Euro-Americans. In the convergence of
religions on display at the World's Parliament of Religions, attendees had the option
to choose—perhaps for the first time—between competing religious paths. This is
one consequence of globalized modernity, the awareness of difference resulting from
once-disparate people coming into contact with one another, which in turn necessitates the negotiation of difference. This negotiation includes the possibility of individuals embracing alternatives—alternative sociopolitical systems, alternative identities,
alternative religions—and it is this embrace of alternatives and rejection of modernity
that defines aspects of the postmodern (Chapter 8). Of course, there is continuity
between the modern and postmodern, "postmodernity is still post-*modernity*, still
shot through with its constitutive contradictions" (Ivy 2005, 328), its simultaneous
critique and embrace of the past resulting in articulations of the Buddhist tradition at
once familiar and new.

Whereas colonial empires would eventually give way to modern nation-states, their
underlying economic imperative remained in place. That is, the trade networks established by the Dutch or the British are essentially the foundation upon which modern
global capitalism is built. It is this context that allows for the global flow of capital, commerce, and persons. The United States did not sail its navy into Tokyo Harbor in 1853
to conquer the island nation; it did this to secure trade rights (Figure 37). The opening
of Japan not only allowed for the exchange of products, it also allowed for the movement of persons. From the 1880s through the early decades of the twentieth century,
tens of thousands of Japanese immigrants would arrive first in Hawai'i and later at the
West Coast of the mainland, bringing with them their Buddhist traditions (Chapters 3
and 6). These living traditions, physical buildings populated with practicing Buddhists
and encountering American culture first-hand, add a layer of complexity to the largely
intellectual flow of information between Japanese and American scholars and academics of an earlier era.

FIGURE 37 *Japanese print depicting Commodore Perry landing in Tokyo, circa 1861. (Courtesy Library of Congress.)*

It should not be surprising that the US Navy was deployed to secure trade routes. Military conflicts are as much about economics as they are about territory and ideology. Even the largely ideological Cold War between the United States and the USSR was about economics—capitalism versus communism. In this war of words, the rhetorical logic of lowering restrictions to immigration and valorizing American exceptionalism led to the passage of the Hart-Celler Act of 1965 (Chapter 4). Whereas the architects of this legislation may have been focused on Eastern Europe, other Cold War engagements in Asia would create the conditions for tens of thousands of Asian Buddhist immigrants and refugees to arrive on American shores by the century's end.

Reverse flows of persons and capital are also made possible by these global systems of capitalism. Long before he traveled to colonial Ceylon, Olcott was able to communicate with Buddhists there via letters and the distribution of newsletters and pamphlets (Chapter 2). Fenollosa was able to travel to Japan in the late 1800s, secure a post at the University of Tokyo, and eventually return to Boston with an impressive collection of Japanese Buddhist art (Chapter 9). The same Cold War politics that caused Vietnamese, Khmer, and Laotian refugee crises also created new opportunities for Americans to travel abroad, either through military service, the Peace Corp, or tourism. Spiritual seekers and pilgrims were then able to study and practice Buddhism in its Asian contexts and bring these teachings home to establish new communities (Chapter 5). Contemporary Asian Buddhist missionaries have capitalized on modern telecommunications networks to promote a wide array of Buddhist causes from disaster relief out of Taiwan (Chapter 6) to the promotion of new religious movements from Japan (Chapters 6 and 7). This confluence of capital and communication, immigration and diaspora, pilgrimage and tourism combines in the United States, forever altering the US Buddhist landscape with a seemingly endless variety of traditions and communities from nearly the whole of Asia.

Once rooted in their new American contexts, Buddhists express themselves according to their local environments. The local contexts of the United States may be regionally based while also affected by and contributing to translocal discourses and movements, cultural flows not confined to "Buddhism" or even religion. In postwar America, the avant garde appropriated Buddhist themes and ideas into Beat poetry and experimental music (Chapters 3 and 9), a discourse made possible by larger critiques of normative American suburban culture. Whereas these movements would eventually be subsumed into more established Zen Buddhist traditions and lineages (Chapter 6), other forms of cultural adaptation would come later in the convergence of Buddhist and secular discourses. While insight meditation finds a home in traditionally defined Theravada communities and their decedents (Chapter 5), these practices have also been deployed in the service of nonreligious ends such as psychotherapy and even business success (Chapter 8). Criticism of such appropriation and adaptation is invariably framed in another local dialect, that of American progressivism that lies at the heart of the engaged Buddhist movement (Chapter 11). Despite its origins in Asia, engaged Buddhism is as indebted to explicitly Buddhist sources as it is to deep ecology and the American environmentalist movement.

US Buddhist *sanghas* do not exist in vacuums, isolated from larger cultural and political discourses; on the contrary, they must engage with, are shaped by, and in turn contribute to ongoing American cultural discourses. This is self-evident when US Buddhism is approached from the point of view of identity politics. The language of race and representation has contributed much to the development of US Buddhism. Race-based immigration and naturalization laws determined what US Buddhism would look like through the first half of the twentieth century, largely restricting it to a small minority of Japanese and Chinese immigrants. The repeal of these laws in 1965 would have the opposite effect. The persistent division in popular and scholarly literature between "two Buddhisms" has resulted in activist responses that seek to reclaim an explicitly Asian American identity. These discourses have been joined by feminist and queer theorists and activists engaged in confronting patriarchy in Buddhist *sanghas*, reviving the *bhiksuni* lineage of female monastics, and challenging heteronormative readings of Buddhist practices and institutions (Chapter 10). Such articulations of Buddhist identity perhaps only make sense in this specific context, once again drawing our attention away from the global, to the local.

Nevertheless, these local instantiations of culture are invariably picked up and spread across global networks, contributing to a modern global Buddhist discourse. Observers have noted the peculiar penchant of US advertisers and marketers for cashing in on Buddhism's cultural cachet in the promotion of "Zen and the art of ..." products. There is growing evidence that this cultural cachet may be part of a feedback loop to Asia where marketers in Buddhism's homeland reproduce this cultural narrative, once again drawing our attention away from the local, to the global.

Thus, US Buddhism is best viewed as a broad set of locally specific traditions with connections to all parts of Asia, an active participant in and recipient of modern global Buddhist discourses expressed in various local contexts.

Conclusion: The beginning

US Buddhism is expressed variously in the personal and the communal, from the quiet and contemplative to the political and engaged. Large, nationally dispersed traditions established in the 1800s are joined by communities who exist solely in the virtual worlds of the Internet. Monastic traditions upholding the *vinaya* are in dialogue with secular meditation teachers working in hospitals and prisons. Retreat centers can be found in the remote corners of New Mexico, seemingly isolated from the world, and yet owing their existence to Asian Buddhist diasporas and political affairs half a world away. On a quiet street corner in Oakland, California, a young woman offers fruit and flowers at a small, make-shift Buddhist shrine, alone and unnoticed. On the other side of the globe, a delegation of US Buddhist leaders is invited to participate in the Pontifical Council for Interreligious Dialogue where they discuss social justice and ecological issues with Pope Francis. US Buddhism is complex and multifaceted, a set of related practices, communities, discourses, and persons.

Does this then describe the elephant of US Buddhism, answer the question of what makes American Buddhism *American*? Hardly—it merely gestures toward the beginning of an answer, the start of a journey. The question can only be answered in its fullness by asking more questions.

What were the historical causes and conditions that first brought Buddhism to the West's awareness? How did colonialism, trade, and international politics bring Buddhists to the United States? And once here, what cultural forces did they encounter that shaped and reshaped their communities and their practices? Why should some forms of Buddhism, such as Zen, become so popular in the 1950s while others, such as Pure Land, remain so hidden from mainstream awareness? How did US political and military engagements in Asia post–World War II forever redraw the American Buddhist landscape? What impact did the counterculture of the 1960s and 1970s have on burgeoning Buddhist communities? And why should some new Buddhist movements be more readily accepted than others? Where is the line between Buddhist and non-Buddhist art? And who gets to decide? Are these questions related in some way to issues of identity? Or, to put it another way, who owns culture? How and why have Buddhists chosen to engage the social and ecological suffering of the world? Are these engagements in line with classically defined Buddhism, or are they a marriage between Eastern and Western cultural discourses? Are such developments little more than modern adaptations to the tradition, aberrations from the past that reframe Buddhism in a globalized world?

These are the starting points for future research agendas, points of departure for your own journeys into the rich landscape of US Buddhism.

DISCUSSION QUESTIONS

1. In what ways does "the modern" refer to a temporal period? How is it also a discourse or a rhetoric not connected to any particular age?

2. What does it mean to refer to Buddhism as discursive subject and translocative object?

3. What does a focus on regional specificity reveal about US Buddhism? How does a focus on translocal connection change our image of US Buddhism?

SUGGESTIONS FOR FURTHER READING

Beyer, Peter. 2006. *Religions in Global Society*. London: Routledge.

Blackburn, Anne M. 2010. *Locations of Buddhism: Colonialism and Modernity in Sri Lanka*. Chicago: The University of Chicago Press.

Ivy, Marilyn. 2005. "Modernity." In *Critical Terms for the Study of Buddhism*, ed. Donald S. Lopez, 311–331. Chicago: The University of Chicago Press.

McMahan, David L. 2008. *The Making of Buddhist Modernism*. New York: Oxford University Press.

Quli, Natalie E. F., and Scott A. Mitchell. 2015. "Buddhist Modernism as Narrative: A Comparative Study of Jodo Shinshu and Zen." In *Buddhism beyond*

Borders, ed. Scott A. Mitchell and Natalie E. F. Quli, Albany: State University of New York Press.

Taylor, Charles. 2001. "Two Theories of Modernity." In *Alternative Modernities*, ed. Dilip Parameshwar Gaonkar, 172–196. Durham, NC: Duke University Press.

Tweed, Thomas A. 2012. "Tracing Modernity's Flows: Buddhist Currents in the Pacific World." *The Eastern Buddhist* 43 (1&2): 35–56.

Glossary

S-Sanskrit; P-Pali; C-Chinese; J-Japanese; T-Tibetan; K-Korean; V-Vietnamese

abhidharma (S), *abhidhamma* (P):   Third branch of the Buddhist canon (*tripiṭaka*); whereas the *sūtra* literature presents the teachings in a more narrative way, the *abhidharma* literature offers a systematic, highly analytic and technical explication of the teachings.

abhiṣeka (S), *abhiseka* (P):   "Anointing," a ceremony in Vajrayāna traditions wherein esoteric knowledge is ritually passed from teacher to student.

ācārya (S), *acariya* (P):   Master or teacher, specifically a dharma master as opposed to one who teaches monastic precepts.

āgama (S/P):   A set of mainstream Buddhist texts that roughly correspond with the Pali *nikāya*.

ahiṃsā (S/P):   Nonviolence or non-harming.

Ajātaśatru (S), Ajātasattu (P), Ajase (J):   In Buddhist literature, Ajātaśatru was prophesied to kill his father and supporter of the Buddha, King Bimbisāra. Aided by the Buddha's cousin and rival, Devadatta, in some accounts Ajātaśatru succeeds; in others, he attempts to kill his mother. Eventually, overcome with remorse, he becomes a follower of the Buddha and provides financial support for the sangha.

ālayavijñāna (S):   In Yogācāra, the "storehouse consciousness," wherein karmic seeds are deposited, which form the basis for later experiences and rebirth.

Amitābha (S), Amida (J):   The Buddha of "infinite light," and sometimes referred to as Amitāyus ("infinite life"), a Buddha who resides in the western pure land of Sukhāvatī. Whereas Amitābha makes an appearance in a number of different Mahāyāna sutras, he is the central Buddha in what have become known as the three pure land *sūtras*. Practices in devotion to this Buddha which developed in India became foregrounded in China; in Japanese, distinct pure land schools emerged, notably Jōdo Shū and Jōdo Shinshū.

Amitāyus (S):   See Amitābha.

Ānanda (S/P):   Cousin and principle disciple of the Buddha; at the First Council, Ānanda was responsible for reciting from memory the *sūtras*.

anātman (S), *anattā* (P):   "No self" or "nonself," more generally insubstantiality, a marker (along with impermanence and *duḥkha*) of existence.

arhat (S), *arahant* (P):   One who has attained the highest level of awakening, will enter full *paranirvāṇa* at death, and not be reborn.

āryāṣṭāṅgamārga (S), *ariyāṭṭhaṅgikamagga* (P):   The Eightfold Path which leads to the cessation of suffering or *nirvāṇa* consisting of: right (1) views, (2) intention, (3) speech, (4) conduct, (5) livelihood, (6) effort, (7) mindfulness, and (8) concentration.

Aśoka (S), Asoka (P) (c. 300–232 BCE):   Indian Mauryan emperor who, following a
   protracted and bloody war, turned to the dharma; his stone inscriptions are among
   the earliest known forms of writing in India and make many references to the
   Buddha, dharma, and *saṅgha*. Celebrated as the first patron of Buddhism.

asura (S/P):   Literally "non god" but most often translated as "demigod," a violent
   and malevolent being in one of the six realms of rebirth (*saṃsāra*).

Avalokiteśvara (S), Guanyin (C), Kannon/Kanzeon (J), Chenrézik [Spyan ras gzigs] (T):
   The bodhisattva of compassion, a central figure in Mahāyāna texts, and an attendant
   of the Buddha Amitābha. Depicted in both male and female forms, prominent leaders and teachers in Tibet, including the Dalai Lama, are believed to be incarnations
   of Avalokiteśvara.

Avataṃsaka Sūtra (S):   Central text for the Chinese Huayan school, this colossal text
   presents an intricate and complex image of an infinite cosmos of interconnected
   world systems that forms the basis of all reality.

avidyā (S), *avijjā* (P):   Ignorance, the root cause of *duḥkha*.

Bhaiṣjyaguru (S):   The "Medicine Buddha" who resides in an eastern pure land, often
   portrayed in a triad with the Buddhas Śāykamuni and Amitābha.

bhikṣu (S), *bhikkhu* (P):   "Home-leaver"; one who has left the home life and entered
   into a Buddhist monastic order, a monk.

bhikṣuṇī (S), *bhikkhunī* (P):   Female equivalent of *bhikkhu*, a nun.

Bimbisāra (S):   King who ruled at the time of the Buddha; featured in a number of narrative accounts usually concerning his son Ajātaśatru's attempts at patricide.

Bodhgayā: The location of the Buddha's awakening.

bodhi (S/P):   "Awakening," the knowledge that liberates one from *saṃsāra*.

bodhi tree: The tree under which the Buddha sat when he attained awakening.

bodhicitta (S):   "Thought of awakening," usually reference to one's initial intention to
   attain awakening.

bodhisattva (S), *bodhisatta* (P):   "Awakening being," originally merely a reference to
   one who has aspired to become a Buddha (e.g., Gautama Siddhārtha before attaining awakening and in his previous incarnations). In Mahāyāna, used rhetorically in
   contrast to the *arhat* ideal of the mainstream schools and later ascribed specific
   qualities and powers.

buddha (S/P):   "Awakened one." Whereas most commonly associated with the historical buddha (Gautama Siddhārtha or Śākyamuni Buddha), the Buddha claimed to
   be only the most recent buddha in a long line of awakened beings over many eons,
   and many other buddhas are specifically named in canonical texts.

buddhadharma (S), *buddhadhamma* (P):   The teachings of the Buddha.

buddhadhātu (S):   "Buddha-element," the innate potential within sentient beings for
   awakening; see also *tathāgatagarbha*.

buddhakṣetra (S):   Buddha filed, a realm of a buddha. See also pure land.

buddhanature: See *buddhadhātu*, *tathāgatagarbha*.

buddhavacana (S/P):   "Word of the buddha," reference both to teachings delivered by
   the Buddha and teachings considered authoritative.

Budai (C), Hotei (J):   Commonly known as the "laughing Buddha" and in the West
   often mistaken for the historical Buddha, Budai is a Chinese representation of
   the future Buddha Maitreya and a symbol of luck and happiness in East Asian folk
   customs.

cakra (S), *cakka* (P): "Circle" or "wheel," a symbol used to represent various aspects of Buddhism, most commonly the dharmawheel or *dharmacakra*.

cakravartin (S), *cakkavattin* (P): "Wheel-turning-king," or universal monarch; in Buddhism, one who rules in accordance with the dharma.

Caodong zong (C), Sōtōshū (J): Chan lineage brought to Japan by Dōgen in the thirteenth century; one of the more influential Zen lineages in the United States.

catvāry āryasatyāni (S), *cattāri ariyasaccāni* (P): The four noble truths, though, the phrase would be more appropriately translated as "the four truths known by the spiritually noble"; the core insight of the Buddha's awakening. The four truths are (1) the truth of suffering (*duḥkha*), (2) the cause of suffering, (3) the cessation of suffering, (4) the path (*āryāṣṭāṅgamārga*).

Chan (C), Zen (J), Sŏn (K), Thien (V): Chinese school of Buddhism purported to have been established by Bodhidharma as early as the fifth century. Chan is the Chinese rendering of the Sanskrit *dhyāna*, or meditation.

dāna (S/P): "Giving" or "generosity," a core Buddhist virtue, refers both to the material support given by the laity to the *saṅgha* as well as the gift of the dharma itself.

Devadatta (S/P): Cousin and rival of the Buddha who enlisted Ajātaśatru in several assassination attempts against the Buddha as well as Ajātaśatru's father and mother.

Dhammapada (P): A collection of sayings of the Buddha in verse that forms part of the *Khuddakanikāya* (see *nikāya*); the work remains a popular text in modern translation.

dhāraṇī (S): Short phrases that serve as mnemonic devices for specific teachings; a *dhāraṇī* is said to encapsulate lengthier texts and thus those who memorize and recite them are, in effect, reciting the the root teachings themselves.

dharma (S), *dhamma* (P): (1) Teaching, specifically the teachings delivered by the Buddha as part of the path (*mārga*) to awakening; (2) from the root "to hold" or "to maintain," dharma literally means factor or element. Thus, one meaning of the term is a constituent element of phsyco-physical reality. Early Buddhist exegesis was concerned with disclosing the full range of dharmas that make up the universe, and understanding the essential nature of these elements. It was in reaction to this undertaking that early Mahāyāna tradition emphasized the emptiness (*śūnyatā*) of all dharmas.

dharmacakra (S), *dhammacakka* (P): "Wheel of dharma," or the wheel of the teachings, as in the Buddha's first sermon called the "turning of the wheel of the dharma."

dharmadhātu (S): See pure land.

Dharmaguptaka (S): An early mainstream school of Indic Buddhism; its *vinaya* was translated into Chinese in the fifth century and became the standard throughout East Asia.

dharmakāya (S): See *trikāya*.

dhyāna (S), *jhāna* (P), *chan* (C), *zen* (J): "Meditative absorption," a mental state characterized by the complete withdrawal from external sensory input brought about by single-minded concentration on a physical or mental object. The meditative states of advanced practitioners came to be viewed as necessary for the attainment of awakening and were propagated in China where they became foregrounded in the Chan school.

Dīpaṃkara (S), Dīpaṅkara (P):   The first of twenty-four Buddhas said to precede
   Śākyamuni Buddha and before whom he vowed to attain awakening an endlessly
   long time ago.
Dīpavaṃsa (P):   Pali canonical text concerning Buddhism's introduction to Sri Lanka.
dorje [rdo rje] (T):   See *vajra*.
duḥkha (S), *dukkha* (P):   Suffering or unsatisfactoriness, the first of the four noble
   truths.
Dunhuang: On the crossroads of Buddhism's entry into China, an oasis town on the
   Silk Road and important archeological site; the nearby complex of caves holds some
   of the most spectacular Buddhist statuary and paintings in the world.
dzogchen [rdzogs chen] (T):   "Great perfection," a meditative practice associated primarily with the Nyingma school of Tibet.
eightfold path: See *āryāṣṭāṅgamārga*.
enlightenment: See *nirvāṇa*.
five houses, seven schools of Zen: A way of describing traditional Chan schools and
   lineages that developed during the Tang Dynasty (618–907) in China. Over time, many
   schools and houses were absorbed into other lineages, particularly Caodong and Linji.
Flower Adornment Sūtra: See *Avataṃsaka Sūtra*.
four noble truths: See *catvāry āryasatyāni*.
Gaṇḍavyūha (S):   Sometimes a separate *sūtra*, the final chapter of the *Avataṃsaka
   Sūtra*; tells the story of a young man's spiritual journey through a series of
   fifty-three teachers (*kalyāṇamitra*) who represent the fifty-three stages of the
   bodhisattva path.
Gandhāra: An area of ancient India, now part of northern Pakistan and southwest
   Afghanistan, which was a crossroads between Europe, the Middle East, and India.
   It is widely believed that due to these cross-cultural connections that important
   developments in Buddhist art arose, most notably the creation of Buddha images.
Gautama Siddhārtha (S), Gotama Siddhattha (P):   The given name of the historical
   Buddha; in the Pali tradition, he is usually referred to as Gotama Buddha; in the
   Mahāyāna he is more commonly known as Śākyamuni Buddha.
Guhyasamājatantra (S):   An important tantric text, especially in Tibet, and an exemplar of the often transgressive and antinomian character of *tantras* more generally.
gong'an (C), *kōan* (J):   Whereas kōan have become well known in the English-
   speaking West as paradoxical or "unsolvable riddles" (e.g., what is the sound of
   one hand clapping?), *gong'an* study and practice involved the examination of classical texts and accounts of Chan ancestors and masters. Correctly interpreting and
   uncovering the meaning of these accounts forms the basis for deeper meditative
   insights into the true nature of reality. *Kōan* are foregrounded in the Rinzai school
   of Japanese Zen.
guru (S):   A religious guide or teacher, sometimes synonymous with *kalyāṇamitra*.
   The central importance of a guru is fundamental to Vajrayāna Buddhism from whom
   one learns proper rituals and doctrinal knowledge.
hanamatsuri (J):   A Japanese spring festival celebrating the birth of Śākyamuni
   Buddha. See also *vesak*.
Heart Sūtra: See *Prajñāpāramitāhṛdaya Sūtra*.
hīnayāna (S):   Pejorative term for mainstream schools of Indic Buddhism
   by the Mahāyāna. Whereas hīnayāna is still sometimes used to describe

preliminary or preparatory practices as a prerequisite for perfection of wisdom practice (*prajñāpāramitā*), the term should be avoided in reference to non-Mahāyāna schools.

homa (S):   An esoteric purification fire ritual.

Huayan (C):   School of Chinese Buddhism based on the *Avataṃsaka Sūtra*. Whereas the school's importance was eventually displaced by Chan meditation and pure land traditions, its cosmology and textual exegesis are widely influential across East Asia.

jātaka (S/P):   "Birth stories," stories about past incarnations of Gautama Siddhārtha, which collectively form a narrative leading toward his eventual awakening.

jhāna (P):   See *dhyāna.*

Jizō (J):   See Kṣitigarbha.

Jōdo Shinshū (J):   A Japanese pure land tradition established by the decedents and disciples of Shinran (1173–1263), a disciple of Hōnen, which rose to prominence in the fifteenth century.

Jōdo Shū (J):   A Japanese pure land tradition established by Hōnen (1133–1212).

Kālacakratantra (S):   Often erroneously translated as "Wheel of Time," the *Kālacakratantra* is a tantric text composed in the early eleventh century. The *tantra* conveys a rather apocalyptic story of Buddhism's decline and resurgence in India, and its associated *maṇḍala* are presumed to be powerfully efficacious in thwarting enemies.

kalpa (S), *kappa* (P):   An eon, used sometimes to denote specific period or time, almost always of unimaginably long duration.

kalyāṇamitra (S), *kalyāṇamitta* (P):   "Good/noble friend," one who is extremely knowledgeable in doctrine and practice, often a prerequisite for one's own path of practice.

Kannon (J):   See Avalokiteśvara.

Kapilavatsu (S), Kapilavatthu (P):   The hometown of Gautama Siddhārtha where he spent his youth before beginning his search for awakening.

karma (S), *kamma* (P):   "Action," a term common to most Indic religious systems referring to actions and their corresponding effects either in the immediate future or leading to future rebirth in the six realms of saṃsāra. Buddhism foregrounds the moral aspect of karma and links it explicitly to intention; with intention, beings accomplish actions of body, speech and mind that have positive, negative, or mixed positive/negative consequences.

karuṇā (S/P):   Compassion or empathy; as opposed to *maitrī*, *karuṇā* is the desire for others to be free of suffering.

kleśa (S), *kilesa* (P):   Affliction or defilement; *kleśa* defile the mind and prevent one from attaining awakening. They therefore need to be controlled, removed, or transformed to progress along the path.

kōan (J):   See *gong'an.*

koṭi (S/P):   Essentially the "end" of a scale, usually rendered as one hundred thousand, ten million, one hundred million, or an infinity; often paired with *kalpa* in Buddhist literature to express an unimaginably long duration of time.

Kṣitigarbha (S), Dizang (C), Jizō (J):   The "earth store" bodhisattva revered particularly in East Asia as one who saves suffering beings from the hell realms; in his Japanese form as Jizō, he is known as the protector of children and travelers.

Kuśunagari (S), Kusinārā (P):   The city in which the Buddha died and passed into *parinirvāna*. Following his death, his relics were temporarily housed in a *stūpa* before being divided among eight kingdoms; an important pilgrimage site.

lama [*bla ma*] (T):   Tibetan term for guru.

Linji zong (C), Rinzaishū (J):   Chinese school of Chan brought to Japan in the twelfth century by Eisai (1141–1215); one of the two most influential schools of Zen in Japan.

Lotus Sūtra: See *Saddharmapundarīka Sūtra*.

Lumbinī: The location of the Buddha's birth; an important pilgrimage site.

Madhyamaka (S):   Literally the "middle way," school of Indian Buddhism that traces its roots to the work of the second century monk Nāgārjuna and best known for its articulations of emptiness (*śūnyatā*) and two truths doctrines.

Mahākāśyapa (S), Mahākassapa (P):   One of the principal disciples of the Buddha known for his superior ascetic and moral abilities; convened the First Council after the Buddha's death wherein the *sūtra* and vinaya were recounted; considered the first patriarch of the Chan school.

Mahāmaudgalyāyana (S), Mahāmoggallāna (P), Mulien (C), Mokuren (J):   Along with Sāriputra, one of the Buddha's first disciples renowned for his supernatural abilities. In a Chinese *sūtra* known as the *Ullambana Sūtra*, Mulien is seen using these powers in an attempt to rescue his mother from the realm of hungry ghosts. In Japan, the story became the basis for the summer *obon* festival.

Mahāparinibbāna Sutta (P):   The canonical Pali account of the death of the Buddha, his final advice to his disciples, his passing into *parinirvāna*, and what the community did with his remains.

Mahāparinirvāna Sūtra (S):   Sanskrit and Mahāyāna account of the death and *parinirvāna* of the Buddha; while the text overlaps with its Pali equivalent, it differs significantly, mostly in regards to its focus on the true nature of the Buddha and the *tathāgatagarbha*.

Mahāprajāpatī (S), Mahāpajāpartī (P):   Aunt and step-mother of Gautama Siddhārtha who raised the boy following his mother's death; the first woman to request admittance into the monastic *sangha*.

Mahāvairocana Sūtra (S):   An esoteric *sūtra* of great importance to the East Asian Vajrayāna traditions that focuses on the Buddha *Mahāvairocana*, the personification of universal truth of the dharma, often associated with the sun.

Mahāyāna (S):   Literally "great vehicle," a tradition of Buddhism that distinguished itself from the mainstream Buddhist schools around the beginning of the common era by focusing on the doctrine of emptiness (*śūnyatā*) and the bodhisattva path. Exported from India and spread widely across Asia, Mahāyāna traditions came to dominance in Central and East Asia.

mainstream Buddhist schools: Term used by modern scholars to refer to non-Mahāyāna Indian Buddhist traditions, traditionally eighteen in number.

Maitreya (S), Metteya (P):   The predicted next Buddha to be born into this world after the dharma has disappeared completely. See also Budai.

maitrī (S), *mettā* (P):   "Loving-kindness," the wish for others' well-being and happiness.

mālā (S/P); *nenju/ojuzu* (J):   "Garland," or a string of beads often used for counting the recitations of prayers, *mantra*, or the *nenbutsu*.

manas (S/P):   Mind or consciousness. In Yogācāra sometimes used as a shortened form of *kliṣṭamanas*, or "afflicted mentality," the consciousness responsible for mistakenly creating a sense of self.

maṇḍala (S):   Literally circle, *maṇḍala* may iconographically represent various aspects of reality, awakening, or the cosmos itself. In Vajrayāna practice, one may construct a physical *maṇḍala* or visualize entering one as part of a larger tantric ritual.

mantra (S):   A syllable or string of syllables that may or may not be syntactically meaningful, usually in Sanskrit, the recitation of which is both powerfully efficacious and represents some aspect of the dharma. Included in many Mahāyāna sūtras (see *Prajñāpāramitāhṛdaya Sūtra*), mantra are particularly important in Vajrayāna traditions.

mappō (J):   See *mofa*.

Māra (S/P):   The personification of evil in Buddhism, said to have unsuccessfully tempted Gautama Siddhārtha from his pursuit of awakening.

mārga (S), *magga* (P):   Literally "path," mārga forms a central metaphor for Buddhism as a path left by the Buddha for a way to awakening.

Māyā (S/P):   Also Mahā Māyā, the mother of Gautama Siddhārtha who died shortly after childbirth.

Meru (S/P):   See Sumeru.

mettā (P):   See *maitrī*.

mikkyō (J):   "Secret teachings," Japanese term for esoteric Buddhism (see Vajrayāna).

mindfulness: See *smṛti*.

mofa (C), *mappō* (J):   Term for the "final dharma" period, the age in which the true dharma will gradually fade and disappear from our world. In this context, more expedient means for awakening are needed, and in medieval Japan, several teachers advocated single-practice traditions more suited to these times.

mudrā (S), *muddā* (P):   A gesture, usually of the arms and hands, with symbolic significance such as the "earth-touching gesture" of Śākyamuni Buddha symbolizing the earth bearing witness to his awakening. *Mudrā* are often employed in esoteric practice.

Mūlasarvāstivāda (S):   A sub-sect of the Sarvāstivāda school of mainstream Buddhism. Its associated *vinaya* became the basis for Tibetan monastic traditions.

nāga (S/P):   A serpent or dragon common in Buddhist literature.

nam-myōhō-renge-kyō (J):   The Japanese title of the *Saddharmapuṇḍarīka Sūtra* or *Lotus Sūtra*, chanted by the Nichiren school.

nenbutsu (J):   See *nianfo*.

nenju (J):   See *mālā*.

nianfo (C), *nenbutsu* (J):   Chinese translation of the Sanskrit Buddhānusmṛti (see *smṛti*), literally the recollection or keeping in mind the qualities of the Buddha. Generally, the term refers to the recitation of the name of a specific Buddha, most commonly the Buddha Amitābha, and forms the central practice of pure land Buddhism.

nikāya (S/P):   (1) "Collection" or "group," *nikāya* may refer to the collection of teachings contained in the *sūtras* of the Pali canon (see *tripiṭaka*); (2) "group" in the sense of a school especially used in reference to the mainstream Buddhist schools.

Is also used contemporarily to denote specific monastic lineages within Theravāda Buddhism.

nirmāṇakāya (S):   See *trikāya.*

nirvāṇa (S), *nibbāna* (P):   The goal of the Buddhist path (*mārga*), variously translated as enlightenment or awakening, from the Sanskrit "to blow out" as in "a flame blown out by the wind," and therefore more properly translated as "extinction," specifically the extinction of the desires that allow one to be freed from the realm of rebirth (*saṃsāra*).

obon (J):   A Japanese summer festival to honor the spirits of one's ancestors and linked to the story of Mokuren as told in the *Ullambana Sūtra* (see Mahāmaudgalyāyana). Imported to the United States via Japanese immigrants, obon celebrations are an important part of most Japanese-derived Buddhist ritual calendars.

ojuzu (J):   See *māla.*

padma (S), *paduma* (P):   A lotus flower; because the lotus blooms above stagnant, muddy waters, it has come to represent the clear and pure mind that grows out of the impurity of *saṃsāra*, thus becoming one of the most frequent symbols across the Buddhist tradition.

pagoda: See *stūpa.*

pāramitā (S), *pāramī* (P):   "Perfection," a virtue or quality developed by a bodhisattva on the way toward awakening usually enumerated in a list of either six or ten including: (1) generosity (*dāna*), (2) morality, (3) patience, (4) effort, (5) concentration (*dhyāna*), (6) wisdom (*prajñā*), (7) skillful means (*upāya*), (8) vows, (9) power, and (10) knowledge of the true dharma.

parinirvāṇa (S), *parinibbāna* (P):   Final *nirvāṇa* entered into at death when there remain no causes for rebirth.

prajñā (S), *paññā* (P):   Wisdom, but more specifically an accurate awareness and understanding of reality as it is.

prajñāpāramitā (S), *paññapāramī* (P):   Literally the perfection of wisdom, a term that is used to describe the Buddha's (or any bodhisattva's) training prior to awakening (see *pāramitā*); it can also refer specifically to the knowledge of emptiness (*śūnyatā*). In this later sense, it is directly related to a the same-named genre of literature that explicates central Mahāyāna doctrines as well as the bodhisattva path.

Prajñāpāramitāhṛdaya Sūtra (S):   Known in English as the *Heart Sutra*, perhaps the most concise of all the *prajñāpāramitā sūtras*, told as a response by Avalokiteśvara to Śāriputra on how to perfect the *pāramitās*. The bodhisattva's response includes the famous line that "form is emptiness, emptiness is form," as well as the *mantra*, "*gate-gate-paragate-parasamgate-bodhi-svaha.*"

prātimokṣa (S), *pāṭimokkha* (P):   The section of *vinaya* texts that includes the specific rules or codes of conduct for monastics. Every two weeks, the codes are recited in an *uposadha* ceremony wherein the monks or nuns assembled are expected to confess any transgressions of the monastic rules.

pratītyasamutpāda (S), *paṭiccasamuppāda* (P):   Conditional origination; foundational Buddhist teaching on the conditioned nature of all existence and core insight of the Buddha on the night of his awakening.

pratyekabuddha (S), *paccekabuddha* (P):   "Solitary buddha"; term for one who has attained awakening without instruction. Pratyekabuddhas generally do not teach others what they have learned because they have failed to develop the requisite compassion for other sentient beings.

preta (S), *peta* (P): Hungry ghost; one of the six realms of rebirth (*saṃsāra*).

pūjā (S): Offerings—both the offerings themselves and the ritual ceremonies during which offerings are made.

pure land: English term with several separate but related meanings: in general, it may be used to refer to a *buddhakṣtra* or realm in which a Buddha exits. More commonly, pure land refers to the specific pure land of the Buddha Amitābha, Sukhāvatī, and those traditions devoted to his related texts and practices.

Rāhula (S/P): Gautama Siddhārtha's son, born shortly before he left to pursue awakening; later, Rāhula became a disciple of the Buddha.

rinpoche (T): Tibetan honorific title used when addressing a teacher or lama.

Rinzaishū (J): See Linji zong.

Saddharmapuṇḍarīka Sūtra (S): In English, the *Lotus Sūtra*, a central text of Mahāyāna Buddhism that sets forth the primacy of the "one vehicle" teaching, that all Buddhist practices lead to the same fundamental understanding of awakening.

Śākyamuni (S), Sakkamuni (P): "Sage of the Sākya clan," the most common epithet for the historical Buddha, especially in Mahāyāna, to distinguish him from other Buddhas.

samādhi (S): Concentration, specifically the necessary ability to fix one's mind on an object of concentration during meditative practice.

śamatha (S), *samatha* (P): Calmness or serenity; often paired with *vipaśyanā*, *śamatha* is the mental serenity generated through the cultivation of *samādhi* and necessary for insight.

saṃbhogakāya (S): See *trikāya*.

saṃsāra (S/P): The round of rebirth, usually divided into six realms: (1) various hell realms; (2) hungry ghosts (*preta*); (3) animals; (4) humans; (5) angry or wrathful demigods (*asuras*); and (6) the heavenly realms of the gods. If nothing else, *nirvāṇa* is the release from *saṃsāra* and its attendant suffering.

saṅgha (S/P): Community. The term is sometimes used to refer specifically to the community of monastics; in other cases, especially in the modern West, the term often refers to all members of a Buddhist community, both lay and monastic.

Śāriputra (S), Sāriputta (P): Along with Mahāmaudgalyāyana, a primary disciple of the Buddha who figures predominately in many texts, including the *Prajñāpāramitāhṛdaya Sūtra*.

Sārnāth: City near Benares in India where the Buddha is said to have delivered the first turning of the wheel of dharma; an important pilgrimage site.

sesshin (J): From the Chinese characters for "touching heart and mind," in Zen traditions, an extended *zazen* meditation retreat.

shikantaza (J): "Just sitting," a style of meditation advocated by Dōgen and later Sōtōshū Zen tradition wherein the act of sitting meditation is itself an expression of awakening.

Shingonshū (J): Japanese esoteric school established by Kūkai in the ninth century.

skandha (S), *khandha* (P): Aggregates of being; traditionally, five are listed: (1) form, (2) feeling or sensation, (3) perception, (4) mental formations, and (5) consciousness. Of these five, only form (*rūpa*) is material; the rest collectively are referred to as "name" and involve some aspect of mental activity. None of these has a self, and it is the mind's mistaken association with one or the other of them as a self that is the principle cause of *duḥkha* and being bound to *saṃsāra*.

smṛti (S), *sati* (P):   Most often translated as mindfulness, a central aspect of Buddhist meditation practice; generally, mindfulness refers to the ability to remain focused on some object or the body, but it can also be used in the sense of "to keep in mind," as in *nianfo*.

Sŏn (K):   See Chan.

Sōtōshū (J):   See Caodong zong.

śramaṇa (S), *samaṇa* (P):   A renunciant or mendicant; the historical Buddha represented one of many *śramaṇa* traditions that are explicitly mentioned in Buddhist sources, including Jainism.

śrāvaka (S), *sāvaka* (P):   A disciple of the Buddha; in later Mahāyāna the term was used somewhat pejoratively in juxtaposition with the more idealized bodhisattva.

stūpa (S), *thūpa* (P):   A reliquary that contains the remains of the Buddha, Buddhist saints, or patriarchs. Exported across Buddhist Asia, the Tibetan chörten and the East Asian pagoda are examples of *stūpa*.

Śuddhodana (S); Suddhodana (P):   Father of Gautama Siddhārtha who, when hearing that his son was destined to become either a great king or a great religious leader, conspired to keep him distracted from the spiritual life with all manner of sensual pleasures.

Sukhāvatī (S):   Literally "land of bliss," the name of the pure land established by Amitābha Buddha. The realm is an ideal practice place as it is free from the distractions of this world and may be accessed either via advanced meditative practice or, more commonly, rebirth.

Sumeru (S/P):   The mythical "world mountain" that exists at the center of this world system around which the various continents and their inhabitants dwell.

śūnyatā (S):   Most commonly translated as "emptiness," *śūnyatā* is not to be confused with nothingness or the idea that things do not exist. Rather, as explicated by Nāgārjuna and other Madhyamaka thinkers, *śūnyatā* refers specifically to the false sense of individuality or identity that are given to beings and phenomena. Building on *pratītyasamutpāda*, because the world is conditioned, all phenomena lack—that is, are empty of—an autonomous or individual essence.

sūtra (S), *sutta* (P):   Along with the *abhidharma* and the *vinaya*, one of the three divisions of the Buddhist canon or *tripiṭaka*. *Sūtra* are teachings delivered by the Buddha or with his sanction and were said to have been recited from memory by Ānanda at the First Council, and as a result *sūtras* begin with the famous phrase "Thus have I heard," before setting out the time, location, and those in attendance for the delivered teaching.

tantra (S):   A classification of texts that are esoteric in nature (as opposed to the exoteric *sūtras*) that contain instructions for *homa* rituals, *maṇḍala* construction, and *abhiṣeka* initiation ceremonies, all central aspects of Vajrayāna practice.

tathāgata (S/P):   Either the "thus gone" or the "thus come" one; one of the most common epithets of the Buddha.

tathāgatagarbha (S):   Literally "womb of the *tathāgata*," a term that may have originally referred to the latent potentiality in sentient beings for awakening but that took on greater and greater importance in Mahāyāna and East Asian Buddhism as a way of explaining how it was possible for imperfect, impure beings to attain a pure state of awakening.

tathatā (S): Suchness; the world as it is, free of all (human) conceptualizations of it.

Tendaishū (J): see Tiantai zong.

thangka (T): Traditional Buddhist painting most associated with Tibet and Nepal often depicting a Buddhist deity or *maṇḍala*.

Theravāda (P): The "way of the elders"; whereas Theravāda traces it origins to the mainstream school Sthaviranikāya, the term itself did not come into widespread use until the modern era to designate the variety of Pali-based Buddhisms that have dominated South and Southeast Asia since the eleventh century.

Therīgāthā (P): "Verses of the female elders," a collection of some seventy-three poems by female disciples of the Buddha, including his stepmother, Mahāprajāpatī.

Thien (V): See Chan.

three afflictions: A standard list of afflictions (*kleśa*) sometimes called the three poisons (*triviṣa*) of greed, hatred, and ignorance that either need to be removed or controlled to attain awakening.

three bodies: See *trikāya*.

three jewels: See *triratna*.

three pure land *sūtras*: Whereas Amitābha Buddha appears in a number of Mahāyāna texts, later Japanese pure land tradition groups three specific texts together as uniquely authoritative: (1) the *Larger* and (2) *Shorter Sukhāvatī-vyuha Sūtras* and (3) the *Visualization Sūtra*.

Tiantai zong (C): A major school of East Asian Buddhism that took the *Saddharmapuṇḍarīka Sūtra* as foundational, systematized by Zhiyi in the sixth century and exported to Japan several centuries later. In Japan, where it is known as Tendaishū, the school became one of the largest and most politically influential schools from roughly the ninth century on. The founders of Japanese Pure Land, Zen, and Nichiren schools all first studied as Tendai monks.

tonglen [*gtong len*] (T): A meditation practice whereby, as the meditator inhales, he or she imagines all the suffering of all sentient beings entering the meditator's body; on the exhale, the meditator imagines all his or her happiness and merit entering the bodies all sentient beings.

trikāya (S): A central Mahāyāna doctrine concerning the three bodies or three aspects of a buddha, namely: (1) the *nirmāṇakāya*, or the physical form a buddha takes in the world; (2) the *saṃbhogakāya*, or the "reward body," wherein a buddha can manifest all manner of supernormal abilities; and (3) the *dharmakāya*, or "truth body." In later Mahāyāna and Vajrāyāna Buddhism, the *dharmakāya* became an object of devotion in itself as a manifestation of reality, sometimes associated with *tathatā*.

tripiṭaka (S), *tipiṭaka* (P): "Three baskets," a term used in reference to the Buddhist canon, traditionally divided into the *sūtra*, *vinaya*, and *abhidharma*.

triratna (S), *tiratana* (P): Alternately *ratnatraya*, three jewels, three treasures, or triple gem; the three objects of veneration, namely (1) the Buddha, (2) the dharma, and (3) the *saṅgha*. One of the most common practices across Buddhist traditions is the formal "going for refuge in the three jewels" wherein Buddhists, both monastic and lay, formally recite that they will take refuge in, seek guidance from, or abide by the three jewels.

tulku [*sprul sku*] (T):   Tibetan translation of the Sanskrit *nirmāṇakāya* and used more generally to refer to an incarnate lama, that is, lamas who have been recognized as the reincarnation of some previous teacher.

tuṣita (S), *tusita* (P):   A heaven in Buddhist cosmology where a bodhisattva resides before becoming a Buddha.

two truths: From the Sanskrit *satyadvaya*, ultimate and conventional truth refer to the world as it is in suchness (*tathatā*) and the world as perceived by unawakened sentient beings, respectively.

Upāli (S/P):   Disciple of the Buddha who was responsible for reciting the *vinaya* at the First Council.

upāsaka (S/P):   A male lay disciple of the Buddha.

upāsikā (S/P):   A female lay disciple of the Buddha.

upāya (S/P):   Usually translated as "skillful means" (*upāyakauślya*), refers to the pedagogical efficacy of the Buddha and advanced bodhisttavas of tailoring teachings to the specific needs of suffering sentient beings.

Vaidehī (S), Videhī (P):   Wife of Bimbisāra and mother of Ajātaśatru.

Vairocana (S):   One of five transcendent buddhas, in the *Avataṃsaka Sūtra*, he is the personification of universal truth. A central object of devotion in Vajrayāna traditions and sometimes equated with Mahavairocana (see *Mahavairocana Sutra*).

vajra (S), *dorje* [*rdo rje*] (T):   Variously translated as diamond or thunderbolt, the *vajra* is both a weapon and symbol of unbreakable power. As a ritual object, the *vajra* is often paired with a bell where it symbolizes *upāya* as opposed to *prajñā*.

Vajrayāna (S):   A term used to refer to tantric or esoteric forms of Buddhism in distinction from hīnayāna and Mahāyāna. Vajrayāna traditions are characterized by the centrality of tantric texts and their associated practices, including *dhāraṇī*, *mantra*, *maṇḍala*, and so forth.

vesak: From the Pali *vesākha*, also sometimes spelled wesak, holiday commemorating the birth, enlightenment, and death of the Buddha, ordinarily held in the late spring (see also *hanamatsuri*).

vinaya (S/P):   The section of the Buddhist canon (*tripiṭaka*) that deals with monastic regulations, both texts that set out the specific rules as well as narrative accounts that explain how the rules came to be.

vipaśyanā (S), *vipassanā* (P):   Literally "insight," but more specifically insight as the direct awareness of impermanence, suffering, and no-self; often paired with *śamatha* with which it forms two sides of Buddhist meditative practice. Classical commentaries suggest that *śamatha* leads to *jhāna* whereas *vipassanā* leads to true awakening, and whereas the former is not a prerequisite for the later, *vipassanā* mediation requires a level of meditative ability normally associated with *śamatha*.

Visuddhimagga (P):   The "Path of Purification"; in Pali-based Buddhism, foundational exegetical text written by Buddhaghosa in the fifth century in Sri Lanka.

yāna (S):   Literally "vehicle," used especially by Mahāyāna and later traditions metaphorically as a vehicle that conveys one toward awakening.

Yaśodharā (S), Yasodharā (P):   Wife of Gautama Siddhārtha and mother of Rāhula. Along with Mahāprajāpatī, one of the first women to join the monastic *saṅgha*.

yoga (S):   Term generally used to describe any spiritual discipline; in Buddhism, this may refer to any training or contemplative practice.

Yogācāra (S):   Together with Madhyamaka, a foundational Mahāyāna philosophical school. Whereas Yogācāra translates loosely as "practice of yoga," the school has come to be known as the "consciousness only school" for its detailed analyses of consciousness and especially *ālayavijñāna*.

zazen (J):   Seated meditation, the primary practice of most Zen schools, and refers mostly to the specific posture of seated meditation with one's legs crossed and eyes lightly closed.

Zen (J):   See Chan.

zendō (J):   Literally "place of zen," a meditation hall.

Timeline

1853–1878 Establishment of Chinese Temples in San Francisco, West Coast, and Hawai'i.

1875 The Theosophical Society is founded in New York by Henry Steel Olcott and Madame Helena Petrovna Blavatsky.

1882 Passage of the Chinese Exclusion Act barring immigration from China until World War II.

1889 First Japanese Buddhist Temple in Hawai'i (Jodo Shinshu).

1890 Ernest Fenollosa returns to Boston from teaching in Japan and gifts a large collection of Japanese Buddhist art to the Museum of Fine Arts.

1893 World's Parliament of Religions held in Chicago as part of the World Columbian Exposition; in attendance are: Anagarika Dharmapala, Yatsubuchi Banryu, Shaku Soyen and his assistant D. T. Suzuki, among others.

1898 The North American Buddhist Mission (later renamed the Buddhist Churches of America) is established in San Francisco.

1900 The Dharma Sangha of the Buddha is established by non-Japanese members of the NABM in San Francisco.

1907 "Gentlemen's Agreement" between United States and Japan limited Japanese immigration only to the wives or children of Japanese already living in United States.

1912 Shingon Koyasan Betsuin is established in Los Angeles.

1913 Soto Zen Mission of Hawai'i established.

1924 Immigration Act barring immigration from most of Asia and the Middle East.

1927 Soto Zen Mission (Zenshuji) in Los Angeles is established.

1931 Nyogen Senzaki opens his "floating *zendo*" in Los Angeles.

1931 Zen Buddhist Society of America established in New York.

1934 Soto Zen Temple in San Francisco's Japantown established; this is the temple to which Shunryu Suzuki was assigned in 1959.

1935 Relics of the Buddha are gifted to the NABM by the King of Siam (Thailand); a new building is constructed with a stupa on its roof to house the relics, completed in 1938.

1941 Japanese attack on Pearl Harbor.

1942–1946 Internment of Japanese Americans.

1944 At a meeting in the Topaz Internment Center in Utah, the NABM officially incorporates as the Buddhist Churches of America.

1944 A nonsectarian Buddhist temple is established in Chicago; though "nonsectarian," the community has strong ties to Jodo Shinshu (Ohtani) and Zen.

1949 The Buddhist Studies Center opens in Berkeley to train ministers for the BCA.

1950 The People's Liberation Army enters Tibet, annexing the country for China.

1950 D. T. Suzuki takes up a teaching post at Columbia University, begins to have a large impact on the spread and popularization of Zen in the United States.

1950s The "Zen Boom"; as a result of Suzuki's work, Alan Watts' publications, and the work of Beat Generation poets and writers, Zen becomes highly visible and popularized in the United States.

1957 Cambridge Buddhist Association is founded and directed by a number of Buddhist teachers over the years including: Hisamatsu Shinichi (Rinzai Zen), Masatoshi Nagatomi (Jodo Shinshu), Maurine Stuart (Rinzai Zen), and George Bowman (Korean Chogye).

1958 Tibetan Buddhist Learning Center opens in New Jersey.

1959 Sino-American Buddhist Association, precursor of the Dharma Realm Buddhist Association, is established in Hong Kong by Chan Master Hsuan Hua.

1959 The Diamond Sangha is founded in Hawai'i by Robert Aitken, a lineage holder in the Sanbo Kyodan school of Zen.

1960 The president of Soka Gakkai, Daisaku Ikeda, visits the United States and encourages Japanese American Nichiren Buddhists (many of whom are wives of US servicemen) to spread Nichiren Buddhism; eventually, their organization becomes SGI-USA.

1962 The San Francisco Zen Center is established by Shunryu Suzuki.

1966 Thich Nhat Hanh visits the United States, meets with Martin Luther King, who later nominates him for a Nobel Peace Prize.

1964 The Buddhist Association of the United States is established in the Bronx, New York, eventually building a large monastic complex in upstate New York.

1965 The Hart-Celler, or the Immigration and Nationality Act, is passed, ending immigration exclusion laws and allowing a large influx of immigrants from Asia.

1966 The Washington Buddhist Vihara established in Washington, DC, with the support of the Sri Lankan government.

1966 San Francisco Zen Center opens a monastic training center, Tassajara Zen Mountain.

1966 The Buddhist Studies Center changes its name to the Institute of Buddhist Studies.

1967 Zen Center of Los Angeles established by Taizan Maezumi who later establishes the White Plum Asanga and whose numerous students establish communities of their own across the country.

1969 Nyingma Meditation Center in Berkeley established by Tarthang Tulku.

1970 Chögyam Trungpa Rinpoche arrives in the United States.

1970 International Buddhist Meditation Center established by Thich Thien-An in Los Angeles.

1972 Korean Zen Master Seung Sahn establishes a Zen Center in Providence, Rhode Island, eventually renamed the Kwan Um School of Zen.

1972 Wat Thai established in Los Angeles.

1972 Gold Mountain Monastery, headquarters of the Dharma Realm Buddhist Association, is formally opened in San Francisco's Chinatown by Hsuan Hua.

1973 Chögyam Trungpa founds Vajradhatu, a new school of Buddhism derived from Nyingma and Kagyu traditions/practices.

1974 Naropa Institute (later renamed Naropa University) is established by Vajradhatu in Boulder, Colorado.

1975 The Fall of Saigon brings a formal end to the US-Vietnam War and begins a refugee crises that spreads across South East Asia, which in turn leads to a large number of Vietnamese, Lao, Hmong, and Khmer refugees to enter the United States.

1975 Insight Meditation Society is established in Barre, Massachusetts.

1976 City of 10,000 Buddhas is opened by the Dharma Realm Buddhist Association.

1976 Council of Thai Bhikkhus is organized in Denver, Colorado.

1976 Dai Bosatsu Zendo Kongo-ji is opened in Lew Beach, New York, by Eido Tai Shimano.

1978 Buddhist Peace Fellowship is founded.

1979 The Institute of Chung-Hwa Buddhist Culture Meditation Center (later Chan Meditation Center) is established in Elmhurst, New York, by Sheng-Yen Cheng (of Dharma Drum).

1979 Jon Kabat-Zinn begins adapting mindfulness meditation techniques for stress reduction programs at the University of Massachusetts Medical School.

1980 Dhammodaya Monastery, the first Burmese Buddhist temple in America, is established in Los Angeles.

1980 The Dharma Vijaya Buddhist Vihara is established in Los Angeles.

1980 The Zen Mountain Monastery is established in New York by John Daido Loori.

1984 Richard Baker, Suzuki's heir at the San Francisco Zen Center, resigns his position following revelations of an extramarital affair.

1985 Institute of Buddhist Studies affiliates with the Graduate Theological Union.

1986 Lt. Col. Ellison Onizuka, a Hawaiian-born Jodo Shinshu Buddhist and the first Asian American to reach space, killed in the space shuttle *Challenge* disaster.

1987 Chögyam Trungpa dies.

1988 Hsi Lai Temple is established in Hacienda Heights, California.

1990s Buddhist communities grow and expand, establishing new temples across the country; Buddhism is generally believed to be the fastest growing religion of the decade.

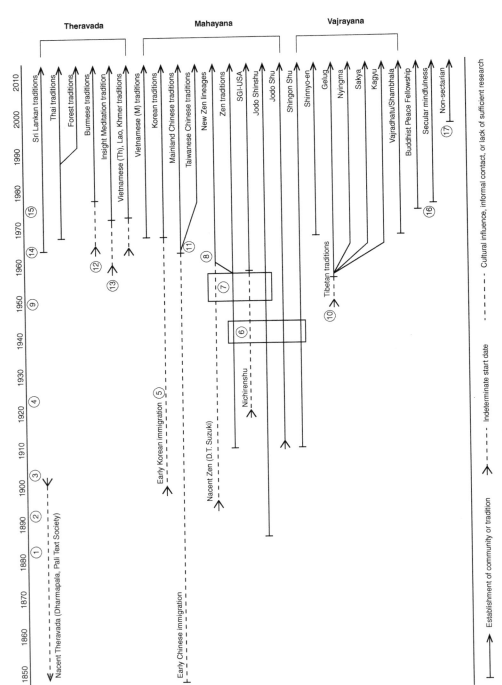

FIGURE 38 *Timeline of Buddhism in the United States.*

Theravada Mahayana Vajrayana

Sri Lankan traditions
Thai traditions
Forest traditions
Burmese traditions
Insight Meditation tradition
Vietnamese (Th), Lao, Khmer traditions
Vietnamese (M) traditions
Korean traditions
Mainland Chinese traditions
Taiwanese Chinese traditions
New Zen lineages
Zen traditions
SGI-USA
Jodo Shinshu
Jodo Shu
Shingon Shu
Shinnyo-en
Gelug
Nyingma
Sakya
Kagyu
Vajradhatu/Shambhala
Buddhist Peace Fellowship
Secular mindfulness
Non-sectarian

Nacent Theravada (Dharmapala, Pali Text Society)

Early Korean immigration

Nacent Zen (D.T. Suzuki)

Nichirenshu

Early Chinese immigration

Tibetan traditions

→ Establishment of community or tradition

↗ Indeterminate start date

- - - - Cultural influence, informal contact, or lack of sufficient research

1990 Hsi Lai Temple establishes University of the West in Rosemead, California.

1990 Ösel Tendzin, Trungpa's heir, dies of complications from HIV; within the decade, Vajradhatu is reorganized as Shambhala International.

1991 Dalai Lama gives teachings and performs the Kalachakra Initiation in New York City.

1991 *Tricycle: The Buddhist Review* begins publication.

1996 Members of Hsi Lai Temple are prosecuted for violating campaign finance laws following a luncheon attended by then-Vice President Al Gore.

1998 Shinnyo-en sponsors its first lantern-floating ceremony in Honolulu, Hawai'i.

2001 The East Bay Meditation Center opens in Oakland, California.

2006 The Jodo Shinshu Center opens in Berkeley, California.

2007 Mazie Hirono (D-HI) becomes the first Buddhist congresswoman.

2008 Noah Levine opens the first Against the Stream meditation center in Los Angeles, California.

2009 Revelations that Eido Shimano has been sexually harassing and abusing students leads to his resignation from the New York Zen Center a year later.

2011 Four nuns receive full Theravada monastic ordination in Northern California, capping more than a decade of work to legitimize female monastic ordination.

2011 Genpo Merzel resigns as a teacher in the White Plum Asanga following revelations of his extramarital affairs.

2014 Congresswoman Hirono (D-HI) is elected to the US Senate.

Notes to Figure 38

1   Chinese Exclusion Act (1882).
2   World's Parliament of Religions, Chicago (1893).
3   Gentlemen's Agreement, limiting Japanese immigration (1907).
4   Immigration Act excluding virtually all immigration from Asia (1924).
5   Evidence of Korean immigration as early as Japanese immigration; more research is needed on Korean Buddhist communities pre-1965.
6   World War II Japanese American internment (1941–1946).
7   Zen boom and the popularization of Zen Buddhism (1950s).
8   Branching off from Japanese-American Zen communities and benefiting from the Zen boom, several new communities of Zen are established in the 1960s and 1970s.
9   People's Liberation Army enters Tibet, annexes country for China (1950).
10 Following the Chinese occupation of Tibet, Tibetan refugees begin entering the United States in small numbers in the mid-1950s and early 1960s.
11 During World War II, immigration restrictions are lifted for Chinese nationals; following the communist and cultural revolutions (ending 1949 and 1976), large

numbers of Chinese immigrants enter the United States both from mainland China and Taiwan.

12   Following a coup d'état (1962), Burmese refugees begin immigrating to the United States; immigration records are incomplete; the first dedicated Burmese Theravada temples opens in 1980.

13   During the 1960s, Americans begin heading to Asia as part of the Peace Corps, the military, or as tourists, and begin learning meditation techniques from primarily Burmese and Thai teachers.

14   Hart-Celler Immigration reform act (1965).

15   Fall of Saigon (1975).

16   In 1979, Jon Kabat-Zinn establishes a mindfulness and stress reduction clinic at the University of Massachusetts Medical School marking the beginning of an increasing number of secular mindfulness programs.

17   By the end of the twentieth century, nonsectarian or pan-sectarian Buddhist communities begin to emerge, including the East Bay Meditation Center (est. 2001) and Against the Stream (est. 2008).

Lineages

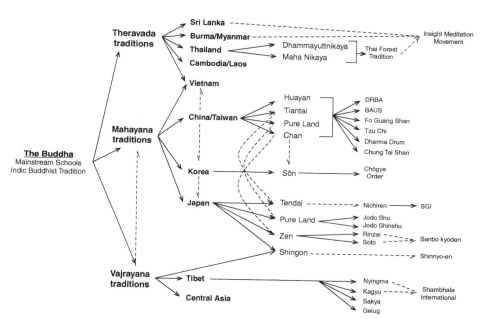

FIGURE 39 *Major Buddhist lineages with a US presence.*

Notes

Introduction

1 See http://www.rcms2010.org.
2 The Pew Forum released a follow-up survey in 2015 using the same methodology as the original, and thus the same limitations. No significant changes were reported in its profile of US Buddhists. See: http://www.pewforum.org/religious-landscape-study/.

Chapter 1

1 The exact date of the Buddha's birth is somewhat contested. According to tradition, it is 624 BCE. Recent scholarship, however, places his birth more than a century later in 566 or 448 (Robinson and Johnson 1997, 11).
2 From the *Assutava Sutta*: http://www.accesstoinsight.org/tipitaka/sn/sn12/sn12.061.than.html.

Chapter 4

1 I am indebted to Courtney Bruntz for bringing the wealth of Plains Buddhism to my attention.
2 For an exhaustive and ongoing account of the controversy as well as how it impacted the broader US Zen Buddhist scene, see the "Eido Shimano Collection" at Sweeping Zen: http://sweepingzen.com/category/featured-content/eido-shimano-collection.

Chapter 5

1 In 1989, the military *junta* controlling Burma changed the country's name to Myanmar. As some opposition groups did not recognize the military's right either to rule the country or change its name, they have chosen to retain the name Burma. As a result, various international organizations and countries use Burma and Myanmar interchangeably. In popular US Buddhist sources, Burma is preferred, and I have followed suit.
2 See http://www.dhamma.org/en/about/goenka.
3 In addition to these two main branches of Thai Buddhism, other forms of Buddhism exist in the country, including Mahayana, and new lineages have developed recently, including the Dhammakaya; though this group is extremely influential in parts of Thailand, they have not had a large impact in the United States.

Chapter 6

1 See http://zmm.mro.org/zen-kids-celebrate-buddhas-birthday-at-zmm for more information on the Zen Mountain Monastery; see http://www.sfgate.com/bayarea/johnson/article/Buddha-seems-to-bring-tranquillity-to-Oakland-5757592.php for the Oakland street-corner shrine; and I am indebted to Anne Spencer for knowledge of the Idaho chapter of SGI-USA.
2 A third school of Japanese Zen, Obaku, was established in the mid-seventeenth century. Obaku Zen is smaller and less known outside of Japan than Rinzai and Soto, and has no presence in the United States. See Baroni 2000.
3 See http://zmm.mro.org/about/history-of-zmm-and-mro/.

Chapter 7

1 It should be noted that scholars of Japanese esoteric Buddhism (*mikkyo*) generally do not use the term Vajrayana. Whereas the history and development of tantric Buddhism in East Asia generally and Japan in particular is well worth more sustained attention, it is well beyond this current project (see Payne 2006). My decision to bring Japanese esoteric schools into conversation with Tibetan tantric schools is to highlight their divergent trajectories in the American context.
2 There is a growing Tendai movement in the United States that has been actively engaging non-Japanese populations and is in need of more sustained research; I am indebted to Aaron Proffitt for his insights on this subject.
3 "*Sesshin*" in this context should not be confused with the Zen use of the Japanese homophone "*sesshin*," which refers to a long meditation period or retreat.
4 There is evidence that the Chinese government has supported protest groups against the Dalai Lama as part of their larger campaign to discredit the Tibetan leader's political cause. For one example, see: http://www.lionsroar.com/global-anti-dalai-lama-buddhist-sect-disbands/.
5 In addition to Wylie's contribution to the academic study of Tibetan Buddhism, it is worth noting the work of the late E. Gene Smith whose Tibetan Buddhist Resource Center in Cambridge, Massachusetts, is currently at work digitizing Tibetan texts. Further, in addition to Robert Thurman, Jeffrey Hopkins also studied with Kalmyk teachers and monks in the Gelug tradition before establishing the University of Virginia's Tibet Center.

Chapter 8

1 See http://www.againstthestream.org/about-us/who-we-are/ and http://www.againstthestream.org/about-us/our-tradition/.
2 See http://www.mindfulschools.org.
3 My thanks to Dan Bammes for this insight.
4 See http://secularbuddhism.org and http://secularbuddhism.org/faq/.
5 "Arunlikhati" has, to my knowledge, never publicly revealed her/his gender and has purposefully obfuscated her/his identity in other ways including the suggestion that "I could be a black woman on the other side of the world—but my writing on the issues of Asians in Western Buddhism would still be true."

See https://web.archive.org/web/20121320083000/http://www.tricycle.com/blog/
who-angry-asian-buddhist-interview-arunlikhati.

6 See https://web.archive.org/web/20121320083000/http://www.tricycle.com/blog/
who-angry-asian-buddhist-interview-arunlikhati.

7 On the Pew Forum's original estimates, see http://religions.pewforum.org/portraits; for
a corrective from the Pew, see http://www.pewforum.org/2012/07/19/asian-americans-
a-mosaic-of-faiths-religious-affiliation/; for the Angry Asian Buddhist's critique see http://
www.angryasianbuddhist.com/2010/04/stop-using-pew-study.html.

Chapter 9

1 See http://www.angryasianbuddhist.com/2012/01/buddha-toilet-brush-holder.html.

Chapter 10

1 See http://encyclopedia.densho.org/Ozawa%20v.%20United%20States/.
2 See http://www.tricycle.com/feature/white-trash-buddhist; and http://
engagedbuddhism.net/category/class/.
3 Chenxing Han's forthcoming work on young-adult Asian American Buddhist
experiences throws into sharp relief generational changes, differences, and
continuities. See http://chenxinghan.org/about/.

Chapter 11

1 See http://www.buddhistpeacefellowship.org/our-work/training-and-education/the-
system-stinks/.
2 See http://www.buddhistpeacefellowship.org/10-years-later-resisting-us-war-on-iraq/;
and http://liberatedlifeproject.com/2012/04/my-most-beautiful-thing-taking-a-stand-for-
what-you-believe/.
3 See http://www.lionsroar.com/white-house-buddhist-leadership-conference-hozan-
allan-senauke/, http://hardcorezen.info/i-wish-i-could-agree/3553, and http://www.
buddhistpeacefellowship.org/can-we-critique-us-militarism-when-we-benefit-from-it/.
4 See https://www.youtube.com/watch?v=DK7m2CMgl2E.
5 See http://theidproject.org/blog/patrick-groneman/2011/10/17/being-present-meditation-
occupy-wall-street; http://www.buddhistpeacefellowship.org/occupy-oakland/; and
http://www.buddhistpeacefellowship.org/category/occupy-movement-blog/.
6 Several important works have well documented the central role of women Buddhist
leaders including Boucher 1988 and Haas 2013. See also: http://www.oxfordbibliographies.
com/view/document/obo-9780195393521/obo-9780195393521-0207.xml.

Chapter 12

1 See http://ccare.stanford.edu/research/current-research/#firsttab; and http://www.
sfgate.com/health/article/Stanford-studies-monks-meditation-compassion-3689748.php.
2 See: http://www.againstthestream.org/about-us/our-tradition/.

Bibliography

Abe, Stanley K. 1995. "Inside the Wonder House: Buddhist Art and the West." In *Curators of the Buddha: The Study of Buddhism Under Colonialism*, ed. Donald S. Lopez, 63–106. Chicago: University of Chicago Press.

Adams, Sheridan, Mushim Ikeda-Nash, Jeff Kitzes, Margarita Loinaz, Choyin Rangdrol, Jessica Tan, and Larry Yang, eds. 2000. *Making the Invisible Visible: Healing Racism in Our Buddhist Communities*. Woodacre, CA: Spirit Rock.

Almond, Philip C. 1988. *The British Discovery of Buddhism*. Cambridge: Cambridge University Press.

Ama, Michihiro. 2011. *Immigrants to the Pure Land: The Modernization, Acculturation, and Globalization of Shin Buddhism*. Honolulu: University of Hawai'i Press.

Ama, Michihiro. 2015. " 'First White Buddhist Priestess': A Case Study of Sunya Gladys Pratt at the Tacoma Buddhist Temple." In *Buddhism beyond Borders*, ed. Scott A. Mitchell and Natalie E. F. Quli, Albany: State University of New York Press.

Amstutz, Galen. 1997. *Interpreting Amida: History and Orientalism in the Study of Pure Land Buddhism*. Albany: State University of New York Press.

Anālayo, Bhikkhu. 2014. "Karma and Female Birth." *Journal of Buddhist Ethics* 21: 108–151.

Anderson, Richard C., and David A. Harper. 2014. "Dying to Be Free: the Emergence of 'American Militant Buddhism' in Popular Culture." In *Buddhism and American Cinema*, ed. John Whalen-Bridge and Gary Storhoff, 133–156. New York: State University of New York Press.

Appadurai, Arjun. 1996. *Modernity at Large: Cultural Dimensions of Globalization*. Minneapolis: University of Minnesota Press.

Arai, Paula. 2011. *Bringing Zen Home: The Healing Heart of Japanese Women's Rituals*. Honolulu: University of Hawai'i Press.

Asai, Senryō, and Dunan Ryûken Williams. 1999. "Japanese American Zen Temples: Cultural Identity and Economics." In *American Buddhism: Methods and Findings in Recent Scholarship*, ed. Duncan Ryûken Williams and Christopher S. Queen, 20–35. Richmond, Surrey: Curzon.

Asato, Noriko. 2010. "The Japanese Language School Controversy in Hawaii." In *Issei Buddhism in the Americas*, ed. Duncan Ryûken Williams and Tomoe Moriya, 45–64. Urbana: University of Illinois Press.

Bankston, Carl L. III, and Danielle Antoinette Hidalgo. 2008. "Temple and Society in the New World: Theravada Buddhism and Social Order in North America." In *North American Buddhists in Social Context*, ed. Paul David Numrich, 51–85. Boston: Brill.

Barnhill, David Landis. 2010. "Gary Snyder's Ecosocial Buddhism." In *How Much is Enough?: Buddhism, Consumerism, and the Human Environment*, ed. Richard K Payne, 83–120. Somerville, MA: Wisdom Publications.

Baroni, Helen. 2000. *Obaku Zen: The Emergence of the Third Sect of Zen in Tokugawa, Japan*. Honolulu: University of Hawai'i Press.

Baroni, Helen. 2012. *Love, Rōshi: Robert Baker Aitken and His Distant Correspondents*. New York: State University of New York Press.

Bartholomeusz, Tessa. 1998. "Spiritual Wealth and Neo-Orientalism." *Journal of Ecumenical Studies* 35 (1): 19–33.

Batchelor, Stephen. 2012. "A Secular Buddhism." *Journal of Global Buddhism* 13: 87–107.

Bechert, Heinz. 1984. "Buddhist Revival in East and West." In *The World of Buddhism*, ed. Heinz Bechert, and Richard Gombrich, 273–285. London: Thames and Hudson.

Beek, Kimberly. 2015. "About vs. Of." https://buddhistfictionblog.wordpress.com/2013/03/01/about-vs-of/ (accessed January 1, 2015).

Beek, Kimberly. 2015. "Telling Tales Out of School: the Fiction of Buddhism." In *Buddhism beyond Borders*, ed. Scott A. Mitchell and Natalie E. F. Quli, 125–142. Albany: State University of New York Press.

Bell, Catherine M. 1992. *Ritual Theory, Ritual Practice*. New York: Oxford University Press.

Beyer, Peter. 2006. *Religions in Global Society*. London: Routledge.

Bielefeldt, Carl. 2005. "Practice." In *Critical Terms for the Study of Buddhism*, ed. Donald S. Lopez, 229–244. Chicago: The University of Chicago Press.

Bielefeldt, Carl, Wendy Cadge, Jan Nattier, Charles S. Prebish, and Donald K. Swearer. 2001. "Tensions in American Buddhism." *Religion and Ethics Newsweekly*. http://www.pbs.org/wnet/religionandethics/week445/buddhism.html.

Bjerken, Zeff. 2005. "On Mandalas, Monarchs, and Mortuary Magic: Siting the Sarvadurgatiparisodhana Tantra in Tibet." *Journal of the American Academy of Religion* 73 (3): 813–841.

Blackburn, Anne M. 2010. *Locations of Buddhism: Colonialism and Modernity in Sri Lanka*. Chicago: The University of Chicago Press.

Blum, Mark. 2009. "The Transcendentalist Ghost in EcoBuddhism." In *TransBuddhism: Transmission, Translation, Transformation*, ed. Nalini Bhushan, Jay L. Garfield, and Abraham Zablocki, 209–238. Amherst Northampton: University of Massachusetts Press in association with the Kahn Liberal Arts Institute of Smith College.

Blum, Mark. 2011. "Kiyozawa Manshi: Life and Thought." In *Cultivating Spirituality: A Modern Shin Buddhist Anthology*, ed. Mark Blum and Robert F Rhodes, 55–65. Albany: State University of New York Press.

Boucher, Sandy. 1988. *Turning the Wheel: American Women Creating the New Buddhism*. San Francisco: Harper and Row.

Braun, Erik. 2013. *The Birth of Insight: Meditation, Modern Buddhism, and the Burmese Monk Ledi Sayada*. Chicago: University of Chicago Press.

Braun, Erik. 2015. "The United States of *Jhāna*: Varieties of of Modern Buddhism in America." In *Buddhism beyond Borders*, ed. Scott A. Mitchell and Natalie E. F. Quli, Albany: State University of New York Press.

Brown, Candy Gunther. 2015. "Textual Erasures of Religion: the Power of Books to Redefine Yoga and Mindfulness Meditation as Secular Wellness Practices in North American Public Schools." *Mémoires du livre/Studies in Book Culture*. 6 (2): http://www.erudit.org/revue/memoires/2015/v6/n2/1032713ar.html.

Bush, Mirabai. 2011. "Mindfulness in Higher Education." *Contemporary Buddhism* 12 (1): 183–197.

Busto, Rudiger V. 2002. "Disorienting Subjects: Reclaiming Pacific Islander/Asian American Religions." In *Revealing the sacred in Asian and Pacific America*, ed. Jane Iwamura and Paul Spickard, 9–28. New York: Routledge.

Buswell, Robert E, ed. 2005. *Currents and Countercurrents: Korean Influences on the East Asian Buddhist Traditions*. Honolulu: University of Hawai'i Press.

Butler, Judith. 1990. *Gender Trouble: Feminism and the Subversion of Identity*. New York: Routledge.

Cabezón, Jose Ignacio. 1998. "Homosexuality and Buddhism." In *Queer Dharma: Voices of Gay Buddhists: Volume 1*, ed. Winston Leyland, 29–44. San Francisco: Gay Sunshine Press.

Cadge, Wendy. 2004. "Gendered Religious Organizations." *Gender and Society* 18 (6): 777–793.

Cadge, Wendy. 2005. *Heartwood: The First Generation of Theravada Buddhism in America*. Chicago: University of Chicago Press.

Cadge, Wendy, and Sidhorn Sangdhanoo. 2005. "Thai Buddhism in America: An Historical and Contemporary Overview." *Contemporary Buddhism* 6 (1): 7–35.

Campbell, Patricia Q. 2011. *Knowing Body, Moving Mind: Ritualizing and Learning at Two Buddhist Centers*. New York: Oxford University Press.

Castro, Don. 2015. "In the Spirit of Mottainai." *Wheel of Dharma* 37 (4): 1.

Ch'en, Kenneth. 1964. *Buddhism in China: A Historical Survey*. 1st Princeton paperback, 2nd printing ed. Princeton: Princeton University Press.

Chananie, Steven. 1982. "Belief in God and Transcendental Meditation: The Problem of Defining Religion in the First Amendment." *Pace Law Review* 3 (1): 147–167.

Chandler, Jeannine. 2015. "Invoking the Dharma Protector: Western Involvement in the Dorje Shugden Controversy." In *Buddhism beyond Borders*, ed. Scott A Mitchell, and Natalie E. F. Quli, 75–91. Albany: State University of New York Press.

Chandler, Stuart. 1998. "Chinese Buddhism in America: Identity and Practice." In *The Faces of Buddhism in America*, ed. Charles S. Prebish, and Kenneth Tanaka, 14–30. Berkeley: University of California Press.

Chandler, Stuart. 2004. *Establishing a Pure Land on Earth: The Foguang Buddhist Perspective on Modernization and Globalization*. Honolulu: University of Hawai'i Press.

Chandler, Stuart. 2005. "Spreading Buddha's Light: The Internationalization of Foguang Shan." In *Buddhist Missionaries in the Era of Globalization*, ed. Linda Learman, 162–183. Honolulu: University of Hawai'i Press.

Chapman, David. 2011. "The Crumbling Buddhist Consensus: Overview." https://meaningness.wordpress.com/2011/06/07/the-crumbling-buddhist-consensus-overview/ (accessed November 15, 2014).

Chappell, David W. 1987. "Is Tendai Buddhism Relevant to the Modern World?" *Japanese Journal of Religious Studies* 14 (2–3): 247–266.

Cheah, Joseph. 2011. *Race and Religion in American Buddhism: White Supremacy and Immigrant Adaptation*. New York: Oxford University Press.

Chen, Carolyn. 2008. " 'True Buddhism is Not Chinese': Taiwanese Immigrants Defining Buddhist Identity in the United States." In *North American Buddhists in Social Context*, ed. Paul David Numrich, 145–161. Boston: Brill.

Chryssides, George D., and Benjamin E. Zeller, eds. 2014. *The Bloomsbury Companion to New Religious Movements*. London: Bloomsbury Academic.

Chuong, Chung Hoan, and Minh Hoa Ta. 2003. "Vietnamese Americans." *Asian-Nation: the Landscape of Asian America.* http://www.asian-nation.org/vietnamese.shtml (accessed May 21, 2014).

Clarke, J. J. 1997. *Oriental Enlightenment: The Encounter between Asian and Western Thought.* London: Routledge.

Cole, Alan. 2009. *Fathering Your Father: The Zen of Fabrication in Tang Buddhism.* Berkeley: University of California Press.

Coleman, James William. 2001. *The New Buddhism: The Western Transformation of an Ancient Tradition.* New York: Oxford University Press.

Collins, Steven. 1990. "On the Very Idea of a Pali Canon." *Journal of the Pali Text Society* 15: 89–126.

Connelly, Louise. 2012. "Virtual Buddhism: Buddhist Ritual in Second Life." In *Digital Religion: Understanding Religious Practice in New Media Worlds*, ed. Heidi A. Campbell, New York: Routledge.

Corbyn, Zoë. 2014. "Is San Francisco Losing Its Soul?" *The Guardian.* http://www.theguardian.com/world/2014/feb/23/is-san-francisco-losing-its-soul (accessed April 21, 2015).

Corless, Roger. 2000. "Gay Buddhist Fellowship." In *Engaged Buddhism in the West*, ed. Christopher S. Queen, 269–279. Boston: Wisdom Publications.

Corless, Roger. 2004. "Toward a Queer Dharmology of Sex." *Religion and Culutre: An Interdisciplinary Journal* 5 (2): 229–243.

Cornille, Catherine. 2000. "New Japanese Religions in the West: Between Nationalism and Universalism." In *Japanese New Religions in Global Perspective*, ed. Peter B Clarke, 10–34. Richmond, Surrey: Curzon Press.

Crenshaw, Kimberlé. 1989. "Demarginalizing the Intersection of Race and Sex: A Black Feminist Critique of Antidiscrimination Doctrine, Feminist Theory and Antiracist Politics." *University of Chicago Legal Forum.* 139: 139–167.

Crenshaw, Kimberlé. 2010. "Intersectionality and Identity Politics: Learning from Violence Against Women of Color." In *Feminist Theory: A Reader*, ed. Wendy K. Kolmar and Frances Bartkowski, 482–491. 3rd ed. Boston: McGraw-Hill Higher Education.

Crooms, Stephen. 2013 "Understandable but Unacceptable: A Buddhist Analysis of The New Jim Crow." *Turning Wheel Media.* http://www.buddhistpeacefellowship.org/understandable-but-unacceptable-a-buddhist-analysis-of-the-new-jim-crow/ (accessed April 21, 2015).

Dake, Mitsuya. 2010. "Pure Land Buddhism and Its Perspective on the Enviroment." In *How Much is Enough?: Buddhism, Consumerism, and the Human Environment*, ed. Richard K. Payne, 63–82. Somerville, MA: Wisdom Publications.

Darlington, Susan M. 2003. "Buddhism and Development: The Ecology Monks of Thailand." In *Action Dharma: New Studies in Engaged Buddhism*, ed. Christopher S. Queen, Charles S. Prebish, and Damien Keown, 96–109. London: RoutledgeCurzon.

Darlington, Susan M. 2009. "Translating Modernity: Buddhist Response to the Thai Environmental Crisis." In *TransBuddhism: Transmission, Translation, Transformation*, ed. Nalini Bhushan, Jay L. Garfield, and Abraham Zablocki, 183–207. Amherst Northampton: University of Massachusetts Press In association with the Kahn Liberal Arts Institute of Smith College.

Dart, John. 1989. "Buddhist Sect Alarmed by Reports that Leader Kept His AIDS a Secret." *Los Angeles Times*, March 2, 1989.

Davidson, Ronald M. 2002. *Indian Esoteric Buddhism: A Social History of the Tantric Movement*. New York: Columbia University Press.

de Beauvoir, Simone. 1949. *Le deuxième sexe*. Paris: Gallimard.

Deveaux, Tynette. 2014. "Commentary: No More Secrets." *Buddhadharma: The Practitioner's Quarterly* 13 (2): 7.

Donner, Neal. 1987. "Suddent and Gradual Intimately Conjoined: Chih-i's T'ien-t'ai View." In *Sudden and Gradual: Approaches to Enlightenment in Chinese Thought*, ed. Peter N. Gregory, 201–226. Honolulu: University of Hawai'i Press.

Douglas, Mary. 2005. *Purity and Danger: An Analysis of Concept of Pollution and Taboo*. New York: Routledge.

Du Bois, W. E. B. 2012. *Black Reconstruction in America: Toward a History of the Part of which Black Folk Played in the Attempt to Reconstruct Democracy in America, 1860–1880*. New Brunswick: Transaction Publishers.

Duff, David. 2000. *Modern Genre Theory*. Harlow, England: Longman.

Eastman, Elizabeth. 2009. "Incense at a Funeral: The Rise and Fall of an American Shingon Temple." In *TransBuddhism: Transmission, Translation, Transformation*, ed. Nalini Bhushan, Jay L. Garfield, and Abraham Zablocki, 68–85. Amherst Northampton: University of Massachusetts Press In association with the Kahn Liberal Arts Institute of Smith College.

Eastman, Janet. 2008. "Buddhamania: The Religious Symbol as Decoration? It's Complicated." *Los Angeles Times*, June 12, 2008.

Eaton, Joshua. 2014. "People's Climate March." *Tricycle: The Buddhist Review*. http://www.tricycle.com/blog/peoples-climate-march-buddhists (accessed April 20, 2015).

Eck, Diana L. 1999. "Foreward." In *American Buddhism: Methods and Findings in Recent Scholarship*, ed. Duncan Ryûken Williams and Christopher S. Queen, ix–xi. Richmond, Surrey: Curzon.

Eck, Diana L. 2006. "From Diversity to Pluralism." http://pluralism.org/encounter/challenges (accessed May 21, 2014).

Eldershaw, Lynn P. 2007. "Collective Identity and the Postcharismatic Fate of Shambhala International." *Nova Religio* 10 (4): 72–102.

Faure, Bernard. 1998. "The Buddhist Icon and the Modern Gaze." *Critical Inquiry* 24 (3): 768–813.

Faure, Bernard. 2004. *Double Exposure: Cutting across Buddhist and Western Discourses*. Trans. Janet Lloyd. Stanford: Stanford University Press.

Fisher, Danny. 2013 "Let's Talk Aboout Sex." *Off the Cushion*. http://www.patheos.com/blogs/dannyfisher/2013/03/lets-talk-about-sex/ (accessed April 20, 2015).

Fisher, Danny. 2014a. "Interview: Ajahn Brahm, the Alliance for Bhikkhunis' Michael Bratton and Donna McCarthy, and Ayya Santussika." *A People's Buddhism*. https://archive.org/details/DrDannyFisher (accessed May 20, 2015).

Fisher, Danny. 2014b. "Interview: Ven. Bhikkhu Bodhi and Cat Jaffee." *A People's Buddhism*. https://archive.org/details/DrDannyFisher (accessed April 20, 2015).

Fronsdal, Gil. 1998. "Insight Meditation in the United States: Life, Liberty, and the Pursuit of Happiness." In *The Faces of Buddhism in America*, ed. Charles S. Prebish and Kenneth Tanaka, 164–180. Berkeley: University of California Press.

Geekie, Constance Lynn. 2008. "Soka Gakkai: Engaged Buddhism in North America." In *North American Buddhists in Social Context*, ed. Paul David Numrich, 203–224. Boston: Brill.

Gethin, Rupert. 1998. *The Foundations of Buddhism*. New York: Oxford University Press.

Gethin, Rupert. 2001. *The Buddhist Path to Awakening: A Study of the Bodhi-Pakkhiyā Dhammā*. Oxford: Oneworld.

Gilpin, Richard. 2008. "The Use of Theravada Buddhist Practices and Perspectives in Mindfulness-based Cognitive Therapy." *Contemporary Buddhism* 9 (2): 227–251.

Girardot, Norman J. 2002. *The Victorian Translation of China: James Legge's Oriental Pilgrimage*. Berkeley: University of California Press.

Gleig, Ann. 2012a. "Queering Buddhism or Buddhist De-Queering?" *Theology & Sexuality* 18 (3): 198–214.

Gleig, Ann. 2012b. "Wedding the Personal and Impersonal in West Coast Vipassana: A Dialogical Encounter between Buddhism and Psychotherapy." *Journal of Global Buddhism* 13: 129–146.

Gleig, Ann. 2014. "From Buddhist Hippies to Buddhist Geeks: The Emergence of Buddhist Postmodernism?" *Journal of Global Buddhism* 15: 15–33

Gombrich, Richard F. 1988. *Theravāda Buddhism: A Social History from Ancient Benares to Modern Colombo*. New York: Routledge.

Gombrich, Richard F., and Gananath Obeyesekere. 1988. *Buddhism Transformed: Religious Change in Sri Lanka*. Princeton: Princeton University Press.

Green, Paula. 2000. "Walking for Peace: Nipponzan Myohoji." In *Engaged Buddhism in the West*, ed. Christopher S. Queen, 128–158. Boston: Wisdom Publications.

Green, Ronald S. 2014. *Buddhism Goes to the Movies: Introduction to Buddhist Thought and Practice*. London: Routledge.

Gregory, Peter N. 2001. "Describing the Elephant: Buddhism in America." *Religion and American Culture* 2 (2): 233–263.

Grieve, Gregory P. 2015. "The Middle Way Method: A Buddhist-Informed Ethnography of the Virtual World of Second Life." In *Buddhism, the Internet, and Digital Media: The Pixel in the Lotus*, ed. Gregory P. Grieve and Daniel M. Veidlinger, 23–39. New York: Routledge.

Grieve, Gregory P., and Daniel M. Veidlinger, eds. 2015. *Buddhism, the Internet, and Digital Media: The Pixel in the Lotus*. New York: Routledge.

Gross, Rita M. 1993. *Buddhism after Patriarchy: A Feminist History, Analysis, and Reconstruction of Buddhism*. Albany: State University of New York Press.

Gyallay-Pap, Peter. 2006. "Reconstructing the Cambodian polity: Buddhism, Kingship, and the Quest for Legitimacy." In *Buddhism, Power and Political Order*, ed. Ian Harris, 71–103. New York: Routledge.

Gyatso, Janet. 2005. "Sex." In *Critical Terms for the Study of Buddhism*, ed. Donald S. Lopez, 271–290. Chicago: The University of Chicago Press.

Gyatso, Janet. 2014. "In the Face of Tragedy." *Tricycle: The Buddhist Review*. http://www.tricycle.com/blog/face-tragedy (accessed May 21, 2014).

Gyatso, Tenzin. 1999. *Ethics for the New Millennium*. New York: Riverhead Books.

Haas, Michaela. 2013. *Dakini Power: Twelve Extraordinary Women Shaping the Transmission of Tibetan Buddhism in the West*. Boston: Shambhala Publications.

Habermas, Jürgen. 1985. "Modernity—An Incomplete Project." In *The Anti-Aesthetic: Essays on Postmodern Culture*, ed. Hal Foster, 3–15. Seattle: Bay Press.

Hackett, Paul G. 2013. *Theos Bernard, The White Lama: Tibet, Yoga, and American Religious Life*. New York: Columbia University Press.

Hallisey, Charles. 1995. "Roads Taken and Not Taken in the Study of Theravada Buddhism." In *Curators of the Buddha: The Study of Buddhism under Colonialism*, ed. Donald S. Lopez, 31–61. Chicago: University of Chicago Press.

Hammond, Phillip E., and David W Machacek. 1999. *Soka Gakkai in America: Accommodation and Conversion*. New York: Oxford University Press.

Haney, Dawn. 2014. "Buddhist Blockade against Police Militarization." *Turning Wheel Media*. http://www.buddhistpeacefellowship.org/the-four-noble-truths-in-our-world-truth-3-the-cessation-of-the-suffering-of-caste/ (accessed April 20, 2015).

Harding, John S., Victor Sogen Hori, and Alexander Soucy. 2014. *Flowers on the Rock: Global and Local Buddhisms in Canada*. Montreal: McGill-Queen's University Press.

Harrison, Paul. 1995. "Searching for the Origins of the Mahāyāna: What Are We Looking For?" *The Eastern Buddhist*. n.s., 28 (1) : 48–69.

Hickey, Wakoh Shannon. 2010. "Two Buddhisms, Three Buddhisms, and Racism." *Journal of Global Buddhism* 11: 1–25.

Hickey, Wakoh Shannon. 2015. "Two Buddhisms, Three Buddhisms, and Racism." In *Buddhism beyond Borders*, ed. Scott A. Mitchell and Natalie E. F. Quli, 35–56. Albany: State University of New York Press.

Higgins, Winton. 2012. "The Coming of Secular Buddhism: A Synoptic View." *Journal of Global Buddhism* 13: 109–126.

Hopkins, Jeffrey. 1997. "The Compatibility of Reason and Orgasm in Tibetan Buddhism: Reflections of Sexual Violence and Homophobia." In *Que(e)rying Religion: A Critical Anthology*, ed. Gary David Comstock and Susan E. Henking, New York: Continuum.

Hori, Victor Sōgen., John S. Harding, and Alexander Duncan Soucy, eds. 2010. *Wild Geese: Buddhism in Canada*. Montreal: McGill-Queen's University Press.

Huang, Julia C. 2005. "The Compassion Relief Diaspora." In *Buddhist Missionaries in the Era of Globalization*, ed. Linda Learman, 185–208. Honolulu: University of Hawai'i Press.

Hubbard, Jamie. 1995. "Upping the Ante: budstud@millenium.end.edu." *Journal of the International Association of Buddhist Studies* 18 (2): 309–322.

Hubbard, Jamie. 1998. "Embarrassing Superstition, Doctrine, and the Study of New Religious Movements." *Journal of the American Academy of Religion* 66 (1): 59–92.

Hunt-Perry, Patricia, and Lyn Fine. 2000. "All Buddhism is Engaged: Thich Nhat Hanh and the Order of Interbeing." In *Engaged Buddhism in the West*, ed. Christopher S. Queen, 35–66. Boston: Wisdom Publications.

Hurst, Jane. 1998. "Nichiren Shōshū and Soka Gakkai in America: The Pioneer Spirit." In *The Faces of Buddhism in America*, ed. Charles S. Prebish, and Kenneth Tanaka, 79–98. Berkeley: University of California Press.

Imamura, Jane Michiko. 1998. *Kaikyo: Opening the Dharma: Memoirs of a Buddhist Priest's Wife in America*. Honolulu: Buddhist Study Center Press.

Ivy, Marilyn. 2005. "Modernity." In *Critical Terms for the Study of Buddhism*, ed. Donald S. Lopez, 311–331. Chicago: The University of Chicago Press.

Iwabuchi, Kōichi. 2002. *Recentering Globalization: Popular Culture and Japanese Transnationalism.* Durham: Duke University Press.

Iwamura, Jane. 2010. *Virtual Orientalism: Asian Religions and American Popular Culture.* New York: Oxford University Press.

Jaffe, Richard M. 2001. *Neither Monk nor Layman: Clerical Marriage in Modern Japanese Buddhism.* Honolulu: University of Hawai'i Press.

Jenkins, Steven. 2009. "Compassionate Violence." *Institute of Buddhist Studies Podcast.* http://podcast.shin-ibs.edu/?cat=55 (accessed September 18, 2015).

Jerryson, Michael K., and Mark. Juergensmeyer, eds. 2010. *Buddhist Warfare.* New York: Oxford University Press.

Johnson, Lyndon B. 1965. "Remarks at the Signing of the Immigration Bill, Liberty Island, New York." *The American Presidency Project.* http://www.presidency.ucsb.edu/ws/?pid=27292 (accessed May 21, 2014).

Josephson, Jason Ānanda. 2006. "When Buddhism Became a 'Religion': Religion and Superstition in the Writings of Inoue Enryō." *Japanese Journal of Religious Studies* 33(1): 143–168.

Kapstein, Matthew. 2000. *The Tibetan Assimilation of Buddhism: Conversion, Contestation, and Memory.* New York: Oxford University Press.

Kashima, Tetsuden. 1977. *Buddhism in America: The Social Organization of an Ethnic Religious Organization.* Westport: Greenwood Press.

Kassor, Constance. 2009. "Buddhism in American Prisons." In *TransBuddhism: Transmission, Translation, Transformation*, ed. Nalini Bhushan, Jay L. Garfield, and Abraham Zablocki, 55–67. Amherst Northampton: University of Massachusetts Press in association with the Kahn Liberal Arts Institute of Smith College.

Kaufman, Leslie. 2008. "Making Their Own Limits in a Spiritual Partnership." *New York Times*, May 15, 2008.

Kaza, Stephanie. 2000. "To Save All Beings: Buddhist Environmental Activism." In *Engaged Buddhism in the West*, ed. Christopher S. Queen, 159–183. Boston: Wisdom Publications.

Kaza, Stephanie. 2010. "How Much is Enough?: Buddhist Perspectives on Consumerism." In *How Much is Enough?: Buddhism, Consumerism, and the Human Environment*, ed. Richard K. Payne, 39–62. Somerville, MA: Wisdom Publications.

Kemper, Steven. 2005. "Dharmapala's *Dharmaduta* and the Buddhist Ethnoscape." In *Buddhist Missionaries in the Era of Globalization*, ed. Linda Learman, 22–50. Honolulu: University of Hawai'i Press.

Kennedy, John F. 1963. "Remarks to Delegates of the American Committee on Italian Migration." *The American Presidency Project.* http://www.presidency.ucsb.edu/ws/?pid=9269 (accessed May 21, 2014).

Keown, Damien. 2012. "Buddhist Ethics: A Critique." In *Buddhism in the Modern World*, ed. David L. McMahan, 215–231. New York: Routledge.

Ketelaar, James Edward. 1990. *Of Heretics and Martyrs in Meiji Japan: Buddhism and its Persecution.* Princeton: Princeton University Press.

Kim, Karen Chai. 2008. "A Religious Minority within an Ethnic Minority: Korean American Buddhists." In *North American Buddhists in Social Context*, ed. Paul David Numrich, 163–183. Boston: Brill.

King, Richard. 1999. *Orientalism and Religion Post-Colonial Theory, India and 'the Mystic East'*. New York: Routledge.

King, Sallie B. 2005. *Being Benevolence: The Social Ethics of Engaged Buddhism*. Honolulu: University of Hawai'i Press.

King, Sallie B. 2012. "Socially Engaged Buddhism." In *Buddhism in the Modern World*, ed. David L. McMahan, 195–213. New York: Routledge.

Klein, Anne C. 2008. *Meeting the Great Bliss Queen: Buddhists, Feminists, and the Art of the Self*. Ithaca: Snow Lion.

Koppedrayer, Kay. 2002. "Reading Pema Chdrn." *Contemporary Buddhism* 3 (1): 51–79.

Kraft, Kenneth. 2000. "New Voices in Engaged Buddhist Studies." In *Engaged Buddhism in the West*, ed. Christopher S. Queen, 485–511. Boston: Wisdom Publications.

Kukura, Andrew, Jenny Phillips, and Anne Marie Stein. 2008. *The Dhamma Brothers*. [film] New Light Production.

Lavine, Amy. 1998. "Tibetan Buddhism in America: The Development of American Vajrayana." In *The Faces of Buddhism in America*, ed. Charles S. Prebish and Kenneth Tanaka, 99–115. Berkeley: University of California Press.

Layman, Emma McCloy. 1976. *Buddhism in America*. Chicago: Nelson-Hall Publishers.

Le, C. N. 2001. "The 1965 Immigration Act." *Asian-Nation: The Landscape of Asian America*. http://www.asian-nation.org/1965-immigration-act.shtml (accessed May 21, 2014).

Le, C. N. 2009. "Reflections on a Multiracial Buddhist Retreat." http://www.asian-nation.org/headlines/2009/07/reflections-multiracial-buddhist-retreat/ (accessed September 25, 2014.

Leighton, Taigen Daniel. 2008. "Zazen as an Enactment Ritual." In *Zen Ritual: Studies of Zen Buddhist Theory in Practice*, ed. Steven Heine and Dale Stuart Wright, 167–184. New York: Oxford University Press.

Lin, Irene. 1999. "Journey to the Far West: Chinese Buddhism in America." In *New Spiritual Homes: Religion and Asian Americans*, ed. David Yoo, 134–165. Honolulu: University of Hawai'i Press in association with UCLA Asian American Studies Center, Los Angeles.

Lopez, Donald S. 1998. *Prisoners of Shangri-La: Tibetan Buddhism and the West*. Chicago: University of Chicago Press.

Lopez, Donald S. S., ed. 2002. *A Modern Buddhist Bible: Essential Readings from East and West*. Boston: Beacon Press.

Lopez, Donald S. 2008. *Buddhism and Science: A Guide for the Perplexed*. Chicago: University of Chicago Press.

Lugo, Luis, ed. 2008. *U.S. Religious Landscape Survey: Religious Affiliation: Diverse and Dynamic*. The Pew Forum on Religion and Public Life. Pew Research Center.

Lugo, Luis, and Alan Cooperman, eds. 2012. *Asian Americans: A Mosaic of Faiths*. The Pew Forum on Religion and Public Life. Pew Research Center.

MacNell, Lillian, Adam Driscoll, and Andrea N Hunt. 2014. "What's in a Name: Exposing Gender Bias in Student Ratings of Teaching." *Innovative Higher Education* 40 (4): 1–13.

MacQueen, Graeme. 1998. "Changing Master Narratives in Midstream: Barlaam and Josaphat and the Growth of Religious Intolerance in the Buddhalegend's Westward Journey." *Journal of Buddhist Ethics* 5: 144–166.

Masaaki, Hattori. 2005. "Realism and the Philosophy of Consciousness-Only." In *Buddhism: Yogācāra, the Epistemological Tradition and Tathāgatagarbha*, ed. Paul Williams, 36–64. London and New York: Routledge Press.

Masatsugu, Michael K. 2004. *Reorienting the Pure Land: Japanese Americans, The Beats, and the Making of American Buddhism, 1941–1966*. PhD diss., University of California, Irvine.

Masatsugu, Michael K. 2008. " 'Beyond this World of Transiency and Impermanence': Japanese Americans, Dharma Bums, and the Making of American Buddhism during the Early Cold War Years." *Pacific Historical Review* 77 (3): 423–451.

McIntosh, Peggy. 2004. "White Privilege and Male Privilege: A Personal Account of Coming to See Correspondences through Work in Women's Studies." In *Oppression, Privilege, and Resistance: Theoretical Perspectives on Racism, Sexism, and Hetersexism*, ed. Lisa Heldke and Peg O'Connor, 317–327. New York: McGraw-Hill.

McKinley, Alexander. 2014. "Fluid Minds: Being a Buddhist the Shambhalian Way." *Buddhist Studies Review* 31 (2): 279–291.

McLuhan, Marshall. 1964. *Understanding Media; The Extensions of man*. 1st ed. New York: McGraw-Hill.

McMahan, David L. 2002. "Repackaging Zen for the West." In *Westward Dharma: Buddhism beyond Asia*, ed. Charles S. Prebish, and Martin Baumann, 218–229. Berkeley: University of California Press.

McMahan, David L. 2008. *The Making of Buddhist Modernism*. Oxford; New York: Oxford University Press.

McMahan, David L. 2015a. "Buddhism and Multiple Modernities." In *Buddhism beyond Borders*, ed. Scott A. Mitchell, and Natalie E. F. Quli, 181–195. Albany: State University of New York Press.

McMahan, David L. 2015b. "Mindfulness as Self-Cultivation in Ancient and Modern Contexts." Keynote Presentation. Mindfulness and Compassion: The Art and Science of Contemplative Practice. San Francisco. June 5.

McRae, John R. 2003. *Seeing Through Zen: Encounter, Transformation, and Genealogy in Chinese Chan Buddhism*. Berkeley: University of California Press.

Meade Sperry, Rod. 2013. "Run, Beasties, and Constant Craving." *Shambhala Sun* 21 (4): 60–69.

Midal, Fabrice. 2004. *Chögyam Trungpa: His Life and Vision*. Trans. Ian Monk. Boston: Shambhala Press.

Mitchell, Scott A. 2008. *Taking Refuge in the Dharma: Post-Colonialism, Ritual Theory, and American Buddhist Studies*. PhD diss. Graduate Theological Union, Berkeley.

Mitchell, Scott A. 2010. "Locally Translocal American Shin Buddhism." *Pacific World: Journal of the Institute of Buddhist Studies* 3 (12): 109–126.

Mitchell, Scott A. 2012. " 'Christianity is for Rubes; Buddhism is for Actors': U.S. Media Representations of Buddhism in the Wake of the Tiger Woods' Scandal. *Journal of Global Buddhism* 13: 61–79.

Mitchell, Scott A. 2014a. "The Ritual Use of Music in US Jōdo Shinshū Buddhist Communities." *Contemporary Buddhism* 15 (2): 1–17.

Mitchell, Scott A. 2014b. "The Tranquil Meditator: Representing Buddhism and Buddhists in US Popular Media." *Religion Compass* 8 (3): 81–89.

Miyata, Koichi. 2002. "Critical Comments on Brian Victoria's 'Engaged Buddhism: A Skeleton in the Closet?'" *Journal of Global Buddhism* 3: 79–85.

Montrose, Victoria Rose. 2014. "Floating Prayer: Localization, Globalization, and Tradition in the Shinnyo-en Hawaii Lantern Floating." *Journal of Religion in Japan* 3 (2–3): 177–197.

Mowe, Sam. 2011. "Making Tantric Practice Available to the Masses: The Kalachakra for World Peace." *Tricycle: the Buddhist Review*. http://www.tricycle.com/blog/making-tantric-practice-available-masses-kalachakra-world-peace-2011 (accessed November 13, 2014).

Mrozik, Susanne. 2013. " 'We Love Our Nuns': Affective Dimensions of the Sri Lankan *Bhikkhunī* Revival." *Buddhist Ethics* 20: 57–95.

Mullen, Eve. 2001. *The American Occupation of Tibetan Buddhism: Tibetans and Their American Hosts in New York City*. Münster; New York: Waxmann.

Mullen, Eve. 2006. "Tibetan Religious Expression and Identity: Transformations in Exile." In *Materializing Religion: Expression, Performance and Ritual*, ed. Elisabeth Arweck and William J. F. Keenan, 175–189. Burlington: Ashgate.

Mullen, Eve. 2014. "Buddhism, Children, and the Childlike in American Buddhist Films." In *Buddhism and American Cinema*, ed. John Whalen-Bridge and Gary Storhoff, 39–52. New York: State University of New York Press.

Nattier, Jan. 1991. *Once Upon a Future Time: Studies in a Buddhist Prophecy of Decline*. Berkeley: Asian Humanities Press.

Nattier, Jan. 1995. "Visible and Invisible: On the Politics of Representation in America." *Tricycle: The Buddhist Review* (Fall): 42–49.

Nattier, Jan. 2009. "Gender and Hierarchy in the *Lotus Sūtra*." In *Readings of the Lotus Sutra*, ed. Stephen F. Teiser, and Jacqueline Stone, 83–106. New York: Columbia University Press.

Nguyen, Cuong Tu, and A. W. Barber. 1998. "Vietnamese Buddhism in North America: Tradition and Acculturation. "In *The Faces of Buddhism in America*, ed. Charles S. Prebish, and Kenneth Tanaka, 129–146. Berkeley: University of California Press.

Nhat Hanh, Thich. 1987. *Being Peace*. Berkeley: Parallax Press.

Nishimura, Arthur. 2008. "The Buddhist Mission of North America 1898–1942: Religion and its Social Function in an Ethnic Community." In *North American Buddhists in Social Context*, ed. Paul David Numrich, 87–106. Boston: Brill.

Nobutaka, Inoue. 2012. "Media and New Religious Movements in Japan." *Journal of Religion in Japan* 1 (2): 121–141.

Normand, Lawrence, and Alison Winch. 2013. *Encountering Buddhism in Twentieth-Century British and American Literature*. London: Bloomsbury Academic.

Numrich, Paul David. 1996. *Old Wisdom in the New World: Americanization in Two Immigrant Theravada Buddhist Temples*. Knoxville: University of Tennessee Press.

Numrich, Paul David. 1998. "Theravāda Buddhism in America: Prospects for the Sangha." In *The Faces of Buddhism in America*, ed. Charles S. Prebish and Kenneth Tanaka, 147–161. Berkeley: University of California Press.

Numrich, Paul David. 2003. "Two Buddhisms Further Considered." *Contemporary Buddhism* 4 (1): 55–78.

Numrich, Paul David. 2008. "North American Buddhists: A Field of study?" In *North American Buddhists in Social Context*, ed. Paul David Numrich, 1–17. Boston: Brill.

Omi, Michael, and Howard Winant. 1986. *Racial Formation in the United States: From the 1960s to the 1980s*. New York: Routledge & Kegan Paul.

Omi, Michael, 2014. *Racial Formation in the United States*. 3rd ed. New York: Routledge & Kegan Paul.

Oppenheimer, Mark. 2010. "Sex Scandal Has U.S. Buddhists Looking Within." *New York Times*, August 20, A13.

Osborne, Peter. 1995. *The Politics of Time: Modernity and Avant-Garde*. London: Verso.

Padgett, Douglas M. 2000. " 'Americans Need Something to Sit On,' or Zen Meditation Materials and Buddhist Diversity in North America." *Journal of Global Buddhism* 1: 61–81.

Painter, Nell Irvin. 2010. *The History of White People*. New York: W. W. Norton.

Panish, Jon. 1994. "Kerouac's The Subterraneans: A Study of 'Romantic Primitivism'." *Melus* 19 (3): 107–123.

Payne, Richard K. 2005. "Hiding in Plain Sight: The Invisibility of the Shingon Mission to the United States." In *Buddhist Missionaries in the Era of Globalization*, ed. Linda Learman, 101–122. Honolulu: University of Hawai'i Press.

Payne, Richard K. ed. 2006. *Tantric Buddhism in East Asia*. Boston: Wisdom Publications.

Payne, Richard K. 2010. "Introduction: Just How Much is Enough?" In *How Much is Enough?: Buddhism, Consumerism, and the Human Environment*, ed. Richard K Payne, 1–16. Somerville, MA: Wisdom Publications.

Payne, Richard K. 2012a. "Buddhism and the Powers of the Mind." In *Buddhism in the Modern World*, ed. David L. McMahan, 233–256. New York: Routledge.

Payne, Richard K. 2012b. "Why 'Buddhist Theology' Is Not a Good Idea: Keynote Address for the Fifteenth Biennial Conference of the International Association of Shin Buddhist Studies, Kyoto, August 2011." *The Pure Land* n.s., 27.

Payne, Richard K. 2014. "Corporatist Spirituality." http://rkpayne.wordpress.com/2014/02/18/corporatist-spirituality/ (accessed November15, 2014).

Payne, Richard K. 2015. "Afterword: Buddhism beyond Borders: Beyond the Rhetorics of Rupture." In *Buddhism beyond Borders*, ed. Scott A. Mitchell and Natalie E. F. Quli, 217–239. Albany: State University of New York Press.

Pepper, Tom. 2012. "Comfort-Food Buddhism." http://speculativenonbuddhism.com/2012/08/24/comfort-food-buddhism/ (accessed September 25, 2014).

Perreira, Todd. 2004. "Sasana Sakon and the New Asian American: Intermarriage and Identity at a Thai Buddhist Temple in Silicon Valley." In *Asian American Religions: The Making and Remaking of Borders and Boundaries*, ed. Tony Carnes and Fengang Yang, 313–337. New York: New York University Press.

Prebish, Charles S. 1979. *American Buddhism*. North Scituate, MA: Duxbury Press.

Prebish, Charles S. 1993. "Two Buddhisms Reconsidered." *Buddhist Studies Review* 10 (2): 187–206.

Prebish, Charles S. 1998. "Introduction." In *The Faces of Buddhism in America*, ed. Charles S. Prebish and Kenneth Tanaka, 1–10. Berkeley: University of California Press.

Prebish, Charles S. 1999. *Luminous Passage: The Practice and Study of Buddhism in America*. Berkeley: University of California Press.

Prothero, Stephen R. 1995. "Introduction." In *Big Sky Mind: Buddhism and the Beat Generation*, ed. Carole Tonkinson, 1–20. New York: Riverhead Books.

Prothero, Stephen R. 1996. *The White Buddhist: the Asian odyssey of Henry Steel Olcott.* Bloomington: Indiana University Press.

Prothero, Stephen R. 1997. "The Good Shepard." *Tricycle: the Buddhist Review.* http://www.tricycle.com/feature/the-good-shepherd (accessed May 29, 2014).

Prothero, Stephen R. 2001. "Boomer Buddhism." *Salon.com.* http://www.salon.com/2001/02/26/buddhism (accessed May 16, 2014).

Purser, Ron, and David Loy. 2013. "Beyond McMindfulness." *The Huffington Post.* www.huffingtonpost.com/ron-purser/beyond-mcmindfulness_b_3519289.html?view=print&comm_ref=false (accessed July 22, 2013).

Queen, Christopher S. 2000. "Introduction: A New Buddhism." In *Engaged Buddhism in the West*, ed. Christopher S. Queen, 1–31. Boston: Wisdom Publications.

Quli, Natalie. 2008. "Multiple Buddhist Modernisms: Jhāna in Convert Theravāda." *Pacific World Journal* 10 (1): 225–249.

Quli, Natalie. 2009. "Western Self, Asian Other: Modernity, Authenticity, and Nostalgia for 'Tradition' in Buddhist Studies." *Journal of Buddhist Ethics* 16: 1–38.

Quli, Natalie E. F., and Scott A. Mitchell. 2015. "Buddhist Modernism as Narrative: A Comparative Study of Jodo Shinshu and Zen." In *Buddhism beyond Borders*, ed. Scott A. Mitchell and Natalie E. F. Quli, 197–215. Albany: State University of New York Press.

Reader, Ian. 2008. "Buddhism and the Perils of Advocacy." *Journal of Global Buddhism* 9: 83–112.

Ream, Amanda. 2014. "Why I Disrupted the Wisdom 2.0 Conference: The Organizer behind the Demonstration Speaks Out." *Tricycle: The Buddhist Review.* http://www.tricycle.com/blog/why-i-disrupted-wisdom-20-conference (accessed November 15, 2014).

Ritzer, George. 2007. *The Globalization of Nothing 2.* Thousand Oaks, CA.: Pine Forge Press.

Robertson, Roland. 1992. *Globalization: Social Theory and Global Culture.* London: Sage.

Robinson, Richard H., and Willard L. Johnson. 1997. *The Buddhist Religion: A Historical Introduction.* 3rd ed. Belmont, CA: Wadsworth.

Said, Edward. 1978. *Orientalism.* 1st ed. New York: Pantheon Books.

Salgado, Nirmala S. 2004. "Religious Identities of Buddhist Nuns: Training Precepts, Renunciant Attire, and Nomenclature in Theravada Buddhism." *Journal of the American Academy of Religion* 72 (4): 935–953.

Santos, Fernanda. 2012. "Mysterious Buddhist Retreat in the Desert Ends in a Grisly Death." *New York Times*, June 6, 2012; page A10.

Schedneck, Brooke. 2011. "Forest as Challenge, Forest as Healer: Reinterpretations and Hybridity within the Forest Tradition of Thailand." *Pacific World: Journal of the Institute of the Institute of Buddhist Studies* 3 (13): 1–24.

Schedneck, Brooke. 2014. "Noah Levine: Punk Rocker and Buddhist Meditation Teacher." In *Buddhists: Understanding Buddhism Through the Lives of Practitioners*, ed. Todd Lewis, 107–114. West Sussex: Wiley Blackwell.

Schober, Juliane. 2006. "Colonial Knowledge and Buddhist Education in Burma." In *Buddhism, Power and Political Order*, ed. Ian Harris, 52–70. London; New York: Routledge.

Seager, Richard Hughes. 1999. *Buddhism in America.* 1st ed. New York: Columbia University Press.

Seager, Richard Hughes. 2015. "Dharma Images and Identity in American Buddhism."
    In *Buddhism beyond Borders*, ed. Scott A. Mitchell and Natalie E. F. Quli, 113–124.
    Albany: State University of New York Press.
Shachtman, Noah. 2013. "In Silicon Valley, Meditation is No Fad. It Could Make Your
    Career." *Wired*. http://www.wired.com/2013/06/meditation-mindfulness-silicon-valley/2/
    (accessed April 21, 2015).
Sharf, Robert H. 1995a. "Sanbōkyōdan: Zen and the Way of the New Religions." *Japanese
    Journal of Religious Studies* 22:3–4: 417–457.
Sharf, Robert H. 1995b. "The Zen of Japanese Nationalism." In *Curators of the
    Buddha: The Study of Buddhism Under Colonialism*, ed. Donald S. Lopez, 107–160.
    Chicago: University of Chicago Press.
Sharf, Robert H. 2002. "On Pure Land Buddhism and Ch'an/Pure Land Syncretism in
    Medieval China." *T'oung Pao* Second Series,88, fasc. 4/5: 282–331.
Sharf, Robert H. 2005. "Ritual." In *Critical Terms for the Study of Buddhism*, ed. Donald
    S. Lopez, 245–270. Chicago: The University of Chicago Press.
Shields, James Mark. 2011. "Sexuality, Blasphemy, and Iconoclasm in the Media Age."
    In *God in the Details: American Religion in Popular Culture*, eds. Eric Mazur and Kate
    McCarthy, 80–102. London: Routledge.
Shiramizu, Hiroko. 1979. "Organizational Mediums: A Case Study of Shinnyo-en."
    Japanese Journal of Religious Studies 6 (3): 413–444.
Silk, Jonathan A. 2002. "What, if anything, is Mahāyāna Buddhism? Problems of
    Definitions and Classifications." *Numen* 49 (4): 355–405.
Simmer-Brown, Judith. 2000. "Speaking Truth to Power: The Buddhist Peace Fellowship."
    In *Engaged Buddhism in the West*, ed. Christopher S. Queen, 67–94. Boston: Wisdom
    Publications.
Simmer-Brown, Judith. 2002. "The Roar of the Lioness: Women's Dharma in the West."
    In *Westward Dharma: Buddhism Beyond Asia*, ed. Charles S. Prebish, and Martin
    Baumann, 309–323. Berkeley: University of California Press.
Skilling, Peter. 2006. "King, *Sangha* and Brahmans: Ideology, Riutal and Power in
    Pre-Modern Siam." In *Buddhism, Power and Political Order*, ed. Ian Harris, 182–215.
    London; New York: Routledge.
Slater, Don. 2002. "Social Relationships and Identity Online and Offline." In *Handbook of
    New Media: Social Shaping and Consequences of ICTs*, ed. Leah Lievrouw and Sonia
    Livingstone, 533–546. London: Sage Publications.
Snodgrass, Judith. 1998. "Buddha no Fukin: The Deployment of Paul Carus' Gospel of
    Buddha in Meiji Japan." *Japanese Journal of Religious Studies* 25: 319–344.
Snodgrass, Judith. 2003. *Presenting Japanese Buddhism to the West: Orientalism,
    Occidentalism, and the Columbian Exposition*. Chapel Hill: University of North
    Carolina Press.
Snyder, Gary. 1996. *Mountains and Rivers without End*. New York: Counterpoint.
Spencer, Anne C. 2014. "Diversification in the Buddhist Churches of America:
    Demographic Trends and Their Implications for the Future Study of US Buddhist
    Groups." *Journal of Global Buddhism* 15: 35–61.
Sperling, Elliot. 2004. "The Tibet-China Conflict: History and Polemics." *Policy Studies* 7.
Stone, Jacqueline I. 2003. "Nichiren's Activist Heirs: Sōka Gakkai, Rishhō Kosekai,
    Nipponzan Myōhōji." In *Action Dharma: New Studies in Engaged Buddhism*, eds.

Christopher S. Queen, Charles S. Prebish, and Damien Keown, 63–94. London; New York: RoutledgeCurzon.

Suh, Sharon A. 2004. *Being Buddhist in a Christian World: Gender and Community in a Korean American Temple.* Seattle: University of Washington Press.

Suh, Sharon A. 2015. *Silver Screen Buddha: Buddhism in Asian and Western Film.* London: Bloomsbury Academic.

Suzuki, Daisetz Teitaro. 1967. "An Interpretation of Zen Experience." In *The Japanese Mind: Essentials of Japanese Philosophy and Culture,* ed. Charles A. Moore, 122–142. Honolulu: University of Hawai'i Press.

Tanabe, George J. 1998. "Glorious Gathas: Americanization and Japanization in Honganji Hymns." In *Engaged Pure Land Buddhism: Challenges Facing Jōdo Shinshū in the Contemporary World: Studies in Honor of Professor Alfred Bloom,* ed. Kenneth Tanaka and Eisho Nasu, 221–240. Berkeley: WisdomOcean.

Tanaka, Kenneth K. 1998. "Epilogue: The Colors and Contours of American Buddhism." In *The Faces of Buddhism in America,* ed. Charles S. Prebish and Kenneth Tanaka, 287–298. Berkeley: University of California Press.

Tanaka, Kenneth K. 1999. "Issues of Ethnicity in the Buddhist Churches of America." In *American Buddhism: Methods and Findings in Recent Scholarship,* ed. Duncan Ryûken Williams and Christopher S. Queen, 3–19. Richmond, Surrey: Curzon.

Taylor, Charles. 2001. "Two Theories of Modernity." In *Alternative Modernities,* ed. Dilip Parameshwar Gaonkar, 172–196. Durham, NC: Duke University Press.

Taylor, Charles. 2011. "Western Secularity." In *Rethinking Secularism,* ed. Craig J. Calhoun, Mark Juergensmeyer, and Jonathan VanAntwerpen, ix, 311. New York: Oxford University Press.

Tebbe, Adam Kōshin. n.d. "Gengo Akiba." http://sweepingzen.com/gengo-akiba-bio/ (accessed September 25, 2014).

Thomas, Stephanie. 2013. "Dispatch from the Front Lines: Resisting Keystone XL and Tar Sands." *Turning Wheel Media.* http://www.buddhistpeacefellowship.org/dispatch-from-the-front-lines-resisting-keystone-xl-and-tar-sands/ (accessed April 21, 2015).

Tomalin, Emma. 2006. "The Thai Bhikkhuni Movement and Women's Empowerment." *Gender and Development* 14 (3): 385–397.

Trinlae, Bhikṣuṇī Lozang. 2010. "The Mūlasarvāstivāda Bhikṣuṇī Has the Horns of a Rabbit: Why the Master's Tools Will Never Reconstruct the Master's House." *The Journal of Buddhist Ethics* 17: 311–331.

Tsomo, Karma Lekshe. 2002. "Buddhist Nuns: Changes and Challenges." In *Westward Dharma: Buddhism beyond Asia,* ed. Charles S. Prebish and Martin Baumann, 255–274. Berkeley: University of California Press.

Tweed, Thomas A. 1992. *The American Encounter with Buddhism, 1844–1912: Victorian Culture and the Limits of Dissent.* Bloomington: Indiana University Press.

Tweed, Thomas A. 1999. "Night-Stand Buddhists and Other Creatures: Sympathizers, Adherents, and the Study of Religion." In *American Buddhism: Methods and Findings in Recent Scholarship,* ed. Duncan Ryûken Williams and Christopher S. Queen, 71–90. Richmond, Surrey: Curzon.

Tweed, Thomas A. 2002. "Who is a Buddhist? Night-Stand Buddhists and Other Creatures." In *Westward Dharma: Buddhism beyond Asia,* ed. Charles S. Prebish and Martin Baumann, 17–33. Berkeley: University of California Press.

Tweed, Thomas A. 2008a. *Crossing and Dwelling: A Theory of Religion.* Cambridge: Harvard University Press.

Tweed, Thomas A. 2008b. "Why Are Buddhists So Nice? Media Representations of Buddhism and Islam in the United States Since 1945." *Material Religion* 4 (1): 91–93.

Tweed, Thomas A. 2009. "Crabs, Crustaceans, Crabiness, and Outrage: A Response." *The Journal of the American Academy of Religion* 77 (2): 445–459.

Tweed, Thomas A. 2011. "Theory and Method in the Study of Buddhism: Toward 'Translocative' Analysis." *Journal of Global Buddhism* 12: 17–32.

Tweed, Thomas A. 2012. "Tracing Modernity's Flows: Buddhist Currents in the Pacific World." *The Eastern Buddhist* 43 (1&2): 35–56.

Tweed, Thomas A. 2015. "Theory and Method in the Study of Buddhism: Toward a Translocative Analysis." In *Buddhism beyond Borders*, ed. Scott A. Mitchell and Natalie E. F. Quli, 3–19. Albany: State University of New York Press.

Tworkov, Helen. 1991. "Many Is More." *Tricycle: The Buddhist Review* (Winter): 4.

Urubshurow, David. 2013. "From Russia with Love." *Tricycle: The Buddhist Review* 23 (2): 46–53; 103–105.

Usuki, Patricia Kanaya. 2007. *Currents of Change: American Buddhist Women Speak Out on Jodo Shinshu.* Berkeley: Institute of Buddhist Studies.

Van Esterik, Penny. 1999. "Ritual and the Performance of Buddhist Identity among Lao Buddhists in North America." In *American Buddhism: Methods and Findings in Recent Scholarship*, ed. Duncan Ryûken Williams and Christopher S. Queen, 57–68. Richmond, Surrey: Curzon.

Vásquez, Manuel A. 2009. "The Limits of the Hydrodynamics of Religion." *The Journal of the American Academy of Religion* 77 (2): 434–445.

Vásquez, Manuel A., and Marie Friedmann Marquardt. 2003. *Globalizing the Sacred: Religion across the Americas.* New Brunswick: Rutgers University Press.

Veidlinger, Daniel M. 2006. *Spreading the Dhamma: Writing, Orality, and Textual Transmission in Buddhist Northern Thailand.* Honolulu: University of Hawai'i Press.

Veidlinger, Daniel M. 2015. "Introduction." In *Buddhism, the Internet, and Digital Media: The Pixel in the Lotus*, ed. Gregory P. Grieve and Daniel M. Veidlinger, 1–20. New York: Routledge.

Verchery, Lina. 2007. *The Trap: Fisherman and Buddhist Monks on Cape Breton: Two Worlds, One Idea.* [Film] Montreal, PQ: National Film Board.

Victoria, Brian Daizen. 1997. *Zen at War.* 1st ed. New York: Weatherhill.

Victoria, Brian Daizen. 2001. "Engaged Buddhism: A Skeleton in the Closet?" *Journal of Global Buddhism* 2: 72–91.

Walker, Colette. 2014. "The Ki of Dow: Adaptations from Japanese Buddhist Aesthetics in the Art Pedagogy of Arthur Wesley Dow." American Academy of Religion Annual Meeting: Arts, Literature, and Religion Section. San Diego, California.

Wallis, Glenn. 2012a. "Why X-Buddhism?" *Speculative Non-Buddhism: Ruins of the Buddhist Real.* http://speculativenonbuddhism.com/categories/. (accessed November 15, 2014).

Wallis, Glenn. 2012b. "On the Faith of Secular Buddhists." *Speculative Non-Buddhism: Ruins of the Buddhist. Real.* http://speculativenonbuddhism.com/categories/. (accessed November 15, 2014).

Washington, Peter. 1995. *Madame Blavatsky's Baboon: A History of the mystics, Mediums, and Misfits Who Brought Spiritualism to America.* New York: Schocken Books.

Watson, James L. 2006. "McDonald's in Hong Kong: Consumerism, Dietary Change, and the Rise of a Children's Culture." In *Golden Arches East: McDonald's in East Asia*, ed. James L Watson, 77–109. 2nd ed. Stanford: Stanford University Press.

Watts, Alan. 1967. *This Is It, and Other Essays on Zen and Spiritual Experience.* New York: Pantheon Books.

Wayman, Alex. 2013. *The Buddhist Tantras: Light on Indo-Tibetan Esotericism.* London: Routledge.

Webster, David. 2012. *Dispirited: How Contemporary Spirituality Makes Us Stupid, Selfish and Unhappy.* Winchester: Zero Books.

Wedemeyer, Christian K. 2013. *Making Sense of Tantric Buddhism: History, Semiology, and Transgression in the Indian Traditions.* New York: Columbia University Press.

Wells, Keiko. 2002. "Shin Buddhist Song Lyrics Sung in the United States: Their History and Expressed Buddhist Images (1), 1898–1939." *Tokyo daigaku taiheiyō* 2: 75–99.

Wells, Keiko. 2003. "Shin Buddhist Song Lyrics Sung in the United States: Their History and Expressed Buddhist Images (2), 1936–201." *Tokyo daigaku taiheiyō* 3: 41–64.

Whalen-Bridge, John. 2014. "What is a 'Buddhist Film?'" *Contemporary Buddhism* 15 (1): 44–80.

Whalen-Bridge, John, and Gary Storhoff, eds. 2009. *The Emergence of Buddhist American Literature.* Albany, NY: State University of New York Press.

Whalen-Bridge, John, and Gary Storhoff, eds. 2011. *Writing as Enlightenment: Buddhist American Literature into the Twenty-First Century.* Albany, NY: State University of New York Press.

Whalen-Bridge, John, and Gary Storhoff, eds. 2014. *Buddhism and American Cinema.* New York: SUNY Press.

Williams, Dunan Ryûken. 1997. "Animal Liberation, Death, and the State: Rites to Release Animals in Medieval Japan." In *Buddhism and Ecology: The Interconnection of Dharma and Deeds*, eds. Mary Evelyn Tucker and Duncan Ryûken Williams, 149–162. Cambridge: Harvard University Press.

Williams, Dunan Ryûken. 2002. "Camp Dharma: Japanese-American Buddhist Identity and the Internment Experience of World War II." In *Westward Dharma: Buddhism Beyond Asia*, ed. Charles S. Prebish and Martin Baumann, 191–200. Berkeley: University of California Press.

Williams, Dunan Ryûken. 2003. "Complex Loyalties: Issei Buddhist Ministers during the wartime Incarceration." *Pacific World: Journal of the Institute of Buddhist Studies* 3 (5): 255–274.

Williams, J. Mark G., and Jon Kabat-Zinn. 2011. "Mindfulness: Diverse Perspectives on its Meaning, Origins, and Multiple Applications at the Intersection of Science and Dharma." *Contemporary Buddhism* 12 (1): 1–18.

Williams, J. S., and J. B. Wright. 2015. "The Geography of Buddhism in the Four Corners States." *Journal of Cultural Geography* 32 (3): 1–27.

Williams, Paul. 1996. "Dorje Shugden. " *The Middle Way* 71 (2): 130–132.

Williams, Paul. 2009. *Mahāyāna Buddhism: The Doctrinal Foundations.* London; New York: Routledge.

Wilson, Jeff. 2011. "What is Canadian about Canadian Buddhism?" *Religion Compass* 5 (9): 536–548.

Wilson, Jeff. 2012a. " 'All Beings Are Equally Embraced by Amida Buddha': Jodo Shinshu Buddhism and Same-Sex Marriage in the United States." *Journal of Global Buddhism* 13: 31–59.

Wilson, Jeff. 2012b. *Dixie Dharma: Inside a Buddhist Temple in the American South.* Chapel Hill: University of North Carolina Press.

Wilson, Jeff. 2014. *Mindful America: The Mutual Transformation of Buddhist Meditation and American Culture.* New York: Oxford University Press.

Wilson, Jeff. 2015. "Regionalism within North American Buddhism." In *Buddhism beyond Borders*, ed. Scott A. Mitchell, and Natalie E. F. Quli, 21–33. Albany: State University of New York Press.

Wilson, Liz. 2012c. "Buddhism and Gender." In *Buddhism in the Modern World*, ed. David L. McMahan, 257–272. New York: Routledge.

Winfield, Pamela D. 2014. "New Wine in Old Bottles? Questioning the Category of New Religious Movements (NRMs)." *CrossCurrents* 64 (2): 170–179.

Wuthnow, Robert. 2005. *America and the Challenges of Religious Diversity.* Princeton: Princeton University Press.

Wuthnow, Robert, and Wendy Cadge. 2004. "Buddhists and Buddhism in the United States: The Scope of Influence." *Journal for the Scientific Study of Religion* 43 (3): 363–380.

Yamada, Shôji. 2009. *Shots in the Dark: Japan, Zen, and the West.* Chicago: University of Chicago Press.

Yamauchi, Jeff. 1997. "The Greening of Zen Mountain Center: A Case Study." In *Buddhism and Ecology: The Interconnection of Dharma and Deeds*, ed. Mary Evelyn Tucker and Duncan Ryûken Williams, 249–265. Cambridge: Harvard University Press.

Yü, Chün-fang. 2000. *Kuan-yin: The Chinese Transformation of Avalokiteśvara.* New York: Columbia University Press.

Yu, Eui-Young. 1988. "The Growth of Korean Buddhism in the United States, with Special Reference to Southern California." *The Pacific World: Journal of the Institute of Buddhist Studies* 4: 82–93.

Zhou, Min. 2003. "Chinese Americans." *Asian-Nation: The Landscape of Asian America.* http://www.asian-nation.org/chinese.shtml (accessed May 21, 2014).

Zürcher, E. 2007. *The Buddhist Conquest of China: The Spread and Adaptation of Buddhism in Early Medieval China.* 3rd ed. Leiden: Brill.

Index

CPSIA information can be obtained
at www.ICGtesting.com
Printed in the USA
LVHW061559060822
725343LV00005B/8